COLUMBIA

CAPITAL CITY OF
SOUTH CAROLINA

1786-1936

EDITED BY

HELEN KOHN HENNIG

PUBLISHED BY

THE COLUMBIA SESQUI-CENTENNIAL COMMISSION

Columbia, S. C.
The R. L. Bryan Company, Printers
1936

[iii]

Carolina Engraving Company, Engravers
Columbia, S. C.

EDITOR'S NOTE

I T IS with great pleasure and pride that this volume is presented
to the public. For the hundred and fifty years of its existence
Columbia has developel along lines which should occasion nothing
but satisfaction to her well-wishers and it is a matter of great delight to me that I have had the opportunity to present this history
of my native city.

The work of writing this history has been done by others, by
men and women who have shown an unusual degree of devotion
and ability. It has not been an easy task—the time and space have
been very limited but we have just pride in the accomplishments of
our staff of authors. If slight inaccuracies have crept in, if there are
omissions, please bear with us, for they are small in the sum total of
the history of a city for a century and a half. Each chapter has been
a labor of love, for which the authors have received no compen-
sation, except the knowledge of a work well done.

The Sesqui-Centennial Commission has stood solidly behind this
publication and to them goes what credit it may bring.

The Historical Committee has worked unceasingly to make this
book accurate and interesting. We hope it may prove a starting point
into further research into the history of Columbia which will result in the publication of new material and the corrections of any
errors which may have crept into this. Each and every member has
seen each chapter, in manuscript. To every member the thanks of
the Commission and of the editor are offered for their interest and
their service.

To the Mayor and the Council of Columbia, and to the Richland
County Legislative Delegation go our especial thanks, for by their
vision and encouragement, this celebration of the founding of the
capital of South Carolina is made possible.

My most sincere and appreciative thanks are extended to Mrs.
Arney R. Childs, who has not only written a chapter in the book,
but has labored for uncounted hours in the tedious work of editing.

When Columbia celebrates her Bi-Centennial, when she attains
to the glory which is hers, may her citizens find this volume a true
history of her accomplishments to this date.

HELEN KOHN HENNIG

Columbia, S. C.,
December 17, 1935.

SESQUI-CENTENNIAL COMMISSION

Hon. James H. Hammond, Chairman
Hon. L. B. Owens, Treasurer
Mrs. Julian Hennig, Secretary
Hon. Jeff B. Bates
Mr. J. Macfie Anderson
Mr. William Lykes, Jr., Ex Officio
Mr. Ames Haltiwanger
Mr. C. S. Lemon, Ex Officio

HISTORICAL COMMITTEE

Mrs. Julian Hennig, Chairman
A. S. Salley
Mrs. Arney R. Childs
Dr. E. L. Green
Robert Moorman
R. L. Meriwether
Miss Sadie Magill
Fitz Hugh McMaster
W. E. Gonzales
J. M. Bateman
James H. Hammond, Ex Officio

MAYOR AND CITY COUNCILMEN

Dr. L. B. Owens, Mayor
Hon. Gary Paschal
Hon. W. D. Barnett
Hon. W. P. Eleazer
Hon. Colin S. Monteith, Jr.

RICHLAND COUNTY DELEGATION

Hon. Jeff B. Bates, Senator
Hon. Patrick H. Nelson
Hon. Ben E. Adams
Hon. T. Pou Taylor
Hon. W. P. Donelan
Hon. Jake D. Hill
Hon. O. D. Seay

CONTENTS

LIST OF ILLUSTRATIONS

PAGE

LIST OF ILLUSTRATIONS—Continued

PAGE

Grateful acknowledgment is made for material supplied for illustrations to:

Allen University, Mr. J. M. Bateman, Benedict University, Columbia Chamber of Commerce, Daughters of the American Revolution of Columbia, Dr. R. W. Gibbes, Mrs. James H. Hammond, Mr. James Hunter, Mr. August Kohn, Jr., Mr. David Kohn, Mrs. A. E. Legare, Mr. Maurice Matteson, Mr. William Shand, Mr. B. F. Taylor, Tomlinson Engineering Company, University of South Carolina Library, Mrs. George Waring.

[x]

FOREWORD

WILLIAM ELLIOTT GONZALES

On a plateau on the western shoulder of the Andes in southern Peru is that country's most beautiful city. On the banks of a stream flowing through the town are trees and flowers of the temperate zone. A few miles to the east volcanic Mount Misti raises its snow-capped head eighteen thousand feet above the sea, and while the sun paints rose tints upon Misti's frozen crown, spirals of smoke ascend from the hidden furnace in the mountain's depths.

Away to the west, across endless grey billows of desert mountains, the Pacific beats upon a rock-guarded shore. Legend says that in bygone ages a band of travelers, weary with their pilgrimage across vast treeless piles of dust-strewn rocks, came to this oasis in the shadow of the great mountain, and one who bided there gave them greeting in the Quechua tongue, "Arequipa," the meaning being, "Rest thou here." So there they tarried and named the spot on which a city grew, Arequipa—a place for rest.

But in this age none contemplates a city as a place where the battles and struggles, the victories and defeats of life may or should be escaped. It presents a field on which those contests having the greatest complexities are unceasingly waged. Civilization is advancing and in the modern city are its problems concentrated. There is development and evolution. Where a people are conscious of their responsibilities, their developed character is stamped upon their community in the character of their collective works and achievements.

It is given to this generation of South Carolinians, and particularly of those in Columbia, to speculate upon what was in the minds of the legislators of this State who a hundred and fifty years ago instructed commissioners "to lay off a tract of land two miles square . . . on the Congaree River."

The primary purpose, of course, was to establish where were then fields and forests, the official "capital," in the centre of South Carolina, where a state house would be built so that legislators could conveniently meet. By their votes and a few strokes of a pen they made a "city" without citizens. One wonders if looking into the future they visualized the Columbia of today, thrilled with human joys, aching with human sorrows? Did the crystal glass then reveal to them a Columbia of schools and colleges; of libraries, churches and hospitals; of charities and benevolencies; of traffic and trade; a Columbia whose people are the composite of those gathered from every county of South Carolina, from a score of states of the Union, and from perhaps a score of foreign countries; a friendly and a liberal-minded people?

Did the legislators of a century and a half ago have a vision of the struggles of those who would people the city they so readily created; of that so slow development for three-quarters of a century until Columbia attained a position of business, educational and social importance then to be stricken by grim-visaged war, and blasted by fire that left utter, stark ruin? Did they see those following decades of battling for economic existence when Columbia's people could give little thought to lifting their community, so that the light of finer things might shine upon and out of their city?

Numbers of citizens of the South Carolina capital of today have been asked, What one thing in the past few decades has contributed most to Columbia's growth and development? A variety of answers have been given, each having to do with some constructive undertaking. There was merit in each claim. But the fundamental truth is that each one of these city-developing achievements, through a half century, was due to intelligent, far-seeing, patriotic thought, and persistent effort of some son, native or adopted, of Columbia; or of some group of such sons.

Columbia's outstanding, incomparable asset is in that Spirit of Columbia which has entered into the hearts of so many of the men and women who have come here, to make a city of homes, where "good neighbors" live. Not only have they entered into the life of the city, but they have contributed tremendous motive power which has driven through the notable accomplishments. They have given inspiration to development in the higher spheres of life.

Here is not "Arequipa," but the City of Endeavor.

ORIGIN AND EARLY DEVELOPMENT

By A. S. Salley

SOON AFTER the first settlement was effected within South Carolina in 1670, traders going to all parts of the province speedily realized that the site upon which Columbia was subsequently built was a natural gateway to all sections of the province above the "fall line" in the rivers. As a consequence, a factory was established on the south side of the river at "the Congarees" and a fort was built nearby and garrisoned in 1718 in order that goods for the Indian trade might be stored there and protected while in the process of distribution.

By an Act of May 11, 1754, the General Assembly authorized the establishment of a ferry connecting the settlement on the south side of the Congaree with the high ground on the north side.[1] Settlements increased on the north side and its superiority over the south side soon became apparent. About this time the settlement on the south side was called Granby.

Prior to the Revolution opposition of the British Lords Commissioners of Trade and American Plantations prevented the newly established settlements of the Up-Country from having a proper voice in the government of South Carolina. At the outset of the Revolution the promoters thereof divided the Up-Country up by natural boundaries—with little consideration to apportionment by population—into election districts, and accorded their inhabitants representation in the extra-legal legislative bodies which were directing the revolution. The constitutions of the new government made those subdivisions legal and all of the people of the state came into an equal share in the government.

With the close of the war the idea of changing the seat of government to a central location rapidly developed. In 1783 General Sumter laid out a town on the high hills of the Santee and, with the hope of making it the seat of government, called it Stateburgh. In 1785 a resolution was adopted by the General Assembly to have a legislative committee to investigate the feasibility of locating the seat of government at a central point of the state and report back at the next session. The committee offered its report in the House of Representatives March 1, 1786, and recommended Camden. By a vote of 68 to 54 the House rejected the report.

---

[1] Thomas Cooper and D. J. McCord, eds., *Statutes at Large of South Carolina,* Columbia, 1786-1841, IX, 175-177.

[1]

John Lewis Gervais, senator from the election district of Ninety Six and a former Charleston merchant—a man of unusual vision—on March 6, 1786, introduced into the Senate "A Bill for removing the seat of government from Charleston, and for other purposes therein mentioned." [2] It was given its first reading and ordered printed in all of the gazettes.

The bill provided for the election by the General Assembly of commissioners who were authorized to lay off six hundred and fifty acres of land near Friday's Ferry on the Congaree River, on the plain of the hill whereon James and Thomas Taylor resided, into lots of half an acre each with such shape and form and with convenient streets of such dimensions as they should think just and necessary for the establishment of a town. Four acres were to be reserved for public buildings, and as soon as the money arising from the sale of one-fourth of the lots should become due, the commissioners were

directed to contract for building a State House with convenient rooms for the General Assembly, courts of justice, secretary of State, treasury, surveyor general and other public offices and a convenient house for the residence of the governor. Every purchaser of a lot was required to build thereon a good two-story wood or brick house, with brick or stone chimneys, not less than thirty feet long and

State House in Charleston before Columbia was made the Capital

eighteen feet wide in the clear, within the space of two years from the date of purchase; and failing therein to forfeit the lot. James and Thomas Taylor were allowed to reserve two acres each, if they so desired. No name was proposed for the town, but a blank space was left to be filled in by the General Assembly.

---

[2] Journal of the Senate of South Carolina, MS., March 6, 1786.

On March 9th, the bill came up in the Senate for its second read-ing. Senator Vander Horst wanted the provision for the site stricken out and wanted the commissioners selected to recommend a central place. Senator DeSaussure wanted Manigault's plantations or Belle-ville on the south side of the Congaree near McCord's Ferry and offered Manigault's plantation as a substitute for Friday's Ferry, but his substitute was rejected.[3]

When the question of naming the town was reached, Senator Vander Horst said he thought every new town laid out should have a typical name affixed to it, as this town would be without the pale of justice, where there would be no sheriff, where the laws would be laughed at, and where the lawless would gather, and suggested that it be called the Town of Refuge.

Gervais said he had no objection to its being a town of refuge, but not in an opprobrious manner. He hoped that in this town the oppressed of every land might find a refuge under the wings of Columbia. That was the first intimation in the open discussion that Columbia was the name to be supported by the proponents of the bill.

Senator Barnwell thought if this name were derived from Columbus it would be raking up the ashes of the dead. He preferred that the town be named for a living hero of immortal memory by the name of Washington. When put to a vote Columbia received a majority. On the final vote to send the bill to the House it carried 11 to 7.

On Tuesday, March 14th, the House took up the bill for a second reading. Dr. John Budd, of Charleston, said that while he would like to have the capital remain in Charleston, in justice to the rest of the state he would vote for the bill. He hoped that if the house determined upon removing the seat of government, that the Act for that purpose would expressly direct that the streets should be at least sixty feet wide. This precaution was necessary in a warm climate, and if carefully adhered to could not fail to prove highly beneficial to the health of the residents of the town. He further stated that no man then living could prophesy what the future in street traffic was going to be. His suggestion was incorporated into the bill. Another suggestion from two Charleston members brought an amendment to substitute two miles square in place of 650 acres.

General Stephen Bull, of Beaufort, wanted a more convenient location. He offered to survey the section himself, during the recess.

---

[3] Journal of Senate, MS., March 9, 1786.

Dr. Budd wanted the capital placed at the centre of population, taxes and duties. He wished the town well, and, as a proof of it, said he intended to bring before the next meeting of the General Assembly a plan for promoting and encouraging manufactures, without which, he said, an inland town like this could never be expected to become great or flourishing.

General Sumter said he had served on the committee appointed at the last session to examine sites and that the committee had found that Friday's Ferry was above the center of the state. He said that on former occasions he had not mentioned the place he considered the most convenient because he possessed land there, but when he considered that his delicacy or modesty might prove injurious to the public, he stood forward to propose the High Hills of Santee. He gave a warm, animated picture of that part of the state and pointed out the variety of advantages that would accrue from the seat of government being fixed there. He said Friday's Ferry was far from being as wholesome or healthy as was generally supposed; that the country about it was a barren, sandy soil, producing no other timber than pine, a wood he claimed unfit for answering all the purposes of building; that to the westward and southwestward of it the lands were mostly worn out, so that many of the planters were not within ten miles of any others; that navigation, so necessary and essential to commerce, was extremely bad in some parts of the Congaree; that in that respect the Wateree had an advantageous superiority, in addition to extending much higher up; that the water was good and the air wholesome on the High Hills; that the produce proved the superiority of the soil, which even admitted of great improvement.

Mr. Patrick Calhoun, from Senator Gervais's own election district, said that fatal experience proved that all places situated upon the confluence of rivers were unwholesome, from the marshes with which they were commonly surrounded. He was of opinion that the lands around the High Hills were "to the full" as broken and barren as those near Friday's Ferry. He wished that the place for the seat of government should be as westerly as possible, because the land there was rich and capable of producing excellent yellow pine. He had seen a saw mill some years ago three or four miles from Friday's Ferry with seven saws working at once and all around were streams capable of working mills of different kinds. This place was out of danger of freshets which frequently swept away in a night the hope of industrious planters. In his opinion Friday's Ferry was more central than the High Hills of Santee.

Edward Rutledge and General Charles Cotesworth Pinckney opposed Friday's Ferry and favored a place on the Orangeburgh side of the Congaree near Colonel William Thomson's place.

Judge Henry Pendleton, representing Saxe-Gotha, but a resident of Charleston, favored Friday's Ferry. On the question as to place being put, the vote was sixty-five for Friday's Ferry, sixty-one against. After several amendments had been adopted the bill was returned to the Senate for a third reading, by a large majority.

On Friday, March 17th, the bill came up in the house for its third reading, after the senate had given it a third reading and returned it to the house. Edward Rutledge moved to amend by striking out "Taylor's Hill," and inserting "within two miles of the confluence of the Congaree and Wateree Rivers." He said he was opposed to any change at all, but, as a majority wanted a change, he wanted the new town convenient to the building materials that would be needed to construct.

Commodore Gillion said he favored the change because the people wanted it, but that he did not expect any such advantages in trade as had been predicted, or of a very large town developing, because it was at the mouths of the canals

Colonel Thomas Taylor

that great towns would be built and trade flourish. The Low-Country representatives mustered a majority for the amendment, but the Senate refused to concur and the bill went to conference. In conference each set of conferees refused to give in to the other, and

Rutledge reported to the House that its conferees had refused to
recede, but the country representatives were so afraid of postponing
action that enough of them deserted Rutledge to carry a motion to
recede from the amendment and pass the bill, which was ratified
March 22nd as:

"AN ACT to appoint Commissioners to purchase Land for the
purpose of building a Town, and for removing the Seat of Government thereto."

The preamble recites:

"WHEREAS, the continuing the seat of government in the city of
Charleston is productive of many inconveniences and great expense
to the citizens of this State; for remedy whereof:" [4]

The Commissioners were "authorized and required to lay off a
tract of land of two miles square, near Friday's Ferry, on the
Congaree River, including the plain of the hill whereon Thomas and
James Taylor, Esquires, now reside, into lots of half an acre each, and
the streets shall be of such dimensions, not less than sixty feet wide,
as they shall think convenient and necessary, with two principal
streets, running through the centre of the town at right angles, of
one hundred and fifty feet wide; which said land shall be, and the
same is hereby declared to be, vested in the said commissioners, and
their lawful successors, for the use of this State."

They were to "first value the said land, allowing a generous price
for the same in its present state, without reference to its future or
increasing value," and pay that price to the owners out of the first
moneys arising from the sale of the lots to be sold under directions
to be given.

They were to reserve a square or squares of eight acres "for the
purpose of erecting such public buildings as may be necessary," in
such part of the planned town "as shall be most convenient and
ornamental" and then "sell one-fifth of the remainder" of the lots
to the highest bidder, at a price not less than twenty pounds each
lot, giving three months public notice in the *State Gazette,* on a
credit of twelve months, taking bond with sufficient security, for
the purchase money."

As soon as they should be possessed of such funds from the sale
of lots, or by subscription, loan, or otherwise, they were "to contract
for the building of a State House, with convenient rooms for the

---

[4] *Statutes at Large,* IV, 751–752. This account of the debates on the bill
has been derived from contemporaneous newspaper files in the Charleston
Library.

reception of the General Assembly, courts of justice, and the officers necessarily required for each, secretary of the State, treasury, surveyor general, and such other public officers as may be appointed by law, and also a convenient house for the residence of the Governor or Commander-in-chief for the time being"; the contract to be let to the lowest bidder, who should be able and willing, giving good bond and surety, with sufficient penalty, to erect, and complete the same "on the most frugal plan, which, in the opinion of the commissioners, the honor and interest of the state will admit of."

Every purchaser of a lot was obligated "to build thereon a frame, wood, stone, or brick house, not less than thirty feet long and eighteen feet in the clear, with brick or stone chimneys, within the space of three years from the time of such purchase," any purchaser failing therein to forfeit and pay annually five per cent. upon the purchase money of each lot bought until he should have complied with the directions of the Act.

Thomas and James Taylor, or any other owners of the land who then had dwelling houses within the limits of the two miles square,[5] were permitted, if they chose, to reserve two acres each, on what was then their own property, including their dwellings, the same not to be included in the value of the land; provided that they should not be at liberty to build thereon in any way inconsistent with the plan of the town, nor claim any property in the land which might happen to fall within the limits of any of the streets.

It was provided that as soon as the public buildings should be erected, either in whole or in part, in such manner as should be sufficient to accommodate the General Assembly and officers of the executive departments, the town was to become the seat of government of the State.

That five commissioners were to be elected by joint ballot of the Senate and House of Representatives, who should give bond, to be approved by the governor, in the sum of five thousand pounds each, who should be allowed a commission of two and one-half per cent. on the sales of the town lots in lieu of all expenses except the surveyor's charges for laying out the town; that vacancies on the board of commissioners should be filled by the governor.[6]

The commissioners named by the General Assembly were Commodore Alexander Gillon, of Charleston, Judge Henry Pendleton, of Saxe-Gotha, General Richard Winn, of Winnsborough,

---

[5] There were other owners of land within the four square miles acquired by the state: Stephen Curry, Nathan Center, John Comty, Sharp and Patrick.

[6] *Statutes at Large*, IV, 751–752.

Colonel Richard Hampton, of Saxe-Gotha and Colonel Thomas Taylor, who lived on the site of the proposed town.

The Charleston Morning Post and Daily Advertiser for March 24, 1786, announced:

"The commissioners appointed to lay out Columbia will meet on the 21st of next month, at Taylor's Hill, for the purpose."

The same paper for May 1, 1786, announced:

> A gentleman lately arrived from the neighborhood of Friday's Ferry informs that the new town called Columbia appears in a very forward way of being soon erected; saw mills are building on every stream within its vicinity, and such an opinion is entertained of the utility of this new undertaking that land thereabout has risen 150 per cent.

The same paper for May 23rd announced that the commissioners had appointed the first sale of lots to take place in Charleston, September 2nd, following.

In laying out the town the commissioners divided the two miles each way into ten streets to the mile making ten blocks to each mile, giving a total of forty blocks. The streets were laid out slightly northwest and southeast. The streets parallel with the main central avenue running north and south, Assembly Street, were named for the general officers who served in this state during the Revolution. Those running east and west and parallel with Senate Street, the other central avenue, were given various names appropriate to contemporaneous history and industry. The streets east of Assembly and parallel thereto were

Compass used by John Gabriel Guignard in Original Survey of Columbia

named for the general officers of the militia of South Carolina with the exception of the two easternmost streets which were named for Lieutenant-Colonel John Laurens of the Continental Line of South Carolina and Colonel William Harden of the Upper Granville County regiment of the militia of South Carolina. They were in order Richardson, since changed to Main, Sumter, Marion, Bull, Pickens, Henderson, Barnwell and Winn, since changed to Gregg, Laurens and Harden. The streets running parallel to Assembly on the west were named after Continental generals who served in South Carolina except the last street, which was named for Colonel Owen Roberts, who was colonel of the 4th regiment (artillery) of the South Carolina Line, Continental Establishment, who was killed at the battle of Stono, June 20, 1779. These were in order Gates, Lincoln, Gadsden, Wayne, Pulaski, Huger, Williams, Gist, Pinckney and Roberts. Of these only Generals Gadsden, Huger and Pinckney and Colonel Roberts were South Carolinians. The streets lying south of Senate and parallel thereto were Pendleton, named for Judge Henry Pendleton who was conspicuous in promoting the passage of the bill to establish Columbia; Medium, Devine, named for a citizen of the new town; Green, also named for a citizen of the new town, Blossom, which was probably a compliment to the cotton industry just starting in the State; Wheat, Rice, Tobacco and Indigo, which were productive commodities of the State at the period. The last street was Lower Boundary Street, 150 feet wide, which has since been changed to Heyward Street. After the opening of the South Carolina College the name of Medium Street was changed to College and at a later date Indigo Street was changed to Whaley in compliment to W. B. Smith Whaley, who built several large cotton mills in that section of Columbia and did great service in developing manufacturing in Columbia.

The streets parallel to Senate on the north were Gervais, named for John Lewis Gervais, the author of the first bill to establish the seat of government here; Lady, after Mrs. Martha Washington, wife of General George Washington; Washington, after General Washington; Plain, to preserve the name of one of the Taylor plantations which had been absorbed by the town; Taylor, after Colonel Thomas Taylor; Walnut, Laurel, Richland, after another Taylor plantation; Lumber and Upper Boundary. Walnut was changed to Blanding about a century ago, in compliment to Colonel Abram Blanding, who built the first water works for the city, planted many willow oaks, of which some are still standing, and did other great services to the city. Lumber has since been changed to honor John C. Calhoun. Plain has been changed to honor General Wade Hampton and Upper Boundary has been changed to Elmwood Avenue—the only one of the six 150-foot avenues to which the term avenue is applied.

REMOVAL FROM CHARLESTON

When the session of the General Assembly of 1789 adjourned it "adjourned to the first Monday in January next then to meet at the seat of government after a sitting of sixty eight days."

On Monday, January 4, 1790, the General Assembly met in Columbia "In pursuance of an adjournment of Friday March the 13th, 1789"[7] and the following proclamation of his Excellency the Governor—Charles Pinckney—declaring that:

> In Consequence of a letter from the Commissioners for Erecting public buildings at Columbia dated in 29th,, Ult⁰,, Confirming their Report of the 29th,, of May last—I have thought fit to issue this Proclamation, hereby notifying to the Secretary of the State—the Surveyor General—the Commissioners of the Treasury, and the Auditor General, that they are to prepare themselves, together with all the Records Documents and papers belonging to their respective Offices, to remove on the first day of December next to Columbia, pursuant to the Act of the Legislature in that case made and provided—And I do hereby Summon the Honorable the Members of the Senate and House of Representatives to Convene at the said Town of Columbia on the first Monday in January next that being the day to which they at present stand adjourned.

In May, 1790, a convention of the people of South Carolina met in the state house in Columbia and began the framing of a new

The State House at Columbia, taken from Rives's Tavern, May, 1794

constitution for the state. The constitution was completed and ratified on June 3rd and the convention adjourned.

---

[7] House Journal, MS., March 13, 1789, January 4, 1790.

EXPANSION AND DEVELOPMENT

By an act passed December 16, 1797, an inspection and warehouse for the inspection and reception of tobacco in accordance with the laws of the State was provided for Columbia.[8] The commissioners named in the act were: Timothy Rives, Alexander Purvis, George Wade, Benjamin Waring and Swanson Lunsford.

M. L. Kinard Home, One of Oldest in Columbia

By an act of December 21, 1798, "all free white inhabitants" of Columbia "who shall have paid a tax of one dollar the preceding year, toward the support of government" were accorded the right to vote for seven commissioners of streets and markets of Columbia. Their duties were prescribed by the act.

By an act ratified December 18, 1802, the commissioners for disposing of the State's lands in Columbia were authorized and directed to cancel the bond given by George Wade for the purchase of two acres in the square bounded by Richardson, Devine, Sumter and Green streets; that given by William Cunnington for the square bounded by Sumter, Green, Marion and Medium streets; that given by Thomas Rhett Smith for the square bounded by Sumter, Blossom, Marion and Devine; that given by Ezekial Pickens for the square bounded by Marion, Devine, Bull and Green streets, and that given by Bartlee Smyth for the square bounded by Marion, Green, Bull and Medium streets, upon their producing to the commissioners

---

[8] *Statutes at Large,* V, 311–312.

"certificates from the board of trustees" of the South Carolina College that they had conveyed thereto the said lots and squares. The commissioners were also authorized and directed to convey to the trustees the square bounded by Sumter, Devine, Marion and Green streets; that bounded by Marion, Blossom, Bull and Devine, and the half square adjoining Wade's lots in the square bounded by Richardson, Devine, Sumter and Green streets. The trustees were empowered to close up all or any part of Green, Marion or Devine streets lying within the bounds of Bull, Blossom, Sumter and Medium streets.

By an act of December 17, 1803, provision was made for the commissioners to transfer other lands to in lieu thereof, or purchase from the holders, the two squares bounded by Medium, Sumter, Pendleton and Bull streets and convey them to the trustees of the South Carolina College.[9]

In the Appropriation Act of 1816 the commissioner of Columbia was "authorized and required to convey to the trustees of the Columbia Academy, all unsold lots and squares of land lying in the outer town of Columbia, east of Bull-street, south of Senate-street, west of Harden-street, and north of Lower Boundary-street; and also all such lots and squares as include the marsh north of Senate-street, and eastward of the town: And that the streets within the said limits be, and they are hereby, vested in the said trustees, who shall have power to dispose of the same, reserving always the right of way to such as now are, or hereafter may become, the owners of lots, squares or portions of land within the said limits." [10]

A considerable acreage of the portion of the original town so sold off was acquired by Robert Stark. It lay between Harden, Senate, Barnwell, and Green. He also acquired some of the low ground north of Senate Street. James Sanders Guignard acquired most, if not all, of the land between Stark's holdings and Bull street and James Gregg acquired a large acreage to the south of Green Street. These lands were used for farming purposes until the eighties when their owners began to lay out streets and sell off lots. Some of the streets of the original plan were reopened by the owners of the land to the full width of one hundred feet during the nineties. During the early years of the twentieth century other streets were opened in that property. Some of them were made narrower than those on original plan; while others did not coincide with the existing streets of which they were continuations.

---

9 *Ibid.*, V, 464.
10 *Ibid.*, VI, 53.

ANTE-BELLUM COLUMBIA

By Susan Markey Fickling

H APPENINGS in Columbia in the early 1800s are hard to
find. Curiously enough, an issue of an early paper published here states that on Tuesday, January 16, 1816, the
temperature was 10 degrees below freezing inside a close, tight
room, and never rose 6 degrees during the day.[1] However, early
evidence appears of the hospitality in the little capital city. "All
that I can say at present is that I have met with distinguished
attention, undissembled kindness, and the most friendly hospitality
from those to whom I brought letters of recommendation. In the
literary circles to which I have gained admission, I find much good
sense, some philosophy, and an abundance of patriotism," writes a
resident stranger.[2] Although the town had only about 250 houses
with nearly 1,000 population, the Columbians were generally polite
to strangers, most of the people "being in a public way."[3] They
were intensely interested in the creditable part their country played
in the War of 1812, where the "superior courage and skill of our
seamen over the lords of the ocean have given us ample reason to be
proud of our doings on the sea. . . . Great Britain lost more
ships (she undoubtedly lost more honor) in our little brush with her
than in the French Revolution."[4]

Those were the days when a pump stood at the Court House corner on Main street to supply the needs of the citizens and to fill the
firemen's buckets in time of fire. Candles were kept burning at night,
though flint and steel could be used to strike a light in case of
emergency.[5] Interest in sanitation made the Town Council request
Dr. Gibbes to prepare a genuine chloride of lime to be sold at cost,
or supplied free to those who applied to the Town Marshal.[6] Bathing as a means to health was urged,[7] and a bath house connected
with the water works was opened to visitors.[8] A gymnasium at the
Town Hall advertised that Mr. Houtonville's "mode of instruction
in the various branches of self defense is calculated to give satisfac-

---

[1] *Columbia Telescope,* January 16, 1816.
[2] *Ibid.,* February 27, 1816.
[3] *Ibid.,* May 14, 1816.
[4] *Ibid.,* January 23, 1816.
[5] E. J. Scott, *Random Recollections of a Long Life,* Columbia, 1884, p. 30.
[6] *Columbia Telescope,* September 11, 1832.
[7] *Ibid.,* July 24, 1829.
[8] *Southern Chronicle* (Columbia), May 12, 1841.

tion." [9] An effort was made to reduce the number of licenses to the "dram sellers of the town" who sold liquor not only to freemen but to slaves as well;[10] the Town Council was petitioned to withhold licenses from all persons who retail spirits on the Sabbath.[11] A legislative statute made it possible for every citizen of Columbia to feel a deep anxiety for the suppression of gambling here "where the flower of the rising generation, the rich hope of parents and of the state are concentrated . . . where every temptation held out to youth should be a temptation to the acquirement of science and literature . . . the improvement of morals, character and sentiment." [12] When two members of the legislature were sent to Washington to lobby for funds for the railroad company, the hope was expressed in Columbia that "their success would be such as to warn future adventurers from this new career." [13]

To raise supplies, to regulate the working of the streets, and for other purposes, the Intendant and Wardens of Columbia levied a tax of 12½ cents per $100 on all town real estate, and owners were to pay 5 cents extra tax, if they were not subject to patrol duty, the assessments to be made by the Town Clerk. A tax of 12½ cents on every slave in town, $5 on a pleasure carriage, $3 on a wagon, $2 on a sulky, $2 for exemption from work on the streets, $4 tax on mechanics, $5 on every livery stable carriage—these added to the town's income. Licenses were secured from the Town Marshal who received 75 cents on collections, while the Town Clerk got 50 cents for each execution. All taxes were to be paid by August 1.[14] Then, as now, Sheriff's sales were held before the Court House, where farm lands, lots, homes, negroes, furniture, horses, etc., were offered for cash.[15] Citizens complained about horses and mules running loose in the streets, and demanded a new ordinance with a penalty similar to the one prohibiting hogs running at large.[16]

Two presidential elections especially appealed to Columbians. Jackson's inauguration on March 4, 1829, was observed with joy and hilarity; the fine spring day was begun with a discharge of cannon; at night, illuminations, bonfires, sky rockets and transparencies were seen everywhere. About one hundred gentlemen enjoyed a

[9] *Ibid.,* October 8, 1840.
[10] *Columbia Telescope,* May 22, 1829.
[11] *Ibid.,* May 22, 1829.
[12] *Ibid.,* June 26, 1829.
[13] *Ibid.,* March 16, 1829.
[14] *Southern Times and South Carolina State Gazette* (Columbia), May 25, 1832.
[15] *Ibid.,* May 25, 1832.
[16] *Southern Times* (Columbia), April 12, 1830.

dinner given by Mr. John McColl. The whole town rejoiced that a "man of the people" had reached the highest office.[17] The Fourth of July, 1830, was celebrated with beating of drums and firing of salutes. A military parade ended at the Presbyterian church where a large and enthusiastic audience of both sexes showed their cordial approval of the "truly Carolinian sentiments of the orator." The barbecue near Governor Taylor's spring featured many toasts complimentary to the national government.[18] However, the election of 1840 was the most exciting known to Columbia.[19] As early as July, the papers were flooded with laudatory articles about Harrison and

Residence of John Gabriel Guignard, built about 1790, Southwest Corner Senate and Pickens

Tyler.[20] The Richland Guards celebrated the Fourth of July with a barbecue, where thirteen regular and seventeen volunteer toasts favored Harrison. In August, the Democratic Republican leaders sent a letter to the Whig party suggesting that each party select two candidates to represent the district in the next legislature, and the ticket be sustained by joint vote, thus avoiding the agitation and excitement of a contest, but as the Whig party committee had dissolved, nothing was done.[21]

[17] *Columbia Telescope,* March 6, 1829.
[18] *Southern Times,* July 5, 1830.
[19] Julian A. Selby, *Memorabilia,* Columbia, 1905, p. 127.
[20] *Southern Chronicle,* July 2, 9; September 10, 1840.
[21] *Ibid.,* September 3, 1840.

Sentiment was about equally divided in Columbia, though the activities of the Whigs were more spectacular. For weeks before the election, both parties assembled at the beating of a drum after dark, paraded Main street, each keeping to its own side of the street to prevent collision. The Democrats, led by Jesse DeBruhl, wore red caps and had their headquarters in the Coleman Theatre.[22]

The Whigs had organized early in September at the Town Hall in Columbia, where they had set forth twenty objections to Van Buren, pledged their support to Harrison, named a ticket, and ended with a barbecue, followed by fourteen regular toasts and seventy-six volunteer ones;[23] their meetings were held in Carolina Hall, featured by log cabins, coon-skin caps, hard cider, and excited oratory.[24] In spite of poetry [25] and toasts, the election passed off quietly.[26] Although the Whigs carried triumphantly Richland district, the Columbia precinct went to Elmore, DeSaussure, Hopkins, and Douglass, the Democratic candidates,[27] another case of the country versus the town. The Democrats contested the election,[28] and the *Chronicle* published a list of twenty-six illegal voters in Columbia, so a new election was ordered, the box not to be opened for two days.[29] The Whig candidates, Adams, Threadwell, Black, and Wade, were re-elected.[30] At a meeting of the Tippecanoe Club in Columbia on February 17, 1841, nine delegates were appointed to attend the inauguration of General Harrison.[31] Hardly a month later, the Whigs gathered in Carolina Hall, where a series of resolutions expressed their regret for the "great national bereavement in the death of the President," and their "confidence in the principles, patriotism, and intelligence of the present head of the government." [32]

Columbia early became interested in providing banking facilities for the up-country. In 1812, the Legislature chartered the Bank of the State of South Carolina with headquarters in Charleston.[33] A

[22] Scott, *Random Recollections,* p. 151.
[23] *Southern Chronicle,* September 10, 1840.
[24] Selby, *Memorabilia,* p. 127.
[25] A lady, Boston born and educated, living in Columbia, wrote a poem of twelve stanzas to the tune of "Auld Lang Syne" in praise of Harrison, and a toast to William C. Preston, which were not read at the Whig Convention in Macon because pressure of business prevented. *Southern Chronicle,* September 10, 1840.
[26] Scott, *Random Recollections,* p. 152.
[27] *Southern Chronicle,* October 15, 1840.
[28] *Ibid.,* October 22, 1840.
[29] *Ibid.,* December 3, 1840.
[30] *Ibid.,* December 10, 1840.
[31] *Ibid.,* February 17, 1841.
[32] *Ibid.,* April 28, 1841.
[33] Robert Mills, *Statistics of South Carolina,* Charleston, 1826. p. 213.

De Bruhl House Designed by Robert Mills, 1820, Northeast Corner, Laurel and Bull

branch at Columbia was authorized by an Act of December 9, 1812, and was shortly afterwards opened in the brick basement of the old State House.[34] In 1816, William E. Hayne was elected cashier.[35] In 1830, Judge Colcock was a candidate for its president, as the "state of his health rendered necessary less laborious duties than a seat on the Appeal Bench." [36] Notices appeared in the papers from time to time that a part of the principal must be paid at each renewal of notes.[37] In 1841, the mother bank in Charleston elected the following officers for the branch in Columbia: President, R. H. Goodwyn; Cashier, M. A. Moore, and twelve directors.[38] At a later date, a building was erected north of the City Hall, at the northeast corner of Washington and Main streets, set back in an open area, as a protection against fire and burglars. The branch bank remained until 1865.[39]

[34] W. A. Clark, *The History of Banking Institutions Organized in South Carolina Prior to 1860,* Columbia, 1922, p. 28.
[35] *Columbia Telescope,* February 20, 1816.
[36] *Southern Times,* May 24, 1830.
[37] *Columbia Telescope,* October 16, 1829; *Southern Times* and *State Gazette,* October 8, 1831.
[38] *Southern Chronicle,* June 16, 1841.
[39] Clark, *History of Banking Institutions,* p. 98.

In the summer of 1830, a notice appeared in the paper that a meeting of the citizens of Columbia would take place early in September for the purpose of getting up a petition to the Legislature for a bank charter. "As this is a matter of general interest, and particularly beneficial to the planters of the neighborhood and the upper country, who find a market in this place, it is confidently expected that they will co-operate in furthering the views of the merchants and other citizens of Columbia, before the Legislature and in taking up the necessary stock . . . there are very sanguine prospects of success in the proposed project." [40] However, their hopes were in vain, for the bill was defeated, the reason being given that it would injure the Bank of the State, although re-charters were allowed two banks in Charleston.[41] It was a serious matter to the merchants and planters of the back country,[42] and they voiced their feelings in no uncertain terms. "Why not allow the centre and capital of the state to have *one* bank? Is it because they wish to lay the whole back country under contribution to Charleston? A bank, situated in Columbia, would in some degree equalize—the conveniencies and advantages which are derived from the use of banks, The branch bank rarely gives a check on any bank but its principal— seldom on that—Columbia begins to feel of some importance and wishes to transact business on her own account." [43] Their protests bore fruit, for at the next meeting of the Legislature, an act was passed, December 17, 1831, to establish a "Bank in the town of Columbia," [44] and the Commercial Bank began its long and honorable career. Through commissioners at nearly every court house in the state, its twenty thousand shares of stock at $25 per share were soon subscribed; $5 to be paid at the time, and the rest in quarterly installments.[45] On September 11th, thirteen directors were elected by the stockholders,[46] and these men immediately organized, and chose Col. A. Blanding as president.[47] Though it had to suspend payments in 1837, this bank was one of the nine out of twenty in the state which did not suspend specie payments in 1857.[48] E. J.

---

[40] *Southern Times* and *State Gazette,* August 2, 1830.
[41] *Ibid.,* December 20, 1830.
[42] *Ibid.,* December 20, 1830.
[43] *Ibid.,* December 7, 1830.
[44] Clark, *History of Banking Institutions,* p. 105.
[45] *Southern Times* and *State Gazette,* April 6, 1832.
[46] *Columbia Telescope,* September 11, 1832.
[47] Col. Blanding, a Northern man by birth, married a daughter of Chancellor DeSaussure. He never mingled in politics, but was a useful, enterprising, and public-spirited citizen. Scott, *Random Recollections,* p. 69.
[48] Clark, *History of Banking Institutions,* p. 226.

Scott, who entered the bank as teller in 1839,[49] tells us as cashier in 1852,[50] that "In the fall and winter months, we assisted in moving the crops by advancing to purchasers of cotton for their drafts . . . we loaned freely to approved planters on six months' time in anticipation of their crops. The law limited the rate of bank interest . . . to six per cent per annum, and we observed it strictly." [51] From 1837 to 1850, no banks were chartered, but in 1852, the Exchange Bank of Columbia at the corner of Main and Taylor Streets, opened with J. V. Tyler as president.[52] Selby says there were eleven banking establishments destroyed in the burning of Columbia.[53]

By far the most important political events in Columbia prior to 1860 were the three conventions of 1832, 1833, and 1852, for these affected national interests. In 1824, R. Y. Hayne wrote to C. C. Pinckney that "no threat of forcible resistance to the National Government should ever be resorted to." [54] On July 2, 1827, a meeting was held in Columbia to protest against the proposed increase in the tariff.[55] Thomas Cooper believed that Congress could regulate commerce for revenue, defense, and retaliation, but not for unequal protection, which favored the manufacturers and burdened the agriculturists.[56] Sentiment in Columbia vigorously asserted the rights of the state, but a second anti-tariff meeting on August 21st showed a more moderate temper.[57] During the next two years the questions of nullification, secession, and slavery were the principal topics of discussion. When in 1827, Dr. Cooper wrote that it was time to "calculate the value of the Union," [58] he made articulate the theory of State Rights in Columbia. When Congress adjourned in 1830, without amending the tariff of 1828, the *Southern Times* in Columbia published in almost every issue, articles and editorials advocating nullification as the only means of relief.[59] By August, the question of a convention was fairly before the people.[60] On September 20, 1830, a so-called State Rights meeting was held in

---

[49] Scott, *Random Recollections,* p. 146.
[50] *Ibid.,* p. 165.
[51] *Ibid.,* pp. 165-166.
[52] Clark, *History of Banking Institutions,* p. 173.
[53] Selby, *Memorabilia,* p. 154.
[54] Theodore D. Jervey, *Robert Y. Hayne,* New York, 1909, p. 182, note.
[55] Dumas Malone, *The Public Life of Thomas Cooper,* New Haven, 1926, p. 306.
[56] *Ibid.,* p. 292.
[57] *Ibid.,* p. 316.
[58] *Ibid.,* p. 309.
[59] *Southern Times,* May 10, 13, 17, 20, 31; June 10, 17, 1830.
[60] *Southern Times* and *State Gazette,* August 12, 16, 1830.

Columbia, which though largely local, represented the up-country. The majority favored a convention and prompt action, but many were opposed to nullification.[61] Much to the surprise of the convention party, the fall elections sent only two of their number to the legislature from Richland District.[62] When that body convened on November 22, 1830, it was over two weeks before Mr. Seabrook, chairman of the Committee on Federal Relations, brought in a bill for a convention.[63] The Senate voted for it 23 to 18 but it was lost in the House.[64]

By July, 1831, the State Rights and Free Trade party had organized associations over the state, and within two months, twenty-two meetings had been held.[65] Politics was the business of the day. On December 5, a convention met in Columbia with delegates from

Slave Warehouse of Charles Mercer Logan, Near His Residence, Corner of Senate and Assembly Streets

thirty associations, whose business was to spread information about the American system, the interests of the South, and its constitu-

---

[61] C. S. Boucher, *The Nullification Controversy in South Carolina,* Chicago, n. d., p. 93.
[62] *Southern Times* and *State Gazette,* October 14, 1830.
[63] *Ibid.,* December 4, 1830.
[64] *Ibid.,* December 17, 1830.
[65] Boucher, *Nullification Controversy,* p. 124.

tional and confederate rights. Ten thousand copies of the address to the people of the state were to be printed, and an enthusiastic proprietor of stage coach lines offered to transmit free all packages sent by State Rights associations.[66] "I saw General James Blair, William Drayton, and Mr. Mitchell, members of Congress, burnt in effigy by a mob in the Main St. of Columbia in the days of nullification."[67] The Union men were not idle. Joel R. Poinsett, Jackson's confidential agent, arrived in Columbia in October, 1830, and after consultation with Union sympathizers resolved to organize a Union party.[68] They held a convention in Columbia, September 10, 1832, in the Presbyterian Church with 147 members present.[69] They denounced nullification but offered to join the State Rights party in any constitutional resistance to the tariff.[70]

A great jollification took place at Isaac Coleman's theatre in Columbia over the election in October, 1832, of candidates in favor of nullification—General Adams and Colonel Preston. The crowd marched to greet the principal nullifiers—Colonel James Gregg, Dr. Cooper, and Colonel J. J. Chappell.[71] Though the popular vote was distributed over coastal and up-country, the Union party with its 17,000 members carried few districts. Governor Hamilton immediately called an extra session on October 22, sending a message recommending a convention. The bill was passed, October 26, by a vote of 96 to 25 in the House, 31 to 13 in the Senate.[72] The Convention assembled in Columbia, November 19, 1832, in the House of Representatives, with 156 members,—five from Richland District, Pierce M. Butler, William C. Clifton, Sterling C. Williamson, Sr., James Adams, and John G. Brown.[73] President Hamilton appointed a committee of twenty-one with Charles J. Colcock chairman. An ordinance to nullify certain Acts of Congress was the special order of November 24, when it was passed by 136 to 26; the ordinance was to go into effect February 1, 1833; January 31, 1833, was appointed a day of prayer; then the convention adjourned, subject to the call of the president.[74] The legislature reassembled at once, and passed laws to carry out "the peaceable remedy of nullification."[75]

---

[66] *Ibid.*, p. 26.
[67] Scott, *Random Recollections*, p. 17.
[68] Boucher, *Nullification Controversy*, p. 98.
[69] *Columbia Telescope*, September 11, 1832.
[70] Boucher, *Nullification Controversy*, p. 203.
[71] Scott, *Random Recollections*, p. 29.
[72] D. F. Houston, *A Critical Study of Nullification in South Carolina*, New York, 1896, p. 107.
[73] *Journal of the Convention of 1832*, Columbia, 1860, p. 8.
[74] *Ibid.*, p. 79.
[75] Houston, *Nullification in S. C.*, p. 112.

The Union men called a convention in Columbia on December 10, while the legislature was still in session, and organized Washington Societies for self-defense and protection, under the leadership of Poinsett, who made it clear that Jackson approved his plans.[76] On February 13, 1833, Hamilton issued a call for the convention to

J. J. Seibels Home—One of the Oldest in Columbia

reassemble on March 11, to consider the Virginia mediation and the changes made in the tariff by Congress. The second session, presided over by Governor Hayne, received Benjamin Watkins Leigh, who presented the resolutions of the Virginia Assembly, together with a letter from Governor Floyd to Governor Hayne.[77] By March 16, the committee of twenty-one presented a report that the "Ordinance of November 24, 1832, have no force or effect," [78] and March 18, 1833, this historic convention dissolved, feeling it had accomplished its primary purpose of tariff reduction.[79]

On December 20, 1850, an act was passed to call a convention of the people of South Carolina, and appoint delegates to a Southern Congress.[80] This convention met April 26, 1852, in Columbia, with 149 delegates, and elected Governor John R. Means president—he pled for "a healing of division for upon the union of our states

[76] Boucher, *Nullification Controversy*, p. 246.
[77] *Journal of the Convention*, p. 87.
[78] *Ibid.*, p. 110.
[79] *Ibid.*, p. 134.
[80] *Journal of the Convention of 1852*, Columbia, 1852, p. 137.

. . . depends our destiny." [81] On April 30, an ordinance declaring the rights of the state to secede from the Federal Union was adopted 136 to 19. Eighteen deputies were elected to a Southern Congress, four by the legislature, and two from each of the seven districts.[82] However, other Southern states refused to join in such a congress, which left South Carolina in the unenviable position of "having declared the right of secession, without the support of the other slave-holding states, upon whose joint action would depend the pressure to be brought upon the Federal Government." [83]

[81] *Ibid.*, p. 140.
[82] *Ibid.*, p. 169.
[83] *Ibid.*, p. 155.

CONFEDERACY AND RECONSTRUCTION

By Charles Edward Cauthen

Professor of History, Columbia College

"THE ELECTION of Lincoln," said Dr. Thornwell, " . . . is nothing more nor less than a proposition to the South to consent to a Government, fundamentally different upon the question of slavery from that which our fathers established . . . secession becomes not only a right but a bounden duty."[1] Such was the sentiment which by the fall of 1860 had come to prevail in South Carolina. In Columbia there were few who disagreed. Some, like Wade Hampton,[2] might doubt the wisdom or necessity of such a step, but secession was in the air "like a spiritual contagion" which the reluctant found it difficult to resist.[3] And when the die had been cast men like Hampton threw themselves with enthusiasm into the cause of the state. There were a few northern men employed in the construction of the new State House who left when war came, and one prominent business man who was whipped, tarred and feathered, and driven out,[4] but these were exceptions. Long after the war twenty-two Richland citizens in filing claims for indemnity against the United States swore that they had been sympathetic with the Union cause,[5] but such sympathy, if it existed, was no doubt carefully concealed during the war.

Columbia, as the capital of the state, was naturally the scene of intense excitement, as the legislature met November 5th, chose Presidential electors, and on the 12th, unanimously ordered an election of delegates to a convention to assemble in Columbia on December 17th. The streets were filled with excited audiences as prominent men spoke from hotel balconies and porches on the great topic of the day.[6] Even the annual address of the president of the State Agricultural Society was devoted to a ringing defense of secession and a denunciation of the "vulgar, coarse, and insolent [Republican] party, restrained by no oath, restricted by no Constitution, and only impelled by hatred to the slaveholder and his slave."[7] Zealous college

---

[1] J. H. Thornwell, *The State of the Country*, n. p., 1861, p. 4.
[2] David Duncan Wallace, *The History of South Carolina,* New York, 1934, 111, 158.
[3] William Dallam Armes, ed., *The Autobiography of Joseph LeConte,* New York, 1903, p. 179.
[4] J. F. Williams, *Old and New Columbia,* Columbia, 1929, pp. 42, 103.
[5] Charleston *News and Courier,* November 24, 1873.
[6] *South Carolinian,* November 14, 1860.
[7] *Ibid.*

students expelled Francis Lieber, former professor in the College, but now at Columbia University, from honorary membership in the Euphradian Society and ordered his bust and portrait removed from the hall because he supported Lincoln.[8] On December 17th at the First Baptist Church met what LeConte thought was the "gravest, ablest, and most dignified body of men" he had ever seen brought together,[9] and before adjournment to Charleston because of a near-by case of small-pox,[10] the convention unanimously declared its intention to "forthwith secede" from the Federal Union.[11] News of the passsage of the ordinance December 20th caused a tremendous demonstration in Columbia. Bonfires were lighted, cannon fired, and bells rung. Minute Men, wearing the blue ribbon rosettes of the order on their hats, paraded.[12]

Secession Convention, First Baptist Church, December 7, 1860

Columbia took, through her representatives, a prominent part in the events accompanying secession. Maxcy Gregg was one of the committee of seven appointed to draft the ordinance,[13] and W. F. DeSaussure was on that which prepared the address to the people

[8] Wallace, *op. cit.,* 111, 152–153.
[9] *Autobiography of LeConte,* p. 180.
[10] Wallace, *op. cit.,* 111, 154 and note.
[11] *Journal of the Convention of the People of South Carolina Held in 1860, 1861 and 1862* . . ., Columbia, 1862, p. 11.
[12] Williams, *Columbia,* p. 97; *The Centennial Celebration of the Granting of the Charter to South Carolina College* . . ., Charleston, 1902, p. 53.
[13] *Convention Journal,* p. 23.

of the Southern States.[14] Ex-Governor James H. Adams, who had spoken eloquently for secession in the convention was one of the three Commissioners dispatched to Washington to negotiate with Buchanan [15] and John S. Preston was sent as Commissioner to Virginia where he delivered a notable address to the convention in that state as it considered secession.[16]

Preparation for a possible clash at Fort Sumter and the outbreak of war began at once; Governor Pickens, under authority granted by the convention and legislature, proceeded to raise a force of ten regiments of South Carolina Volunteers.[17] In these early military measures, Columbia played an honorable part. Dr. Robert W. Gibbes as early as December 28th organized the Department of the Surgeon General and conducted it in a highly efficient manner until the following June when he turned over his duties to Confederate authorities.[18] Maxcy Gregg was appointed Colonel of a regiment composed of men who had volunteered for six months, for the generally understood purpose of taking Fort Sumter.[19] From January 3rd until Sumter fell he was busy with his regiment about Charleston.[20]

Into the first regiments went numbers of Columbia men. Company A of Gregg's Regiment, for example, was the Richland Volunteers, Captain D. B. Miller.[21] In Colonel Joseph B. Kershaw's 2nd South Carolina Rigiment were two of the several volunteer companies which existed in Columbia in the years before secession —namely the Governor's Guards, Captain Wm. H. Casson, and the Columbia Grays, Captain William Wallace.[22] Even earlier had gone two others, the Columbia Artillery and Richland Rifles. Several more of these military organizations seem not to have gone as companies

---

[14] *Ibid.*, p. 21.
[15] *Ibid.*, p. 59.
[16] Published in *Addresses Delivered Before the Virginia State Convention by . . . and Hon. John S. Preston, Commissioner from South Carolina, February, 1861,* Richmond, 1861.
[17] *The Statutes at Large of South Carolina,* Columbia, 1836—, XII, 726; *Convention Journal,* pp. 123, 137, 140-142, 150-151; *The War of the Rebellion, A Compilation of the Records of the Union and Confederate Armies,* Washington, 1880-1901, Serial No. 126, p. 689. Hereafter cited O. R.
[18] MS Report of Dr. R. H. Gibbes, Surgeon General of South Carolina, 1861, in cellar of State House, Columbia, S. C.
[19] D. Augustus Dickert, *History of Kershaw's Brigade . . .,* Newberry, 1899, p. 15.
[20] *Dictionary of American Biography,* New York, 1928—, VII, 598.
[21] Clement A. Evans, ed., *Confederate Military History,* Atlanta, 1899, V, 496.
[22] John M. Bateman, *A Sketch of the History of the Governor's Guards of Columbia, S. C. . . .,* Columbia, 1905, pp. 10-11, 17.

Camp Sorghum, Where Federal Prisoners Were Kept
From Harper's Weekly, April 1, 1865

but from time to time members went as individuals.[23] This was true
of the Company of South Carolina College Cadets, reorganized in
the fall of 1860. When the bombardment of Fort Sumter began they
were unable to get permission to go as a company, disbanded, reorganized, and paying their own fare to Charleston, were accepted by
Pickens and saw service on Sullivan's Island before Sumter surrendered.[24]

Meanwhile Columbia, though not in the war zone, took on a
somewhat military atmosphere, as troops passed through the mobilization camp, first at the Fair Grounds and then at Lightwood Knot
Springs near Killians.[25] Throughout the war this Camp of Instruction was located here, as was the state office of the Bureau of
Conscription. Various other Confederate agencies had offices in the
city, such as those of commissary, quartermaster, paymaster and
medical departments.[26] Temporary encampment of troops from
time to time in and about the city, the prison camp, and the almost

[23] Williams, *Columbia*, pp. 44-45, 97.
[24] *Centennial South Carolina College*, pp. 54-55.
[25] Williams, *Columbia*, p. 102.
[26] Directory in *Daily Southern Guardian*, September 8, 1863.

constant passage of troops through Columbia were additional re-
minders of the struggle being waged at more distant points.

No attempt can here be made to trace Columbia's part in South
Carolina's remarkable record. A few of her citizens attained high
rank and served with notable brilliance in the southern cause. Among
them was Wade Hampton, South Carolina's only Lieutenant-General
with permanent rank [27] and one of the really great captains of the
Confederacy. Brigadier-General Maxcy Gregg, whom Lee described
at the time of his death at Fredericksburg, as one of the Confederacy's "noblest citizens" and one of the army's "bravest and most
distinguished officers," [28] was another. Brigadier-General John S.
Preston likewise rendered notable service as Superintendent of the
Bureau of Conscription.[29] But in addition to these, hundreds of

Hampton Mansion Being Occupied by Federal Officers, 1865

other officers and privates served with no less devotion, if in less
conspicuous places, the cause they loved.[30]

---

[27] Wallace, *op. cit.*, III, 220.
[28] Quoted by Evans, *op. cit.*, V, 400.
[29] *Dictionary of American Biography*, XV, 202-3.
[30] "The first to die for Southern independence" was Wm. M. Martin, from
exposure, at Ft. Moultrie, February 21, 1861. Wallace, *op. cit.*, III, 167,
citing inscription in Washington Street church yard. The second shot fired at
Ft. Sumter was by Lieut. W. H. Gibbes, of Columbia. *Ibid.*, p. 166, note.

Living conditions in Columbia during the war involved much inconvenience, hardship, and even actual suffering. Besides the sorrow over loss of loved ones, there came many other difficulties resulting largely from the deranged economic system of a country at war, blockaded, and embarrassed by an unsound currency.

The excitement and uncertainties of secession brought in the first year of the war a slump in business [31] during which prices remained more or less normal.[32] By the fall of 1861, however, scarcity of goods appeared, attended by a revival of business [33] and rising prices. As early as November 19, 1861, Dr. Thornwell was writing from Columbia, "There is no bacon in this part of the country; . . . We have been supplementing our small stock of coffee with rye, but we shall soon have to come down to sassafras." [34] Conditions became, of course, much worse as the war continued. As energies were diverted to military activities necessities of life became scarcer. Paper money depreciated as its quantity vastly increased and as confidence in the ultimate success of the Confederacy waned. As prices soared from these natural causes a loud cry was raised against "speculators," "extortionists," and "forestallers." So great was the criticism, for example, of Saluda Factory prices, that the owners decided in 1862 to sell out at half price to be relieved from what Dr. R. W. Gibbes called the "unjust, unkind and un-Christian attacks." [35] Confederate societies were agitated in 1863 to sustain Confederate currency and boycott speculators.[36] The city council passed ordinances to regulate service charges and to prevent purchase of produce in Columbia for resale at other points.[37] In spite, however, of denunciation of hoarding by producers and consumers alike [38] prices continued to rise. In the spring of 1864 when prices temporarily tumbled, eggs were $2.50 per dozen, butter $7.00 and beef $5.00 per pound.[39] By January, 1865, Confederate money was being refused as payment for provisions and flannel cloth was $40.00 a yard.[40] Under such conditions wholesale stealing of pigs and poultry occurred and bur-

[31] *Mercury,* February 6, 1860, quoting Columbia *Guardian.*
[32] Williams, *Columbia,* p. 104.
[33] Wallace, *op. cit.,* III, 167.
[34] Benj. Morgan Palmer, *The Life and Letters of James Henley Thornwell,* Richmond, 1875, p. 498.
[35] *Charleston Daily Courier,* December 18, 1862.
[36] *The Southern Enterprise* (Greenville), November 12, 1863, quoting *South Carolinian.*
[37] *South Carolinian,* March 5, May 2, 1863.
[38] *Ibid.,* April 21, 29, 1864.
[39] *Ibid.,* April 19, May 5, 1864.
[40] "How They Lived in South Carolina", *Living Age,* October 5, 1867, p. 39.

glaries increased.[41] At the end of 1864, when there were no longer
gas lights, the streets became quite unsafe, murders and robberies
being common occurrences.[42] Soldiers' families suffered. As a wife
wrote *The Guardian,* they were helpless on a soldier's monthly pay
of $11.00 when wood cost $34.00 per cord and extortionate prices
were demanded for all articles by both merchants and farmers.[43]

Attempts to afford the necessary relief were never quite adequate.
Something was done through Boards of Relief established by the
legislature in various counties of the state. For example, 1,152 per-
sons of Richland County were on the Board of Relief rolls in 1864.[44]
Ladies' Associations and other private charities did what they could.
A Corn Association, established April, 1863, undertook to sell bread

Old Saluda Factory

to the poor at low prices and by September was furnishing about two
thousand persons.[45] At the end of the year was also established the

[41] *South Carolinian,* February 25, March 6, 16, 17, May 6, November 2,
1864.

[42] *Ibid.,* December 23, 28, 29, 31, 1864.

[43] Wallace, *op. cit.,* III, 193, citing *Guardian,* October 14, 1863.

[44] *Report of the Comptroller General to the Legislature of South Carolina,
November, 1864,* Columbia, 1864, p. 22.

[45] *Guardian,* September 15, 1863, for an appeal signed by M. LaBorde.

Columbia Mutual Supply Association, with a paid-in capital stock of nearly $100,000.00 designed to furnish goods to stockholders and the poor at low rates.[46] But the *South Carolinian,* November 4, 1864, said distress in the city was greater than the public realized. Hundreds of hungry and cold refugees were pouring into the city and the suffering of the masses was extreme, especially for lack of fuel.

There was, on the other hand, a considerable degree of gaiety and entertainment. In their efforts to raise funds for hospital and relief work the women of the city either staged or sponsored one entertainment after another. One of the first concerts in the state was that one given by a music class of young girls under sixteen about June of 1861, from which was realized the sum of $150.00.[47] Until the very end of the war concerts continued, with amateur or professional performers. Contemporary newspapers described them as well attended and sometimes very elaborate, with admission in cases as high as $5.00.[48] Free band concerts for a time were given twice weekly at Sidney Park. Military companies paraded and serenaded officers and citizens. Sometimes a military review, as that of the Hampton Legion at the race course in May, 1864, was made a grand social occasion with everybody turning out to enjoy the display. There was a tournament by twenty-five Knights of the Legion followed at night by an elaborate hop and supper at the City Hall. Once a great barbecue on the Asylum grounds was given by the ladies to the Hampton men with an address of welcome by Dr. Palmer and a speech by Hampton himself.[49] On another occasion a great reception was given to General Kershaw, followed by a supper described as "handsome and brilliant."[50] Lectures, picnics, "Grand Select Soires," fetes, and "Grand Tableaux," furnished additional diversion.[51] Columbia, said the *South Carolinian* (April 22, 1864), was one of the liveliest places in the Confederacy.

The most elaborate and colorful social event of the war in Columbia was the Great Bazaar in the State House in January, 1865. There had been other fairs and bazaars, notably the Young Ladies' Gunboat Fair of 1862, which raised a considerable sum for the "Palmetto

[46] *Ibid.,* November 10, 11, 16, 20, 23, 25, 1863; November 4, 1864.
[47] *South Carolina Women in the Confederacy,* Columbia, 1903-7, I, 18-19.
[48] Advertisements and accounts frequently appear in newspapers, *e. g.* *South Carolinian,* April 14, 20, 21, 27, 30, June 19, July 8, 9, 20, August 23, October 19, November 2, 12, 25, 27, 1864; *Guardian,* January 2, 1865.
[49] *South Carolinian,* April 17, 20, 30, May 5, 6, June 19, 1864.
[50] *Guardian,* February 9, 1864.
[51] *South Carolinian,* February 19, May 4, 5, 24, September 8, November 1, 1864.

State." [52] But the Great Bazaar was much more ambitious. As early as May 31, 1864, a circular signed by Mrs. M. A. Snowden, Miss Eliza T. Hayne of Charleston; and by Mrs. John Fisher, Mrs. F. H. Elmore and Mrs. A. W. Leland of Columbia announced the project. In the fall this was followed by another appeal and definite arrangements made.[53] Railroads offered free transportation [54] for the goods which began to pour in from all parts of the state. "For a week, the old State House was a transformation scene, brilliant and changing. Each southern state was represented by name, having booths arranged tent-shape, draped with the Confederate colors, and surmounted by the shield or coat of arms of the state represented." [55] Almost every article the Confederacy could boast was there on display besides "youth, beauty, joyous laughter, fuss, feathers and fun." [56] The splendor of this great carnival was really remarkable under war conditions, and its financial success is indicated by the $350,000.00 raised for the Confederate cause.[57]

No small portion of Columbia life during the war was in connection with various efforts to afford care and relief of sick and wounded soldiers in Columbia and at the front. A notable pioneer in this work was Rev. Robert W. Barnwell of the South Carolina College. As early as March, 1861, he had collected several thousand dollars, and in June went to Virginia where he labored in behalf of the soldiers until his death, two years later. His appeals to the public of South Carolina for money and supplies met a ready response and enabled him to establish the Hospital Aid Association which, with headquarters at Charlottesville and later at Richmond, established depositories near government hospitals and with many loyal helpers ministered to the wounded and sick. By November, 1862, supplies worth over $200,-000.00 and over $50,000.00 in cash had been received.[58]

Meanwhile the need of a more effective organization became apparent. With the winter of 1862 approaching it was learned that South Carolina soldiers in Virginia were ragged and destitute. Public meetings in Columbia October 8th and 20th established the Central Association for the Relief of Soldiers of South Carolina designed to

[52] South Carolina Women in the Confederacy, I, 132; see South Carolinian, April 11, 1862.
[53] South Carolina Women in the Confederacy, II, 64-5, 77-8.
[54] South Carolinian, November 25, 1864.
[55] South Carolina Women in the Confederacy, I, 217.
[56] Ibid., I, 243-247.
[57] Jas. G. Holmes, ed., Memorials to the Memory of Mrs. Mary Amarintha Snowden . . ., Charleston, 1898, p. 8.
[58] Detailed account in Report of the South Carolina Hospital Aid Association in Virginia, 1861-1862 . . . Richmond, 1862, passim, The Mercury and other newspapers published weekly and quarterly reports.

Confederate Bill, Signed "M. Gist," Later Mrs. Malvina Waring of Columbia

stimulate and co-ordinate relief efforts over the state. Dr. Maximilian LaBorde, who was very active in the work from the outbreak of the war, was made chairman of the central committee, which included ten other prominent Columbians. A stirring address was published in the newspapers, read from pulpits, and broadcast in pamphlet form.[59] Contributions poured in from Columbia and Richland "in one full constant stream of gushing benevolence." [60] Within a few weeks, from the state as a whole, supplies worth over $150,000.00 had been forwarded and a request to the legislature brought an appropriation of $200,000.00.[61] Much larger amounts were appropriated in 1863 and 1864 [62] and the Central Association, guided by Columbians, remained until the end of the war the chief agency for soldier relief.

Columbia women from the first were quite active in all relief efforts. As early as January, 1861, they were sending lint and linen to Dr. Gibbes for the hospitals at Charleston.[63] No less than six groups formally organized for war work [64] and practically every woman in the city, high or low, had a part in the achievements. Members of these societies made quantities of clothing, collected vast amounts of supplies and money, established hospitals, aided refugees

---

[59] *Central Association for the Relief of the Soldiers of South Carolina. The Plan and Address adopted by the citizens of Columbia, October 20, 1862,* Charleston, 1862, p. 3.

[60] *Memorial of Hon. John Townsend . . . on Behalf of the Central Association . . .* n. p., n. d., pp. 1-3.

[61] *Reports and Resolutions of the General Assembly . . . 1862,* Columbia, 1862, pp. 183-184.

[62] *Ibid.,* 1863, pp. 405, 409 ; 1865, p. 16.

[63] *Mercury,* January 30, 1861.

[64] *South Carolina Women in the Confederacy,* I, 22, 79, 84, 89, 93, *passim;* Mrs. Campbell Bryce, *Reminiscences of the Hospitals of Columbia, S. C., during the . . . Civil War,* Philadelphia, 1897, pp. 29-31.

and needy families of soldiers, and on occasions made sandbags [65] or even a few bullets and cartridges.[66]

Hospital work was especially notable. At the old Fair Grounds they established, soon after the war began, a hospital to care for the sick from the camp near the city. It was shortly taken over by the government but they continued to visit it and assist in every possible way. In the summer of 1862 this hospital was transferred to the buildings of South Carolina College where it operated until the end of the war, in spite of considerable agitation for the reopening of the college.[67]

Meanwhile, in the latter part of 1861 was established what is said to have been the first wayside hospital in the world. Members of the Young Ladies Hospital Association canvassed the town, and, with funds secured, established a "Soldiers' Rest" in a small room of the Charlotte Depot (E. Blanding St.). Soon the project was taken over by the older women and transferred to the South Carolina Railroad Depot (W. Gervais), where an adequate building was available. Here the "Rest" became the Wayside Hospital and was widened into a soldiers' home where 75,000 men are said to have been sheltered or fed or given temporary medical attention before resuming their journey.[68] It received support from all over the state and in the latter part of the war was aided by state funds.[69]

In the latter part of 1862 was established, on Laurens Street, near the Charlotte Depot, the Ladies' Hospital. It seems to have been small, but admitted about 1,000 patients in its first year.[70]

In all of this relief work the women of Columbia rendered heroic and devoted service. No list of the names of those most active, even if space allowed, could be compiled without injustice, for there were few who did not share in this labor of love.

The political life of Columbia during the war was comparatively quiet; on only a few occasions did the public mind seem to become greatly disturbed. Once, in 1862, the people became much excited in the controversy over the Executive Council. This body which had been given almost unlimited power by the convention was severely

[65] *South Carolinian,* August 3, 1864.
[66] Bryce, *Reminiscences,* p. 4.
[67] M. LaBorde, *History of the South Carolina College,* Charleston, 1874, pp. 483-5, 501-2.
[68] *South Carolina Women in the Confederacy,* I, 81–86, 93–95; Bryce, *Reminiscences,* pp. 13–19; Mary B. Chestnut, *A Diary from Dixie,* New York, 1929, pp. 205-206; *South Carolinian,* March 10, 1864; Location of Wayside is given by Williams, p. 75, as "just across the railroad from the Columbia Hospital". Contemporary newspapers locate it near S. C. & Greenville R. R. depot (Gervais St.)—*South Carolinian,* May 2, 1863.
[69] *Reports and Resolutions,* 1865, pp. 20-21.
[70] Bryce, *Reminiscences,* pp. 17, 19, 28; *South Carolinian,* May 2, 1863.

condemned by the people and press of Columbia and under a state-wide attack had to be discontinued.[71] Again, in 1864, Columbians were greatly stirred over a letter written by their congressman, W. W. Boyce, to President Davis proposing an armistice and a convention of all the states to discuss peace.[72] An immense gathering of Boyce's Richland constituents, after listening to his defense, utterly repudiated the proposal and indignantly requested his resignation.[73]

Perhaps the greatest Confederate handicap in the effective prosecution of the war was the difficulty, under blockade conditions, of obtaining adequate supplies for the army. The Confederacy made remarkable attempts to overcome this difficulty through the manufacture at home of the needed articles. In Columbia there was a considerable amount of this war-time industry.

The scarcity of powder was early apparent, and one of the first attempts to produce the necessary nitre for its manufacture was made in Columbia by the state authorities. Five acres of land (now part of the State Hospital property)[74] were leased from Dr. Parker, sheds erected, and work begun.[75] In November, 1863, three hundred sixty beds were processing, with the oldest about to mature, when the legislature authorized sale of the property to the Confederate Government.[76]

At the same time part of the Columbia Canal was leased to the Confederacy,[77] and powder works erected just above the Congaree Bridge, where they operated until Sherman took the city.[78] On the Congaree, just below the bridge, the Confederate Government operated an important armory. Other material manufactured in Columbia for the army included bomb-shell, cannon-ball, swords, bayonets, silver-plated copper buttons, wool hats, leather shoes,[79] at least one order of 500 pairs of wooden-soled cloth shoes,[80] tents and knapsacks.[81] The Saluda Factory, recently enlarged and equipped with wool machinery,[82] also sold to the government, and employed

[71] For Columbia sentiment see *South Carolinian*, April 11, 1862; *Courier*, July 9, 1862; *The Camden Confederate*, December 12, 1862.
[72] *Courier*, October 13, 1864, for the letter.
[73] *South Carolinian*, October 19, 1864.
[74] Williams, *Columbia*, p. 109.
[75] *Convention Journal*, pp. 608-610.
[76] *Reports and Resolutions*, 1863, pp. 157, 402.
[77] *The Statutes at Large of S. C.*, XII, 133.
[78] Williams, *Columbia*, pp. 109-110.
[79] *Ibid.*, pp. 107, 108, 110.
[80] *Courier*, February 11, 1863. These were sold at $5.00 a pair, and were manufactured by C. A. and R. G. Chisolm.
[81] *O. R.*, Serial No. 127, p. 490.
[82] Williams, *Columbia*, p. 90; *Courier*, December 18, 1862.

about 1,000 workers in 1862.[83] Important, too, was the sock factory operated by John Judge and Company, (S. E. corner of Main and Calhoun), employing twenty-five persons in the manufacture of needles, seventy persons in the mill, and five hundred or more in their homes to cut the tubing, let in heel and toe, and hem.[84] Yarn for this factory is said to have been produced by a little cotton mill "down back of Sidney Park." [85]

Another important war-time enterprise was the Confederate laboratory for the manufacture of medicines. Situated at the old Fair Grounds, superintended by Dr. Joseph LeConte, and later by Dr. James Woodrow, this laboratory was the army's greatest source of supply.[86] Columbia was also the chief producer of another government necessity—Confederate notes and bonds. There were four establishments engaged in this large-scale enterprise. In the latter part of the war the clerical force for the signing, numbering, counting, and handling of this paper was moved from Richmond to Columbia

Shields Foundry, Arsenal Hill, Where Arms and Munitions for the Confederacy Were Made

and a number of Columbia women found employment in the work.[87] There was also a cotton card factory established by the state near the

[83] *Convention Journal*, p. 355.
[84] *Courier*, April 12, 1864.
[85] Williams, *Columbia*, p. 110.
[86] *Autobiography of LeConte*, p. 184; Marion W. Woodrow, ed., *Dr. James Woodrow as Seen by his Friends* . . . Columbia, 1909, Part 1, pp. 20-22; Williams, *Columbia*, p. 102.
[87] Williams, *Columbia*, p. 105, gives locations.

State House in 1863, the machinery having been obtained abroad by James G. Gibbes on one of his trips to Europe as state agent.[88]

The population of Columbia largely increased as a result of these enterprises, and even more from the many refugees who poured into the city. Columbia became also at the end of the war a place to which public and private treasure was sent for safety. For example, the Bells of St. Michael's,[89] rare books of the Charleston Library,[90] the magnificent printing establishment of Evans and Coggswell,[91] immense quantities of silver plate, banks with government and private funds, valuable papers, and possessions of all kinds were moved to this supposedly safe place,[92] not only from lower South Carolina but from Georgia as well.[93]

Into this crowded city of perhaps 20,000 [94] people and untold wealth came Sherman in February, 1865. Having completed his

Plant Used for Printing Confederate Money, Later Dispensary and Present U. S. Seed Loan Building

famous "March to the Sea," he turned toward South Carolina with an army "crazy to be turned loose," he said,[95] on the precipitator of "rebellion."

As the army approached Columbia the greatest confusion existed within the city. "The roads leading out of the town were crowded to

[88] *Reports and Resolutions*, 1863, p. 151; *Ibid.*, 1865, p. 78; *Courier*, April 11, 1863.
[89] *Reports and Resolutions*, 1865, p. 78.
[90] *Courier*, September 8, 1863.
[91] *Ibid.*, February 20, 1864.
[92] Mary S. Whilden, *Recollections of the War 1861-1865*, Columbia, 1911, p. 8.
[93] *South Carolinian*, November 22, 1864.
[94] *Ibid.*, March 6, 1864.
[95] *O. R.*, Serial No. 92, p. 702.

excess by terrified fugitives." [96] Terrible was "the press, the shock, the rush, the hurry." [97] And as Sherman threw shells into the city from across the Congaree on February 16th, rioters and robbers began to steal what they could in spite of the existence of martial law.[98] During the night of Thursday 16th, Governor Magrath and other officials withdrew from the city followed by most of the Confederate troops. At daylight Friday the city was startled by an explosion set off accidentally by plunderers at the South Carolina Railway depot on lower Gervais Street. Some thirty-five persons were killed and the depot and contents destroyed by fire. Disorder continued as commissary and quartermaster stores were thrown open and eager soldiers took what they could.[99]

About nine o'clock General Wade Hampton, in command of the cavalry remaining in the city, prepared to withdraw and directed

"Logan's Corps Crossing The Saluda River Above Columbia, South Carolina"
From Harper's Weekly, April 15, 1865

Mayor Goodwyn to surrender the city. With three councilmen the Mayor proceeded in a carriage, with a white flag, towards the Broad River Road, as the last Confederate troops were moving through the northern outskirts of the city. Meanwhile Sherman had proceeded up the Congaree, crossed the Saluda at the factory, and had put a detachment across the Broad on pontoons. This detachment, under Colonel Stone, was met by Mayor Goodwyn and received the sur-

---

[96] Columbia Board of Trade Pamphlet, *Columbia, S. C., The Future Manufacturing and Commercial Center of the South,* Columbia, 1871, p. 15. Hereafter cited Columbia Board of Trade, 1871.
[97] [W. G. Simms], *Sack and Destruction of the City of Columbia, S. C. . . .* Columbia, 1865, p. 10.
[98] Wallace, *op. cit.,* III, 208.
[99] Simms, *op. cit.,* pp. 11-12, Scott, *op. cit.,* pp. 175-6.

"General Sherman and Staff Crossing Broad River, South Carolina."
From Harper's Weekly, April 15, 1865

render of the city. Promising, in accordance with Sherman's orders to General Howard to protect citizens and respect private property, Stone proceeded down Main Street, followed before noon by Sherman and his staff.[100]

The nightmare of events between the entrance of Sherman's army on the morning of Friday 17th and the dawn of Saturday 18th cannot be related here. The correspondent of the *New York Herald* said: "I will simply observe that the night of Friday, Feb. 17, would have cracked Alaric's brain if he had witnessed it." [101] Citizens were robbed and dwellings plundered throughout the afternoon by a drunken and disorderly soldiery. This continued as darkness fell and as fire almost simultaneously broke out in various parts of the city. Driven by high winds, the fire was not subdued until the greater part of the city lay in ashes, and old men, women and children were left shocked and shivering in its streets and vacant lots. Eighty-four of about a hundred and twenty-four blocks in the heart of the city had hardly a building left.[102] "Where formerly stood buildings which

---

[100] [Simms], *op. cit.,* pp. 12-13; Wallace, III, 204; Scott, *op. cit.,* p. 176; James Ford Rhodes, *History of the United States,* . . . New York, 1928, V, 96-97.

[101] John Porter Hollis, *The Early Period of Reconstruction in South Carolina,* Johns Hopkins University Studies in Historical and Political Science, Series XXIII, Nos. 1-2, Baltimore, 1905, p. 23, note.

[102] Simms, *op. cit.,* describes graphically the losses. A detailed catalogue of buildings destroyed with location is given. pp. 58-76.

were the boast and pride of the people, nothing was visible save their charred and misshapen remains, or a wilderness of chimneys, lifting their blackened faces to heaven in solemn protest against the wrongs of a stricken and outraged community." [103] All property of military value which escaped was later officially destroyed.[104]

Space does not permit a review of the controversy over who was responsible for the barbarous burning of Columbia. Hampton immediately after the event definitely charged Sherman with permitting, if not ordering the destruction.[105] Sherman, in his official report, claimed Hampton left cotton, fired by his order, burning in the street and that a high wind carried the blaze over the city. This was indignantly denied by Hampton at once.[106] Official reports of Union officers in a few cases partially supported Sherman's charge, while others stated that the fire was set by drunken soldiers, escaped Federal prisoners, citizens or negroes.[107] Various eye witnesses, notably

Columbia In Flames, From Leslie's Weekly, April 1, 1865

W. G. Simms and Dr. D. H. Trezevant, wrote accounts highly unfavorable to Sherman for Columbia papers and, in 1867, a mass

---

[103] Columbia Board of Trade (1871), p. 20.
[104] *O. R.* Serial No. 99, pp. 502-3, for list.
[105] *Ibid.,* pp. 596-597.
[106] *Letter of Gen. Wade Hampton, June 24, 1873,* Charleston, 1888, p. 4. This is a reprint of original to *Baltimore Enquirer.*
[107] Rhodes, *op. cit.,* V, 92-95, citing *O. R.*

The Burned City, 1865, Looking North From the Capitol

meeting of Columbia citizens appointed a committee to take evidence. This committee, composed of men of unimpeachable integrity, took more than sixty depositions, abstracted the damaging evidence in a report, and filed the documents in the city archives.[108] When a mixed Commission examined in 1873 a British claim for cotton destroyed at Columbia, testimony of Federal officers and others was taken to determine liability, if any, of the United States. This testimony inspired a spirited letter from Hampton to the *Baltimore Enquirer* in which contrary evidence was convincingly set forth. To this material has been constantly added much in the form of memoirs, reminiscences, etc., to make the literature on the destruction of Columbia quite extensive. It has been frequently examined with somewhat varying results.

From this mass of literature a few conclusions may be safely drawn. The cotton origin theory of the fire must be dismissed as utterly untenable. Whether the fires were set mainly by Sherman's soldiers or by escaped prisoners [109] is not a difficult problem, for the

[108] Chancellor James P. Carroll, *Report of the Committee Appointed to Collect Testimony.* . . . Columbia, 1893.
[109] See Col. Stone's statement in *Hampton letter,* 1873, pp. 16-17.

number of prisoners left in the city was too small to have played more than a negligible part,[110] and there is too much unimpeachable testimony of persons who saw the soldiers at work.

That the soldiers acted without official orders from Sherman is clear, but while assuring the inhabitants of the perfect safety of the city,[111] he failed to take proper precautions against what he had every reason to fear and did fear; [112] and somehow his soldiers, according to General Howard, received the impression that the destruction of the city would be "peculiarly gratifying to General Sherman." [113] It may be seriously doubted whether reasonably energetic efforts were made to check the spread of the conflagration and restore order. A recent student of the question even concludes that the high wind was a negligible factor in the efforts to curb the spread of the fire as only "formal gestures" were made to extinguish it.[114]

RECONSTRUCTION

To the people of Columbia Sherman's fateful visit was the climax, and end, of the war. The surrender, shortly afterward, of Lee in Virginia and Johnston in North Carolina, was merely an epilogue to a tragedy which was already completed.

The condition of the city after the federal occupation was acute. With 1,386 [115] buildings in ashes the problem of shelter itself must have been a serious one for many people. But far more alarming was the lack of food. General Sherman, at the request of the mayor and a committee of citizens, agreed to leave 500 cattle, some salt, and medicine. The medicine, besides a pint of castor oil, is said to have been only enough to fill a large cigar box, and though the cattle were extremely poor, this meat for several weeks prevented the greatest suffering.[116] Prompt steps were taken under the energetic leadership of Acting Mayor J. G. Gibbes [117] to provide for the hungry, and for three months a committee distributed to seven or eight thousand persons a daily ration consisting of a small quantity of

---

[110] Jas. D. Hill, "The Burning of Columbia Reconsidered", *The Atlantic Monthly Quarterly,* Vol. XXV, 279-81.

[111] *Hampton Letter of 1873,* pp. 7-8; Simms, *op. cit.* p. 13.

[112] Rhodes, *op. cit.,* V, 97. Sherman several times before coming to Columbia referred in official letters to the "insatiable desire to wreck vengeance" on South Carolina, *e. g., O. R.* Serial 92, pp. 702, 799, 741-3.

[113] *Hampton Letter of 1873,* p. 12, Wallace, *op. cit.,* III, 209-210.

[114] Hill, *op. cit.,* pp. 281-282. Cf. Rhodes, *op. cit.,* V, 95.

[115] Hollis, *op. cit.,* p. 23 citing Simms list; Yates Snowden, *Marching with Sherman . . .,* Columbia, 1929, p. 25, gives the number as 1,426.

[116] Scott, *op. cit.,* pp. 193, 195.

[117] *Ibid.* Later, on the resignation of Goodwyn, Gibbes was elected to the office by the council—*Columbia Daily Phoenix,* May 27, 1865.

beef and meal.[118] The problem of feeding the population was, of course, greatly increased by the inadequate transportation facilities of a city which had been a railroad center but was now some thirty miles from the nearest line.[119] Neighboring cities, however, sent by wagon much needed supplies. Augusta sent many loads of provisions[120] and help came from such towns as Charlotte, Chester, Greenville, and Sumter.[121] But the *Phoenix,* April 15, reported much continued suffering. Appeals for relief to the legislature (called by

Raising the Stars and Stripes Over the Capitol at Columbia, South Carolina
From Harper's Weekly, April 8, 1865

Governor Magrath to meet April 25th at Greenville) were made by a public meeting and city council.[122] In May and June, however, con-

[118] Carroll, *op. cit.,* p. 18; Scott, *op. cit.,* p. 195; *Phoenix,* June 2, 1865.
[119] Sidney Andrews, *The South Since the War: As Shown by Fourteen Weeks of Travel and Observation in Georgia and the Carolinas,* Boston, 1866, p. 29.
[120] Scott, *op. cit.,* p. 194, states that 18 loads were largely stolen before being put across the river. Rhodes, *op. cit.,* V, 98 note, tells of a report from Augusta that by March 16, that city had contributed $180,000 in money and $50,000 in provisions.
[121] *Phoenix,* March 21, 1865.
[122] *Ibid.,* April 8, 11, 17, 22.

ditions improved. The war over, northern merchants began to extend credit to old customers, and cotton found a market at good prices. Building began on a modest scale and in mid June the *Phoenix* spoke of shops opening every day as regular wagon lines brought in new stocks. At the end of June some twenty-five stores were open and ready to supply anything from "fish-hooks to elephants." In July, said the same journal, business was brisk and houses were going up all over the city.[123] But all of this commendable enterprise was on a small scale. Sidney Andrews in September thought $20,-000.00 would buy the stock of all the merchants in the city and the new buildings, while numerous, were of the cheaper sort.[124]

Meanwhile civil authority passed to the military. Under orders from General Gillmore, a part of the 25th Ohio Regiment appeared on May 25th; the same day Governor Magrath was arrested on the charge of high treason, to be sent to Fort Pulaski, Savannah. The citizens, on the invitation of the military, appeared in large numbers at headquarters (south side of college campus) to take the oath of allegiance to the United States, and the 25th Ohio was praised for its excellent behavior.[125] Good order prevailed except for frequent robberies apparently committed by negroes. The latter, however, seem to have been otherwise orderly, the *Phoenix* commending them for their conduct at an elaborate July 4th celebration to which they came from all over the county.[126]

The people of Columbia seem to have entered into the conciliatory reconstruction plans of President Johnson hopefuly and sincerely. There were some, it is true, who considered emigration to Mexico, or Brazil, or Venezuela to escape the consequences of emancipation.[127] A prominent citizen of Columbia, Mr. C. R. Bryce, was authorized by the Venezuelan government to issue 2,500-acre land grants to South Carolina citizens, and Wade Hampton in the summer of 1865 received many requests to lead an exodus to some foreign country. In refusing, he patriotically said that the very fact that the state was passing through a terrible ordeal "should cause her sons to cling more closely to her." [128] Columbians generally recognized the wisdom of accepting the verdict of the sword and appreciated the advantages promised by the re-establishment of civil government in the state. Said the *Phoenix;* ". . . we have suc-

[123] *Ibid.,* May 16, 27, June 2, 5, 15, 24, July 3, 14, 22, 24, 29.
[124] Andrews, *op. cit.,* p. 34.
[125] *Phoenix,* May 25, 26, 27, 1865.
[126] *Ibid.,* July 6, 14, 26, August 11, 22, etc., 1865.
[127] *Autobiography of LeConte,* p. 239.
[128] F. B. Simkins and R. H. Woody, *South Carolina During Reconstruction,* Chapel Hill, 1932, pp. 239-240.

cumbed, we are submissive. There is not a dog among us so conceited as to suppose he has a tail at all."[129]

To the convention of 1865 Richland elected such outstanding citizens and soldiers as F. W. McMaster, A. R. Taylor, William Wallace, and Wade Hampton, though the latter, spending the summer in Cashiers Valley, received notice too late to attend.[130] He was highly sympathetic with the efforts of the state to meet the conditions of the Johnson plan, and preferred to avoid public office lest his name discredit that plan among the Radicals at the North. He, therefore, refused to run for governor, and when a movement began to elect him anyway, urged his friends over the state not to support him. Many thought that he had been elected, but the official count showed Orr 9,928, Hampton 9,185.[131]

Unfortunately Congress in December, 1865, refused to seat representatives of the southern state governments reconstructed under Johnson's plan. Seizing upon the Black Codes as a justification of their claim that emancipation had not really been accepted at the South, the Radicals began a contest with the President and his moderate supporters, which did not end until their program was adopted in the notorious Reconstruction Acts of 1867.

In July, 1867, soon after the passage of the Reconstruction Acts the Republicans organized in a convention held in Columbia. As a result of this meeting the negroes all over the state were soon organized into Union Leagues which became the chief agency for mobilizing and controlling the negro vote.[132] Since the negroes of the state greatly outnumbered the whites it was not difficult for their leaders to control the whole process of reconstructing the state. In the convention of January, 1868, which drew up a new state constitution incorporating negro suffrage, there were seventy-six negroes to forty-eight whites. The Richland delegation of four had three negroes, Beverly Nash, S. B. Thompson, C. M. Wilder.[133] Two-thirds of the negro members being former slaves, mostly illiterate, they took small part in the proceedings. But Nash, ex-slave and hotel porter, coal-black, corrupt, ignorant—in spite of considerable native ability, was rather prominent. Thompson drew attention

[129] September 14, 1865. See also May 19, 26, 27, July 12, 24, 29, August 11, 1865.
[130] John S. Reynolds, *Reconstruction in South Carolina, 1865-77*, Columbia, 1905, p. 16. The convention met, appropriately, in the Baptist Church in Columbia. The legislature which met soon afterwards used the library and chapel of S. C. College, *Ibid.*, pp. 16, 20-21.
[131] *Ibid.*, p. 20; Hollis, *op. cit.*, p. 43.
[132] *Ibid.*, pp. 77, 83.
[133] Reynolds, *op. cit.*, pp. 78-79.

by his resolution for the removal of the efficient superintendent of the penitentiary.[134]

In the election of 1868, Richland, with 2,812 black and 1,236 white registered voters,[135] went to the Radicals. To the legislature (which met in Janney's Hall)[136] was sent a negro delegation; Nash to the Senate and Wilder, Thompson, Simmons, Goodson to the House.

The House of Representatives in Radical Days

Thomas J. Robertson became United States Senator for the short term, being re-elected by the legislature in 1870.[137]

Richland County helped maintain negro majorities in the legislature until the end of the Radical regime. Only in 1874 did the Conservatives succeed in capturing one seat in the legislature and then only as a result of a factional contest between the two negro candidates for the Senate. The Nash faction won after making a

---

[134] Hollis, *op. cit.*, p. 85; Simkins and Woody, *op. cit.*, pp. 91, 132-133; Reynolds, *op. cit.*, p. 80.
[135] *Ibid.*, p. 74.
[136] Simkins and Woody, *op. cit.*, p. 120.
[137] *Ibid.*, pp. 108, 110-111, 157-158.

bid for Conservative support by offering one seat in the legislature, the probate judgeship and a trial justiceship in Columbia.[138] Nash, who was thus returned to the Senate, was easily the most prominent Columbia negro in public life and one of the most conspicuous in the state. He began his political career as a magistrate in Columbia as an appointee of General Canby,[139] was a member of the constitutional convention of 1868, and state senator 1868-1876. He impressed a northern visitor as the leading Republican in the Senate and a man of great ability.[140] An effective speaker, "always ready with a story or anecdote,"[141] he became chairman of the important Senate Finance Committee, and served on the boards governing the lunatic asylum, the penitentiary, and the state orphan home; he was Republican elector in 1876.[142]

The same majority which kept Nash in the Senate elected Radicals to local county offices. In many cases ignorance alone disqualified them for their duties. For example, Rev. N. E. Edwards, colored, defeated a capable white man in 1870 for School Commissioner. This officer was official head of public instruction in the county and enjoyed the power of appointing two other persons to serve with him as a Board of Examiners for teachers. How unfitted he was for such duties is indicated by the following sentence from one of his official letters: "The foller ring name person are Rickermended to the Boarde . . . for the Hower Schoole Haveing Given fool sat es fact shon in thi tow Last years." [143]

The negro and his white allies controlled city as well as county officers. The city, unlike the county, had a white majority, but as early as June 19, 1868, General Canby, for no apparent reason, removed the mayor and aldermen of Columbia and appointed a council which included three negroes.[144] During the first year of Radical rule the whites regained complete control, but in order to overcome the white majority, the Legislature, in the session of 1869-1870, extended the limits of the city to include the negro suburbs. This gave control in municipal elections to the Negro and resulted in the

---

[138] *Ibid.,* pp. 283-284.

[139] *Ibid.,* p. 71. Canby had removed J. T. Zealy after an altercation between two Columbia youths and two northern visitors, whose political activities were offensive, on the ground that insufficient bond was required. *Ibid.,* pp. 67-68; Simkins and Woody, *op. cit.,* p. 69.

[140] James S. Pike, *The Prostrate State: South Carolina under Negro Government,* New York, 1874, p. 34.

[141] Simkins and Woody, *op. cit.,* pp. 132-133.

[142] Reynolds, *op. cit.,* pp. 123, 366, 489-490.

[143] *Ibid.,* p. 122.

[144] The three whites appointed at the same time were gentlemen of good standing. *Ibid.,* p. 98.

election of a Radical council which proceeded to duplicate on a smaller scale the recklessness of the state legislature. The "wildest schemes of useless extravagance and waste" were concocted. Under the guise of the necessity of rebuilding the city, application was made to the legislature for permission to issue $250,000.00 of bonds. In spite of protests from the taxpayers the legislature consented, but with the proviso that the total indebtedness of the city should not exceed $600,000.00. The debt was increased nevertheless from $360,000.00 to $850,000.00 in four years with not more than $75,000.00 expended for permanent improvements.[145] The police force at one time during this period is said to have included only one white man besides the chief.[146]

The history of Columbia during the carpet-bag régime becomes almost the history of reconstruction in South Carolina, for in no other period of the state's history was attention so centered on the drama being enacted at the capital. But the story of inefficiency, extravagance, and amazing corruption which characterized the state government between 1868 and 1877 cannot here be detailed. Almost every conceivable scheme for diverting public funds into private pockets was practiced.[147] And it was of course natural that the negro, suddenly raised to political power, should claim social recognition as well, especially since it served the interest of his political allies to encourage racial consciousness as a means of promoting political solidarity. While the whole State felt the effect of these aspirations, it was in Columbia that their evidences were most apparent.

With the inauguration of the Ohio carpet-bagger R. K. Scott as governor in 1868 there appeared a new social régime, more distasteful to the old families than all the financial and political scandals of the reconstruction period. Almost immediately at the governor's receptions began the mingling of white and black as both crowded about his "luxurious refreshment tables" with "no invidious distinctions." [148] Leading politicians of the two races walked arm-in-arm down Main Street and disappeared together into eating-house and amusement place.[149] Wives of colored politicians "from their carriages summoned clerks to exhibit there to them the goods which they were purchasing with the public's money."[150] The Preston mansion, acquired by Governor Moses with down payment of $15,000.00 re-

145 *Ibid.*, p. 126; Scott, *op. cit.*, pp. 205-207.
146 Williams, *Columbia*, p. 137.
147 Convenient summary is Reynolds, *op. cit.*, Chap. X.
148 Simkins and Woody, *op. cit.*, p. 369.
149 Reynolds, *op. cit.*, p. 501.
150 Wallace, *op. cit.*, III, 263-264.

ceived as a bribe for signing a $450,000.00 printing bill,[151] became the center of official society, as Moses "gave a series of notorious receptions" and "enveloped the colored belles and dandies in the garish splendor of an ostentatious age." One of the guests has left us a description: "The colored band was playing 'Rally 'Round the Flag' . . . Supper was announced, and you ought to have seen the scrambling for the table. Social equality was at its highest pitch. It was amusing to see Cuffy reaching across the table and swallow

Wade Hampton's Garden, Columbia, South Carolina
From Harper's Weekly, November 11, 1865

ing grapes by the bunch, champagne by the bottle, and turkey, ham and pound-cake by the bushel." [152] Another social center was the elegantly furnished home of the mulatto Rollin sisters. Here. in a somewhat more refined and literary atmosphere, the educated sisters entertained with an "air of good taste" leading politicians of both races.[153] Less elite was Murphy's "evil all night house in Gervais Street." [154]

---

[151] *Ibid.,* p. 290.
[152] Simkins and Woody, *op. cit.,* p. 370.
[153] *Ibid.,* pp. 368-369; Claude G. Bowers, *The Tragic Era,* New York, 1929, pp. 351-353.
[154] Alfred B. Williams, *Hampton and His Red Shirts, South Carolina's Deliverance in 1876,* Charleston, 1935, p. 392.

Quite different were the circles in which the old families moved. In the first days of peace, society had been quite gay. Everybody was poor, but with the young men furnishing a fiddler and the hostess lemonade and cake, fun was inexpensive.[155] With the coming of the Radicals, however, the houses of the old families became strangely silent with "little merriment floating out of the open windows on the night."[156] As the "Gig Society" drove to the parade grounds to listen to the band,[157] the old residents remained quietly at home. Natives who joined the Republicans were scorned in the spirit of the Euphradian Society which expelled certain members for having "lowered their dignity and station as true gentlemen of Carolina."[158] On the other hand the greatest sympathy was shown those who suffered at the hand of the Radicals. When a group of reputed Klansmen were arrested in Laurens and jailed in Columbia the most prominent men and women of the city made the prison almost a social center as they visited and showed every attention to the victims. "During all our *four weeks* sojourn in their midst," wrote one, "we never ate one morsel of jail rations, and our larder was kept constantly supplied with the best the market could afford." [159]

The rebuilding of Columbia went forward slowly after 1865. In the fall of 1866 building was reported brisk but many unsightly chimneys and other evidences of the fire remained. As late as 1870 Main Street was still only half rebuilt and the Congaree bridge was as yet not replaced, flat boats being used for crossing.[160] In 1873, while Main Street was again restored, many squares in other parts of the city were vacant,[161] and not until the end of reconstruction may rebuilding be said to have been largely achieved.[162] Business recovered somewhat more rapidly as politicians spent freely the public's money. The stores on Main Street in 1876 were well worthy, says one observer, both in appearance and stocks, of a city of 100,000 people.[163]

Efforts of the whites to control the state government were unsuccessful through eight long years. The attempt to prevent the

[155] *Autobiography of LeConte*, p. 236. Military officers and their families then stationed in the city were not included. Columbia men were cordial, but their wives scornful. *Ibid.*; Andrews, *op. cit.*, p. 35.
[156] Bowers, *op. cit.*, p. 348; Pike, *op. cit.*, p. 107.
[157] *Ibid.*, p. 79.
[158] Reynolds, *op. cit.*, p. 99. For the University under negro control see *ibid.*, pp. 231-237.
[159] John A. Leland, *A Voice From South Carolina. Twelve Chapters Before Hampton. Two Chapters After Hampton. With a Journal of a Reputed Ku-Klux and an Appendix*, Charleston, 1879, pp. 99-107.
[160] Simkins and Woody, *op. cit.*, p. 279.
[161] Pike, *op. cit.*, p. 108.
[162] Simkins and Woody, *op. cit.*, p. 279.
[163] Williams, *Hampton*, p. 69.

calling of a constitutional convention failed in 1868; the ratification of this Radical document and the election of a black legislature were effected in spite of white opposition; protests to Washington availing nothing at all.[164] Scott, by organizing the negroes into militia companies, defeated the program of the Union Reform party which had hoped to coax negroes into the white man's party in 1870; conventions of taxpayers in 1871 and 1874 called attention to abuses without tangible results; the Ku-Klux Klan was disrupted by martial law and wholesale arrest.[165] It seemed to "Honest John" Patterson, who had paid legislators $50.00 to $2,500.00 a vote for his election to the United States Senate in 1872, that there were "still five years of good stealing in South Carolina,"[166] but he calculated without the Red Shirts.

As the election of 1876 approached there was considerable disagreement among Conservatives as to their proper course. Many felt that support should be given to cultured Governor D. H. Chamberlain; although he was a Maine carpet-bagger, who earlier as attorney general had been involved in some of the greatest irregularities, he had nevertheless as governor since 1874 made a valiant fight for reform, and with some success. Others, believing that thoroughgoing reform could never be effected by the Radical organization and yearning for white-man government, advocated a straight-out fight for offices from "Governor to Coroner." Two incidents played into the hands of the straight-outs. One was the election by the legislature, in spite of Chamberlain's bitter opposition, of W. J. Whipper and ex-governor F. J. Moses, Jr., to circuit judgeships. The elevation of such bestial and dissolute men to the bench was the crowning insult to decent government and convinced many of the impotence of Chamberlain ever to control his party. The other incident was the passion-stirring Hamburg riot in July, 1876, which demonstrated the necessity of ending a régime which tolerated a militia composed entirely of negroes. A great wave of determination to "storm Hell," if need be, swept the state.[167]

The Democratic Executive Committee immediately called a convention for August 15th, 1876, in Columbia. Richland and Columbia

---

[164] Columbia men were prominent in the campaign of 1868. Hampton was chairman, John P. Thomas the leading spirit, and F. W. McMaster and J. D. Pope members, of the executive committee which waged the fight. Thomas, J. G. Gibbes, and L. D. Childs carried the protest to Washington where Thomas made a strong supporting speech before the Reconstruction Committee. Thomas and S. L. Leaphart were candidates on the state ticket. Reynolds, *op. cit.*, pp. 89, 93-94.

[165] Simkins and Woody, *op. cit.*, pp. 86-89, 107-109, 182, Chap. XVII.

[166] Reynolds, *op. cit.*, p. 229.

[167] Williams, *Hampton*, pp. 27-38; Wallace, *op. cit.*, III, 301-306.

went overwhelmingly for the straight-out plan, sending a delegation headed by Hampton completely committed to it.[168] The convention nominated Hampton ; all Democratic factions united for the straight-out fight. There remained, however, a division of opinion as to the fundamental issue of the campaign and the proper method of waging it. One group, in accordance with Hampton's views held that the issue was simply that of good government and that the negro should be persuaded by peaceful means to join the whites in its accomplishment. The other group, led by General M. W. Gary, held that the issue was a contest between races for supremacy and that the "Mississippi Plan" of intimidation, and if need be force, should be adopted. In the campaign that followed both methods were effectively used.[169]

The Red Shirt campaign of 1876 was the most colorful and dramatic in South Carolina history. It began even before the meetings in the up-country. There Chamberlain was forced to divide time and listen to abusive denunciations of himself and his party, while mounted and armed men surrounded the stand and a hostile audience noisily interrupted and insulted him. So humiliating were these experiences that later the Republican nominees did not take part in a series of joint debates to which the Democrats invited them. The Democrats, however, continued throughout the campaign to appear in force at Republican meetings, demand division of the time and in every way possible attempt to discredit the speakers before their negro audiences.[170]

Meanwhile Hampton spoke at huge county campaign meetings over the state. Beginning at Anderson September 2nd and ending at Columbia November 4th, great crowds, with Red Shirts much in evidence, gathered to do him honor and promote enthusiasm.[171]

The whites, in order to prevent Federal interruption, were anxious to avoid outbreaks of violence and in many cases showed remarkable discipline and forbearance. It is surprising that so few collisions occurred in a campaign so intense. There were a few, as in Charleston where negroes attacked whites as they were guarding negro speakers of a Democratic Club. More serious were the Ellenton riots and the Cainhoy Massacre in Charleston County.[172]

Columbia and Richland were well represented among the leaders of the campaign. Besides Hampton, Richland had on the State

[168] Williams, *Hampton,* pp. 58-59.
[169] Wallace, *op. cit.,* III, 306.
[170] Wallace, *op. cit.,* III, 307-8.
[171] Williams, *Hampton, passim.*
[172] Wallace, *op. cit.,* III, 308-11.

ticket Hugh S. Thompson, (Superintendent of Education), and S. L. Leaphart (Treasurer). Colonel A. C. Haskell was chairman, and Richard O'Neal, Jr., was a member of the Executive Committee which managed the campaign.[173] Haskell proved a skillful manager and Hampton was almost a perfect candidate. A war hero, immensely popular all over the state, his character and disposition particularly fitted him for leadership in such a campaign. He had been among the very few who in 1865 had advocated a limited negro suffrage, and throughout the Radical régime he had stood for friendly and normal relations with the negroes. His conciliatory speeches during the campaign did much to swing negro votes into the Democratic column, while his qualities as a fearless and skillful leader in a desperate cause strongly appealed to the whites.[174]

The people of Columbia stood squarely behind their idol. Even the merchants, who profited greatly from Radical extravagance, were enthusiastic straight-outs. "On the principle of 'easy come, easy go' the official thieves were good spenders. . .As a place of fast living, by the thieves and their friends, the capital was a gathering place for immoral women of both colors and all styles and varieties from everywhere in the country. These, too, bought lavishly and for cash. Yet every business man was for honest, economical government and the turning out of wasters, good and profitable customers as they were. There were no more determined or earnest straight-outs in the State than the Columbia merchants, standing for what they believed to be the general good and for righteousness and decency, regardless of their own pocket nerves. This position was shared by the saloons, of which there were some forty or fifty. . .the business men of Columbia, big and little, high and low, good and bad, lost more money from the over-throw of Reconstruction than any other group of men in the State and did it with eyes open and gladly and proudly."[175]

Four great Hampton demonstrations were staged in Columbia during the campaign. The first coincided with the Convention and was for the double purpose of influencing the nomination[176] and answering threats of Republican leaders that no such demonstration would be allowed in Columbia. It was described as the finest celebration since 1860, but it was probably the "biggest and wildest array" Columbia had ever seen, with a great military display and

---

[173] Reynolds, *op. cit.,* pp. 351-353.
[174] Wallace, *op. cit.,* III, 231, 235, 237; Simkins and Woody, *op. cit.,* pp. 491, 497.
[175] Williams, *Hampton,* pp. 69-70.
[176] Simkins and Woody, *op. cit.,* p. 490, note.

a torch-light procession over a mile long. Again, when Hampton passed through Columbia September 21st, on his way to Darlington from the upcountry, he was given a great ovation. And when the speaking tour ended with the meeting November 4th in Columbia the demonstration exceeded anything which had occurred in a most spectacular campaign. Northern newspaper men said they had never seen anything that approached it. Hundreds of evergreen cables were stretched across Main Street, and at intervals were great arches, one of which was surmounted by a full-rigged ship with Hampton at

Hampton Carried Through the Streets After His Election as Governor
The Hatted Figure in Foreground is that of General Wilie Jones

the helm. The Columbia Flying Artillery, which since the order to disband the rifle clubs, now described itself as the "Hampton and Tilden Musical Club, with four twelve-pounder flutes," began firing salutes at sunrise. The procession was elaborate, one float showing a tall palmetto tree with a rattlesnake curled around its trunk and a coon-skin labeled "Chamberlain's Hide" nailed to a nearby post. The Fair Grounds were packed to the fences as Hampton and others spoke. At night the celebration continued with parade, transparencies, fireworks and a general hurrah. A fourth demonstration came when on the 9th of November returns seemed to indicate that Hampton was elected. The city went "stark, staring crazy with joy." Everybody quit work and proceeded to celebrate.[177] But the results from Richland were disappointing—Chamberlain had a majority of 1,422.[178]

The eyes of the world were on Columbia as the dispute over the election raged; for Tilden's as well as Hampton's title was involved. The returns showed a Hampton majority of 1,134 and 64 Democrats elected to the legislature with 60 Republicans. But there were charges of corruption on each side and the Republican Returning Board declared the election in Edgefield and Laurens invalid, thus giving the Republicans their claim to 59 in the legislature to 57 Democrats. The Democrats claimed, as did the Supreme Court, that the Returning Board had no such authority.[179]

In order to enforce the Republican contention Chamberlain, on the night before the legislature assembled in January, placed United States troops in the State House. Next day the Edgefield and Laurens members, marching with the Democrats to the door, were refused admission; whereupon the Democrats retired to Carolina Hall [180] and elected W. H. Wallace of Union, speaker. E. W. M. Mackey became speaker of the Republicans. The contest became intense and dangerous when a few days later the Democrats marched to the State House and into the hall, before the Republican doorkeeper realized their intention. When the Mackey House members entered a few minutes later Wallace refused to vacate the speaker's chair. Each speaker requested his Sergeant-at-Arms to remove the other and bloodshed seemed imminent as members crowded forward to protect their officers. But trouble was avoided when a Democrat proposed a committee of adjustment. For four days and nights this strange and threatening situation continued, as both sides attempted in vain to

---

[177] Williams, *Hampton,* pp. 79, 85, 216, 357-359, 372.
[178] Reynolds, *op. cit.,* p. 394.
[179] Wallace, *op. cit.,* III, 313–315.
[180] Located at rear of present Court House between Main and Sumter, about opposite present Western Union office.

Carolina Hall, the Place of Meeting of the Wallace House
From Leslie's Illustrated Newspaper, December 30, 1876

conduct business in defiance of the other. Finally, to avoid bloodshed the Wallace House retired again to Carolina Hall. Both houses declared elected, and inaugurated, their respective candidates and dual government continued until President Hayes withdrew the military support on which Chamberlain's tenure depended. On April 10th, 1877, Chamberlain retired, and Columbia was rid of the carpet-baggers.[181]

---

[181] Wallace, *op. cit.*, III, 318-321.

GOVERNMENT: MUNICIPAL, STATE AND FEDERAL

George A. Buchanan, Jr.

A LL CITIES, greater and lesser, have their governments and their problems in government. To Columbia, however, government is meat and drink. Born of government, it has existed and grown by and for government. County seat for Richland County, capital of South Carolina, center of a multiplicity of federal agencies, it revolves around government with its State House, its court houses, its city, county, state and federal office buildings, its governmental institutions and instrumentalities. Its big business is government, its woes governmental, its prosperity governmental prosperity; its tragedy is that government, upon which its peace and sustenance depend more than upon anything else, is too often the other face of politics, which is the tragedy of all capitals.

Established by the Act of March 22, 1786,[1] Columbia was the product of that conflict, which is the stuff of politics, between coastal region and interior, low country and up country that developed out of the diversity of interests in practically all of the original colonies.[2]

Original Seal of City of Columbia

In 1789 the General Assembly provided for the removal of the public records, those relating to the districts of Charleston, Georgetown and Beaufort excepted, to Columbia on and by December 1, 1789, the required public buildings in the new capital being ready.[3] By May 27 the commissioners, named to lay out the town on Taylor's Hill, near Friday's Ferry, reported in a letter to Governor Charles Pinckney that the carpenter had "engaged to compleat" the State House within two months and in accordance with this report, confirmed by later advices, Governor Pinckney issued his proclamation November 2, 1789, calling upon the state officers to prepare themselves and their papers for removal to Columbia and summon-

---

[1] Thomas Cooper and David J. McCord, *Statutes at Large of South Carolina*, 9 vols., Columbia, 1836-1841, V, 102-103.
[2] David Duncan Wallace, "Constitution of 1790 in South Carolina's Development," *History of South Carolina*, ed. by Yates Snowden, 5 vols., Chicago, 1920, I, 505-523.
[3] Cooper, *Statutes*, V, 102-103.

ing the members of the Senate and House to meet the first Monday in January in the new State House.[4]

On January 4, agreeably to this proclamation, the General Assembly held its first session in Columbia, distinguished for the fact that it issued the call for the constitutional convention, which also meeting in Columbia, gave South Carolina the constitution, signed June 3, 1790, that was, with amendments enacted in 1808 and 1816, to determine the State's government for seventy-five years. The renewal of the dispute as to the site of the capital almost disrupted the convention, but ended in the constitutional confirmation of Columbia's title "until otherwise determined by the concurrence of two-thirds of both branches of the whole representation." James Green Hunt, son-in-law of Colonel Thomas Taylor and a delegate to the convention, made the motion to have Columbia fixed as the permanent capital and on May 20 it came up for consideration. General C. C. Pinckney immediately moved the previous question, his motion being defeated 105 to 104 to reveal the delegates as practically evenly divided on the issue. The vote to name Columbia in the constitution as the permanent seat of the government was carried, 109 to 105,[5] but before this could be done a committee, representing both sections of the State, had worked out the compromise, embodied also in the constitution, whereby there were to be two State Treasurers, one for the up country, one for the low country; the Surveyor-General and the Secretary of State were to maintain offices both in Columbia and Charleston; the Court of Appeals was to meet in both Columbia and Charleston; and the Governor, although he was required to reside in the capital during the legislative sessions, might at other times make his residence where he should elect.[6]

Columbia's career as the city of government had been definitely begun although it had itself no government other than the General Assembly. The board of five commissioners, after 1806 appointed by the Governor [7] who had until then been empowered merely to fill vacancies during the recess of the Legislature, continued in office until by the Act of December 17, 1808,[8] it was supplanted by a single commissioner, Thomas Taylor, Jr.[9] The commissioners exercised

[4] Journal of House of Representatives, MS, January 7, 1790.
[5] Edwin L. Green, *History of Richland County*, Columbia, 1932, I, 152.
[6] Wallace, "Constitution of 1790," p. 513.
[7] Cooper, *Statutes*, V, 525.
[8] *Ibid.*, p. 589.
[9] Green, *History of Richland County*, I, 151. Green gives the date of the change as 1805; the act abolishing the old commission, the method of selection of the members of which had been changed in 1806, was not passed however until December, 1808, as a part of the Act to Raise Supplies, &c for that year.

no ordinary governmental functions however; they were the authors of the form of the city. To them, incidentally, is due Columbia's one hundred foot streets, an improvement upon the provision of the founding Act, written into it on the suggestion of Dr. John Budd, Representative from Charleston, that the streets should be not less than sixty feet wide, "with two principal streets running through the center of the town, at right angles, of one hundred and fifty feet wide." These two are, of course, Assembly and Senate streets, although the early inhabitants of the town preversely made Richardson Street (now Main), the principal business street, which it remains. In one particular the commissioners were a bit overzealous and in laying out the town so arranged the two-mile square as to include a fair bite of the river, in which they sold some lots,[10] a circumstance cited to the city's later advantage in the case of *State, ex rel. Bridge Co. v. Columbia,* 27 S. C., 137, in which the city's title to that portion of the river was upheld.

A visitor to Columbia from Connecticut, Edward Hooker, in 1805 described the first State House: [11]

"The State House is placed on an eminence directly in the center of the township. . . . The principal street is Richardson Street which runs on the east side of the State House: although State Street which runs on the west side was designed by the commissioners who planned the town, for the principal one. . . . The State House though made with two fronts was, however, so constructed as to present its handsomest front to the west. Yet public choice has so far disregarded the original plan that State Street is even to this time, to a considerable extent over-run with bushes. . . . The State House is very large on the ground, but yet so low as to be entirely void of anything like just proportion. It has only two stories, and one of these is partly below the natural surface of the ground, and is of brick plaistered over. The lower story is appropriated to the Treasurer's, Secretary's and Surveyor-General's offices. There are several other rooms, which, as far as I can learn, are used for little else than lodging rooms for the goats that run loose about the streets, and which, as the doors are never shut, have at all times free access. The Court House is a much handsomer building. . . .

"The Senate and Representative Chambers though not magnificent are finished in a better style than the exterior of the edifice would

---

[10] *Ibid.,* p. 150.

[11] The material for the following section on the State House was supplied by J. Mauldin Lesesne, Head of the History Department, Greenville High School.

authorize one to expect. They are furnished with handsome carpets, tables and chairs—with elegant maps of the United States and of each state in the Union—also of Europe and Asia—with a plan of Charleston and another of Columbia. The latter is executed in a very neat manner by a young Mr. Waring of this town who presented one to each house. The Legislature in return made him a compliment of an hundred dollars.

"There is considerable elegance, bordering on magnificence, about the seats of the President of the Senate and Speaker of the House. The curtains for the windows, before which the chairs are placed on an elevated and commanding stand, are quite rich and beautiful to the eye." [12]

This original State House, where the first Legislature had met in Columbia in January, 1790,[13] continued to be used until its destruc-

State House, about 1855

tion by fire in February, 1865, during Sherman's occupation of the city.[14]

The building had deteriorated so considerably by 1850, however, that Governor Seabrook felt that the state records were not safe there.[15] The General Assembly recommended that a fire-proof build-

---

[12] "Diary of Edward Hooker, 1805-1808," *American Historical Association Report for 1896*, Washington, 1897, pp. 854-57.
[13] *Senate Journal, 1790*, MS.
[14] *Reports and Resolutions, 1865*, p. 78.
[15] *Senate Journal,* 1850, p. 61.

ing for the records be erected near the State House,[16] but a joint committee to decide upon the recommendation went further, and plans were drawn for this fire-proof structure as the northern wing of a complete new State House.[17]

Work on the new north wing was begun at once, and the corner stone was laid on December 15, 1851.[18] In December, 1852, the commission appointed to superintend the building asked for $50,000.00, part of which was to be used for a new section of the Capitol, following the plans submitted by P. H. Hammarskold. The appropriation was granted, and the Legislature was thereby committed to the building of a new State House.[19] The strongest single influence in bringing this about, was probably that of Benjamin Fanueil Hunt, a native of Massachusetts, who was then a member of the House of Representatives from Charleston.[20]

The next December the commission reported that work was progressing rapidly, giving the public the cheapest and most magnificent public building in the United States;[21] $250,000.00 was asked to continue the work, and a bond issue was provided by the Legislature for this amount.[22] This was the beginning of the long series of bond issues which placed a heavy debt upon the state.

During 1854 the old State House was removed slightly to the southwest to make room for the new building. In May, when the foundation of the new State House was completed and the walls were well above ground, the commissioners found cracks in the masonry which the architect could not explain. They appealed to Governor John L. Manning who engaged John R. Niernsee as consulting architect.[23] He examined the building and reported that its defects were due to the use of inferior materials and poor workmanship. The commission, convinced that there was either fraud or extreme carelessness, dismissed Hammarskold and the contractors for the brick and stone work.[24] The loss to the State was estimated at approximately $75,000.00,[25] and there was serious doubt whether the project should be given up or continued.

---

[16] Reports and Resolutions, 1850, p. 158.
[17] Ibid., 1851, p. 273.
[18] House Journal, 1851, pp. 229-31.
[19] Reports and Resolutions, 1852, p. 217.
[20] Edwin Scott, Random Recollections of a Long Life, Columbia, 1884, p. 40.
[21] Reports and Resolutions, 1853, pp. 133-35.
[22] Statutes at Large, XII, 307-8.
[23] Mr. Niernsee, a native of Germany, had come to the U. S. and located in Baltimore where he enjoyed an enviable reputation.
[24] Reports and Resolutions, 1854, pp. 130-32.
[25] Ibid., p. 137.

The Legislature decided to continue, with important changes suggested by Niernsee. The building was to face north and south instead of east and west as originally planned.[26]

In December, 1855, the supervision of construction was put in the hands of a paid commissioner, elected by joint ballot.[27] General James Jones [28] was elected and gave complete satisfaction in the position until he resigned to enter the service of the Confederacy.

One of his first acts was the engagement of Mr. Niernsee.[29] The architect moved to Columbia in June, 1856, and thereafter gave his

State House, as planned by Niernsee

full time to the work.[30] The State House was completed largely according to the plans of Mr. Niernsee except for the substitution, by a later architect, of the dome for Niernsee's rectangular tower.

The chief period of uninterrupted work took place from 1856 to 1861. During these years the Legislature issued annually over a quarter of a million dollars in stocks or bonds to finance the enter-

---

[26] *Ibid.*, pp. 283-84.
[27] *Ibid.*, 1855, p. 348.
[28] *House Journal, 1855*, p. 255.
[29] *Reports and Resolutions*, 1856, p. 163.
[30] *Ibid.*, p. 167.

prise. The paper was usually sold at or near par by the Bank of the State of South Carolina. It bore interest (payable semi-annually) at the rate of 6% and the date of maturity ranged from twenty to thirty years. The building peak was reached for the fiscal year 1860 when over $425,000.00 was expended and an average of 498 persons were employed. The average number employed from 1856 to 1861 was about 375, of whom about three-fifths were negroes.[31]

Practically all of the granite came from the Granby quarry near the Congaree River. A railroad slightly more than three miles long was constructed to the quarry in 1857.[32] Over this road were hauled fifty-six blocks weighing up to 56 tons.[33] Almost all the work in the quarries was done by negro slaves, while the finished stone work was done by white laborers. The finished granite work and all the marble work was let on contract to Sisson and Dougherty who worked faithfully even during the trying days of the Confederate War.[34]

Most of the work on the building was suspended on March 15, 1861, since the bonds for financing it could not be sold. The slaves were still kept in the quarries and the polishing and shaping of the finer stone continued.[35]

When Sherman's army shelled Columbia from Lexington Heights, ten shells struck the unfinished State House, four falling inside the building and the rest striking the outer wall. The next day the old State House was burned in the city-wide conflagration. The heat from the old building caused a portion of the new structure to crumble, but this damage was insignificant compared with the destruction of materials on the grounds. Practically all of the finished granite, marble and wrought iron was destroyed. Even the construction machinery and the plans of the architect were ruined. But the great monolithic columns, then on the ground, escaped the general destruction, and today adorn the north and south porticoes. After salvaging what he could from the wreckage, Mr. Niernsee estimated the loss to the state at $700,000.00.[36]

The war had left the people of the State bankrupt, but a roof was placed on the unfinished building and the Legislature was able to

---

[31] These are facts compiled from the reports of the commissioner, and the architect, to the legislature for the inclusive years and found in *Reports and Resolutions*. The bond issues were taken from *Statutes at Large*.
[32] *Reports and Resolutions*, 1857, p. 225.
[33] *Reports and Resolutions*, 1860, p. 226.
[34] *Ibid.*, 1859, p. 125; *Ibid.*, 1863, p. 110.
[35] *Ibid.*, 1861, pp. 160-61.
[36] *Reports and Resolutions, 1865*, pp. 77-79.

Incomplete Structure of State House, 1865

use the new State House for the first time in 1869.[37] The radical group, who governed South Carolina from 1868 to 1876, did no more for the State House building, but, within a four-year period spent over $200,000.00 on furniture for it, which a later inventory valued at only $17,715.00.[38]

When the Democrats resumed control in 1877, they were occupied for a number of years in restoring the credit of the State, but by 1882 they again took up the completion of the State House. Governor Hugh S. Thompson was very much interested in the enterprise and conferred with Mr. Niernsee who had returned to Baltimore to live. In 1884, the sum of $75,000.00 was appropriated to begin construction with Mr. Niernsee in charge, but he died in June, 1885, and J. C. Neilson of Baltimore was appointed to complete the building.[39] Mr. Neilson became involved in a political controversy which ended in his dismissal, and Frank Niernsee, son of the original architect, was selected to replace him.[40] He completed this work in 1891, although the porticoes were not yet in place.[41]

Yet another building program had to be adopted before the State House was to appear as it does today. In 1900 the Legislature decided to add the porticoes and the tower. A commission appointed

---

[37] *House Journal Regular Session, 1869-70,* p. 17.
[38] *Reports and Resolutions, 1877-78,* p. 1026.
[39] *House Journal,* 1885, p. 26.
[40] *Reports and Resolutions,* 1888, II, 893.
[41] *Ibid.,* 1891, II, 459.

Frank P. Milburn of Charlotte as architect.[42] Mr. Milburn changed the original tower to a dome. He completed his work in 1902, and although J. Q. Marshall, a member of the commission, objected violently the commission accepted the work on May 23, 1902.[43]

Mr. Marshall then took his fights to the Legislature and succeeded in getting a new commission appointed with himself as chairman and Mr. C. C. Wilson of Columbia as architect.[44] Mr. Wilson corrected some of the shabby work of the former architect and made a number of improvements from 1903 to 1907.[45]

Thus the work which began in 1851 was completed in 1907. The total cost to the State was approximately $3,000,000.00.[46] The state government has long ago outgrown the building. A number of proposals have been made for enlargement, but it is feared that any addition may destroy the symmetry of the beautiful structure.

State House, 1895

Columbia's government, independent of the general state law, dates from the act of December 16, 1797,[47] "to establish roads and ferries, etc.," one of the provisions of which created a board of nine commissioners of streets and markets in the interest of the "convenience

[42] *Ibid.,* 1903, II, 1157-1159; *Statutes at Large,* XXIII, 501.
[43] *Reports and Resolutions, 1903,* II, 1243-44.
[44] *Ibid.,* 1904, I, 717.
[45] *Ibid.,* 1905, V, 182; *Ibid.,* 1907, III, 373; *Ibid.,* 1908, III, 446.
[46] This figure is derived by taking the reports of the various commissioners and architects to the legislature. It includes Sherman's estimated destruction and does not account for the funding arrangement of 1873.
[47] Cooper, *Statutes,* V, 379.

and comfort of the inhabitants of Columbia." The nine commissioners, who were vested with all the authority within the limits of Columbia that "the Commissioners of the town of Georgetown are vested with, within the limits of Georgetown," were elected neither by the Legislature nor by the town's citizens but were named in the act itself: Benjamin Waring, John Calvert, Thomas Fitzpatrick, Samuel Green, Joshua Benson, Burrage Purvis, Swanson Lunsford, George Wade and John Taylor. Of these, constituting the first Columbia government, one, John Taylor, was afterwards governor of South Carolina, and another, Benjamin Waring, was elected secretary of state. Swanson Lunsford, who died August 7, 1799, has the distinction of being buried on the State House grounds (near the southeastern corner.) [48]

This was far from either effective or self government and the following year the act creating the street and market commission was repealed and another act, providing for the election of seven

Old Market, Built After 1865, Razed 1913

commissioners of streets and markets, was passed. The nine-member commission itself had petitioned the assembly for the change, setting forth that "the powers invested in them . . . are not sufficiently extensive and complete, and not fully calculated for the well-governing and regulating the streets and markets of the said town." The election in which all free white inhabitants of the town who had paid a tax of $1.00 or more towards the support of the

---

[48] Bateman, pp. 31-32. Green, *History of Richland County*, I, 178.

state government were permitted to vote, was fixed for the first Monday of the following April, Simon Taylor, Swanson Lunsford and Samuel Green being named as the managers of the election. The commissioners, vested with all the powers of commissioners of the roads, were given authority as a local governing body to pass "such rules and regulations, within the said town, as they may deem proper and requisite for the promotion of the quiet and safety of the inhabitants"; they were empowered to levy and collect fines, to grant tavern and liquor licenses, to fine and expel all keepers of gaming tables, to collect, through a clerk of the market to be selected by them, rents on the market stalls and fees for recording marks and brands of all cattle butchered and sold. The money so derived from these miscellaneous licenses and fees—the town's first revenue source—was appropriated for the upkeep of streets and the market, the clerk's salary and the salaries of any other officers named to carry out the purposes of the act. The surplusage remaining, if any, it was provided, was to be paid over to trustees of the Columbia Academy, for which provision had been made in the act of December 21, 1792, and of which Abram Blanding was the head.[49]

When Richland County had been created in 1785 the act required that at a point near the center of the county a court house, a pillory, whipping post and a jail should be built. And on Monday, August 6, 1792, the inhabitants of the county were called to gather at the house of William Sanders Taylor, on Mill Creek, to ballot for a place to erect the county court house.[50] Two years later *The South Carolina Gazette* announced an election for Richland County, to be held the first day at Richland Court House and the second day at Columbia, indicating apparently that some other site than Columbia had been chosen for the court house. Tradition has it that the court house was at Meyer's Hill, now Horrell Hill, and a portion of what is said to be one of the buildings is shown now near the home of Howell Morrell.[51] By the act of December 18, 1799, Columbia became the county seat and John G. Guignard, John Hopkins, Timothy Rivers, John Goodwyn and John Taylor were in 1799 named commissioners to build and repair the court house and gaol.[52] In August, 1800, this commission contracted with Jesse Arthur to erect a gaol in Columbia for $3,570, the work to be done by Septem-

---

[49] Cooper, *Statutes*, V, 332.
[50] *South Carolina Gazette* (Columbia), July 10, 1792, Green, *History of Richland County*, I, 156.
[51] Green, *History of Richland County*, I, 156.
[52] *Ibid.*, p. 201.

Columbia City Hall, 1936

ber 1, 1801.[53] Edward Hooker's diagram [54] locates the building in 1805 as on the southeast corner of Richardson (Main) and Washington streets, apparently, however, in error. It was from the proceeds of the sale of the northeast corner, opposite the first town hall, that the county board of commissioners in 1892 purchased the present Washington and Sumter Street site. Hooker described the first court house as a "much handsomer building (than the State House) of brick, two stories high" while Mills complained that it did not "correspond in . . . appearance with the other buildings" and suggested that a "more spacious and permanent" structure should be erected.[55] This building was torn down about 1850 [56] and the second court house, which was destroyed by the burning of Columbia, took its place also on the northeast corner of Washington and Richardson. The third court house, located at the intersection of Washington and Sumter streets, the contract for which was let in 1872, was razed in 1935 and work was begun December, 1935, on a fourth.

The constitutional convention of 1790 assigned Richland two members of the House and gave the three counties of Richland, Fair-

[53] Miscellaneous Records, MS., B, 168-170. Green, *History of Richland County*, I, 201.
[54] "Diary of Edward Hooker," pp. 853-856.
[55] Robert Mills, *Statistics of South Carolina*, Charleston, 1826, p. 699 *et seq.*
[56] D. P. Robbins, *Historical and Descriptive Sketch of Columbia*, Columbia, 1888, p. 19.

field and Chester one Senator. When the first legislature under the new constitution met January 3, 1791, the Richland representatives were James Green Hunt and Wade Hampton; the senator from the three counties was Colonel Thomas Taylor.[57]

The South Carolina college, established by the act of 1801, had been opened in 1805 and the village during the legislative sessions, if not at other times, had come, as Drayton records, to take on a bustling appearance. The town in its growing pains found the semi-government provided by the street commissioners unsatisfactory. "The inhabitants," Hooker [58] recorded in November, 1805, "have no special privileges at present except a power of making regulations concerning public wells and markets, through the agency of a committee who are styled 'Commissioners of the Streets.' They are however expecting erelong to get from the Legislature a charter of incorporation, which shall confer upon them the same powers with Camden and other little cities or boroughs."

On December 19, 1805, the act, granting the city its first charter, incorporating it as the town of Columbia, was passed. The municipal power was vested in one intendant and six wardens, to be elected annually on the first Monday in April, all persons constitutionally qualified to vote for members of the legislature and resident in the town for one year being declared members of the corporation and entitled to vote. Vacancies were to be filled by special elections, ordered by the intendant and wardens, any four of whom, with the intendant, constituted a quorum of the board. The corporation, through its governing board, was given the authority to levy taxes upon all real taxable property within the town, not to exceed twelve and one-half cents on every $100 of assessed valuation, and might impose fines, not to exceed $12 for each offense. In addition, of course, the board was to collect the licenses and fees which had heretofore been collected by the commissioners of streets and markets.[59]

The first election was held and John Taylor was named the first intendant.[60] The son of Colonel Thomas Taylor and a graduate of New Jersey College at Princeton, Mr. Taylor served as Richland's representative in both branches of the Legislature and was a member of Congress, serving there also in both house and senate; in 1826 he was elected Governor. On April 16, 1832, he died.[61]

---

[57] Green, *History of Richland County*, I, 155.
[58] "Diary of Edward Hooker," pp. 853-856.
[59] McCord, *Statutes*, VIII, 235-237.
[60] *Ordinances of the Town of Columbia*, Columbia, 1823.
[61] Green, *History of Richland County*, I, 182-183.

On May 1, 1806, given in the first publication of the town ordinances (1823) as the date of the election, the first session of the town board was held at which Ordinance No. 1 was passed and ratified. It required the clerk of the market to ring the market bell every evening at 9 o'clock as a signal for all negroes to be at home, prescribed specifications for blacksmith shops within the city limits, than a canter under pain of $1 fine or 20 lashes for a slave, prohibited horses from running at large in the town, established the first speed law prohibiting any horse to be ridden at a gait faster than a canter under pain of $1 fine or, if a slave, 20 lashes, prohibiting false alarms of fire under pain of a $10 fine, licensing billiard tables at $100 a year and liquor shops at $8 a year, fixing the punishment for slaves found drunk or misbehaving in any other manner at 20 lashes, or two hours in the stocks, or 24 hours imprisonment.

Three other ordinances were passed during Mr. Taylor's administration. One, Ordinance No. 2, ratified June 9, 1806, prohibited public shows unless licensed by the intendant or two wardens. The third, passed December 5, fixed the tax levy for the year at twelve and one-half cents, the maximum allowed by the charter. The fourth, passed the same day, provided for the sale of wood from the unsold town lots at 25 cents a cord for pine ready cut and dry, 50 cents a cord for other fire wood, 25 cents a tree for all timber trees and established rental charges for market stalls.

On April 11, 1807, the second intendant, Abraham Nott, was elected.[62]

The first act of his administration, written into the market ordinance, passed May 6, was Columbia's first step towards prohibition —a section forbidding the gift, sale or delivery of "any spirits or other intoxicants" to any negro slave "unless by express permission of the owner or employer of such slave." Also a part of this ordinance was the city's first Sunday law, providing that "no person shall hereafter buy from any negro any corn, peas, fowls or other thing, nor shall sell any articles to any negro on the Sabbath day." Passed the same day was a more general Sunday law prohibiting after June 1 any labor on the Sabbath under pain of a $10 fine, or business under pain of a $12 fine. Slaves violating the ordinance were to receive 20 lashes on the bare back.

The board at its first meeting also acted [63] to set aside the square bounded by Senate, Pendleton, Gadsden and Wayne streets for a burying ground and to prohibit any further burials in the town's

---

[62] *Ordinances of the Town of Columbia,* Columbia, 1823.
[63] *Ibid.*

first cemetery, on the square now occupied by the First Presbyterian Church, for which provision had been made by act of the Assembly, December 21, 1798.[64]

Also during Mr. Nott's administration intruded the until this day unsolved problem of real property tax delinquency. The first town tax act was less than a year old when on July 30, 1807, the town board found that there was need for stern measures to enforce the payment of town taxes. The assessor, whose office filled by election by the board had been created by the town charter, was accordingly required to "hang up at the front door of the court house in Columbia, in the most conspicuous place, a list of the names of all such defaulters." [65] Ten days of such public exposure to scorn was then to be followed by seizure of property for sale. To meet the complaints of those who conceived their property to be assessed too high it was arranged that any taxpayer might "swear off so much thereof as shall be conceived to be overcharged before the intendant and wardens," the assessor being required to accept this declaration under oath without further question. By the following year when Claiborne Clifton was the intendant the delinquent taxpayers got in their inning. A man still had his rights though he might be tardy in paying 12½ cents for every $100.00 of property he owned. And so, by ordinance passed May 28, 1808, the assessor was required, before hanging up his list of tax defaulters, to give three weeks' notice in the *Gazette* of where and when taxes might be paid to him. Tax sales also lost their finality when the assessor was permitted to sell property seized by him for seven years "instead of absolutely and in fee." [66] The tax rate for the first sixteen years of the town's government remained unchanged at 12½ cents on each $100.00, for the reason that the charter act fixed this as the maximum levy. The act of December 14, 1819,[67] amended the charter so as to increase the powers of the intendant and wardens, raising the tax limit to 50 cents on every $100.00 of property and the limit of fines imposed by the town board to $50.00. The next year, therefore, Columbia, James T. Goodwyn being intendant, experienced its first tax increase, the levy being raised from 12½ to 25 cents.[68] In 1821 the rate dropped to 15 cents on each $100.00,[69] but the next year it was up

[64] Cooper, *Statutes*, V, 332.
[65] *Ordinances of Columbia*, 1823.
[66] *Ibid.*
[67] Cooper, *Statutes*, VI, 118.
[68] *Ordinances of Columbia*, 1823, p. 74.
[69] *Ibid.*, p. 78.

again to 20 cents [70] and by 1824 was back at 25 cents.[71] All fines were increased to $50.00 by the ordinance of January 11, 1820.

Columbians of the city's first 20 years, not over-anxious to pay taxes, were also, it appears, somewhat backward in the discharge of their required duty of working the city streets. In 1805 Assembly Street, intended as one of the two principal streets of the town, was, Hooker records, "to a considerable extent overrun with bushes." [72] Almost one out of every four of the early ordinances is concerned with the town board's efforts to see to it that all males in the city performed the street duty required of them. In 1812 the office of warner was created,[73] the holders of which were to make a list of all persons liable to work on the streets and to "warn said persons to meet and work." This failed to solve the problem and what amounts to a street tax of $2.00 was later imposed, payment of which would exempt the citizens from street work as, to this day citizens of the state may upon payment of a nominal road tax be relieved of the responsibility for working the roads which the highway department maintains for them.

The General Assembly, meanwhile, having relinquished the control of other matters of Columbia's economy to the town board, was devoting itself to keeping the city safe from billiards, a form of amusement permitted and licensed in the early days.[74] After the establishment of the college, however, the license, already more than ten times greater than the liquor license charge, was increased to $500.00, apparently designed to be prohibitive.[75] It failed however to prohibit and in 1818 there was inserted in the act to establish the city water system the declaration that the intendant and wardens "shall not hereafter, upon any pretense whatever, issue a license to keep a billiard table in the town of Columbia." [76] At the expiration of licenses already issued billiard tables were declared unlawful in Columbia and within fifteen miles of the town, under pain of a six months sentence to the common jail and a fine of $2,000.00. Four years later the prohibition zone was reduced to a ten-mile radius of Columbia [77] and in 1826 to a five-mile radius. These amendments and retreats were ignored by Mills who in 1826 told how the city's adventure into law-made morals had operated to its citizens' uplift.

[70] Ibid., p. 80.
[71] Ibid., p. 100.
[72] "Diary of Edward Hooker," p. 853.
[73] Ordinances of Columbia, 1823.
[74] Cooper, Statutes, V, 401.
[75] Ibid., V, 612.
[76] Ibid., VI, 103.
[77] McCord, Statutes at Large, IX, 524.

"By law," he records, "billiards and all kinds of gaming tables are prohibited within fifteen miles of Columbia. The beneficial effects of this are evident in the moral habits of the citizens generally and it is important, on account of the number of youth educating there at the public institutions of the place." [78] The very following year, however, the Legislature showed itself as curiously less concerned about the moral habits of Columbians during the summer when, in extending the prohibition limits again to ten miles, it permitted the operation of billiard tables within this restricted area, but not closer to Columbia than five miles, during the months of July, August and September. [79] The pastime of course survived and has long since been made legal in Columbia as elsewhere in the state. [80] Not so fortunate however was the noble game of EO, prohibited by the ordinance of June 16, 1817, for the regulation of tavern keepers. [81]

Where the early sessions of the city board were held, available records do not show—the names of tax delinquents were posted on the county court house door—and it was not until 1818 that provision was made in the acts for the construction of a city hall on a part of the public lot, "on which the gaol in the town of Columbia stands." This, the northwest corner of Richardson (Main) and Washington streets, now the site of the South Carolina National Bank, was conveyed to the city board, Lodge No. 68, Ancient Free Masons, the South Carolina Agricultural Society and the Medical Board of South Carolina. On the lot, eighty feet on Richardson Street and fifty feet on Washington Street, the "grantees, or some one of them" were required within three years to erect a brick or stone building, not less than seventy by forty feet, to be "appropriated to the use of town meetings and meetings of the intendant and wardens." To be housed in the structure when completed was "a large and good town clock,   .   .   .   with bells sufficiently large to be heard throughout the town."

Robert Mills, the architect of the original State Hospital building, who had criticized the court house, found the town hall in 1826 a pleasing structure. "The town hall," he wrote, "has a respectable facade and an excellent clock which ornaments the belfry crowning the roof. The markets are held under the town hall." [82] J. F. Williams, writing in 1929, of his memories of the period from 1856 to 1860, supplies the additional detail that the tower housing the fire

---

[78] Mills, *Statistics,* p. 699, *et seq.*
[79] McCord, *Statutes,* IX, 568.
[80] Furman R. Gresette, ed. *Code of Laws of South Carolina,* Charlottesville, Va., 1932, III, 231-236.
[81] *Ordinances,* 1823, pp. 60-61.
[82] Mills, *Statistics,* p. 699, *et seq.*

bell and town clock extended over the sidewalk. "You went under a large arch over the pavement," he tells, "and could see the clock without going out into the street." [83] Still preserved is a drawing of the building as it was before it was destroyed in the fire of February 17, 1865, during Sherman's occupation of the city.

Passed two days after the enactment of the measure which provided the town with its town hall was the Act of December 18, 1818, intended to empower the intendant and wardens of Columbia to borrow $25,000.00 for the purpose of erecting a waterworks to supply the town with "good water" which in consideration of $5,000.00 to be paid out of the general treasury was to be supplied the State House and all other public buildings without other charge.[84]

The town board did not however undertake the enterprise, but, in accord with the alternative allowed by the Act, entered into an agreement March 12, 1819, with Abram Blanding, its sometime school teacher, to construct the water works and conferred upon him all rights given the town, the right to borrow the $25,000.00 and to levy taxes to repay it excepted, by the Act of 1818. Mr. Blanding on his part contracted to construct the water works and to supply Richardson Street from Senate to Upper Street with water within two years, Sumter, Marion and Bull streets, from Senate to Taylor, within four years. Water for fire hydrants was to be sold to the town at an annual rental of $10.00 a year for each square served, the fire plugs themselves being provided by the town.[85]

Blanding began work, financing the project out of his own resources at a cost of $75,000.00,[86] and by December 13, 1820, the steam engine, purchased from England to pump the water to the elevated reservoirs, was demonstrated before "a large number of the citizens and members of the General Assembly," although, since the reservoirs had not been completed it could not then be put into operation. "A cleaner working piece of machinery," a writer in the Charleston *Courier* recorded, "perhaps is not in the United States. It appeared more like the movement of the celestial system than a human invention." [87]

Mills in 1826 described the completed plant:

"Columbia is amply supplied with spring water which is forced up by a steam power 120 feet from springs issuing from a valley be-

[83] J. F. Williams, *Old and New Columbia,* Columbia, 1929, p. 43.
[84] McCord, *Statutes,* VI, 101.
[85] *Ordinances,* 1823, pp. 86-92.
[86] Bateman, *Scrapbook,* pp. 48-49.
[87] *Courier* (Charleston), December 20, 1820, A. S. Salley, Jr., ed., *South Carolina Historical and Genealogical Magazine,* Charleston, 1904, V, 262.

tween the town and river. It is distributed through the principal
streets in cast iron pipes and then conveyed from these main con-
duits in leaden pipes." [88]

Blanding by his 1819 agreement with the town, signed for the
town by James T. Goodwyn, intendant, and John Bynum, John M.
Creyon, Robert Yates, William Branthwaite, James Young and S.
Guirey, wardens, was "at liberty to charge for the use of water as
much as he   .   .   .   think proper" not to exceed fourteen per cent
per annum upon capital expended, but the venture apparently did
not prove financially successful and Blanding in 1835 sold the works
to the town for about one-third cost.[89]

The water works system since that time has remained a municipal
enterprise. The plant, divers times rebuilt, was moved some time
after 1855, when a $100,000.00 bond issue for a new water works
was authorized,[90] from what is now Seaboard Park, where the water
had been secured from two springs and pumped up to the eminence
of Arsenal Hill. The new plant was fed with spring water until the
pumping station was moved across the canal and water from the
river, as now, was used.[91]

The town in its early days was plagued with fires [92] and the town
board as early as May 12, 1814, was taking steps to reduce the fire
loss by requiring every householder to supply himself with a well if
he were not already supplied with a natural spring and to purchase
and maintain fire buckets, one bucket for each $50.00 of estimated
annual rent,[93] changed the same year to one bucket for each chimney
and an additional bucket for each $1,000.00 over $3,000.00 of property valuation. By the ordinance of November 2, 1816, the organized fire department was born with the creation of the offices of fire
wardens, five of whom were named and empowered to recruit engineers and axemen who were to be paid twenty-five cents an hour
for their work in extinguishing any fire. To encourage the firemen
there was offered also a $10.00 reward to the men operating the first
engine "filled and prepared to discharge." [94]

In 1818 the selection of the fire wardens was ordered to be made
by ballot of the town board as were other municipal officers and the
men of the fire companies were authorized to select for themselves

[88] Mills, *Statistics,* p. 699 *et seq.*
[89] Green, *History of Richland County,* I, 188.
[90] *Statutes,* XII, 353.
[91] Williams, *Old and New Columbia,* p. 57.
[92] *Ordinances,* 1823, pp. 67-68.
[93] *Ibid.,* p. 50.
[94] *Ibid,* p. 57.

"some simple uniform." [95] To encourage citizens to accept willingly the work of firemaster it was provided that no person should be required to serve more than one in any three years and to discourage them from taking the office too lightly the fine for non-performance of duty was increased from $12.00 to such a sum as the board might inflict.[96] In February, 1825, volunteer fire companies having been organized in wards one and two, the fire warden system was abolished, except in ward three until a third volunteer company could be organized, and the captains and lieutenants of the volunteer companies were invested with the powers of fire wardens.[97] The experiment was abandoned as a failure later in the year, the volunteer company in ward one having been disbanded and no volunteer company organized in ward three. The volunteer system was thereupon abolished, November 14, 1825, except for the Vigilant Fire Company

Metropolitan Engine, Purchased for Palmetto Volunteer Fire Company, 1903. From left to right: W. M. Perry, Murdoc McCravey, W. J. Heidt, August Hoefer, George F. Nafey, W. F. Steiglitz

in ward two, and the fire warden plan readopted, with the reward to the first company in action increased to $20.00.[98] The city later,

[95] *Ordinances*, 1823, pp. 66-67.
[96] *Ibid.*, pp. 73-74.
[97] *Ibid.*, pp. 104-105.
[98] *Ibid.*, pp. 118-121.

of course, returned to the volunteer fire company system and the Independent company, organized in 1837; the Palmetto, organized in 1848; the Phoenix, born in 1872, and the Columbia, organized in 1893, were the city's defenders against fire until the establishment of the paid fire department in 1903.[99]

Law enforcement, on the other hand, reached the stage of official organization early in the town's history. In the beginning the town depended upon the state patrol law and the first law enforcement officer, employed by the town, was a marshal, who by ordinance in 1808, was required to go through the town on every Sunday "once in the forenoon and once in the afternoon . . . in order to suppress any riotous or disorderly conduct," always allowing that the rioters would be so careless as to riot at the time of the marshal's passing.[100] The marshal became clerk of the market and on January 1, 1824, the town guard was organized, headed by a captain, elected by the town board.[101] To support the guard an additional five cents tax on real property was levied and for twenty-three days it was law of the town that slave-owners should pay a $1.00 tax on each slave over the age of 15 years for the same purpose.[102] Citizens were exempted from patrol duty upon payment of a $5.00 head tax. June of the same year the guard organization was perfected. Composing it were one captain, at $33.33 1/3 a month; two sergeants, at $20.00 each a month; seven privates, at $18.00 a month.[103] By 1856 there were John Burdell, chief, and nine patrolmen, four on duty at a time, making up the police force.

Created also in June, 1825, was the town board of health, composed of three members from each ward. The board, to which physicians were required to report all cases of contagious or malignant disease, were empowered to direct the town scavengers in the removal of garbage, and were empowered among other things to require citizens to open and ventilate any cellar, house or other inclosure in which "foul air or noxious effluvia originates or are collected." [104]

The town was first divided into three wards by James S. Guignard, Abram Blanding, William Hall, Andrew Wallace and Daniel Morgan, commissioners, by provision of the Act of December 20,

[99] "History of Columbia's Volunteer Fire Department," *Annual State Fireman's Association,* Charleston, 1926, pp. 127-130.

[100] *Ordinances,* 1823.

[101] *Ibid.,* pp. 96-98.

[102] *Ibid.,* p. 99.

[103] *Ibid.,* pp. 107-113.

[104] *Ibid.,* pp. 113-118.

1823, which also gave the town the right to tax personal property and provided for the election of the wardens, two from each ward, by the voters of the wards they represented.[105] The ward election plan however endured only one year and the personal property tax by December 18, 1824, had been limited to twelve and one-half cents tax on each slave and "no other personal property whatever." [106]

Thirty years brought no fundamental change in government and then December 21, 1854, during the second term of William Maybin, intendant, the town was granted its second charter and became thereby the city of Columbia, governed by a mayor and six aldermen, two from each ward, elected each year and collectively designated as the city council, empowered to pass all needful rules, ordinances and regulations. The tax limit was raised to $1.00 on every $100.00 of property valuation and various new taxes, including levies on dogs, on insurance premiums and incomes (ministers and school masters were excused from paying it), were authorized.[107] Four years later an additional ward was created and the number of aldermen was increased to twelve, three from each ward, elected at large. Payment of city taxes was made a prerequisite of the ballot.[108] This Act of 1858 also provided for the establishment of the first work house. In 1859 the term of the mayor and aldermen was increased to two years,[109] the first two mayors, Edward J. Arthur, elected in 1855 and re-elected in 1856, and James D. Tradewell, elected in 1857 and re-elected in 1858, having served two years each by that general consent that sometimes fixes the term of office though no law does.

With the period of the Confederate war and the opening sessions of the secession convention, Columbia became a Confederate city; its military companies went off to war. Those women, children and others, who remained behind endured the hardships that wars involve. Then February 17, 1865, Columbia fell and, the Confederate forces having been withdrawn, Mayor James J. Goodwyn, accompanied by three aldermen proceeded between 8 and 9 o'clock a. m., in the direction of Broad River for the purpose of surrendering the city to General Sherman. The surrender was made to Colonel Stone, leading the advance guard, and by 11 o'clock Columbia was in the hands of Sherman's soldiers. That night the city was destroyed by fire. Sherman continued his march into North Carolina to accept the

---

[105] McCord, *Statutes*, VI, 240.
[106] *Ibid.*, p. 254.
[107] *Statutes*, XIII, 293.
[108] *Ibid.*, p. 614.
[109] *Ibid.*, p. 681.

surrender at Greensboro April 26, 1865, of the last Confederate army in the east. The war was ended.

The Reconstruction period brought the constitutional convention of 1868 and then the orgy of waste and corruption that marked the carpet-bag days. Two mayors, Colonel Gunther and C. H. Baldwin, both appointed by the United States military authorities, were followed by the election of John McKenzie, November, 1868, for a term of four years, the city charter having been amended to this extent by the Act of September 25, 1868. Mayor McKenzie was however legislated out of office by an Act passed February 26, 1870, in which, without regard for the fact that McKenzie's four-year term was not half completed, a new election was ordered for April, 1870. In the ensuing contest, in which voters from territories annexed to the city by the 1870 Act participated although they had not qualified, John Alexander was elected mayor for a two-year term. McKenzie and his aldermen disputed the new council's claim to office and the controversy was finally submitted to the Supreme Court, which in an opinion by Associate Justice Willard, upheld Alexander's right to assume office.[110]

The incorporation of the suburbs into the city had given the Republicans control and an expensive rebuilding program was entered into although obviously all of the money did not go into the rebuilding.

"During the reconstruction period things were in a terrible condition," Williams recalls. ". . . We never had a negro mayor or governor, but most of our aldermen were negroes. . . . At one time there was only one white man on the police force except the chief. . . . Frank Nixon." [111]

The State Hospital, then the Lunatic Asylum, survived the fire as did the College. The asylum, dream of Samuel Farrow, former Lieutenant Governor and Congressman, was provided for by the Act of December 21, 1821, the passage of which was due chiefly to the work of Farrow and William Crafts, neither of whom lived to see the completion of the hospital in 1828, when the first patient, a young white woman, was received. The first superintendents were laymen, little more than head-keepers, and were frequently changed. In 1836 the management was reorganized with the selection of Dr. J. W. Parker as resident physician and superintendent. Dr. Parker served until 1870, when, during the Republican régime Dr. J. F. Ensor, of Maryland, succeeded him. Dr. Ensor in turn was succeeded by

[110] *Ordinances of the City of Columbia,* 1871, Part IV.
[111] Williams, *Old and New Columbia,* p. 137.

by Dr. J. W. Babcock, of Chester,[112] succeeded in 1914 by Dr. Thomas J. Strait, of Lancaster, who held office for only one year. The present superintendent is Dr. C. Fred Williams, of York and Columbia. The institution is now badly overcrowded although there was a time in its first days when the board of regents petitioned the Legislature to make it obligatory that persons having insane people in charge should send them to the asylum for care. The hospital has made use of federal funds to finance needed, but still insufficient, improvements, costing $697,142.00.

The court house having been destroyed, for the period from 1868 to 1874 the county made use of Carolina Hall, erected after the fire, as a temporary substitute, until a new court house could be built. [113] The county board sold the northeast corner lot, on which the court house had stood, for $23,125.00 and purchased the present site on the northwest corner of Washington and Sumter for $5,000.00. The remainder, with additional funds, was used to finance the construction of the new building. The contract was let on December 11, 1872, for $34,623.75 to George W. Davis. It was completed in 1874 and with minor repairs served until 1935 when it was torn down to make way for a fourth court house, to be constructed and equipped at a cost of approximately $300,000.00, of which $140,000.00 is supplied as a public works grant by the federal government. The contractor for the work, which is being done under a commission headed by Clint T. Graydon, is J. C. Heslep.

The city hall was rebuilt on the old site in 1874. The contract price was $65,000.00, but opera house bonds—a theater was incorporated in the building—were issued for $300,000.00, a fairly considerable item in the quadrupling of the city debt during the Reconstruction régime. It was described in 1893 as a "conspicuous landmark on Main Street, but not commensurate with the vast amount expended for its construction." Its destruction by fire March 30, 1899, was hailed as a good riddance of a thing "conceived in sin and born in iniquity." [114] The site on Washington and Main was sold to the Carolina National Bank for $26,100.00 and construction of a new building, combining theater and city hall, at the northeast corner of Gervais and Main, for which the contract was let January 5, 1900, was begun. W. J. May, of Columbia, was the contractor, $38,561.00 the price bid. [115] This building in turn is now to be abandoned by

---

[112] Dr. J. W. Babcock in *Handbook of South Carolina*, Columbia, 1908, pp. 43-63.
[113] *City of Columbia Directory*, 1893.
[114] *The State* (Columbia), March 31, 1899.
[115] *Ibid.*, January 6, 1900.

the city government which in 1934 acquired title to the Federal building at the southwest corner of Main and Laurel streets, which is to be vacated by the federal offices now occupying it when the new federal building behind it on Laurel Street is ready.

The city rebuilding after the fire of 1865 experienced a period of steady growth continuing with the inevitable ups and downs until today. In the fifteen years, 1880-1895, for example, new buildings occupying 1,133 front feet on Main Street were constructed and the assessed valuation of property in the city grew from $3,433,499.00 to $5,405,929.00 [116] In the ten years preceding 1896 the city had spent over $100,000.00 on its water works and was to spend some hundreds of thousands more. Before 1896 the telegraph alarm system for police and fire department had been installed. It was, of course, temporarily disrupted by the burning of the city hall, after which the fire alarm bell was set up on a tower on Assembly Street. Electric street lights had replaced the gas lamps.[117] During the administration of Mayor Sloan, 1894-1898 one hundred and fifteen crossings had been constructed at street intersections for the convenience of pedestrians.[118]

In 1907 after some years of agitation the first step towards the paving of the city streets was taken when in November the contract for paving the sixteen blocks of Main Street from the Union Station to Elmwood was awarded to the Georgia Engineering Company, the work to be done in vitrified brick at a cost of $173,560.00, of which $145,000.00 was to be supplied by the city, the remainder by the street railway company.[119] The first work of paving was begun January 9, 1908, at the Union Station.[120] Controversy developed, however, and the work was stopped. The paving commission had resigned in August, 1907, because of criticism of J. L. Ludlow, the engineer selected by it to have charge of the program. May, 1908, the commissioners' resignations were accepted and a new commission appointed. The new commission's requirements that specifications of the contract be strictly complied with and the resulting controversy led the contractor to withdraw and of the originally planned vitrified brick paving only two blocks on Main, from Rice to Wheat,

---

116 *The State* (Columbia), June 5, 1896.

117 There is recorded in *Columbia, S. C., the Future Manufacturing and Commercial Center of the South,* published by the Board of Trade in 1871, the claim that the "first gas works ever used in the United States were erected in Columbia in 1821 from machinery brought from England by Mr. Ainsley Hall."

118 *The State,* June 3, 1896.

119 *Ibid.,* November 25, 1907.

120 *Ibid.,* January 10, 1908.

United States Post Office

were ever completed. The new commission changed the specifications so as to provide for a bitulithic pavement and, severing connection with Mr. Ludlow, awarded the new contract to George O. Tenney.[121] The new work was begun August 31 and eventually completed for the entire sixteen blocks, although not without some misgivings on the part of citizens disturbed by their discovery that in hot weather impressions could be made on the freshly-laid paving by passing carriages and carts. In 1911, as an experiment, Washington Street, from Assembly to Sumter, and Hampton Street, from Assembly to Sumter, were paved with wood blocks. In 1925, after they had furnished considerable amusement to visitors by buckling up in every heavy rain and, as often as not, floating off in great sections down Main Street's gutters, the blocks were torn up and replaced with asphalt. The paving program, continued with occasional interruptions, as during the World war period, has given Columbia forty-one miles of pavement in one hundred fifty-two miles of streets. Water mains incidentally now run for eighty-seven miles and the city sewer lines one hundred forty-eight miles.[122] The city water works system covers the entire city and in addition serves also the towns of New Brookland and Cayce as well as the Olympia mill village. Until 1935, when it constructed its own water system with federal funds, Eau Claire also secured water from Columbia. Now being spent in improving and extending the water works and sewer systems is $893,000.00 of PWA funds, of which approximately $250,000.00 is a grant from the federal treasury.

The paid fire department was inaugurated January 22, 1903, with the election of W. J. May, chief under the old volunteer system, as

---

[121] *The State,* July 28, 1908.
[122] Records, MS., office W. S. Tomlinson, city engineer.

the first chief.[123] The organization was completed February 1 with
the selection of forty men from the disbanded volunteer companies
as firemen, divided among four companies and four stations. All apparatus was horse drawn. The first piece of motor apparatus, an
automobile for the chief, was put in service December 27, 1910. Six
months later a motor-driven chemical and hose car was purchased;
it was wrecked answering an alarm April 3, 1919. Upon Chief May's
death February 5, 1924, T. M. Danielson was appointed acting chief,
serving until February 26, 1924, when A. McC. Marsh was elected
chief. The present fire department, housed in a single station on
Sumter Street, includes only fifty-two men. It is of course entirely
motor equipped.[124]

When the extravagant 1874 city hall had been built the police station had been included in it and when it was destroyed [125] the police

Governor's Mansion

were forced into temporary quarters. In 1901 the police barracks on
Gervais Street behind the city hall and theater was erected at a
cost of $6,000.00 In 1913 the modern police station and city jail,

---

[123] *The State*, January 23, 1903.
[124] A. McC. Marsh, Letter December, 1935.
[125] Lost in the fire was the "common seal" which, recovered after the destruction of Columbia in 1865, had been presented to the city by General
Hampton during the Centennial celebration in 1891.

1415 Lincoln Street, adjoining the county jail, was completed and the police department moved into it. January, 1935, a short wave radio station, W4XAH, was established and put into service by the department. In 1856 the police department, John Burdell, chief, included nine patrolmen.[126] The present department includes the chief,

Federal Farm Credit Administration Building, 1936

W. H. Rawlinson; an assistant to the chief, W. B. Hughey; six detectives, seven sergeants and fifty-nine patrolmen.

During the period of the participation of the United States in the World War, Columbia was a military concentration point second to few others in the country. Camp Jackson, the military cantonment extending east from the southeastern line of Columbia township, at one time during the war had a population more than double Columbia's of that day. The camp, partially abandoned, is still maintained on a limited scale as a National Guard training center.

Columbia is none the less still an important unit in the federal economy. It is the site of one of the larger Veterans' Hospitals, of the district headquarters of the Federal Farm Credit Administration, state headquarters for practically every one of the so-called alphabetical agencies that have been created by the "New Deal" administration.

---

[126] Williams, *Old and New Columbia*, p. 42.

For several reasons—one of them the fact that it was essentially a governmental city—Columbia went through the depth of the depression with fewer pains than its sister cities of South Carolina. The Roosevelt work and relief program now has given it another fillip. With federal aid a $52,000.00 market shed has been built on Assembly Street south of the 1924 market. The market, a definite municipal asset in bringing to Columbia the produce of South Carolina farms, of the deep South and of the East, includes two 400 foot open sheds containing 160 stalls rented to sellers, so protected, for $6.00 a month. At the State Fair Grounds and also constructed with federal aid is a municipal stadium, now the property of the University of South Carolina. Several of the state institutions at Columbia, which is the location of the Girls' Industrial School, Reformatory for Negro Boys, the Confederate Home, the Home for the Blind, the Penitentiary,[127] State Hospital, State Tuberculosis Sanitorium, and the University (formerly the College), have also been the beneficiaries of PWA and WPA (federal) grants and loans.

The federal administration's spending program (1933-1935), brought also a new element into the city's "relief" problem when federal instrumentalities took over the burden of unemployment and other relief, sending in the cash and goods to be distributed by agencies set up for this purpose. With 1936 the responsibility for the support of "unemployables" falls again upon Columbia's private charities, which throughout the city's existence have been the reliance of the needy and distressed. The Columbia Community Chest, organized in 1912 to co-ordinate the work of raising the needed funds and spending them, assumes the burden. Two charitable agencies of those serving today trace their beginnings back into the farther reaches of Columbia's history—one, the Family Welfare Society deriving from the Ladies' Benevolent Society organized 103 years ago, is a member of the Community Chest; the other, the Hebrew Benevolent Society, was formed in 1826.[128]

Active in pressing the further magnification of Columbia as a governmental center, state and federal, is the Richland delegation to the General Assembly, now comprising one senator, Jeff B. Bates, and

---

[127] Work on the penitentiary on Gist Street was begun during the administration of Governor Orr in 1867, the granite used being quarried from the bed of Broad River. The present superintendent is J. S. Wilson, elected January 13, 1936.

[128] In 1822 the Israelites of Columbia established among themselves a place of burial for their dead, separate from those of any other religious denomination, and in 1826 formed themselves into the Hebrew Benevolent Society. A constitution was adopted and an act of incorporation obtained from the legislature in the year 1834.

six representatives, William P. Donelan, Pat H. Nelson, T. Pou
Taylor, Ben E. Adams, O. D. Seay and Jake D. Hill.

The city's growth—even by 1897 it had been forced to add one
additional ward to increase the total to five ;[129] now there are ten [130]
—gave impetus to a movement for one other fundamental change in
the form of city government and when, after considerable agitation,
the General Assembly February 22, 1910, passed what is known as
the Commission Form of Government Act, the question of Columbia's adoption of the commission system was submitted to the qualified electors for determination.

Balloting April 2, 1910 on the issue, the voters adopted the commission government. The vote, as reported by Robert Moorman,
chairman, J. S. Land and J. W. H. Duncan, commissioners for the
special election, stood: [131] Yeas, 1,310; Nays, 68.

At the ensuing election on April 26, the first mayor and city commissioners under the new system were therefore elected: W. Hampton Gibbes, mayor, and R. W. Shand, R. C. Keenan, R. J. Blalock
and W. F. Steiglitz, councilmen.

Mayor Gibbes was succeeded in 1914—the term of office under
the new law is four years [132]—by L. A. Griffith, who was succeeded
in his turn by R. J. Blalock who was succeeded by W. A. Coleman,
each of whom served one term. In 1926, Dr. L. B. Owens, former
member of the Legislature, was elected mayor. Twice, in 1930 and
in 1934, he has been re-elected. Already he has completed the longest
record of continuous service as head of the city government in its
150 years' existence, John T. Rhett, mayor from 1884 to 1890, being
his nearest rival in office-holding longevity. Members of the city
council are: W. D. Barnett and Gary Paschal, whose terms expire
this year (1936) ; and Colin S. Monteith and W. P. Eleazer, whose
terms expire in 1938, when Mayor Owens' third term will be concluded.[133]

There has been only one significant change in the laws affecting
the city government since the adoption of the commission form of

---

[129] *Statutes,* XXII, 643.
[130] *Revised Ordinances City of Columbia,* 1933, pp. 1-2.
[131] *City of Columbia Annual,* 1910, p. 3.
[132] Which two of the first four commissioners should serve two instead of
four years was a matter of chance, determined by lot, Steiglitz and Blalock
winning the four-year terms—R. J. Blalock verbal recollection, January, 1936.
[133] When the 1930 census moved Columbia into the more than 50,000 population class it had the not anticipated effect of doubling the salaries of the
mayor and commissioners, a circumstance, that, coming during a time of
depression, supplied a lively political issue for the campaign of 1932.—*The
Record* (Columbia), April 3, 12, 16, 1932.

administration. The Act of March 7, 1929, altered the qualifications of voters in city primary elections so as to eliminate the provision that payment of taxes should be a prerequisite of participation in the voting, considerably increasing thereby the number of eligible voters of whom it is now required merely that they should be enrolled as for participation in any other party primary.[134]

State Office Building

The commission system embodies divers improvements over the preceding governmental systems obtaining in Columbia; it establishes the civil service for city employees, for one example; it concentrates power and responsibility, for another. But it is *per se* no cure-all.

"Commission government as applied to Columbia," Mayor Gibbes, the first commission-form mayor, recorded his opinion, "seems to have measurably succeeded, but there is still room for improvement." [135]

It is still a sound judgment.

---

[134] Gressette, *Code of Laws*, 1932, III, 657-662.
[135] *City of Columbia Annual*, 1911, p. 9.

HIGHER EDUCATION

By Edwin L. Green

EDITORIAL NOTE

This paper is purposely brief because of the excellent available secondary material covering the field; such as Edwin L. Green, History of the University of South Carolina, *Columbia, 1916, and other titles which appear in the general bibliography.*

UNIVERSITY OF SOUTH CAROLINA

IN RESPONSE to the recommendation of Governor John Drayton the legislature chartered, December 19, 1801, a college to be located at the seat of government for the purpose of giving to the young men of the state an opportunity of securing an advanced education and to unite the two sections of the state. Thus the South Carolina College came into being. The board of trustees set about to secure plans for the buildings and a site for their location. Robert Mills and Richard Clark were the architects whose plans were accepted, and from whose plans the building committee selected features that were incorporated in the final structures.[1] One building, that on the south side of the campus, later called Rutledge College, was ready for occupancy by the first of January, 1805.

The new institution opened its doors to students on the 10th of January, 1805. Dr. Jonathan Maxcy (1804-20), the president, and Professor Enoch Hanford constituted the faculty, with eight in the student body. William Harper was the first matriculate. By the end of the session twenty-eight students had entered, and two more professors had been employed. When Dr. Maxcy died in 1820, there was a faculty of five, and a student body of one hundred, the capacity of the building. The French language, chemistry and mineralogy had been added to the curriculum. Dr. Thomas Cooper (1820-34), who succeeded Dr. Maxcy, introduced geology and political economy. The nullification agitation and Dr. Cooper's free thinking brought the college to a low ebb, so that a cry resounded through the state to reorganize the institution. This was done in 1835.

A strong faculty under the leadership of President R. W. Barnwell (1835-41), quickly revived the college. The student body grew rapidly, necessitating the erection of new buildings. A wall was

---

[1] For the period prior to 1874 see M. LaBorde, *History of the South Carolina College,* Charleston, 1859; 2nd edit., 1874. Dr. LaBorde is a primary source, as he was a participant in the events he describes as student, teacher, professor.

University Campus—1850

built around the campus to aid in maintaining discipline, and a library building was completed in 1840, the first separate structure of the kind in the country. Under President William C. Preston (1845-51), the student body reached 237 in 1848-49, the largest enrollment in the history of the institution until 1905. In the period preceding 1860 the faculty contained such men at Francis Lieber, student and writer on political science, William Ellet, chemist, who seems to have made the first daguerreotype in the United States, John and Joseph LeConte, scientists, James H. Thornwell, one of the greatest theological thinkers of the age.

At the outbreak of the war the students of the South Carolina College entered the armies of the Confederacy to a man, and on every battlefield was shed the blood of her alumni. Seventeen Confederate generals came from their number. On the 25th of June, 1862, the college buildings were taken by the government for use as a general hospital; the college duties ceased for the remainder of the conflict.

A new charter obtained, December 19, 1865, changed the college into the University of South Carolina, which started on its career January 10, 1866, modeled on the plan of the University of Virginia, its students coming largely from the disbanded armies. The professors were nearly all from the old faculty. It seemed for a time that the university would flourish and surpass its predecessor. Schools of law and medicine were added. But soon the control of the state by the negroes and the carpetbaggers threatened its very existence. The professors gradually departed, resigning or forced out, and when in October, 1873, Henry Elliott Hayne, negro secretary of state, enrolled in the medical school, the students and the remaining members of the old faculty withdrew.[2] Negroes and a few whites of

---

[2] Minutes of board of trustees, MS., October 10, 1873.

alien birth now formed the student body with a faculty drawn from
adventurers. This condition obtained until General Wade Hampton,
as governor, closed the institution in June, 1877, and turned the
keeping of the grounds and buildings over to Hon. Robert W. Barnwell, chairman of the faculty in the university.[3]

After three years the South Carolina College of Agriculture and
Mechanics was opened in the deserted buildings; but two years later
the alumni of the old college and the university succeeded in changing
this into the South Carolina College. Dr. J. M. McBryde was made
president. Under him were Professors Benjamin Sloan, R. Means
Davis, James Woodrow, W. B. Burney, Edward S. Joynes, E. L.
Patton, W. J. Alexander. Others were added as the years passed.
In 1888 the college became a university, but not for long. The movement for a farmer's college brought about the establishment of Clemson College in 1891, with the consequent removal of the agricultural
and mechanical sections of the university to the new institution.
Dr. McBryde resigned; his place was taken by Dr. James Woodrow,
who guided the South Carolina College through the years of trial
resulting from the continued attacks of the followers of the Tillman
movement. He was succeeded by Professor F. C. Woodward. The
desire for education becoming more general in the state, the student
body again passed the 200 mark in 1900. The interest in the secondary
schools was now growing, and a determination to support them
through taxes appeared. High schools were soon sending out more
and better prepared graduates, which caused an increased enrollment
in all colleges.

In 1905 the South Carolina College celebrated its centennial, and
in the following year was granted a charter as the University of
South Carolina. From this time the institution has steadily grown
in departments of instruction, number of professors, and number
of students. Numerous buildings, classrooms, laboratories, dwellings,
dormitories have arisen on the old campus and on "Gibbes Green"
and other parts of the university land. The school of education is
housed in a fine structure, and athletics enjoy Melton and Davis
fields, the gymnasium and field house, the stadium, and a swimming
pool is in course of construction. Although women had been attending the University since 1894, their numbers were small until a
Woman's Building was erected at the beginning of Dr. Melton's
administration, since which they have constituted nearly a third of
the student body.

---

[3] See Edwin L. Green, *History of the University of South Carolina,* Columbia, 1916.

Library, University of South Carolina
Built 1840 (Wings Modern)

The presidents of the present University of South Carolina have been Major Benjamin Sloan, who succeeded Dr. Woodward in 1902; Dr. Samuel Chiles Mitchell, 1908-1913; Dr. William Spenser Currell, 1913-1922; Dr. William D. Melton, 1922-1926; Dr. Davison McDowell Douglas, 1926-31; Dr. Leonard T. Baker, 1931-36.

At present the faculty numbers 85; in the student body are 990 men and 357 women.[4]

The alumni record of service, says President L. T. Baker, has in its roll of honor 3 cabinet officers, 17 United States senators, 24 governors, 11 lieutenant-governors, 106 distinguished jurists, including 35 judges and chancellors, 5 bishops and a large number of noted clergymen, 25 who attained the rank of admiral or general in military service, 50 distinguished men of medicine, several hundred men in education, among them 21 presidents of colleges, 72 deans and professors, 80 school superintendents, and 3 state superintendents of education, and in late years, in response to the special needs of the age, many notable leaders in engineering and industry.[5]

BARHAMVILLE

Elias Marks, M.D., taught young ladies, day students and a few boarders, at the Columbia Female Academy on Washington Street from 1817 to 1827, when on the death of his wife, Jane Barham,

---

[4] Statement of Registrar's office.
[5] *The Gamecock,* Columbia, May 11, 1934.

University of South Carolina

who had taught with him, he decided to establish a school for the higher education of women, and so, after remaining a year longer at the academy, he opened the South Carolina Female Institute a short distance to the northeast of the City at Barhamville, a name derived from that of his wife. Says Professor Davis, the catalogues "give evidence of systematic internal economy and increasing educational range and efficiency according to his theories." [6] He married Julia (Pierpont) Warne in 1833; she had been directress of the institute since 1830. In 1835 "Collegiate" was added to the name of the institute, which was modeled in some measure after "similar institutions in Prussia, Germany and other parts of continental Europe." [7] The school gained wide popularity and reached an enrollment of 124. The curriculum gave four years of college grade of work beyond one academic year required for entrance. Resident graduates could pursue further studies. Thoroughness was insisted on. Walks, entertainments, visits of approved troupes, or singers, and May parties enlivened the routine.

Dr. Marks gave up connection with the institution in 1861 and spent the remainder of his life in Washington. Madam Togno and Madam Sosnowski kept the school going until the war came to an end, when it ceased. A caretaker was in charge of the main building —others had been sold—when it was burned in 1869. [8]

ST. MARY'S COLLEGE

This institution was located on the east side of upper Main Street. It was chartered and started in 1851 with a faculty of President J. J. O'Connell; Vice-president L. P. O'Connell; Professors Julius Posi, Thomas Cleary, Michael Walshe, Richard O'Brien, Charles Montague. The school contained a good library, a collection of paintings and a cabinet of minerals. Respectable youths, irrespective of creed, were free to enter. Boys came from all parts of the South and from Cuba; the day school was full. A threefold curriculum was provided, preparatory, philosophical (arts and science) and commercial. For six years the college flourished, when feeling aroused against the Roman Catholics, according to Dr. O'Connell, almost destroyed it, so that it led a precarious existence until

---

[6] H. C. Davis, "Elias Marks," *Dictionary of American Biography*, XII, New York, 1933.

[7] Miss J. H. Witherspoon, *The State*, March 15, 1903.

[8] Personal communication from Professor H. C. Davis, University of South Carolina.

it perished in the conflagration of February 17, 1865. Efforts to revive it proved futile.[9]

COLUMBIA THEOLOGICAL SEMINARY

The Theological Seminary of the Synod of South Carolina and
Georgia was located in Columbia in December, 1829, and in the
following month Dr. Thomas Goulding and his students came from
Lexington, Georgia, and took up their abode in the building that
had been purchased from Mrs. Ainsley Hall through the efforts of
Colonel Abram Blanding. This house had been planned by the distinguished architect Robert Mills for Ainsley Hall after he had
sold his home in 1823, across the street, to General Wade Hampton.
It bears across the front the date 1828, the year of the foundation
of the seminary. In the course of time it was flanked by two dormitories, Simons Hall and Law Hall, the gifts of Mrs. Eliza Simons
and Mrs. Agnes Law. The small building on the east side of the
campus, which had been built for a stable, became the chapel, and
here Winthrop College began its existence. The iron fence around
the block was erected about thirty years ago by subscriptions for
the purpose.

The first professor added to the faculty after the removal to Columbia was Dr. George Howe, who taught in the seminary for
fifty-two years. His influence was most potent in shaping the curriculum. He became the historian of the Presbyterian Church in
South Carolina. Other prominent men connected with the seminary
were A. W. Leland, C. C. Jones, B. M. Palmer, J. H. Thornwell,
James Woodrow, W. S. Plummer, J. R. Wilson, J. L. Girardeau.

This seminary belonged to the "Old School Calvinism."

On December 7, 1925, the charter was amended to change the
name to "Columbia Theological Seminary" controlled by the synods
of South Carolina, Georgia, Alabama, Florida and Mississippi, and
these moved it on the eve of its centennial to a more central location
at Decatur, Ga.[10] The buildings in Columbia are now used to shelter
a school for missionaries' children.

ARSENAL ACADEMY

In accordance with the act of December 20, 1842, by which the
Arsenal Academy in Columbia and the Citadel Academy in Charleston were created, the board of visitors met in the following Jan-

---

[9] J. J. O'Connell, *Catholicity in the Carolinas and Georgia,* New York, 1879,
pp. 241-262.
[10] W. C. Robinson, *Columbia Theological Seminary,* Decatur, Ga., 1931.

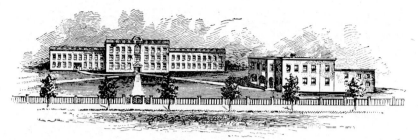

Arsenal Academy—1856

uary and elected officers for the Arsenal Academy: Captain Alfred
Herbert, Superintendent and Principal Professor; 1st Lieutenant
Joseph Matthews, Second Professor; Dr. A. H. Angel, Surgeon;
M. C. Shaffer, Bursar. Eight beneficiary cadets were selected to report
on or before March 20th. The students were formed into a corps
and constituted the guard of the Arsenal at Columbia, which took the
place of the regular guard.

The Arsenal and the Citadel were at first independent of each
other. There were to be eighteen beneficiary students, or, as later
styled, State Cadets, and the same number of pay cadets at the
Arsenal. These numbers were afterwards increased. At first there
were two rectangular buildings extending along the southern side
of the square; in these officers and cadets were lodged, and the
classes were held. In 1852 a three-story brick building, the "main
building," with a wooden parapet, was erected between and uniting
the two original structures. Three years later additional officers'
quarters, a brick tenement building, now known as the Executive
Mansion, was built in front of the main building. A wing was afterward (1858) added to the main building, and in it was the new mess
hall, with kitchen and store room.

An Act of the Legislature, ratified January 28, 1861, united the
two academies under the title, "The South Carolina Military
Academy," and organized the officers and students as "A Public
Guard." The two corps became "the battalion of State Cadets." The
history of the Academy will have to be consulted for their military
service.

The faculty of the Arsenal Academy for 1864 was: Captain John
P. Thomas, superintendent and professor of French; First Lieutenant, J. B. Patrick, professor of mathematics; Second Lieutenant
A. J. Norris, professor of Belles-Lettres and history; Second Lieutenant R. O. Sams, assistant professor of mathematics and French;

A. W. Kennedy, M.D., Surgeon; Second Lieutenant B. H. Knight, Bursar.

On the approach of General Sherman the cadets of the Arsenal Academy were placed in charge of a small battery near the Congaree bridge; but on the firing of this by the Confederates, they returned to their barracks. During the following night, February 16, 1865, officers and cadets marched out with the retreating army of General Beauregard. The corps endured weary marching into North Carolina and back to Greenville, near which it encamped. On the 9th of May it had moved to Newberry, where it was disbanded, thus ending the career of the Arsenal Academy. The buildings except the officers' quarters and some out-buildings, were destroyed in the conflagration of February 17.[11]

COLUMBIA COLLEGE

The Columbia College was chartered December 21, 1854, to give young ladies of Methodist families in South Carolina a college of their denomination. It was not opened until the first Wednesday of October, 1859. A lot had been bought in Columbia where the Columbia Bible College now stands; here the building was erected. Reverend Whiteford Smith was the first president, but resigned in a few months, his work being taken over by Reverend William Martin. Other members of the faculty were Reverend T. E. Wannamaker, E. D'Ovilliers, W. H. Orchard, and assistants Misses Craig and M. A. Dibble. Reverend H. W. Hilliard preached the first baccalaurate sermon and made the graduating address. During the war years the students came from other states: it was thought that Columbia was a safe place. There were 200 boarders and over 100 day students at the close of 1864. On the approach of Sherman the students were hurriedly sent to points of safety. The senior class was graduated in April, 1865, after which the Ursuline Sisters used the building, which had been saved by Professor Orchard, until the end of the year. It was then rented by T. S. Nickerson, who operated it as Nickerson's Hotel until the close of 1872. The trustees having raised sufficient funds, had the building put in order, and the Columbia College started on a new career in 1873.

The eight years following were a struggle for existence; the presidents were Reverends S. B. Jones and J. L. Jones. Presidents O. A. Darby and S. B. Jones conducted the college through thirteen pros-

[11] John Peyre Thomas, *The History of the South Carolina Military Academy*, Charleston, 1893. The author was professor and superintendent of both academies.

perous years from 1881 to 1894. Dr. John A. Rice, from 1894 to 1900, directed his efforts to enlarging the curriculum and making a real college, a work carried on by his successor, Dr. W. W. Daniel, who served the college nobly for sixteen years. Outgrowing its quarters, the college sought another location, which was found just north of Columbia on a tract of forty acres, the gift of F. H. Hyatt and Colonel J. T. Sloan. Here the college began the session of 1905. A fire destroyed the new buildings in 1909, so that for one year Columbia College came back to its old home, then the Colonia Hotel. During Dr. Daniel's administration the student body was nearly trebled.[12] It is at present 368 (November 19, 1935). After the resignation of Dr. Daniel in 1916, President G. T. Pugh directed the college's affairs for four years. Since 1920 the presidency has been held by Dr. J. C. Guilds. Since 1911 the institution has ranked as an "A" grade college.

COLLEGE FOR WOMEN

The South Carolina Presbyterian Institute for young ladies was started by Dr. Neander W. Woods, pastor of the First Presbyterian Church, and a group of elders, in the year 1886; but it did not come into existence until Dr. W. R. Atkinson and a board of directors from Columbia bought the old Hampton, or Preston mansion, and opened the institution October 1, 1890.

Dr Atkinson established a broad curriculum, for he recognized the wide possibilities that were opening up for educated women in professional and social affairs. He was compelled to resign after five years on account of ill health. His place was taken by Dr. Robert P. Pell, ably assisted by Miss Euphemia McClintock. The high standard of Dr. Atkinson was kept up. In 1902 Dr. Pell accepted the presidency of Converse College, and Miss McClintock became head of the institution, which flourished and grew as never before under her guidance. She insisted on high standards of scholarship and secured and held a fine faculty. The enrollment reached 300. In 1910 a self-perpetuating board bought the college, as it was known, to be held in trust for the higher education of women in South Carolina and changed the name to the College for Women. After four years an attempt was made to unite the College for Women with the University of South Carolina. After the failure of this attempt the institution was taken over by the Presbyterian Synod and combined with Chicora College operating at Greenville.

---

[12] E. B. Winn, History of Columbia College, MS., M.A. thesis, University of South Carolina, 1927.

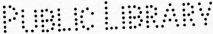

Educational Columbia
Top, Columbia College; Center Left, Ursuline Convent;
Center Right, Lutheran Theological Seminary;
Bottom, Columbia Theological Seminary

The new college was given the name Chicora and located at Columbia in the buildings of the College for Women.[13]

CHICORA COLLEGE FOR WOMEN

From 1915 to 1930 this institution was, under the guidance of Dr. S. C. Byrd and his wife, president and dean, conducted with success until the financial depression destroyed the plans of a larger and stronger college on lands in the southeastern part of Columbia

[13] Maude Moore, History of College for Women, MS., M.A. thesis, University of South Carolina, 1932.

and finally necessitated a union with Queens College, Charlotte, North Carolina, and the removal to that city in 1930.[14]

THE LUTHERAN THEOLOGICAL SOUTHERN SEMINARY

After a varied existence since its beginning in Newberry County in 1831, the Lutheran Theological Southern Seminary was moved in 1911 to Eau Claire on the northern edge of Columbia. It was provided for by the Synod in 1830.[15]

The new building, dedicated on October 11, proving too small, was given over to use as a dormitory, and a second structure, also of granite, was erected in 1926, in which are offices of administration, lecture rooms, library and reading room. The seminary draws students from Virginia, North and South Carolina, Georgia, Florida, Alabama and Mississippi.[16]

Dr. Andrew G. Voigt, a native of Philadelphia and Dean of the Seminary since 1903, served in that office in Columbia until his death in 1933. He was succeeded by Dr. C. A. Freed, D.D., as president and professor of the science of religion and ethics. Other members of the faculty are: Rev. J. B. Moose, Ph.D., systematic and historical theology; Rev. Charles K. Bell, D.D., practical theology; Rev. John W. Horine, D.D. LL.D., Old and New Testament Exegesis.[17]

COLUMBIA BIBLE COLLEGE

Columbia Bible College, youngest of the city's institutions of higher learning, opened in 1923. With legislative authority and with the approval of the State Board of Education, it now grants the degree of B. A. in Biblical Education to its graduates, and has announced work leading to degrees in Theology to begin in the fall. The faculty and board of trustees represent several denominations, the school being chartered as interdenominational. President Robert C. McQuilkin, D. D., heads a staff of twelve faculty members who offer courses in English, history, philosophy, psychology, education, Greek, and music, in addition to the courses in English Bible, theology, biblical interpretation and other subjects designed especially to fit students for effective Christian service.

With an enrollment of only seven at the time of its opening the school has grown so that it now has 145 students registered. Degrees,

[14] *Bulletin of Chicora College for Women,* Columbia, 1930.
[15] S. T. Hallman, ed., *History of the Evangelical Lutheran Synod of South Carolina, 1824-1924,* Columbia, n. d., pp. 60-61.
[16] Historical statement in Catalogue of the Seminary, 1931.
[17] Communication from President Freed's office.

diplomas, and certificates have been given to 122 students. Graduates and former students of the institution are now engaged in Christian service in various parts of Europe, Asia, South and Central America, and in many parts of the United States and Canada.

Columbia Female College, Site of Columbia Bible College

The Bible College has for its motto "To Know Christ and to Make Him Known." Every effort is being made to carry out this high purpose.[18]

---

[18] Statement by J. A. Morris Kimber, Registrar, Columbia Bible College, Columbia, S. C., November, 1935.

PRIVATE SCHOOLS

By Arney R. Childs
Associate Professor of History, University of South Carolina

ORIGIN OF THE COLUMBIA ACADEMIES

THE SETTLEMENT of Columbia came in a general period of educational revival in the state marked by a widespread establishment of academies.[1] As early as 1792 the commissioners of Columbia were authorized to convey to a group of trustees of a "free school" a square of land,[2] and in 1795 these same trustees were incorporated as the academy board.[3] They were made a self-perpetuating body, empowered to purchase, sell or lease lands, conduct lotteries, erect school buildings, and employ teachers. The land grant of 1792 was changed in the act of 1795 by the substitution of two other squares of land for the original grant.[4] Apparently from the very first the academies established by this board were not "free schools," but were endowed institutions with current expenses covered by tuition.[5]

COLUMBIA MALE ACADEMY

An advertisement in a Columbia newspaper of 1879 states that the Columbia Female Academy was established in 1790;[6] but, aside from the land grants of 1792 and 1795, the earliest indication found that either academy was actually in operation is in 1797 when the trustees of the academy (male) announce that they have secured a teacher.[7] By 1816 the division into male and female academies

---

[1] Henry T. Thompson, *The Establishment of the Public School System in South Carolina*, Columbia, 1927, p. 3.

[2] Thomas Cooper and D. J. McCord, eds., *Statutes at Large of South Carolina*, Columbia, 1836-1841, V, 216.

[3] *Ibid.*, VIII, 193. The trustees were: Thomas Taylor, James Taylor, William Montgomery, George Wade, and Benjamin Waring, *Ibid.*

[4] *Ibid.*, pp. 193, 194.

[5] David Duncan Wallace, *The History of South Carolina*, New York, 1934, III, 25. The advertisements current in the newspapers from 1797 to 1883 repeatedly list terms with no mention of free tuition. *City Gazette and Advertiser* (Charleston), January 18, 1797, sets the rate at $30.00 per annum. The endowment came not only from the original grant of land; but from escheated property (*Statutes,* VI, 53); surplusage of certain taxes and fines, (*ibid.,* V, 334); and profits from a public ferry (*ibid.,* IX, 394). Robert Mills, *Statistics of South Carolina . . .,* Charleston, 1826, p. 704, states that the academy began in January, 1798, with A. Blanding as principal.

[6] *The Daily Register* (Columbia), August 1.

[7] *City Gazette,* January 18.

had apparently taken place; and their long and useful history was well begun. It culminated with the transfer in 1883 to the board of commissioners of the City Public Schools of the property of both schools.[8]

An advertisement in 1816 is worth full quotation as it gave details which indicate the general management of the Male Academy in its early years.

> Wanted, a Teacher of talents and character to take charge of the Columbia Academy on the 14th September. The Trustees furnish the Principal of the Academy with a commodious building for the purpose of teaching the Classics; and he is entitled also to the whole of the tuition money. The price of tuition has been fixed at the rate of twenty-five dollars per annum, for the classical scholars, who are taught Reading, Writing, Arithmetic, English Grammar and Geography. Application must be made to the trustees.[9]

Male Academy (Thompson School)

As a result of this advertisement a Mr. Neale was engaged to take charge.[10] Some time before 1824 Robert Edmonds became principal, remaining with the Male Academy until January, 1829.[11]

---

[8] The original lease was for three years. Minutes of the Board of Commissioners, MS, March 24, 1883. The property included the sites of the present High School and Taylor School.

[9] *Columbia Telescope*, September 3, 1816.

[10] *Ibid.*, November 19, 1816.

[11] Mills, *Statistics*, p. 704; *State Gazette and Advertiser* (Columbia), January 20, 1827, January 5, 1828, December 20, 1828.

The trustees thought highly of his work as judged by the public examinations, and spoke of a plan to divide the students into classes and to arrange courses of study.[12] Mr. Edmonds had several assistants: Mr. Knox, Samuel McAliley, and Mr. Summer being mentioned in various advertisements.[13] The academy ran through the summer months and in 1828 had a branch in the sand hills during the season which was considered unhealthy in the city.[14] The rates were somewhat higher than in 1816; "Tuition, (payable quarterly, in advance) in as many branches of an English, Mercantile, Classical and Mathematical Education, as it may be thought advisable for the pupil to study at the same time . . . 12.50." [15]

Mr. Edmonds left Columbia to go to Mt. Zion Academy in Winnsboro and was succeeded by James M. Daniel, who had already made a reputation as a teacher at the Pineville Academy.[16] Daniel remained in Columbia some years, just how long is not clear, and had Thomas Taylor as his assistant in 1830.[17]

Between 1845 and 1855 the Male Academy had a number of principals; among them were: Francis Bulkley, Leslie McCandless, W. H. Campbell, Samuel Jones and James H. Carlisle.[18]

In 1855 Richard Ford, an Englishman, a graduate of Oxford, came to Columbia to take charge of the academy. He was exceedingly popular. Ford remained in charge of the school through the war and during 1866 and part of 1867 continued to teach there with Hugh S. Thompson. He then left Columbia to go to Texas where he died of yellow fever in 1867.[19]

Among older Columbians are many who remember the Male Academy as "Thompson's School," since it was popularly so called

[12] *Ibid.,* July 12, 1828.

[13] Mills, *Statistics,* p. 704; *Gazette,* December 19, 1827, July 12, 1828.

[14] *Ibid.*

[15] *Ibid.,* January 20, 1827.

[16] Neil S. Stevens, *Myological Work of Henry W. Ravenel,* Belgium, 1932, p. 134, speaks of Ravenel coming to Columbia to be under Mr. Daniel. *Columbia Telescope,* January 9, 1829.

[17] *Ibid.,* July 3, 1829; *Times and Gazette* (Columbia), October 18, 1830; *Southern Christian Herald* (Columbia), December 16, 1834. Robert Shand. "Reminiscences of Columbia," 1846-1866, MS. (no title), speaks of "Mr. McDaniel who was the principal in my cradle days (b. 1840) and left a fine reputation behind him when he removed to Florida." No other indication of what became of Mr. Daniel was found.

[18] Wade H. Manning, article on the Thompson School in *The State* (Columbia), December 13, 1908; Shand, MS.; *Southern Chronicle* (Columbia), December 24, 1845; *Telegraph,* December 28, 1847, September 6, 1849, July 30, 1850, September 27, 1850.

[19] Shand, MS.; *The State,* December 13, 1908; *The Daily Carolina Times* (Columbia), October 8, 1857; The *Phoenix* (Columbia), April 23, 1866, April 21, 1867, November 5, 1867.

while Hugh S. Thompson was its principal, 1865-1880. Captain Thompson was an unusually efficient teacher, loved and honored by his pupils and so high in general esteem as to be three times elected State Superintendent of Education, and twice Governor.[20] He associated with himself able assistants, among them: James Wood Davidson, John T. McBride, J. S. Muller, Charles Hemphill, Carl McKinley and Wade Hampton Manning.[21] The school grew rapidly, having at one time as many as 125 pupils.[22] The work was chiefly classical, preparatory to the University and other colleges; but its mathematical courses were advertised as being preparatory to mercantile pursuits.[23]

From 1881 to 1883 Charles H. Barnwell, who had had a private school for boys in Columbia for some years, was principal of the academy.[24] In 1883, as stated above, the property was leased to the public schools.

COLUMBIA FEMALE ACADEMY

The Female Academy may have started its existence coincidently with the Male Academy. However, no specific reference was found prior to 1815.[25] In 1816 the returns from the sale of the escheated property were allocated to the Female Academy.[26] From 1817 to 1828 the principal was Dr. Marks, later well known in connection with the Columbia Female Collegiate Institute at Barhamville. Under Dr. Marks' care the institution flourished. Mills gives the enrollment in 1824 as 110 with 45 boarders; board and tuition were from $175.00 to $200.00 a year, while tuition alone was from $24.00 to $48.00 according to the courses pursued. The usual classical studies, with what were then called the "ornamental branches": music, drawing and "painting on velvet," were offered.[27] Rev. John Rennie succeeded Dr. Marks as principal,[28] and was followed in 1830 by Mrs. S. C. W. Faust, who managed the academy for several years.[29]

---

[20] State Superintendent of Education 1876, 1878, 1880; Governor 1882, 1884.
[21] *Phoenix,* August 27, 1867; September 10, 1869; *The State,* December 20, 1908.
[22] *Ibid.*
[23] *Phoenix,* September 10, 1872.
[24] *Register,* September 6, 1881; September 3, 1882.
[25] *State Gazette,* December 12, 1815, mentions the public examination of the "Young Ladies in Mr. Thompson's" school and invites the legislature to attend.
[26] *Statutes,* VI, 53.
[27] Mills, *Statistics,* pp. 702-703.
[28] *Telescope,* January 9, 1829. This is a long advertisement with details as to courses and terms.
[29] *Times and Gazette,* July 15, 19, August 2, 1830.

The school must have run into financial difficulties in the succeeding years, as it was levied on for a debt which was remitted by the legislature in 1834, when R. S. Gladney, editor of a Presbyterian paper published in Columbia, took it over.[30]

Female Academy, Site of Present Columbia High School

By 1840 the academy had come under the direction of Washington Muller, who was to continue as its principal for twenty years.[31] The building used was on the corner of Washington and Marion streets; it was described as "pleasantly situated . . . with spacious yard and grounds, affording ample room to accommodate boarders, twelve of whom will be received into the family of the Principal." [32] The school must have maintained a large enrollment as Muller frequently mentions a corps of four assistant teachers.[33]

During the war the Misses Jane and Sophia Reynolds took over the academy and Muller went to Lucy Scott Institute, later return-

---

[30] *Southern Christian Herald,* March 18, 1834.

[31] *Chronicle,* October 1, 1840. Muller was a graduate of the South Carolina College and had taught in Charleston before he came to Columbia. *Herald,* December 23, 1834.

[32] *Daily Carolina Times* (Columbia), October 8, 1857.

[33] *Chronicle,* October 1, 1840; October 8, 1857.

ing to Columbia to open an independent private school.[34] The Misses
Reynolds remained in charge until 1879.[35] Under their administration the academy continued to take boarders, who lived with Dr.
and Mrs. William Reynolds. The tone of the advertisements indicates that every expedient was used to keep the institution going
during the lean years of war and reconstruction. Primary classes
were opened to boys as well as girls; afternoon classes in music and
drawing were offered; and tuition rates were lowered to from four
to six dollars a month.

Miss Elmore was principal from 1879 until 1883 when both
academies became a part of the public school system. Miss Elmore
had a corps of assistants,[36] among them a Miss Putnam, whom a
contemporary Columbian remembers as a "long, tall, scrawny old
maid" from Massachusetts.[37]

Inadequate though this treatment of these two academies is, one
must leave with a keen sense of the very real contribution they
made to the cultural life of Columbia. In physical equipment they
were far behind modern standards, though early mention is made of
maps and globes and even "chemical apparatus." The teachers were
of course not professionally trained, but thoroughness of instruction
and rather rigid discipline sent their students to college well prepared to meet the somewhat high standards of the day. Probably
some pioneering was done by the academies in adding subjects not
distinctly of a college preparatory character, such as manual training, calisthenics and bookkeeping, but their finest contribution lies,
as usual, in the influence of very high character of the men and
women who acted as principals and teachers.

OTHER PRIVATE SCHOOLS BEFORE THE WAR

While the two academies probably cared for the needs of much
of what would now be called secondary education, there were any

[34] *Tri-Weekly Carolinian* (Columbia), September 10, 1863, *Phoenix,* September 7, 1869.

[35] *Phoenix,* December 21, 1866; August 28, 1867; September 1, 1868;
September 9, 1869; July 19, 1870; August 9, 1871; September 15, 1872;
September 10, 1873; September 5, 1874; September 10, 1875. This last advertisement claims that the Misses Reynolds were beginning in that year
their 18th session as principals of the academy, which would have made their
connection date from 1857. However, advertisements for 1857 and some
successive years are signed by Washington Muller as principal. (See foot-
notes 32 and 33.) The Misses Reynolds probably had a private school which
they merged with the academy.

[36] *Register,* August 11, 1880.

[37] Letter from B. F. Taylor, November 25, 1935. Mr. Taylor was a pupil
in the primary department. He says he was much interested in a collection
of lichens which Miss Putnam had and that they were "good buddies."

number of other private schools in Columbia, both of elementary and high school rank.

While Robert L. Edmonds was principal of the Male Academy, Mrs. Edmonds conducted a "Female Seminary," large enough to engage all of her time and that of several assistants. In 1827 there were six teachers in all.[38] In rates of tuition and courses it was very like the Female Academy.

Among the many smaller schools running newspaper advertisements from 1820-1840 were those of Miss Blackburn, "daughter of the late eminent professor Blackburn"; Mrs. Eliza B. Mills, who "proposes to receive at her home, opposite the College square, a limited number of young ladies, to whose polite and ornamental education particular attention will be paid"; Mrs. Sanford, corner of Lady and Sumter streets; Allston L. White, a recent graduate of the South Carolina College; Mr. Cooper, a graduate of Cambridge, who left his diploma for inspection in Colonel Maxcy's office; Rev. John Bermingham; Mr. and Mrs. Glass on Plain street; and Mr. and Mrs. Hale, near the corner of Taylor and Sumter streets.[39] This is an incomplete list; and although an editorial of 1834 stated that, "Our Academies are less numerous now than they were a few years back . . . Those that still live are poorly supplied with pupils,"[40] one wonders how there were enough children in Columbia able to pay the tuition rates to support so many schools.[41]

Several interesting private schools of Columbia, not so well known as the two academies, but whose merit is assured by their long years of service, started in this general period, and are considered here although they continued through and after the war. One of the most modest, and yet persistent advertisers, was Mrs. Sarah B. Peck, whose very name somehow suggests the schoolma'am. Her opening announcement appeared in 1827, and from then, with gaps chiefly where newspapers were not available for checking, year after year until 1876 appeared her annual announcement. The forty-nine

---

[38] Mills, *Statistics,* p. 704; *Gazette,* June 23, 1827, August 18, 1827, September 13, 1828.

[39] In the order mentioned above: Mills, *Statistics,* p. 703; *Gazette,* June 23, 1827; January 20, 1827; January 5, 1828; December 15, 1827; February 3, 1827; *Southern Times,* January 29, 1830; July 5, 1830.

[40] *Herald,* August 5.

[41] A population estimate published in the *Southern Chronicle,* August 27, 1840, gives 503 white children. At almost any date between 1820 and 1840, it is easy to locate ten or twelve private schools. Of course the free school figures would have to have come out of this estimate. At the average prevailing rate of $5.00 per month per pupil, the income from the smaller schools was certainly not large.

years of this school capture the imagination, but the records available afford few details.[42]

In point of duration the closest rival to Mrs. Peck's school was that of Dr. and Mrs. Zimmerman, which opened before 1848, was conducted jointly until Dr. Zimmerman's death in 1867, and continued by Mrs. Zimmerman until her own death in 1870. The advertisement of 1848 announces embroidery and waxwork to be taught in the summer and speaks of their "liberal patronage", although they had not resorted to "newspaper puffs" or bombastic titles.[43]

On the State House grounds across from Trinity Church, a Mr. and Mrs. Hassell, "cultivated and accomplished Swedes", conducted a school for girls from 1845 to 1852.[44]

An attempt to bridge the gap between the expensive private schools and the less desirable free schools was made by the Odd Fellows. They conducted what was known as the Palmetto Lodge School from 1844 to 1879 with the avowed purpose of lessening the tuition charges for those able to pay and to educate at no cost indigent children whose applications were passed on by a committee. The first principal of the school was the later eminent president of Wofford College, James H. Carlisle.[45] In 1847 a threat to close the school for lack of suitable housing led to a series of letters in the newspapers, highly commendatory to the school.[46] The legislature was prevailed on to grant a lot to be used for school purposes,[47] and the ladies of Columbia gave a fair which raised over $1,100.00 for the erection of a building.[48] The new building was in use by 1850 and E. E. Bellinger had become principal, succeeding Carlisle who had gone to the Male Academy.[49] Through the succeeding years the school seems to have had difficulty in keeping a principal; frequent advertisements

[42] *Gazette*, January 20, August 18, December 19, 1827; *Southern Chronicle*, August 28, 1844; *Phoenix*, January 4, 1867; August 25, 1868, September 9, 1869, September 28, 1870, September 25, 1872, September 12, 1873, September 16, 1874; *Register*, September 24, 1875, September 7, 1876.

[43] *Telegraph*, March 6, 1848; September 15, 1849, September 17, 1850; *Palmetto State Banner* (Columbia), October 2, 1852; *Daily Carolina Times*, October 8, 1857; *Tri-weekly Carolinian*, September 15, 1863; *Phoenix*, September 15, 1866, September 10, 1867, December 24, 1867, August 9, 1868, September 4, 1870. Obituary, *ibid.*, September 16, 1870.

[44] Shand, MS; *Southern Chronicle*, August 6, 1845; *Daily Telegraph*, October 19, 1849; *Palmetto State Banner*, November 9, 1852.

[45] *Chronicle*, December 31, 1845.

[46] *Telegraph*, October 28, October 30, November 24, November 25, 1847.

[47] *Ibid.*, December 21, 847. The lot was bounded by Lincoln, Gadsden, Plain and Washington streets.

[48] *Ibid.*, December 13, 31, 1847.

[49] *Ibid.*, September 11, 1850.

for applicants appear in the papers and almost every year a new name is signed to the announcement of the opening date.[50] The claim of the Odd Fellows that their school caused a general lowering of tuition rates may have been true, as rates were lowered; however, they did not continue the $25.00 a year price fixed by the act of 1857.[51] The school certainly ran through 1879 and may have continued longer, although no indication to that effect was found.

A complete list of the transitory schools of the ante-bellum period, advertisements of which appeared in the papers, is beyond the compass of this paper. *The Daily Telegraph,* October 19, 1847, published a list for that year which included thirteen schools.

PRIVATE SCHOOLS 1860–1885

As might have been expected, there was apparently a decrease in the number of private schools in Columbia during the war. The two academies, the Zimmerman school, the Palmetto Lodge school all

Barhamville School—About 1850

ran through the war and were supplemented by some transitory schools. Madame Sosnowski, later to take over Barhamville Institute, had a girls' school in Columbia in 1863.[52] Dr. and Mrs. Evans

---

[50] In order the principals were: William Martin, F. W. Pope, R. O. Sams, W. J. Laval, C. O. Trapp, J. J. McCants, R. H. Clarkson, P. A. Cummings, Washington Muller, L. C. Sylvester, Robert A. Lynch, D. B. Clayton. The *Phoenix* carried in August and September of each year the announcement as to term opening.

[51] Rates per term (5 months), $20.00. *Phoenix,* December 30, 1866; by the month, $2.00 to $5.00, *Ibid,* August 26, 1870.

[52] *Tri-weekly Carolinian,* September 29, 1863.

were teaching on "Camden Street [now Taylor], two squares east of Main" in the same year.[53] Mrs. J. C. Englebrecht, who went to Baltimore after the war and was connected with a school for girls there, had a "Select Family School for Young Ladies" on Main street between Laurel and Blanding[54] in 1863-64.

The heydey of the private school movement in point of number of schools established was in the decade immediately after the war. Many of these schools were conducted by women in private homes and were obviously efforts to meet the economic needs of the time. Among schools of this type were those of Mrs. G. T. Mason, Sumter street, south of Lumber; Misses Henry, Henderson street between Senate and Gervais; Miss Olivia McGowan, who continued to have a school at her home on the corner of Taylor and Assembly until 1875; Mrs. S. S. McCully; Mrs. McGregor, "at her residence, the late Orphan House"; Mrs. Levy, corner Bull and Lady; Mrs. Mary S. Monteith, on Stark's Hill; Miss S. G. Huntt, "one door south of the new State Capitol"; Miss Wilbur, and others too transitory to list.[55]

Washington Muller, who has been mentioned above as for many years principal of the Columbia Female Academy, returned to Columbia from Athens, Georgia, in 1866 and opened on the corner of Taylor and Pickens a school called the Columbia Female Seminary.[56] The annual advertisements of this school from 1866-1873 are usually longer and more detailed as to courses, methods and texts than most of the notices of the time. Mr. Muller at one time announced what seems to be a rather ambitious program: "all the branches of a substantial and fashionable education taught according to the most improved systems."[57] What teacher will not agree with him when he says, "cooperation of parents is requested; without which, the wisest schemes of education ever devised may be thwarted by reluctant scholars"?[58] Mr. Muller lived to teach the children of his former pupils.[59]

Many Columbians of today have vivid recollections of Miss Isabel Martin. Some of them may be suprised to know that she opened her

---

[53] *Ibid.,* September 15, 1863.
[54] *Ibid.,* August 27, 1863, August 9, 1864.
[55] *Daily South Carolinian,* September 20, 1866; *Phoenix,* December 13, 1866, August 31, 1867, and succeeding August or September advertisements through 1875; August 10, 1869, August 12, 1866, August 29, 1868, September 24, 1867, September, 1866, 1867, 1868, 1869. Henry Timrod advertised in the *Phoenix,* September 23, 1866, for pupils but did not secure any.
[56] *Phoenix,* September 23, 1866.
[57] *Ibid.,* September 13, 1872.
[58] *Ibid.,* August 1, 1873.
[59] *Ibid.,* September 13, 1872, comment under "local items".

private school before 1866.[60] It was conducted at her home on the corner of Blanding and Henderson streets and ran continuously, first with the Misses Martin as joint principals and after 1880 by "Miss Isabel" alone.[61] The last advertisement noted was in 1889.[62] For many years the music department of the school was under Professor Plate and from time to time there were a number of other assistants. In 1873 there were six teachers besides the Misses Martin, although one or more of these were probably part-time teachers.[63]

Equally well known as teachers were the Misses Elmore who conducted a private school for girls at the corner of Bull and Taylor streets from 1867 to 1879.[64] In that year Miss Ellen Elmore was made principal of the Female Academy which she conducted until 1883. She re-opened her own school the following year and maintained it until 1889. In its later years the school was located at 71 Laurel street. For a number of years Mrs. Thomas Taylor did the music teaching for Miss Elmore, and Mrs. Frank Elmore began in 1873 her school for young children in connection with Miss Elmore's seminary.[65] This was later moved into separate quarters and continued for some years.[66]

During the war the name of Miss Mary Ann Buie, of Edgefield, frequently occurs in the papers in connection with collection for wounded soldiers. After the war, Miss Buie opened a private school in Edgefield which she moved to Columbia in 1870.[67] Much newspaper publicity accompanied this move, Miss Buie's name never appearing, even in an advertisement, without the designation "the soldier's friend". She located the school on the corner of Hampton and Marion streets, and advertised that she would receive free a few Confederate orphans.[68] A year later she appealed for aid to build

[60] *Ibid.*, September 6, speaks of "resuming exercises," etc.
[61] From 1866 through 1874, almost every issue of the *Phoenix* from August 15 to September 15, and again in the latter part of December carries the Martin school advertisement. The *Register* from 1875 to 1885 has similar advertisements.
[62] *Register,* August 23.
[63] *Phoenix,* December 27, 1873. De Hedemann named as French teacher was also on the Male and Female Academy lists for that year. In 1874 Rev. C. R. Hemphill is named by Miss Martin and in the Male Academy advertisements.
[64] Like Miss Martin, Miss Elmore advertised faithfully in the *Phoenix* and then in the *Register.* The first advertisement noted is *Phoenix,* August 15, 1867, the last in the *Register,* September 4, 1888.
[65] *Phoenix,* September 4, 1873.
[66] *Ibid.,* January 3, 1874, September 28, 1877; *Columbia City Directory* (Columbia), 1879-80.
[67] *Phoenix,* September 21, 1870.
[68] *Ibid.,* October 4, 1870.

a "suitable structure".[69] Apparently she received only promises of help and so, in 1872, she moved to Aiken.[70]

The Misses Reynolds have been mentioned above as principals of the Columbia Female Academy. When they left that institution in 1878 they opened a private school for girls variously called, "Sunnyside School", "Eclectic School"; and later changed to the "Reynolds School for Boys".[71] Miss Reynolds' advertisements insist on the thoroughness of their training, and the many years of public patronage sustains her claim. The school continued, at least, to 1892, which gives the Misses Reynolds thirty years of teaching experience in Columbia.

Early in 1871, Mr. Charles H. Barnwell moved to Columbia and established a private school for boys which continued for many years.[72] The school was on the corner of Hampton and Henderson, the playground being the square in front of the present Elks' Home. In 1881 Mr. Barnwell became principal of the Male Academy but returned in a few years to his own school, continuing it until his health failed in 1888.[73]

Among the other schools beginning in this period, and about which little is known except their long service are those of Miss Ellen Janney, Mrs. S. C. A. Scott, Miss Wilbur and Miss LaBruce. Miss Janney taught at her home, 1410 Blanding street, and in 1899, when the last announcement of her school was noted, she was beginning her twenty-fourth year.[74] Mrs. Scott conducted her school at her home on the corner of Blanding and Bull streets certainly from 1881 to 1895 and possibly longer.[75] In 1871 Miss Wilbur announced the

---

[69] *Ibid.*, August 12, 1871.

[70] *Ibid.*, August 1, 1872. The following January 11 a local item says "none of the donations promised to her were ever paid . . . the payment of the same being changed from her appeals to those who are trying to relieve the Methodist Female College of debt."

[71] *Register,* August 17, 1878, August 14, 1879, September 5, 1885, August 31, 1888.

[72] *Phoenix,* December 20, 1870, January 12, 1871. Charles H. Barnwell, now Dean of College of Arts and Sciences, University of Alabama, says that his father's pupils the first year were Woodrow Wilson, James H. Baldwin and "one of the McMaster boys." Personal letter to Prof. E. L. Green, November 8, 1935. It is interesting to note that in 1887 Mr. Barnwell announced that he would be assisted by his son, Charles H. Barnwell, Jr., who had just graduated from college and "has chosen teaching as his profession in life". *Register,* September 5.

[73] *Ibid.,* also his son's letter

[74] *Register,* August 26, 1889, speaks of the 14th session. Annual advertisements follow year after year; the *City Directory* of 1899 lists Miss Janney's school.

[75] *Register,* September 13, 1881, and succeeding years, also *City Directory,* 1895.

reopening of her school on Laurel street and continued the annual advertisements through 1876.[76] The Misses LaBorde enliven the formal announcements of their school which appear each year from 1874 to 1882 with interesting bits as to new courses: "partial introduction of the kindergarten system—Calisthenics".[77] This school was first taught in Chancellor Carroll's house on the corner of Gervais and Marion and later moved to the corner of Laurel and Assembly.[78]

It is impossible to do more than list here the many other schools which dotted Columbia in the years before the public schools were in general favor, and which are still treasured in the memory of older Columbians. Mrs. S. C. Goodwyn began a school during the war and conducted it in various rooms on Hampton, Assembly and Taylor streets.[79] Miss M. A. Bollinger; Miss Barnwell, assisted by her father, Hon. R. W. Barnwell; R. H. Clarkson, who later was a principal of one of the city schools; Mrs. George R. Capers; Miss C. Muller; Mr. C. A. Seabrook, all conducted schools of more than transitory duration.[80]

PRIVATE SCHOOLS SINCE 1885

While the establishment of adequate public schools led to the decrease of private school enrollment, it did not lead to their entire extinction. In the early years of the present century Mr. William Verner conducted a splendid preparatory school for boys in the 1000 block of Barnwell street. After Mr. Verner's health failed, Mrs. Margaret Selby Detyens continued his school at 1428 Taylor street and Mr. A. W. Fogle, in 1905, bought the property of the Verner school and opened the Columbia University School for Boys. He conducted it only a short time. The name was continued by Mr. C. V. Neuffer and the location changed to 1413 Laurel where, in 1908, a

---

[76] Phoenix, September 16, 1871; Register, September 20, 1876.

[77] Ibid., August 19, 1876.

[78] Phoenix, September 3, 1874, and each September following through 1882.

[79] Phoenix, August 26, 1868, September 20, 1890, September 3, 1871, and others.

[80] A list of the newspaper advertisements covering these schools is too long for inclusion. City directories at regular intervals include such lists. The Catholic schools were started as far back as 1857. O'Connell, Catholicity in the Carolinas and Georgia, p. 245. St. Mary's was called a college but took pupils in 1863 only between 9 and 15 years of age. The Ursuline Academy, a finishing school, was for many years after the war outside the city limits of Columbia at "Valle Crucis". Both the Presbyterian and Episcopal churches had parochial schools of brief duration. City Directory, 1895, 1899, 1903, 1904.

roster of pupils shows thirty-one names, among them a number of prominent present-day Columbians.[81]

From 1896 to 1931 was conducted the Bon Air School; for many years by Miss Annie Bonham and later by her sister and niece, Mrs. Gadsden Shand and Miss Roberta Aldrich. Probably no one will question the statements made in *The State* by a former pupil of the Bon Air school that the school was unique and Miss Annie an educational genius.[82] Another beloved private school of the same period was that of Miss Helen McMaster.

Among the private schools in Columbia at present are the primary school of Miss Sue E. Hunt, 2831 Blossom street, and the Davis High School, 1110 Henderson street. Miss Hunt's school was started in 1923 and has taught many beginners since that time.[83] The Davis High School began as a primary school in 1912 and is now an accredited high school. Mrs. Blanche O'N. Davis is the principal; the faculty including Mrs. Davis, Mrs. Alfred Gaillard, Mrs. George Tompkins and Mrs. Margaret Breeland.

Some mention should be made of at least two of the private kindergartens which have meant much to the educational life of Columbia. Miss Louly Shand opened her kindergarten in 1901 and is now teaching children of her former pupils.[84] Miss Lucile Lindsay began her kindergarten in 1911, moving to the present location on Lincoln street in 1918.[85]

The boys and girls of Columbia have in the public schools of today many advantages which their parents and grandparents did not have in the private school period in which they lived. In the physical equipment of the buildings and in the professional training of the teachers the difference is markedly in favor of the public school. However, the very number of private schools before 1885 meant a keen competition for pupils which must have led to the survival of the fittest of the teachers. That many taught ten, twenty and thirty years or more is an indication of their ability. The close association between teacher and pupil, a concomitant of the private school, is hard to attain in public schools with their large enrollment and departmentalization. This intimate teacher-pupil relationship led to the strong sentimental attachment which many of the older

---

[81] Letters from Mrs. Detyens, dated November 21, 1935, and Mr. Fogle, November 12, 1935. Catalogue of the University School of Columbia for the school years 1909-1910. Also *City Directory,* 1906, 1907, 1909, 1910.

[82] November 16, 1932. An editorial in *The State* (n. d. on the clipping, but September, 1931), also comments on what this school meant to Columbia.

[83] Letter from Miss Hunt, November, 1935.

[84] Letter from Miss Shand, November 19, 1935.

[85] Letter from Miss Lindsay, November, 1935.

Columbians feel for the schools of their youth. Men like F. W. Mc-Master and John P. Thomas, Jr., who worked for the beginning of public education, did so, not for the sake of those who were able to attend the private schools, but to meet the needs of those who could not afford the tuition costs.

PUBLIC SCHOOLS

By Orin F. Crow

THE HISTORY of the public schools of Columbia falls into six logical divisions: First, the operation of public schools before 1880; second, the administration of the schools by the school board, 1881-1883; and the administrations of the four school superintendents appointed by the board: D. B. Johnson, 1883-1895; E. S. Dreher, 1895-1918; W. H. Hand, 1918-1928, and A. C. Flora, since 1928.

PUBLIC SCHOOLS BEFORE 1880

Public schools in the city of Columbia became possible by an Act of the General Assembly passed in 1811 commonly known as the "Free School Act". This Act provided for free schools in the state and for the appropriation of state money to aid in their establishment and support. As early as 1800, Governor John Drayton had urged the establishment of public schools for the benefit of the people of the state.[1] Just prior to the passage of the Act, Governor Middleton had urged the necessity of free schools.[2]

The first constitutional provisions for education in South Carolina are found in the Constitution of 1868 (Article X), which established for the first time in the history of the state the offices of state superintendent of education and county commissioners of schools.

It is well-nigh impossible to trace the expenditure of the state's appropriation by the General Assembly from 1811 until 1880, the date of the establishment of the Columbia school district. Some of the state money was used for the support of public schools and some of it was used for the support of "poor scholars" in private schools. Reports now extant give very little information about the detailed expenditure of the free school fund. The reports to the General Assembly were collected by districts. Hence it is impossible to say just how much and under what circumstances free school funds were expended in the area constituting the city of Columbia. In 1826, the faculty of the South Carolina College made a report on the free school system to the General Assembly in which the complaint was made concerning the manner in which the school records were kept

---

[1] House Journal, MS, November 25, 1800, pp. 12-17; see also Senate Journal, MS, November 23, 1802, p. 11.
[2] Senate Journal, MS, December 26, 1811, p. 10.

that "they may be sufficient for a report of the committee satisfactory to the House but more detailed information would be useful to the public." [3]

Under the Act of 1811 [4] public schools were established in the city of Columbia. J. F. Williams reports that he attended such a school prior to 1860.[5] Reynolds indicates that there were white and negro public schools in Columbia in 1871.[6] When the Columbia school board was organized in 1881 it came into control of the Sidney Park School for white children and the Howard School for colored pupils.[7]

UNDER THE SCHOOL BOARD

The school district of the city of Columbia was established by an act of the General Assembly approved 24 December, 1880.[8] The act created a corporation of the inhabitants of the district and gave it the usual corporate powers bestowed by charters. The City Council was ordered to hold an election of school commissioners from each ward of the city who, with one member of the council, were to constitute the board of school commissioners of the school district of Columbia. A new election of commissioners was to be held at each general election of the city. Specific powers granted to the board were enumerated as follows:

1. To discharge the same duties in the city which are required of school trustees in the counties.

2. To determine the studies and class books to be used in the city schools.

3. To cause examinations to be made of teachers for the city schools.

4. To elect and dismiss superintendents and teachers, prescribe their duties and term of office, and to make rules for the government of the schools.

5. To fill vacancies occurring in the board by death, resignation, departure from the state, or refusal to qualify: the said vacancies to be filled from the said wards in which they occur.

6. To establish, when they deem it expedient, a normal school department, and to grant diplomas in said department, which shall entitle the parties holding the same to become teachers in the public schools.

7. To make an annual report to the Superintendent of Education as to the city schools, as is required of commissioners of county schools.

---

[3] *Report of the Faculty of South Carolina College on Free School System,* 1826.

[4] Thomas Cooper, ed., *Statutes at Large of South Carolina,* Columbia, 1836-1839, V, 639-641.

[5] J. F. Williams, *Old and New Columbia,* Columbia, 1929, p. 40.

[6] John S. Reynolds, *Reconstruction in South Carolina,* Columbia, 1905, p. 122.

[7] John P. Thomas, Jr., in *Columbia Graded Schools First Year,* Columbia, 1883, p. 6.

[8] *Statutes at Large of South Carolina,* XVII, Columbia, p. 404.

118

HISTORY OF COLUMBIA

8. To erect suitable buildings for the public schools, to take in charge and keep in order all buildings and property used for school purposes belonging to the said city.

9. To determine the manner in which the tax hereinafter provided for shall be expended in maintaining the city schools.

The County Treasurer was made the treasurer of the board of school commissioners, placed under bond, and empowered to hold and expend school funds only upon the warrant of the commissioners. The school district was authorized to levy a special tax of one mill for the year 1881 and two mills for each succeeding year, provided that a mass meeting of the legal voters of the district approved the levy. The first tax meeting was to be held the fifteenth of February, 1881, and on or before the first day of February of each succeeding year.

No member of the school board was allowed to hold any office authorized by the act. An amendment to the charter was passed by the General Assembly in 1881,[9] providing that no member should hold any *salaried* office and making some changes in the original act concerning the levy and disposition of school funds. The changes provided that the school taxes should be collected with state taxes and should be received by the County Treasurer instead of the City Treasurer. The act of 1880 was further amended in 1883 by adding to the board of school commissioners two persons to be appointed for the same term as the others by the Governor upon recommendation of the board of trustees of the Columbia Male and Female Academy. In 1893 the charter was again changed so as to provide that the office of clerk should be changed to that of secretary, that the County Treasurer's official bond rather than a special bond was extended to the protection of school money and a change in the method of drawing warrants on the school fund.[10]

In 1902 an act was passed providing that the term of office of the commissioners should be four years, half of the elected members to be chosen every two years.[11] Another change was made in 1912 when it was provided that members of the school board should be elected from the city at large rather than by wards.[12]

The first board of school commissioners was set up under the act of 1880 and consisted of the following members; Colonel F. W. McMaster, Messrs. W. J. Duffie, Nathaniel B. Barnwell, J. S.

---

[9] *Ibid.*, p. 558.
[10] *Ibid.*, XVIII, Columbia, 1883, p. 415, XXI, Columbia, 1893, p. 681.
[11] *Ibid.*, XXIII, Columbia, 1902, p. 1218.
[12] *Ibid.*, XXVII, Columbia, 1912, p. 1051; other amendments not discussed: XXVI, Columbia, 1910, p. 904; XXVIII, Columbia, 1914, p. 928.

Muller and J. P. Arthur. The first meeting of the board took place on the first of February, 1881, with all members present. Colonel McMaster was elected chairman and Joseph S. Muller, clerk. The election of a superintendent of schools was postponed and it was determined to call a meeting of the legal voters for the first day of March, 1881, to consider the matter of levying the authorized school tax.

The board of school commissioners began its work in 1881 with little to encourage it except its own zeal for the organization and establishment of an effective public school system. The situation in South Carolina was not dissimilar to that existing in other southern states. The people had little interest in education. Such schools as had been established were in the main pauper schools.[13] The people of means sent their children to private schools and the poor people were too proud to accept what they regarded as the charity of the state.

In the city of Columbia the total attendance for the two years preceding the organization of the school board scarcely averaged five hundred pupils, the large majority of whom were colored children. The length of the session was but a little over three months. The citizens of the city apparently were not interested in the development of a public school system as shown by their refusal in 1881 and again in 1882 [14] to vote the one mill school tax authorized by the act chartering the school district. The only funds available were those derived from the constitutional two mill tax and the poll tax. From these sources the sum of about $1,700.00 was available to organize the school system, provide buildings, equipment and pay its teaching staff. This discouraging situation was met in a heroic manner by the school board under the leadership of Colonel F. W. McMaster, Mr. John P. Thomas, Jr., who became a member of the board after the election of April, 1882, and Dr. E. S. Joynes.[15]

The one mill tax was finally voted. Before the meeting to consider the levy, 31 January, 1883, Mr. Thomas, in a statement to the press, attempted to answer the questions "How are the public schools to obtain the financial support necessary to their full development?"

---

[13] E. P. Cubberley, *Public Education In The United States,* Boston, 1934, p. 97 ff.

[14] Board Minutes, MS, February 7, 1882; B. L. Parkinson, *History of the Administration of the Public Schools of Columbia, S. C.,* Columbia, 1920, p. 17. Bulletin of the University of South Carolina, 1920. Parkinson's pamphlet has been invaluable in the preparation of this sketch.

[15] Dr. Joynes was elected February 1, 1883, to succeed N. B. Barnwell, deceased.

and "What plan is there that will assure the tax payers that the additional taxation will furnish them with good free schools?".[16]

Mr. Thomas gave local taxation as the answer to the first question. He said that the plan had been tried in various parts of the state and that wherever it had been adopted it had given satisfactory results and that no community that had tried this plan had ever repudiated it. He further said that wherever local taxation for school purposes had been tried it had been a popular measure because it made good free schools a reality. He pointed out the success of the

Library, Columbia Theological Seminary, Robert Mills, Architect

system in Charleston, that eight per cent. of the inhabitants of the city were in school, while in Columbia only four per cent. were attending free schools. In answer to the second question Mr. Thomas said that good free schools would be assured by the concentration of school effort in the city. There would be only two schools, one for white and one for colored children. This would concentrate effort and insure efficient inspection, control and direction. "There would be", he asserted, "more uniformity in the methods of instruction and broader opportunity for the well-timed introduction of improvements in methods of instruction, being under one intelligent head, the whole body of the system will be subject to a capable

---

[16] *Columbia Register,* February 1, 1883.

supervision." He prepared a budget to show just how the money would be spent in order to insure good schools. Under the plan proposed by Mr. Thomas, the schools would run for nine months.

The night before the tax meeting, Dr. Joynes made a "strong and vigorous" public address in Temperance Hall to "a large audience of friends and opponents of the proposed system of schools." [17]

The chief credit for arousing the citizens to the point where they would be willing to vote the tax in 1883 after the failures of 1881 and 1882 seems to belong to Colonel F. W. McMaster, Mr. John P. Thomas, Jr., and Dr. Edward S. Joynes. Dr. Joynes, writing in 1912, says:

> This measure was achieved mainly through the efforts and influence of Colonel F. W. McMaster, who is now justly commemorated in the beautiful McMaster School Building, as the Father of Columbia Schools. As I had had some knowledge of a city school system during my earlier residence in Knoxville, Tennessee, and as I had aided Colonel McMaster in his canvass before the people, I was made a member of the School Board and assisted in the first organization of the City Schools.[18]

Mr. Thomas generously stated that "the auspicious opening of the schools under the new law was due in a large measure to the energy, bold perseverance and untiring devotion to the cause displayed by Colonel McMaster." [19]

The pressing problem of housing the schools was solved by an agreement with the board of trustees of the Columbia Male and Female Academy whereby the two buildings of the academy were leased by the Columbia school board. The school commissioners agreed that the academy should have the privilege of naming two members of the board of school commissioners. This part of the agreement was legalized by the General Assembly as has been noted above. The public schools retained control of the academy buildings by successive leases until 1904 when the property was conveyed to the board in perpetuity upon the condition that the academy board be allowed to name two members of the school board for all time.[20] Thus it is that the sites upon which the present Columbia High School and Taylor School are located are not owned in fee simple by the Columbia school board. It seems that the leader in bringing

---

[17] Address by W. H. Hand, "Twenty-five Years of Achievement," *Annual Report,* 1907-08, p. 77; *Columbia Register,* January 3, 1883.

[18] E. S. Joynes, "Origin and Early History of Winthrop College," in *Winthrop Normal and Industrial College Bulletin,* V, Number one, Twenty-fifth Anniversary Number, September, 1912.

[19] *The State,* April 26, 1905. Reprinted in *Annual Report,* 1904-1905, p. 65.

[20] Parkinson, *op. cit.,* 26-29. A copy of the agreement is printed in *Annual Report,* 1903-1904, pp. 54-56.

about the original agreement between the Columbia Academy and the school board was Dr. E. S. Joynes.[21]

At the meeting of the board, 14 April, 1883, it was announced that the Peabody board, through its agent, Dr. J. L. M. Curry, would give a thousand dollars toward the salary of a superintendent of city schools. The board, on motion of Mr. Thomas, decided to add five hundred dollars to the amount subscribed by the Peabody board.

After having committed the people of Columbia to the principle of local taxation for schools and having made arrangements for sufficient housing accommodations and obtaining sufficient money to employ a superintendent, the board was ready to enter the next phase in the development of schools in Columbia. For two years it had operated the schools without a superintendent. Now it was in position to employ someone to direct the establishment of an adequate school system.

SUPERINTENDENT JOHNSON'S ADMINISTRATION

Superintendent D. B. Johnson, of New Bern, North Carolina, was elected superintendent of the Columbia schools on the twenty-third of June, 1883. Superintendent Johnson was, however, not the first choice of the board. The board had elected Mr. E. P. Moses, of Goldsboro, North Carolina, 28 May, 1883. The board accepted Mr. Moses's resignation and reprimanded him for resigning the 20th of June, 1883.

Mr. Johnson was a native of Tennessee and was educated at the University of Tennessee where he was later a member of the faculty.[22] He had organized the graded schools of Abbeville and had completed the organization of the graded schools of New Bern at the time he was elected superintendent at Columbia.

Superintendent Johnson proceeded to the organization of the schools with indefatigable zeal. He personally interviewed, graded and classified the pupils who applied for admission. Buildings were repaired, a janitor was employed, and everything was in readiness by the opening day, 28 September, 1883.[23]

The first school year under Mr. Johnson began optimistically with an enrollment nearly four times as large as that of the previous year. R. H. Clarkson was principal of the male school and Miss O.

---

[21] Dr. Joynes' able appeal to the Academy trustees in behalf of the school board appeared in the *Columbia Register,* March 18, 1883.

[22] He was not called "Doctor" Johnson until the South Carolina College conferred upon him an honorary degree in 1905, ten years after he had left Columbia. *Proceedings of the Centennial Celebration of South Carolina College,* Columbia, 1905, p. 173.

[23] *Columbia Graded Schools First Year,* 1883-1884, p. 9.

A. Garlington was principal of the female school. William M. Dart was principal of the Howard School for both sexes of colored pupils.[24]

The first year was marked by financial difficulties almost insurmountable. The school board had great trouble in meeting its monthly obligations as the year wore on.[25] The expense of conditioning the buildings had drained the resources of the board. To meet this pressing situation several measures were undertaken.[26] Mr. Johnson made a trip North and collected $440.00. The people of Columbia subscribed about $1,000.00. Teachers' salaries were reduced. An "art entertainment" was given and the sum of $152.00 was cleared above expenses.

At the beginning of the year the board decided that instruction would be free to the pupils of the first seven grades. A fee of $2.50 a month was to be charged pupils in Grades 8, 9, and 10.[27] Nonresident pupils were to pay fees in all grades with an increased fee in the last three grades. Collections from this source amounted to $78.00, Superintendent Johnson reported to the board, 5 February, 1884.

In April it was foreseen that, notwithstanding all the measures undertaken by the board, the full term of nine months could not be completed. Accordingly a plan was worked out whereby Superintendent Johnson would undertake the operation of the schools on a tuition basis and divide the fees among the teachers pro rata. The fees charged ranged from $1.00 a month for Grades 1 and 2 to $5.00 a month for Grades 8, 9, and 10.[28] With 329 white children agreeing to attend school at these rates the full nine months of the school session were completed.

In addition to all the work of the first year demanding the attention of the superintendent, Mr. Johnson found time to collect more than 300 volumes as the foundation of a school library.[29] A few of the books were for the profesional improvement of teachers. Two years later Mr. Johnson said of the library: "It is a cherished plan of mine that it shall eventually expand into a free, circulating library for the whole city." [30]

[24] *Ibid.*, p. 8.

[25] Board Minutes, October 30, November 27, 1883, *et seq.*

[26] *Ibid.*, December 20, 1883, February 5, February 15, February 27, 1884, *et seq.* Throughout its history the presentation of bills for payment has been the first order of business at the monthly meetings of the board.

[27] Board Minutes, September 8, 1883.

[28] *Ibid.*, April, 1884.

[29] *Annual Report*, 1884-1885, pp. 12-13.

[30] *Ibid.*, 1885-1886, p. 16.

The school board in the fall of 1884 circulated a petition among the citizens requesting the county delegation in the General Assembly to secure one additional mill in the levy for school support. The extra mill was voted in December, 1884. By the fall of 1885 the financial situation became somewhat easier and the people seemed to be committed to the permanent maintenance of the public school system supported by taxation.[31]

The twin problems of finance and housing continued to beset the Johnson administration, as, indeed, they have every administration since. It was probably in the field of finance that the services of John P. Thomas, Jr., were most valuable and most constructive. On at least one occasion he advanced the amount of money needed to meet the payroll.[32]

Other than establishing the system itself, two significant developments grew out of the Johnson administration. These were the Columbia High School and Winthrop College.

The organization of the Columbia High School was not perfected during the Johnson administration, but as early as his second year, Mr. Johnson began to refer to the last three grades as the high

Columbia High School

school.[33] Boys and girls were housed separately throughout Mr. Johnson's superintendency. In his last annual report, Mr. Johnson suggested that a "separate and distinct High School in the Marion Street School building for both boys and girls" be organized as he

[31] Board Minutes, November 24, 1884; Parkinson, *op. cit.*, p. 43; *Annual Report*, 1884-1885, p. 8.
[32] *Ibid.*, June 6, 1884. Mr. Thomas resigned from the board in 1896 to enter the legislature, having remained a member of the board until it was free of debt. Parkinson, *op. cit.*, pp. 66-67.
[33] *Annual Report*, 1884-1885, p. 12.

had recommended in his two previous annual reports. This measure was possible because of the immediate removal of the Winthrop School from the city. Mr. Johnson felt that such a step

> would enable the teachers to give more time to the classes and to do distinctive High School work. There can be no good objection to co-education in these classes when most schools of this character in this and other States are coeducational, and when the South Carolina College and other male colleges of the State now open their doors to women.[34]

First Home of Winthrop College, Columbia Seminary Grounds

Mr. Johnson's plan was approved at the board meeting of 22 May, 1895, just before he ended his connection with the Columbia city schools.

A normal school was authorized by the act creating the Columbia school district in 1880. In his annual report for 1884-1885, Superintendent Johnson expressed the opinion that "through the high school we shall eventually be able to establish a training school for the purpose of training teachers." [35] It was not until 1886 that definite steps were taken for the establishment of the normal school.

At the meeting of the board, 28th April, 1886, a motion made by Dr. Joynes "to provide, in connection with the city schools, for a course of normal school instruction for the training of teachers" was referred to a committee. The committee made a favorable report on the 26th May, and the board resolved to appoint a committee to memorialize the Peabody board for financial aid in the enterprise. The superintendent was requested to prepare a plan for the operation of a normal department. On the 7th of July, Superintendent

---

[34] *Ibid.*, 1894-1895, p. 17.
[35] Second *Annual Report*, p. 12.

Johnson's report and plan were approved and he was authorized to go to Massachusetts to seek the aid of the Peabody board in person. An appropriation of $1,500.00 a year was obtained from the Peabody board mainly through the influence of the Hon. Robert C. Winthrop, its chairman.[36] At its meeting the 13th of October, 1886, the Columbia school board created the normal school, naming it the Winthrop Training School in honor of Mr. Winthrop and appointed Superintendent Johnson principal of the school with an addition of $500.00 to his salary.

The Winthrop Training School opened 15 November, 1886, in a building borrowed from the Columbia Theological Seminary, which had been constructed for use as a stable and carriage house and which later had been used by the seminary as its chapel. The seminary was not in session at the time.

The evolution of Winthrop Training School into Winthrop College is too long and involved a story to detail here. One item will indicate how precarious was that process at one time. In 1888, when the University of South Carolina was being re-organized an agreement was reached between the University board of trustees and the school board whereby the facilities of the Winthrop Training School and the School of Education, then called the Normal School, of the University were to be made reciprocally available to each other. Mr. Johnson was considered by the University board for the deanship of the new School of Education.[37] He was not elected but if he had been the whole picture of higher education in South Carolina would doubtless have developed differently.

Winthrop Normal and Industrial College of South Carolina was opened in Rock Hill in 1895 with Mr. Johnson as president. The college had been organized in Columbia before its removal to Rock Hill. Thus was brought to a close the administration of Columbia's first superintendent of schools. The committee of inspection, a committee composed of prominent citizens with H. C. Patton as chairman, reported 12th June, 1895, on the condition of the schools at the close of Mr. Johnson's administration. The committee of visitors paid the following tribute to the superintendent:

> In September, 1883, Superintendent Johnson organized the Columbia Graded Schools with some nine hundred pupils and nineteen teachers. In the twelve years of his administration they have grown to over two thousand pupils and more than thirty instructors, trained and skilled in the most improved methods. These schools are held as a model for similar institutions in this state and are the subject of inspection and inquiry

---

[36] Joynes, *op. cit.*, p. 58.
[37] Minutes of the board of trustees, MS, University of South Carolina, May 9, 1888.

from distant cities in other states. A Library of some sixteen hundred volumes has been established and modern equipment for instruction provided. The whole system, as we have it today, Professor Johnson has built from the ground up in twelve years, and with the most limited means at his disposal. From a comparative table of the schools of two hundred and ten cities it appears that, with a single exception, the schools of Columbia are conducted at the lowest expense of any city in the United States.[38]

SUPERINTENDENT DREHER'S ADMINISTRATION

Mr. E. S. Dreher, who entered the Columbia school system in 1889 as a male assistant at the Laurel street school at a salary of $60.00 a month and who became principal of the Laurel street school in 1893, was elected to succeed Mr. Johnson as superintendent.[39] His term of office extended from 1895 until 1918. The most important developments of Mr. Dreher's administration were the organization and establishment of the Columbia High School, the building of several school buildings, the provision for increased financial support and the introduction of semi-annual promotion in the schools.

The Columbia High School was organized as a three-teacher, three-year high school in the fall of 1895 [40] with Mr. C. E. Johnson as principal [41] and Miss F. C. McCants and Miss P. G. Bonham as the other members of the faculty. The school continued as a three-year high school until the session of 1916-17. The first high school commencement took place 10 June, 1897. Before that time the program was called "Closing Exercises of the City Schools." Appearing on the first commencement program,[42] among other items, was an essay by Mr. Edward S. Cardwell, "Some Developments in the Science of Warfare"; a recitation "The Chariot Race" from Ben-Hur, by Mr. John Waites Thomas; and an essay, "The Effects of Lawlessness in South Carolina", by Mr. James A. Cathcart.

By the session of 1901-02 the housing problem became acute. Mr. Dreher reported to the board:

Our school buildings are, indeed, very poor, a fact which I have mentioned in my report from year to year. Small towns all over the state have well-constructed, modern school-houses, others are issuing bonds

[38] *Annual Report,* 1894-1895, pp. 26-27.
[39] Board Minutes, August 3, 1889; *Tenth Annual Report,* 1892-1893, p. 4; Board Minutes, May 22, 1895.
[40] *Annual Report,* 1895-1896, 4, 24.
[41] Principals of the Columbia High School from the beginning have been C. E. Johnson (1895-1901), H. C. Davis (1901-1903), F. E. Hinnant (1903-1906), H. P. Johnson (1906-1908), Lewis Crum (1908-1913), H. A. Wise (1913-1917), A. C. Flora (1917-1928), G. H. Hill (1928-1930), and E. R. Crow since 1930.
[42] *Annual Report,* 1896-1897, pp. 43-44.

for building purposes, but we Columbians have so far done almost nothing for the suitable accommodation of our school children.[43]

Mr. Dreher gave information to the board about the various school buildings.[44] The school buildings in use at that time were: the High School building, "a poorly constructed two-story frame building"; the Washington street school, containing twelve rooms "but only one of them is suited to the purpose for which it is used—the office of your Superintendent"; the Laurel street school, "an unsightly, worn-out, two-story brick building"; Blossom street school, "a small, one-story frame building"; the Howard School, "a rather disreputable, two-story frame building". These five buildings were valued at only $22,500.00. The next year a two-room frame structure was placed on the Washington street school grounds and one room was added to the Laurel street school, but Mr. Dreher said, "The only satisfactory solution of the problem is the erection of new buildings".

The first modern school building erected in Columbia was the Taylor School, completed in 1906.[45] It replaced the Laurel street school. The McMaster School was erected in 1911, Logan School, 1913 (enlarged 1915), Blossom street school, 1916, Columbia High School, 1916. When the Shandon and Waverly sections were annexed to the Columbia school district in 1913 the school board came into possession of the Shandon School, erected in 1909, and the Waverly School, erected in 1911.

The history of Logan School was somewhat different from that of the other buildings erected by the city. The board's committee on school buildings and property reported in 1904 [46] that Charles Logan had devised four acres of land and the sum of $40,000.00 for the purpose of erecting a school for white children to be named the Logan School or Logan High School, the land and the money to be available upon the death of his wife and to be used only for the purpose specified by Mr. Logan. Should a school not be maintained on the site so devised the property will revert to the Logan estate. Mrs. Logan released her claim to the lot in 1912. The Columbia City Council assumed responsibility for $40,000.00 in addition to the $40,000.00 received from the Logans, making the Logan School possible.[47] The acceptance of the Logan terms increased the number of school sites not owned in fee simple by the school board to three.

---

[43] *Ibid.*, 1901-1902, pp. 17-18.
[44] *Ibid.*, pp. 18-19.
[45] For the sources of this paragraph, see the appropriate annual reports.
[46] *Annual Report*, 1903-1904, pp. 10-12.
[47] *Ibid.*, 1911-1912, pp. 11-12; 1912-1913, p. 25.

Logan School, Elmwood Avenue

The special levy for schools remained at two mills from 1885 to 1916 with the exception of the years 1889-95 when the levy was 2½ mills.[48] In 1916 when the need for additional school facilities had become critical, the two-mill levy was increased to five mills by a special election authorized by the General Assembly. The vote in favor of the levy was 253 to 121 against.[49] The amount of this special levy indicates in a general way how strongly the people believed in their schools. In his annual report for 1906, Superintendent Dreher made the following observations about school conditions in the city of Columbia:

> 1. The people of Columbia, as a whole, are indifferent to the importance of a well-educated citizenship. 2. Material prosperity takes precedence of intellectual progress. 3. The horses belonging to the city have strong and conveniently arranged brick buildings in which to rest, while a majority of the school children work in wholly inferior buildings. 4. A course of lectures on the care and protection of school children would be highly beneficial in many ways. 5. By not having better school buildings, the city is without one of the best advertising mediums known to the business world. 6. The annual loss to the city in educational values, industrial achievement, improved economic conditions, increased prosperity, and honorable prestige cannot be estimated.[50]

The increased income produced by the five-mill levy of 1916 eased the financial situation considerably. A bond issue of $250,000.-00 was authorized in 1915 for the purpose of enlarging and building additional schools.[51] The Columbia High School was erected with a part of the proceeds of this issue and the Logan School was en-

---

[48] See *Annual Reports* from 1889 to 1895.
[49] *Ibid.*, 1915-1916, p. 32.
[50] *Ibid.*, 1906-1907, p. 16.
[51] *Annual Report*, 1914-1915, pp. 26-27.

larged by the use of a part of this same fund. Booker T. Washington and Blossom street schools were also erected.[52]

The year 1913-14 saw the introduction of the method of promoting pupils semi-annually.[53] The reasons given for this step were stated by the board's committee on textbooks and courses of study as follows:

> This plan gives a greater flexibility to the classification and promotion of pupils, and it will enable many ambitious and studious pupils to gain from half a year to a year and a half, possibly more, during their school course. It will also encourage slow pupils, because it will be necessary for many of them to repeat a half year only, whereas, under the present system they are forced to repeat an entire year.[54]

Mr. Dreher reported after the first year's operation of the plan that it had "met with the warm approval of the patrons, teachers and pupils of the city." [55]

Mr. Dreher's 24-year term as superintendent of the Columbia city schools came to a close in 1918. In September, 1917, a group of citizens attended a meeting of the board and submitted criticisms on the schools giving their experiences with their own children as a basis for their criticism. One of the citizens, Dr. J. J. Watson, offered the board the sum of $1,000.00 for the purpose of making a survey of the schools. He also offered the interest on certain securities amounting to $500.00 a year to be assigned to the board for five years to increase the salary of the superintendent, provided a certain person was appointed to the position. Dr. Watson asked the board to accept one of the two offers made by him. The board declined to accept the five hundred dollars, but did accept the one thousand dollars for the survey. The survey was made by the United States Bureau of Education. During the progress of the survey, reports were from time to time submitted by the survey committee. Mr. Dreher resigned, 11 June, 1918, after he had been unanimously re-elected for the following year.[56] He said that the conclusions of the survey were "so impractical, so little, and so unfair as to make it really grotesque." He also stated that many of the recommendations made in the survey had been made by him many times in his annual reports. His resignation was accepted and the board passed a resolution of appreciation of Mr. Dreher's services.

---

[52] *Ibid.*, 1915-1916, pp. 19-25.

[53] The plan had been recommended by Ellen Stanley Watkins for elementary schools. *Annual Report*, 1911-1912, p. 34.

[54] *Annual Report*, 1912-1913, p. 19.

[55] *Ibid.*, 1913-1914, p. 38.

[56] For a fuller discussion of the events preceding Mr. Dreher's resignation, see Parkinson, *op. cit.*, pp. 108-110 and Bureau of Education Bulletin, 1918, No. 28, *The Public Schools of Columbia, South Carolina.*

SUPERINTENDENT HAND'S ADMINISTRATION

Mr. W. H. Hand, who for twelve years had held the joint position of professor of secondary education in the University of South
Carolina and state high school inspector, was elected superintendent.[57]
His term of office began 1 August, 1918, and lasted until his death,
7 August, 1928. Mr. Hand's administration covered the period in
which there was a widespread revival of interest in education
throughout the country following the World War. This interest in
Columbia was reflected in greatly increased enrollments, building of
new schools, increased financial outlay, revision of the curriculum,
changes in the school organization, and in general a more effective
school program.[58] In his triennial report for the years 1922-24 [59]
Mr. Hand indicated that the following things among others had been
accomplished by his administration up to that time. In 1922 a bond
issue of $75,000.00 was made to construct an addition to the High
School building. A year later another bond issue of $300.000.00 was
issued for general school improvements. The money from these two
issues was used to enlarge the High School building, to purchase
one-fourth of a city block at Shandon School and to erect an eight-
room building thereon, to add twelve classrooms to the Taylor School
building, to purchase more land and add six classrooms at McMaster
School and to purchase one-half of a city block for the new Howard
School and to erect a twelve-room building thereon. Equipment for
these new buildings was also provided. The general education board
gave $30,000.00 to which the local board added $6,000.00 for the
purpose of erecting an industrial building for negroes. Fences were
placed around the school grounds at Taylor, Shandon, Waverly and
the new Howard schools. The high school day was extended from a
two o'clock closing to a three o'clock closing. The grade school day
was extended to 2:15 o'clock instead of 2 o'clock. Cafeterias were
provided at Columbia High School and at Logan, Taylor, McMaster
and Shandon schools. The curriculum of the first grade through the
eleventh had been revised. "Every white teacher in the system has
made some contribution to this work out of her own experience",
reported Mr. Hand. A testing program was begun in September, 1924. A special school for problem and retarded pupils was organized.

---

[57] *Board Minutes,* July 12, 1918.
[58] Parkinson, *op. cit.,* pp. 110-113, and Elizabeth Peay, W. H. Hand and
His Influence Upon Public Education in South Carolina, MS., pp. 47-62.
Master's Thesis, University of South Carolina, 1932.
[59] *Triennial Report,* 1922-1923, pp. 50-58.

In 1926 another bond issue of $500,000.00 was passed. The proceeds of this issue were to cover a four-year building program.[60]

At the meeting of the board, 1 September, 1926, Mr. Hand proposed the present junior high school system of the city. The Wardlaw Junior High School was erected,[61] and opened in the fall of 1927. A Junior High School for the southeastern section of the city was opened in the old Heathwood building [62] where it remained until the completion of the present Hand Junior High School in 1930.

The Heathwood and Rose Hill sections were annexed in 1927, and a part of the Hyatt Park district was annexed in 1928.[63]

The tax rate was increased to eight mills in 1918, to nine mills in 1919, to ten in 1922, and to fourteen in 1924, where it has remained except for the years 1933 and 1934.[64]

Mr. Hand advocated two policies, among others, which were not finally adopted: the work-study-play or platoon system of schools [65] and the addition of a twelfth year to the school system. In his report to the board, 1 November, 1927, he stated: "My prediction is that Columbia will be in the list of 12-year schools within two years from this date."

SUPERINTENDENT FLORA'S ADMINISTRATION

Upon the death of Mr. Hand, 7 August, 1928, Mr. A. C. Flora, who had been principal of the Columbia High School since 1917, was elected acting superintendent for one year.[66] Mr. J. M. Payne, who had been principal of McMaster School since 1918, became assistant to the superintendent in charge of business affairs.[67] Mr. Flora was elected superintendent in April, 1929,[68] and has held the office ever since.

Mr. Flora's administration has been characterized by rapid growth in enrollment, continuation and enlargement of the building program begun in Mr. Hand's administration, changes in the administra-

[60] Peay, *op. cit.*, p. 41; Mr. Hand's report to the board, May 19, 1926; board minutes, March 1, 1927.
[61] Contract let January 11, 1927. Purchase of Burney lot for Hand Junior school authorized at same meeting.
[62] Report to the board, October 4, 1927.
[63] Board Minutes, February 8, 1927, and June 5, 1928.
[64] See reports for appropriate years and special statement appended to board minutes for February 12, 1935.
[65] Report to the board, February 15, 1927.
[66] Board Minutes, September 4, 1928.
[67] *Ibid.*, November 26, 1928.
[68] *Ibid.*, April 9, 1929.

tive organization, the adoption of modern budgetary record forms, constant curriculum revision, and reduced operating income.[69]

The buildings erected since 1928 include an addition to the Columbia High School, the Hand Junior High School, additions to the Hyatt Park and Logan Schools, the Hamrick School, the A. C. Moore School, the Fannie C. McCants School and a building to house the administrative offices.[70]

The Edgewood school district was added to the city school system in 1930.[71]

Today, Columbia has a large and growing school system, housed in twenty-four buildings, staffed by 380 teachers and administrative

Hall-Preston-Hampton Mansion (College for Women)

officers, an enrollment of 12,775 pupils, and financed at public expense. The school board of 1881, believing as they so thoroughly did in the urgent necessity of public schools, could scarcely have dreamed of what has been wrought.

---

[69] Letter from Mr. Flora dated November 30, 1935.
[70] Board Minutes, October 29, 1929; December 20, 1929; March 4, 1930; April 8, 1930; May 13, 1930; July 3, 1930; December 16, 1931.
[71] *Ibid.,* October 8, 1930.

RELIGION

By Fitz Hugh McMaster

ON "the first map of the City of Columbia, being a copy of the original plan of the city from the survey ordered 1786," the general assembly of the state having decided on March 26, 1786, that the capital of the state should be here, there is no indication that a church was within the limits of the city established.

The same is true of the "map used in 1786, when site of Columbia was under discussion." [1]

The map of Mills' atlas, published in 1826, from surveys of the several counties made in 1820 and 1821, and "improved in 1825 for the atlas," [2] shows only three churches in Richland county. One was near Minervaville, now disappeared, 15 or 16 miles southeast of Columbia, and two others 8 or 9 miles farther, near what is now Eastover. Undoubtedly there were a number of other, possibly small, churches not shown on the map.

The map of Fairfield shows 17 country churches; that of Lexington, 6; of Newberry, 11; of Kershaw, 7. [3]

In the limits of the city as established in 1786, there are in 1935 about 60 places of worship, and, including those in the additions and suburbs of the city, the number is 103, nearest count.

These do not include the Y. M. C. A., established in 1870, and now having 1,600 members with two branches, one for whites at the University and another at Allen University for negroes, and having a plant valued at about $300,000; nor the Y. W. C. A., established in 1912, and now having about 300 members with one branch for the negroes, and property valued at $25,000; nor the Columbia Bible College, founded in 1923, now with 145 students. Since its founding students from 25 denominations coming from half the states in the Union, from Europe, South and Central America, have been enrolled. Twenty-seven of its graduates have gone as missionaries to 17 foreign lands. It is undenominational.

The list does not include the Epworth Orphanage under Methodist control, with more than 300 children, nor the Carolina Home with more than 80 children, drawn from practically every county in the state. Both institutions are under religious influences.

---

[1] Edwin L. Green, *A History of Richland County,* Columbia, 1933, p. 146.
[2] Robert Mills, *Atlas of South Carolina,* Charleston, 1826.
[3] *Ibid.*

The poverty of this community religiously 150 years ago has been transformed into great wealth in the present. However, in the space alloted it is possible only to give the barest outline of those denominations active 100 years ago and to do no more than mention those which began during the last 40 or 50 years.

THE RELIGIOUS ORGANIZATION

At present the Adventists have one white and one negro con gregation; the Baptists have eight white congregations and 23 negro; the Roman Catholic two for whites and a negro mission; the Disciples of Christ, two white; the Congregationalist one white; the Episcopal five white and three negro; the Hebrews two for whites; the Holiness two white and five negro; the Lutherans six white; the Methodists nine white, and eight negro; the Presbyterians five whites and one negro; the Christians one white; the Christian Scientists one white. There are seven religious organizations classed as undenominational, in the city directory, among which are the Church of Latter Day Saints, the Oliver Gospel Mission, and the Salvation Army. There are two undenominational organizations for negroes.

Mills in his chapter on Richland County says: "The Presbyterians were the first religious society established in the district; they erected a church on the banks of Cedar Creek, anterior to the Revolution. The Methodists are the most numerous sect in the district. The Baptists form a respectable number, also the Episcopalians. The Roman Catholics have lately established a church in Columbia, and the Jews are forming themselves into a religious society." [4] The first religious services within the city limits of Columbia, according to Green, were conducted by the Rev. Isaac Smith, "a Methodist minister on the Santee circuit, [who] preached occasionally in 1787 at the house of Col. Thomas Taylor [corner Richland and Barnwell Streets], where Columbia now stands." [5]

The first call of a minister to a charge in Columbia was made March 30, 1794, to Rev. David E. Dunlap. It was signed by Thomas Taylor and Benjamin Waring.[6] Mr. Dunlap, according to Green, "was the son of Samuel Dunlap of the Waxhaw settlement, was a graduate of the Mount Zion College, . . . Winnsboro, and was licensed to preach in April, 1793" [7] (as a Presbyterian). It is not certain that the intention then was to establish a Presbyterian church, and a

[4] Mills, *Statistics of South Carolina*, p. 722.
[5] Green, *A History of Richland County*, p. 128.
[6] George Howe, *History of the Presbyterian Church in South Carolina*, Columbia, 1870-83, I, 595.
[7] Green, *A History of Richland County*, p. 188.

second call, made in September, 1794, was necessary to get the approval of the presbytery.[8]

METHODIST BEGINNING

The following taken from a carefully prepared sketch of "Columbia and Methodism," by Mrs. A. Fletcher Spigner, tells of the beginning of that denominational organization in Columbia:

> In 1802 the Rev. John Harper, an Englishman, ordained to the ministry by John Wesley, held services in the partially completed State House. (Alternating with him was the Rev. David Dunlap, a Presbyterian preacher.) In 1803, Mr. Harper, having served the Methodist ministry for 16 years, located in Columbia where he acquired a home and some property. He immediately set about the organization of a Methodist church.

Washington Street Methodist Church and Sunday School Building

> He organized a unit of membership of six. In the same year in which he located, he deeded to this congregation of six the lot on which the Washington Street Methodist church, its parsonage, and the district parsonage now stand. In 1805 the Washington Street Methodist church was built, being the first Christian house of worship in the City of Columbia." [9]

---

[8] Howe, *History of the Presbyterian Church in South Carolina,* I, 595, says: "The public service of ordination was held in the State House, Robert McCullough acting as Moderator, and John Brown (afterwards D.D.) as clerk of presbytery."

[9] Mrs. A. Fletcher Spigner. "Sketch of Columbia and Methodism, MS."

Green quotes from a diary of Edward Hooker, 1805, tutor in the South Carolina College:

> There is only one church [the Methodist] in the town. People think it *'a very neat, pretty building';* but I am certain there is not a country parish in Connecticut [whence he came], but would disdain not to build a better one, in case they were about to build at all.[10]

Quoting again from Mrs. Spigner:

> In the founding of Methodism in Columbia and the securing of the first members, Bishop Asbury, that mighty pioneer of Methodists in America, had undoubted part as is evidenced in the entries of his Journal, for from 1793 to 1815 are found important references to his journeys to Columbia.
>
> Washington Street was made a station in 1807. The congregations increased in such numbers that, in 1832, although the church which was first built had been enlarged twice already, a brick edifice together with a two-story Sunday school building was erected by Rev. William Capers, afterward bishop and who is known as the founder of missions to the slaves. This stood until 1865 at which time the sacred old place was burned by Sherman's army.
>
> The next year the impoverished congregation salvaged what burned brick they could, and by using with them ordinary red clay or mud mortar constructed, facing Marion Street, a building which served for ten years as the church, but 26 years longer as a Sunday School building.[11]

LATER METHODIST CHURCHES

Again quoting from Mrs. Spigner: "In 1848 there was such growth in the mother church that another church was built on the corner of Marion and Calhoun Streets, facing Marion Street. The erection of this church is attributed to the efforts of Rev. William Martin. This church, together with the parsonage which was next door, was burned in 1898, rebuilt at its present location on Main Street in 1899, Rev. S. H. Zimmerman then being pastor."

> This church has enjoyed rapid growth. At this time(1935) it is not only the largest Methodist church in Columbia, but the largest in the State. It has the distinction of being one of the largest in the Methodist Episcopal Church, South, ranking 19th from the top.
>
> Green Street was established through the agency of Rev. William Martin in 1879. A church was built in 1883 and the present building in 1901.
>
> What is now known as Whaley Street was first organized as Granby Mission in 1896. The present building was erected in 1903. In October, 1935, the handsome educational building was dedicated, Rev. A. B. Ferguson, pastor. This church has at this time a membership of 1500 and has property amounting to $65,000.00.
>
> Shandon was first organized in 1909, and its first church building, located on Maple and Preston Streets, was erected in 1910. In 1931 the

---

[10] Green, *A History of Richland County,* p. 162.
[11] Spigner, "Sketch of Columbia and Methodism."

present location at the junction of Divine Street and Millwood Avenue was secured, and purchase made of the Heathwood school building as the nucleus for the future church plant.

Waverly was established in 1909, and the church built between 1912 and 1915.

Edgewood was established in 1884 through the activities of Mr. and Mrs. Lysander D. Childs. (Bethel Church on the Edgewood charge, one of the oldest churches in the middle country, was established in 1835. Colonel Taylor donated an acre of land and furnished the lumber for the first building, which was destroyed by a forest fire in 1867. The present building was erected the following year.)

Brookland Church was organized in 1892, remodeled as it now stands in 1930 under the pastorate of Rev. A. M. Smith.

College Place was organized in 1913. The present beautiful brick church facing Colonial Drive, and erected at a cost of about $20,000.00, was occupied in 1926.

Palmetto Church was organized in 1924. The equipment is owned by the Methodist members, but the building is the property of the mill.[12]

Epworth Orphanage church was erected in 1902, at a cost of about $6,000.00, after the orphanage had been operated for six years. At the beginning the membership was about 50; at present it is more than 400.

OTHER METHODIST INSTITUTIONS

The Wesley Community House at 1310 Huger Street, operated by the missionary societies of the Methodist churches of the city under the direction of resident deaconess, furnishes training (religious, social, and educational) for more than 10,000 in attendance annually.

The Wesley Foundation is sponsored by Washington Street church for Methodist students at the University of South Carolina and at Columbia College; Rev. W. O. Weldon, director.

The following are the number of members, Sunday school enrollments, and value of church properties, 1934, of the several Methodist churches in Columbia and suburbs: Washington Street, 1,460, 1,045, $275,000.00; Main Street, 2,396, 1,215, $92,000.00; Shandon, 850, 650, $72,500.00; Whaley Street, 1,032, 336, $65,000-.00; Green Street, 663, 369, $137,500.00; Waverly, 301, 166, $12,000-.00; Edgewood, 834, 498, $7,000.00; Brookland, 651, 578, $16,500-.00; College Place, 575, 400, $25,000.00. The aggregates for 1934 are: membership in churches 8,762, enrollments in Sunday schools 5,961, and value of church properties $768,150.00.[13]

---

[12] *Ibid.*

[13] *Minutes of the Twentieth Session of the Upper South Carolina Conference, Methodist Episcopal Church, South,* statistical table. (The College Place Church belongs to the South Carolina Conference.)

THE PRESBYTERIANS

On the tombstone in the southeastern corner of the First Presbyterian churchyard, erected to the memory of the Rev. D. E. Dunlap and his wife, Susannah, who died in the morning and he in the afternoon of September 10, 1804, is the inscription which closes with "The Rev. D. E. Dunlap was ordained and installed pastor of this church June 4th, 1795." These lines were added about 1886. Unfortunately there are no records extant telling of the operations of an organized church.[14]

First Presbyterian Church

After the death of Mr. Dunlap, 1804, there was no pastor until 1809, when the Rev. John Brown, professor of logic and moral philosophy at the South Carolina College, became pastor in April of that year, and effected an organization May 15, 1810, at which time Thomas Taylor, Thomas Lindsay and John Murphy were elected elders, the first elders so far as the records show of the church, and on this date, or thereabouts was the first recorded celebration of the Lord's Supper.[15] The organization has continued uninterruptedly since.

In 1813 the Legislature passed an Act incorporating "The First Presbyterian Church of the Town of Columbia," [16] and at the same session passed an Act providing for the appraisal of "one-half of the old burying ground . . . the property to be conveyed to the First Presbyterian Church and the Protestant Episcopal Church and their

---

[14] See Howe, *History of the Presbyterian Church in South Carolina,* I, 595-6; II, 77-8.

[15] *Ibid.,* II, 253-4.

[16] Thomas Cooper and D. J. McCord, eds., *Statutes at Large of South Carolina,* Columbia, 1836-1841, VIII, 265.

successors in office forever," the Presbyterians and Episcopalians to pay one-half of the appraised value to the Methodists and Baptists, "to finish and complete their churches." [17] This was done. Then it was determined that the Presbyterians should buy the interest of the Episcopalians in the lot,[18] the latter acquiring by gift and purchase the two acres now owned and occupied by Trinity Episcopal Church.

The transactions, together with the building, which was erected, cost the Presbyterians about $8,000.00. The contract for the building was let June, 1813, and the building was dedicated, though not finished, in October, 1814, when Harmony presbytery met in Columbia.[19]

The First Presbyterian Church has had a line of great pastors. Many of them were among the most distinguished men of the South and of most brilliant minds; among these may be mentioned Drs. Thomas Goulding, George Howe, James H. Thornwell, Benjamin Gildersleeve, Benjamin M. Palmer, Joseph R. Wilson, W. S. Plumer, J. L. Girardeau, and Samuel M. Smith. Rev. James Wyly Jackson, D.D., is now pastor of this church and has been for about five years. The church building was erected in 1854. It was greatly enlarged and changed in 1925; this with the building of a Sunday school building and remodeling of recreational building cost something more than $210,000.00. The whole plant with manse is valued at about $425,000.00. Its membership in 1810 was 13; in 1852, 170 white and 33 negroes; in 1869, 140 white, 50 negroes; in 1879, 265 all white. Its present membership is something more than 1,200 and its Sunday school enrollment about 700. In 1869 there were 110 white children on the Sunday school rolls and 325 negroes. There are no negroes either on the church or Sunday school memberships. The negroes have their own organizations.

LATER PRESBYTERIAN CHURCHES

December 23, 1883, a few members of the First Presbyterian Church organized a Sunday school which met in the main building on the old fair grounds (near Logan school). After Sunday school the Rev. John L. Girardeau, D.D., one of the greatest pulpit orators of the South, would preach. From this grew the Arsenal Hill Presbyterian Church. Its first building was on the South side of the 1100 block of Richland Street. Its present church building, northeast

---

[17] *Ibid.*, pp. 268-9.
[18] Howe, *History of the Presbyterian Church in South Carolina*, II.
[19] *Ibid.*, p. 257.

corner of Laurel and Assembly Streets was built in 1904. Its pastor now is Rev. Samuel K. Phillips. Its membership is about 511 and the Sunday school has enrolled 350. The church property has a value of about $100,000.00.

The Shandon Presbyterian church was promoted by Rev. R. B. Grinnan, a returned missionary from China. Dr. W. B. Burney of the University of South Carolina gave two building lots to the church which was organized in 1917 with Rev. W. S. Harden as pastor. Its first church building was on Maple Street. The present church of granite construction was built in 1928. The pastor is the Rev. F. Ray Riddle. The membership is about 600, and the Sunday school enrollment 500.

The Eau Claire Presbyterian Church was regularly organized in 1916, growing out of a mission Sunday school established in the Hyatt Park school building by Dr. and Mrs. R. C. Reed (of the Columbia Theological Seminary) some years previous to 1912. Its pastor now is Rev. R. K. Timmons. It has a membership of about 175 and a Sunday school enrollment of about the same number. Its plant is valued at about $11,500.00.

The Rose Hill Presbyterian Church, on South Saluda Avenue, was organized October 31, 1919, with 30 charter members. The lot on which it is built was given by Dr. William D. Melton, an elder in the First Presbyterian Church, and president of the University of South Carolina at the time of his death. Its membership now is 76 and its Sunday school enrollment about 125. It grew out of a Sunday school which was established in that community by Miss Emily Dick and others.

The New Brookland Presbyterian Church was started about 1895 and the building erected on land given by J. S. Guignard. For a number of years its services were conducted by students from the Columbia Theological Seminary. Its report in 1934 showed 15 members and a Sunday school of about 150 members.

ASSOCIATE REFORMED PRESBYTERIANS

The Associate Reformed Presbyterian Church of Columbia, with its brick church building, 1400 block Laural Street (north side) and a manse, 1809 Bull Street, is known as the Centennial Church of that denomination in South Carolina, as it "was erected as a memorial of the 100th year of the existence of the Associate Reformed Synod of the South." [20]

---

[20] *Centennial History of the Associate Reformed Presbyterian Church*, p. 451.

It was first organized as a mission in Columbia in 1896 by the Rev. J. G. Dale. The church was regularly organized February 1, 1897. The Rev. Robert C. Betts is the pastor now. Its membership is about 400 and its Sunday school enrollment about 225.

In the "History of Ebenezer Lutheran Church," quoting from the report of the Synod in 1843, this reference is made: "Permission has also been granted to ministers of the Associate Reformed Presbyterians, to hold worship occasionally in said church," (Ebenezer Lutheran).[21]

THE FIRST BAPTIST

According to the cover of 1930 Year Book of the First Baptist Church this church was organized in 1807. The historical sketch gives 1809 as the date of its founding, and 1811 as the year in which its house of worship was built on the southeast corner of Hampton (then Plain) and Sumter Streets, the site now of its Sunday school

First Baptist Church, Scene of Secession Convention (Colonnade Modern)

building. This modern addition, joined to the church by a colonnade, was erected in 1930.

---

[21] Gilbert P. Voight, *A History of Ebenezer Lutheran Church, Columbia, S. C.*, Columbia, 1930, p. 18.

[22] *Year Book and Directory, First Baptist Church, Columbia S. C.*, see cover.

Its first pastor was the Rev. Jonathan Maxcy, first president of the South Carolina College, who lies buried in an unmarked grave at the entrance to the driveway in the First Presbyterian churchyard.

In 1841 the First Baptist Church had a membership of 405, of which 49 were white and 360 negroes. Negro converts were baptized by the pastor. In the memorial service a negro deacon served the members of his race.

December 26, 1856, it was determined to build a new church, and the pastor, Dr. James Pettigru Boyce, subscribed $10,000.00 "The present solidly built grand old structure is the enduring monument to his labor," says the historical sketch.[23]

In 1861 the Confederate Secession convention met in this building, before it adjourned to Charleston, so it is said, because of a smallpox outbreak in Columbia.

Almost a new start was made by this church after the Confederate war, which at the close of war had only 33 members, all white. But its membership grew, and during the pastorate of Dr. William C. Lindsay which began in 1877 the church became vigorous and established three other Baptist churches—Park Street, Tabernacle, and South Side. Dr. Lindsay's pastorate continued for 33 years. He resigned in 1910 and was made pastor emeritus. He was one of the most beloved and respected men in Columbia. The present pastor, Dr. John H. Webb, became the pastor in 1927. The church membership is over 1,700, and the Sunday school enrollment about 1,600. The value of the plant, church, Sunday school building, and parsonage exceeds $265,000.00.

A summary of the annual report of this church to the Fairfield Association for 1935 shows total contributions to all objects of $40,688.97.

LATER BAPTIST CHURCHES

The Park Street Baptist Church, Park and Bryan Streets, is a consolidation of the Elmwood Park Baptist and the Second Baptist, done in 1915. The Elmwood Park Church had been organized in 1910, under the leadership of Rev. Carlisle Courtenay, its first pastor. The Second Baptist Church had been organized in 1890, but its building having been burned in 1915, a consolidation of the two churches was made. Its membership in 1935 is 1,138. The Sunday school enrollment is about 1,500. The Rev. Paul Wheeler is the pastor now. The church property is valued at $170,000.00.

The Shandon Baptist Church, corner of Woodrow and Preston streets, was organized in 1909 with 22 members, by the Rev. Carlisle

---

[23] *Ibid.,* p. 3.

Courtenay, who was its first pastor. Its present membership is 1,-058. The present church was built about 1923. Its educational building is of four stories with 70 rooms. The pastor at the present time is the Rev. F. Clyde Helms. The church property is valued at $84,-500.00.

The Tabernacle Baptist, 1517 Gregg Street, has grown out of a mission at 1928 Blanding Street, established by Rev. A. B. Kennedy, when he was assistant pastor of the First Baptist.

The church was organized April 9, 1911, with 102 charter members. Its present membership is 902, and its Sunday school enrollment is 692. To the present it has had one pastor, the Rev. A. B. Kennedy, and one treasurer, J. F. Gaines. Church property is valued at $60,-000.00.

The Eau Claire Baptist church was organized with 13 charter members June 26, 1921, and was first known as Bethel Baptist. The Rev. J. L. Willis is the pastor now. The membership is about 450 and the Sunday school enrollment about 400. Church property is valued at $24,000.00.

The Colonial Heights Baptist church was organized October 1, 1912, by the Rev. Carlisle Courtenay, who served as pastor for a short time. The Rev. F. T. Cox is now the pastor. The membership is about 220.

The Broadway Baptist church, corner of Heyward and Sumter streets, was organized in January, 1915, through the influence of the South Side Baptist church. The present pastor, the Rev. A. Hartley, began his pastorate in 1915. The membership is 306 and the Sunday school enrollment is 350.

LOVELY OLD TRINITY

The fourth church to be organized in Columbia was Trinity Episcopal. The source from which the statements made herein are drawn is the *History and Traditions of Trinity Church,* by Robert Moorman of the Columbia bar, and a devoted member of that church.

The following paragraph is quoted from the sermon of Dr. Robt. Wilson delivered February 10, 1884, in our church at the semi-centennial celebration of Dr. Peter J. Shand's rectorship: "On the 8th day of August, 1812, the first organization of the church in Columbia was accomplished by the action of a meeting composed of John G. and James S. Guignard, Edward Fisher [*sic*], Benjamin R. Waring, Robert Stark, William Harper, Theodore Gaillard, William Braithwaite, Warren R. Davis, Samuel Percival and William Marshall.

The group [above named] enlisted the interest of the Episcopal Society for the advancement of Christianity in South Carolina, and this society sent here as a missionary, Rev. Andrew Fowler. He conducted in 1812 the first Protestant Episcopal service in this City, and this was held in the State House.

Bishop Dehon, on an official visit to this congregation, held services in the State House on May 13, 1813.

This congregation was incorporated by Act of the General Assembly of South Carolina in 1813 under the name 'Episcopal Church of Columbia.' [24]

Mr. Moorman says that it is uncertain how the two acres on which is Trinity church were acquired, but that the best information is to the effect that the northern acre was given by a widow Smythe, and

Trinity Protestant Episcopal Church

the southern acre was acquired by purchase from Colonel James Gregg.[25]

"The first church was a wooden structure, cruciform in shape, and was built on the Northern acre [northwest corner] or Smythe lot. The cornerstone . . . was laid on the 7th of March, 1814, and it was consecrated by Bishop Dehon, December 14, 1814, by the name 'Trinity Church.'

---

[24] Robert Moorman, *History and Traditions of Trinity Church, Columbia, South Carolina,* Columbia, 1925, pp. 3-4. For the act of incorporation see *Statutes at Large of South Carolina,* VIII, 268.

[25] Moorman, *History and Traditions of Trinity Church, Columbia, South Carolina,* p. 4.

"The first Rector called was the Rev. Christian Hanckel," professor of mathematics and natural philosophy at the South Carolina College.[26]

The Rev. Peter J. Shand, D.D., became rector in 1834 and so continued until 1886.

Other rectors who were very prominent throughout the state were Rev. (Gen.) Ellison Capers, D.D., later bishop, and Rev. Kirkman G. Finlay, D.D., later bishop.

The Rev. Henry D. Phillips, D.D., became rector in 1922. The membership is 1,375, and the Sunday school enrollment is 325.

Quoting from Mr. Moorman: "In 1883 the total receipts of this Church was less than $4,000.00. In 1925 our budget is $30,000.00; an increase of 750 per cent." [27]

The parish property is estimated to have a value of about $368,-000.00.

LATER EPISCOPAL CHURCHES

The Episcopal church of the Good Shepherd, south side of 1500 block Blanding street, was organized as a mission by the Rev. H. O. Judd, while he was assistant to Dr. Peter Shand, rector of Trinity. Its first building was on the west side of Barnwell street, north of Richland. This church now has a confirmed membership of 481, a baptized membership of 560. The church school has a membership of 133. Rev. Lewis N. Taylor is the rector.

The value of its church building with the parish house annex and rectory is estimated to be about $50,000.00.

The Rev. A. R. Mitchell was the rector of the Good Shepherd for many years, before going to Greenville.

While rector of the Good Shepherd, he organized St. Timothy's now on the south side of Calhoun, northeast corner of Gadsden, of which the Rev. A. G. B. Bennett is now rector. It has a membership of 198 and property valued at $30,000.00.

While rector of the Good Shepherd the Rev. W. P. Witsell began, about 1905, a union Sunday school in the day school building on Lee street, Shandon, and from this has come St. John's Episcopal church, now on the northeast corner of Wheat and Holly streets, of which Rev. A. Rufus Morgan is rector.

As a church St. John's was organized with a membership coming from only about four families, those of E. R. Heyward, Benjamin Heyward, Robert Jenkins, and George Reaves.

---

[26] *Ibid.*
[27] *Ibid.*, p. 12.

The present church building was erected in 1926. This church
has a communing membership of about 378, and a Sunday school
enrollment of 150. The parish property is estimated to have a value
of $52,000.00.

Trinity Chapel has a membership of 92 and property valued at
$26,000.00. Rev. A. Rufus Morgan is the rector.

ST. PETER'S PARISH

Mills, in his *Statistics,* says: "There are five religious denominations in Columbia. The Methodists, Presbyterians, Episcopalians,
Baptists, and Roman Catholics, whose comparative numbers are in
the order named. The last have been lately formed into a society,
and are now erecting a handsome brick church in the form of a
cross; with tower and spire in front; in the Gothic style of architecture." [28]

From the *History of St. Peter's Parish,* published in 1914 by Rev.
T. J. Hegarty, is taken this account:

> The first Catholics to settle in Columbia, according to the most reliable
> traditions of the parish, were a body of laborers brought to work on the
> canal in 1821. Many of these, either overcome by the excessive heat, to
> which their labor exposed them, or affected by the miasma developed by
> their surroundings, died within a year after their arrival. There being no
> Catholic cemetery in the city, they were buried in potter's field. [About
> where the Atlantic Coast Line freight depot on Gervais street is.] Most
> of those who survived returned North when the work on the canal was
> finished, the few who remained forming the first Catholic congregation
> in Columbia. . . . It was not until 1824 and after many embarrassing
> difficulties that those in charge of the construction were finally able, with
> patient and perservering energy, to make it serviceable as a house of
> worship. . . . The first priest permanently stationed in Columbia was
> Father Corkery.
>
> In 1844 Rev. Edward Quigley was appointed pastor. The first work
> to claim his attention after assuming charge was the renovation of the
> church. . . . The combined efforts of the pastor and his flock soon
> restored and furnished it.
>
> In 1848 Rev. J. J. O'Connell succeeded him. His administration cover-
> ing a period of 23 years. . . . [29]

Father O'Connell established "The St. Mary's College", which
continued with varying success, patronized by Christians of all denominations, until its building on north Main street was occupied
by the Confederate government as a commissary department. The
building and the fine library of the college were burned by Sherman in February, 1865.

---

[28] Mills, *Statistics of South Carolina,* p. 706.
[29] Rev. T. J. Hegarty, *History of St. Peter's Parish.*

The Academy of the Immaculate Conception was established in 1852 by the Sisters of Mercy, and continued until 1858, to be succeeded by the Ursuline Nuns, whom Bishop England brought from the Ursuline convent, Black Rock, County Cork, Ireland, in 1834, into the diocese of Charleston. This continued until 1844 when some members returned to Ireland and others went to Cincinnati. Some

St. Peter's Roman Catholic Church

of the latter group Bishop Lynch persuaded to return to South Carolina in 1858. The building occupied by them, southeast corner of Main and Blanding streets, was burned in the Sherman fire of February, 1865. The nuns occupied the Methodist Female College (now Columbia Bible college, south side 1600 block Hampton street) until August 31. They then went to Valle Crucis (where Heathwood Hall now is) where they remained until 1887 when they moved to what is now known as the Chicora college property, 1600 block Blanding street, north side. They moved to their present home, northwest corner Assembly and Hampton streets, in 1891.

Rev. Thomas J. Hegarty took charge of St. Peter's parish in May, 1895.

vision stores were ransacked and are very limited. We had preaching today in the Sunday school room (the church had been burned), where a mourning congregation assembled, now deprived of their temple." [37]

Mr. Berg "procured four copies of the Presbyterian Psalmodist for the use of the choir." [38]

"On October 1, 1865, a collection of $14.80 was taken and given to the sexton, who had received no pay since 'January, last.' Having lost their own communion vessels at the time of Sherman's visit, the congregation found it necessary to accept the 'plate' of the Presbyterian Church, which was kindly loaned them by that group." [39]

But Ebenezer's struggles are over, and it has a plant in beauty and equipment second to none in the city. It has one of the most beautiful churches in the city. A new Sunday school building was built during the pastorate of Rev. C. A. Freed, D.D. A handsome parsonage, southwest corner of Laurel and Marion streets, and the beautiful church costing about $150,000 were acquired in the present pastorate of Rev. P. D. Brown, D.D. The church property approximates $200,000 in value.

ST. PAUL'S LUTHERAN

St. Paul's Lutheran church, northwestern corner of Bull and Blanding streets, was organized December 12, 1886, with 39 charter members. St. Paul's has had only four pastors—Dr. E. A. Wingard, Dr. W. H. Greever, Rev. J. D. Mauney, and Dr. H. A. McCullough.

The congregation was never a mission. It had the ambition to support itself from the beginning. St. Paul's is noted for its benevolence. In 1934 it paid more money for benevolence than any other Lutheran church in South Carolina. Seldom does it fail to meet its full quota to the South Carolina synod.

The growth of the congregation in membership and equipment has been regular and substantial. Its present resident confirmed membership is 711, a Sunday school of 525, and a junior congregation of 75. The church property is valued at $140,000.

Rev. H. A. McCullough, D.D., has been pastor since 1911.

The Lutheran church of the Ascension, located near the Lutheran Theological seminary, Rev. Karl W. Kinard, pastor, was organized in 1912 and has had a substantial growth. This church was self-

---

[37] *Ibid.*, pp. 31-32.
[38] *Ibid.*, p. 32.
[39] *Ibid.*

supporting from its organization. Dr. W. H. Greever was its first pastor; Dr. C. A. Freed, second, and Rev. Karl Kinard, third and the present pastor. This church has a confirmed membership of 290; Sunday school 225, with church property valued at $50,000.

The Lutheran church of the Incarnation, Shandon, Rev. T. F. Suber, pastor, was organized in 1921. It has a confirmed membership of 314, and a Sunday school of 160. The church property is valued at $40,000.

The Lutheran church of the Reformation, North Columbia, Rev. W. C. Boliek, pastor, was organized in 1926. This congregation has a confirmed membership of 320, and Sunday school of 325, with church property valued at $35,000.

St. Luke's, Olympia, Rev. C. K. Wise, pastor, was organized in 1904. Its confirmed membership is 135; its Sunday school, 175. Its church property is valued at $15,000.

---

[40] A Lost Church: Christ Church, on Blanding Street between Bull and Marion, was consecrated in 1858 and burned in the conflagation in 1865, with a loss to the congregation of $30,000. It was the largest Episcopal Church, except Trinity, outside of Charleston, in South Carolina. The impoverished congregation was unable to rebuild, and even the land was lost in a legal dispute, so the church disappeared from the diocese. *Report of the Committee on the Destruction of Churches in the Diocese of South Carolina during the Late War,* Charleston, 1868, pp. 13-14.

MEDICINE AND HOSPITALS

By Robert E. Seibels, M.D., F. A. C. S.

PHYSICIANS composed a portion of the population of Columbia from the earliest days, as shown by their witnessing wills and becoming executors of estates. There being no medical society, the earlier physicians have left no record of their medical activities.

Dr. Edward Fisher, who was born in Virginia, 1774, and died in Columbia, 1836, was a member of the committee which purchased the site and erected, in 1822, the Mills building, the first structure of the State Hospital for the Insane. He was also a member of the first board of regents of this institution.[1]

Another physician prominent in his extra-medical activities was Dr. Elias Marks, born in Charleston, December 2, 1790, died, June, 1886. He was graduated from the College of Physicians and Surgeons in New York in 1815. He opened a school for young ladies on the northwest corner of Washington and Marion streets, which became so successful that he built, in 1817, the "South Carolina Female Collegiate Institute" about two miles northeast of Columbia at Barhamville. This college had an enrollment of about two hundred and continued until 1861. It numbered among its graduates Miss Pamela Cunningham, founder of the Mount Vernon Association and Martha Bullock, mother of President Theodore Roosevelt.[2]

Several abortive attempts were made to establish a medical school at the University of South Carolina and the profession in Columbia was unusually well represented on the faculty.

The following biographies are given as representative of the educational standards and medical activities of the various periods.

Josiah Clark Nott was born in Columbia, March 31, 1804; he died in New York in 1873. He was graduated from the South Carolina College in 1824. He studied under Dr. James Davis in Columbia and took a course of lectures at the College of Physicians and Surgeons in New York.[3] In 1833 he and Dr. Robert W. Gibbes "established the first Preparatory School of Medicine, by lectures,

---

[1] *100th Annual Report of the South Carolina State Hospital*, Columbia, 1923.
[2] *Handbook of South Carolina*, E. J. Watson, Commissioner, Columbia, 1908, p. 196; Appleton, *Encyclopedia of American Biography*, New York, 1888, IV, 211.
[3] Robert E. Seibels, "Doctor Josiah Clark Nott", *Southern Medicine and Surgery Journal*, January, 1930.

in Columbia; Dr. Nott's lectures were on Anatomy and Surgery,
and Dr. Gibbes's were on Chemistry and Materia Medica." [4] In 1858,
he took a leading part in founding the Medical School at Mobile,
Alabama. The following is a list of his more important writings:
Goupil's *Exposition*, etc.; [5] *Report on Yellow Fever Epidemic in
Mobile;* [6] *Cocyodynia;* [7] *Extirpation of Os Coccyx for Neuralgia;* [8]
*Two lectures on the Connection between the Biblical and Physical
History of Man*, in 1849; *The Physical History of the Jewish Race*,
in 1850; and in collaboration with Glidden, *Types of Mankind*, in
1854; and *Indigenous Races of the Earth*, in 1857. [9]

Maximilian LaBorde, was born at Edgefield, June 5, 1804, and
died November 6, 1873. He graduated at South Carolina College in
1821, at the Medical College of Charleston in 1826, and he was on
the faculty of the South Carolina College from 1842 to his death. [10]

Robert Wilson Gibbes was born at Charleston, July 8, 1809, and
died October 15, 1866. He studied at South Carolina College, but
left without graduating. He graduated from the Charleston Medical
College in 1834. In later years, he trained in his office his son, Dr.
R. W. Gibbes, Jr., Dr. Robert Wilson of Charleston and Dr. Walter
Taylor of Columbia. Besides teaching and practicing successfully,
he was a collector in paleontology, geology, mineralogy, and conch-
ology, and was an able ornithologist. He had a fine collection of
paintings, including several by Sully and a valuable collection of
old engravings presented to him by Charles Fraser. [11]

Alexander Nicholas Talley, whose birth at Washington, Georgia,
took place on October 27, 1827, and whose death was on July 6,
1897, was a Bachelor of Arts from South Carolina College and
a graduate of Charleston Medical College in 1851 and he spent the
following year studying in New York and Paris. [12] With Dr. Huet,
he opened a preparatory medical school at his home on the southwest corner of Washington and Marion streets, the subjects for
dissection being derived from potter's field in true "body snatcher

[4] Maximilian LaBorde, *History of the South Carolina College*, Charleston,
1874, p. 191.
[5] Translation, Columbia, 1831.
[6] *New Orleans Medical and Surgical Journal*, 1848.
[7] *North American Medical Journal*, May, 1844.
[8] *New Orleans Medical and Surgical Journal*, 1844–5.
[9] Seibels, *op. cit.*
[10] Appleton, *op. cit.*, III, 581.
[11] Arney R. Childs, *Robert Wilson Gibbes*, Bulletin of the University of
South Carolina, No. 210.
[12] William B. Atkinson, *The Physicians and Surgeons of the United States*,
Philadelphia, 1878, p. 301.

style." [13] He was also one of the authors of "Confederate States Manual of Surgery." In November, 1862, he became President of the Confederate States Army Board of Medical Examiners. In 1869, he became Professor of the Principles and Practice of Medicine and Obstetrics at the University of South Carolina.[14]

Mills Building, South Carolina State Hospital

Benjamin Walter Taylor was born in Columbia, February 28, 1834, and died December 27, 1905. He was a graduate of South Carolina College in 1855 and of the South Carolina Medical College in 1859. He served as assistant surgeon at Fort Moultrie and to the Hampton Legion. In 1865, he was made director of the Cavalry Corps, Army of Northern Virginia. He was a delegate to the medical congress held in Philadelphia in 1876.[15]

Josiah Fulton Ensor, who was born in Butler, Maryland, December 12, 1834, and who died August 9, 1907, was graduated

[13] J. W. Williams, *Old and New Columbia*, Columbia, 1929, p. 63.
[14] Edwin L. Green, *A History of the University of South Carolina*, Columbia, 1916, p. 90.
[15] Atkinson, *op. cit.*, p. 211.

in medicine from the University of Maryland in 1861. He served as assistant surgeon in the United States Army. In 1868, he became medical purveyor for the Freedmen's Bureau in South Carolina. In 1870, he was appointed superintendent of the State Hospital, where he remained until 1877. In addition to his other duties which were well and faithfully performed, Dr. Ensor was compelled "to give my personal obligations and those of my friends to keep the institution open . . . I have been obliged to give my private notes in order to obtain the necessary subsistance and clothing for our inmates."[16] For the latter ten years of his life he was the postmaster at Columbia.[17]

John Thomson Darby was born at Pond Bluff Plantation, Orangeburg County, December 16, 1836; and he died June 29, 1879. He attended South Carolina College and the Medical College of Charleston and graduated at the University of Pennsylvania in 1858. He was surgeon to the Hampton Legion; later he was medical director of the Army of the West. He served with the Prussian army against Austria in 1866, assisting in the organization of the hospital and ambulance corps. He was Professor of Anatomy and Surgery at

Columbia Hospital, 1895

the University of South Carolina from 1867 until 1874 and Professor of Surgery at the University of the City of New York from 1874 to his death.[18]

---

[16] *Handbook of South Carolina*, p. 55.
[17] *Ibid.*, p. 56.
[18] Kelly & Burrage, *Dictionary of American Medical Biography, New York,* 1928, p. 292.

James Woods Babcock, whose birthplace, on August 11, 1856, was Chester, South Carolina, and whose death was on March 3, 1922, received his Bachelor of Arts degree at Harvard in 1882, and his M.D. at Harvard in 1886. He was superintendent of the South Carolina State Hospital from 1891 to 1914. He founded Waverley Sanitarium in Columbia in 1914, a thirty-five-bed hospital for nervous and mental cases. He was one of the first American physicians to identify pellagra and was associated with Lombroso in Europe, and Lavender and Goldberger of the United States Public Health Service.[19]

Augustus Barton Knowlton was born on April 14, 1868, and died on July 12, 1914. He was graduated with honors from the Medical College of Charleston in 1892. In 1900, following a year's study in London and Berlin, he returned to Columbia where he built and operated the Knowlton Infirmary, which at the time of his death had grown into a seventy-bed hospital. He was especially well known for his success in abdominal surgery.[20]

MEDICAL SOCIETY OF COLUMBIA, SOUTH CAROLINA

The first recorded meeting of the society was on Monday, March 13, 1854.[21] All records of the society were destroyed during the burning of Columbia and the first note in the new records is of a meeting and reorganization in June, 1865. The society became a component part of the American Medical Association in 1904. The present membership embraces all white physicians of Richland County whose qualifications have been acceptable. The present membership is 112.

COLUMBIA HOSPITAL

On May 24, 1892, at a meeting of the United King's Daughters of Columbia, the Columbia Hospital Association was organized on motion of Mrs. David R. Flenniken. The following officers were elected: president, Miss Isabelle D. Martin; vice-presidents, one from each circle of King's Daughters, Mrs. R. S. DesPortes, Mrs. D. R. Flenniken, Mrs. J. A. Meetze, Mrs. George Bearden, Mrs. John A. Willis, Mrs. Coleman Walker, Mrs. John Friday, Mrs. R. E. Seibels, Mrs. T. J. LaMotte, Mrs. C. D. Stanley and Mrs. A.

---

[19] Fielding H. Garrison, *An Introduction to the History of Medicine,* Philadelphia, 1929, p. 705.
[20] *The State,* July 13, 1914.
[21] *Constitution. By-Laws, and Fee Bill of the Medical Society of Columbia, S. C.,* Columbia, 1903.

The Columbia Hospital in 1936

P. Brown; secretary, Miss Lucy Hampton (later Mrs. John C. Haskell), and treasurer, Miss Sophie Carroll.

July 22, 1892, city council granted a 99-year lease on four acres of land for the hospital site. The hospital charter was granted September 17, 1892, and the cornerstone was laid with Masonic rites May 3, 1893, the formal opening being held November 1, 1893.

The original medical and surgical staff was composed of: Dr. A. N. Talley, Dr. B. W. Taylor, Dr. George Howe, and Dr. A. L. Gaubert, assisted by Dr. T. M. DuBose, Sr., Dr. W. M. Lester, Dr. A. Earle Boozer and Dr. Frank W. Ray.

During its early years, the hospital was a community project in the fullest sense, thus the report of the treasurer in 1901 showed income from "gifts, entertainment, boxes in hotels, offerings from all the churches, and an annual contribution of $1,000.00 from the city." Among the disbursements for that year it is of interest to note that the matron's salary was $149.00.

The first large addition to the hospital was made in 1904 and consisted of operating pavilion and private rooms. The funds were raised by ladies of the Endowment Association under the leadership of Mrs. W. C. Wright. Three physicians, through their outstanding ability and statewide reputation gave the hospital its foundation of broad usefulness. These were Dr. LeGrand Guerry, surgeon; Dr. J. J. Watson, diagnostician; and Dr. E. M. Whaley, eye, ear, nose and throat specialist.

In 1909 the 70-bed hospital, entirely free of debt, was turned over to the Columbia Medical Society for future management. The society directed the management of the hospital until 1921 and during this period added two 3-story brick buildings, in the rear of the original building, giving a total of 115 beds in the wards and private rooms.

In 1921 control of the hospital was given to the Legislative Delegation of Richland County which administers it through a board of trustees selected by the delegation and appointed by the Governor.

Since 1922 the nurses' home, "William Weston Hall," has been built and a large portion of the old hospital buildings replaced by new buildings constituting the present plant. The renovated and rebuilt hospital was opened November 1, 1933, and the first patient admitted was Mrs. D. R. Flenniken. Funds have been provided through taxes, contributions from the Duke Endowment Fund, and profits from private patients.

Columbia Hospital now has 275 beds with separate accommodations for colored patients and a training school for white and colored nurses. During 1934, 5,060 patients were admitted. About $35,000.00 is received through taxes for the care of the sick and

Knowlton Infirmary, Forerunner of Present Baptist Hospital

poor and about $35,000.00 additional is now expended each year for non-pay patients, the latter sum being derived largely from the Duke Foundation.

There are 92 white nurses in training and 13 colored. The medical and surgical staff is composed of members of the Columbia Medical Society and the resident staff is one pathologist, one radiologist, two resident surgeons and four internes.[22]

---

[22] *The State,* November 13, 1933.

SOUTH CAROLINA BAPTIST HOSPITAL

This institution (formerly known as the Knowlton Infirmary) was purchased by the South Carolina Baptist State Convention and

opened under their management September 1, 1914. Since that date, there have been admitted to the institution 51,-900 patients, of whom one-third have been without funds and have received free treatment. Additions and alterations have been made and the hospital now has 109 beds. A nurses' training school has been most successful and has 60 student nurses. The visit-

Baptist Hospital

ing staff is appointed from the Columbia Medical Society.[23]

THE DOOR OF HOPE

This institution was founded by J. M. Pike, D.D., May 10, 1898, and offers shelter, prenatal and obstetrical care and aid in finding a useful life. Miss Anna W. Finnstrom became matron in 1898 and served the institution until her death in 1932. Dr. L. K. Philpot was attending physician from 1898-1918, and Dr. D. S. Black from 1918 to the present. This institution takes care of from thirty-five to forty patients a year with an extremely low maternal and infant mortality. Its income is derived from appropriations of Richland County, the City of Columbia, the Community Chest and voluntary contributions.[24]

---

[23] Personal communications from W. H. Whiteside, Nov. 18, 1935.
[24] Annual Report, 1935.

LAW AND THE JUDICIARY

By F. Carlisle Roberts

A LMOST from the founding of the city, and down to the present day, the Columbia bar has been adorned by men of much
legal learning and forensic eloquence, distinguished for their
interest in civic enterprises and for the part they have played in
affairs of state. The capital of the state, and hence the seat of
government, Columbia has continuously gained by the accession of
leading lawyers from other parts of state and nation, desirous of
being near at hand to the Supreme Court, the Legislature, and the
quasi-judicial boards of the state. The United States District Court
likewise sits here, and the location in Columbia of agencies of the
Federal government in ever-increasing numbers has brought a great
many lawyers to the city in the last few years. The growth of Columbia in population and wealth has added to the attractions for
lawyers, with the result that there are now around one hundred
and fifty members of the bar (exclusive of lawyers employed by
Federal agencies), approximately one-seventh of all the lawyers of
the state.[1]

With the exception of John Taylor, Columbia's earliest lawyers
came from other states. John Taylor was the son of that patri-
arch of Columbia, Colonel Thomas Taylor. He practiced for a
few years only, devoting the remainder of his life to politics and
planting; he was elected Governor in 1826. Taylor was a graduate
of Princeton, where he divided first honors with Judge William
Johnson; he studied law in the office of Charles Cotesworth Pinckney.[2] Other early lawyers were: Thomas Henry Egan, of Maryland,
Robert Stark, of Virginia, John Hooker, of Connecticut,[3] Abraham
Nott, of Connecticut, and William C. C. Clifton, of Virginia.[4] Egan,
declared by Chief Justice O'Neall to be, along with Stark, the leading lawyer of the entire Southern District around the year 1800,
had some eleven young men reading law in his office at that time.[5]
Stark, who moved to South Carolina early in life, fought in many

---

[1] Carnegie Foundation for the Advancement of Teaching, *Annual Review
of Legal Education,* New York, 1934, p. 65.
[2] John Belton O'Neall, *Bench and Bar of South Carolina,* Charleston, 1859,
II, 168-170.
[3] *Ibid.,* pp. 247-249.
[4] *Ibid.,* pp. 270-271.
[5] *Ibid.,* pp. 231-232.

Revolutionary battles in this State, was elected Speaker of the House
of Representatives in 1808, and was Solicitor for the Southern

Old Post Office and Federal Building

Circuit 1806-1820.[6] Most
distinguished of the first
lawyers was Abraham
Nott, the first Columbia
lawyer elected to the
bench. Educated at Yale
for the ministry, he
moved to Camden and
there read law under
Daniel Brown. He be-
gan practice in Colum-
bia in 1804, was elected
Law Judge in 1810, and
was president of the
Court of Appeals from
its organization in 1824
until his death in 1830, in which office he had much to do with reorganizing appellate procedure in the state.[7]

The most eminent of Columbia lawyers during the first half of
the nineteenth century were William Harper, Abram Blanding,
and William C. Preston. "These (along with Richard Wild, Longstreet, Petigru and D. L. Wardlaw) were men of the highest rank
—men rarely equalled at any Bar in any country," says O'Neall.
"They were models of legal learning and forensic eloquence." [8]
Chancellor Harper read law in the office of Colonel John Joel Chappell, in Columbia, and became the latter's partner upon his admission
to the bar. He was elected to the Legislature in 1816, and moved to
Missouri in 1818, where he became a chancellor of that state. Returning to South Carolina in 1823, he was elected first official state Reporter. Prievious to that time Henry Junius Nott[9] (later professor
at the South Carolina College) and David J. McCord,[10] and later
McCord alone, had published four volumes of the reports, under
a contract with Faust, the state printer. Harper was appointed to
the United States Senate in 1826, elected Chancellor of South Carolina in 1828, and was promoted to the Court of Appeals, along with
O'Neall, in 1830. Upon the dissolution of the Court of Appeals in

[6] *Ibid.*, pp. 66-73.
[7] *Ibid.*, pp. 121-124.
[8] *Ibid.*, p. 279.
[9] *Ibid.*, pp. 512-513, for sketch of life.
[10] *Ibid.*, 509-511, for sketch of life.

1835, Harper was elected Equity Judge, which he remained until his death in 1847. He was one of the great chancellors of South Carolina.[11] "As a Judge he ranks with Story. As a politician he was one of the prime movers with Calhoun in asserting the independent sovereignty of our state and her determination to resist all unjust infringements of the constitution."[12] Harper was a member of the Nullification Convention in 1832, and drafted the ordinance

Richland County Courthouse, 1872-1935

of nullification.[13] He was the first matriculate at the South Carolina College.[14]

Colonel Abram Blanding, born in Massachusetts, was a student at Brown University under Dr. Maxcy, who was first president of the South Carolina College, and who persuaded Blanding to

---

[11] *Ibid.,* I, 270-274; U. R. Brooks, *South Carolina Bench and Bar,* Columbia, 1908, I, 93.

[12] *The Clariosophic and Euphradian Societies, 125th Anniversary Celebration,* F. Carlisle Roberts, editor, Columbia, 1931, p. 41, from resolutions presented by F. W. McMaster and adopted by the Euphradian Society upon the death of Harper.

[13] *Ibid.,* see also Brooks, *Bench and Bar,* I, 93, and Theodore O. Jervey, *Robert Y. Hayne and His Times,* New York, 1909, p. 319.

[14] Edwin L. Green, *A History of the University of South Carolina,* Columbia, 1916, p. 23.

come to South Carolina. He was interested in internal improve-ments—navigation, roads, canals, railroads, banks. He built a water-works system in Columbia with his own money; was responsible for the establishment of the Presbyterian Theological Seminary in Co-lumbia in 1830; he planted the trees in the center of the street which bears his name.[15] "He was conceded to be first in his profession for fully twenty years. He is one of the few men who, after devoting themselves to other distracting pursuits, could and did return to a successful pursuit of the law." [16]

To William C. Preston, along with Legare, McDuffie, Hayne and Calhoun, is largely attributable the reputation of ante-bellum South Carolina for eloquent speakers.[17] Preston was a fellow-stu-dent of Legare and McDuffie at the South Carolina College,[18] and there, in the halls of the Euphradian Society, first gave promise of extraordinary powers as an orator.[19] He practiced in Columbia from 1822 to 1836, when he was elected to the United States Senate as colleague of Calhoun. He resigned in 1839 or 1840, and returned to the bar.[20] In 1845 he was elected president of the South Carolina College, and the institution saw great growth under his leadership, the student body almost doubling in four years.[21] As a lawyer, Preston's greatness depended not merely upon eloquence; O'Neall states that in his forty years' connection with the bar of the state he "heard as fine legal arguments from Colonel Preston as from any other."[22]

During the second half of the nineteenth century there adorned the Columbia bar a large group of colorful figures, eloquent ad-vocates and sound lawyers. Having served the Confederacy nobly, they were in the thick of the stirring days of redemption of the State from negro rule, and then did gloriously, if more quietly, their part in putting a people on their feet again. Theirs was the last stand of dignity and formal courtesy in dress and speech. With their Prince Albert coats, gold-headed canes, gold snuff boxes and green bags (brief cases) they scarcely could have been otherwise. They were well read in the classics. The great questions of their day had been conducive to fiery oratory, and they carried it over into

---

[15] O'Neall, *Bench and Bar*, II, 236-246.
[16] *Ibid.*, p. 242.
[17] Brooks, *Bench and Bar*, I, 11.
[18] Green, *History U. S. C.*, p. 329. O'Neall was a student there at the same time. O'Neall, *Bench and Bar*, II, 531.
[19] *Clariosophic and Euphradian Societies*, p. 37.
[20] O'Neall, *Bench and Bar*, II, 531-535.
[21] Green, *History U. S. C.*, p. 51.
[22] O'Neall, *Bench and Bar*, II, 533. Brooks places Preston with Petigru as a lawyer. Brooks, *Bench and Bar*, I, 9.

the courtroom—and at a period when auditors had time to listen!
Chancellor James Parsons Carroll,[23] Joseph Daniel Pope, LeRoy
F. Youmans, A. C. Haskell, Cyrus Davis Melton, Samuel W. Melton, Robert W. Shand, F. W. Fickling, E. R. Arthur, F. W. Mc-
Master, Andrew Crawford, Washington A. Clark, W. H. Lyles,
were outstanding lawyers of the period.[24] Patrick Henry Nelson
was unusually successful as a criminal lawyer, and had a great host
of friends.[25] Ben L. Abney, prominent railroad attorney, collected
perhaps the largest private library in the state, consisting of 10,000
volumes, which, upon his death, his distinguished brother, John
R. Abney, presented to the law school of the University of South
Carolina.[26] While it is not our purpose to note recent members of
the bar, it is only fitting that mention should be made of John P.
Thomas, oldest living member of the old Columbia bar. One of its
most distinguished members, he was for years a professor and dean
of the law school of the University of South Carolina.[27]

Joseph Daniel Pope read law under Petigru. He was a striking
figure, with his distinguished carriage, cutaway coat, cane, snuff
box, and colored handkerchief, and he was a forceful speaker, with
a "great, round voice." He, like Chancellor Carroll, was adept at
common law pleading, and had no use for the new code pleading
introduced by the Radical Constitution of 1868.[28] Pope was a signer
of the Ordinance of Secession, was collector of internal revenue
for the Confederacy, and superintended the printing and issuance
of the Confederate currency. He relinquished his large practice in
1884 to reorganize the law school at the University of South
Carolina, where he continued until his death in 1908.[29]

Colonel A. C. Haskell had a fine war record, was chairman of
the Democratic executive committee in 1876, when Hampton was
elected, and was placed upon the Supreme Court in 1877, succeeding
Wright, the negro Judge of Radical days. He resigned in Decem-

---

[23] Brooks, *Bench and Bar,* I, 96-116. See also "Tributes of Respect to Chancellor Carroll," 20 *South Carolina Reports,* IX-XII (1883).

[24] Brooks, *Bench and Bar,* I, 99.

[25] Stated to the writer by Mr. Mark Reynolds of Sumter, S. C., himself
a distinguished lawyer of the time.

[26] *Bulletin of the School of Law, University of South Carolina,* Announcement, 1932-33, p. 6.

[27] Writer's knowledge. See also "Sketch of the Law School of South Carolina University," by Washington A. Clark, 97 *S. C. Reports,* 493, pp. 497-498
(1914).

[28] Stated to the writer by Mr. Mark Reynolds, who was a law clerk in the
office of Pope and Haskell.

[29] See Brooks, *Bench and Bar,* I, 319-327; Green, *History of U. S. C.,*
pp. 108, 130; "Exercises on Presentation of Portrait of the Late Joseph Daniel
Pope," held in the Supreme Court, 1914. 97 *S. C. Reports,* 488-493.

ber of the following year to resume practice.[30] Judge Haskell was
the first lawyer to install a telephone (about 1885), the first to use a
typewriter.[31] He was the brightest lawyer at the bar, in the opinion of
Mr. Mark Reynolds, who was a clerk in his office, but not so well
trained in the law as some others.

Samuel W. Melton had a war record, was Circuit Judge and
United States District Attorney. A careful student of the law, he was
precise in the use of words and an effective speaker.[32] "Rarely, if
ever again, will the Richland Bar number on its roll a member
with that combination of lawyer-like elements which give superiority in the profession, that compact, closely articulated logic,
that brilliant utterance and tongue fence, that sparkling wit, that
captivating humor, that oratorical power, which lie buried in the
grave of Samuel W. Melton." [33]

LeRoy F. Youmans was a member of the Legislature, fought in
the Confederate War, was Solicitor of the Southern Circuit 1865-
68, Attorney General 1877-82, and again in 1906 until his death in
that year. Cleveland appointed him United States District Attorney,
1884-88. Learned in the law, widely read in literature, from which
he quoted easily, he was an effective speaker and a pleasing conversationalist. Youmans was counsel in the important cases before
the Supreme Court involving recognition of the Hampton government, the validity of the enormous bonded indebtedness incurred by
the Radical legislature, and the bills of the State Bank. As Attorney
General he defended in the Federal Courts, persons accused of
having violated the Enforcement Acts of Congress, which pur-
ported to protect the rights of the negro race. He likewise defended
election officials charged with stuffing ballot boxes. In no case was
a conviction secured.[34]

Columbia has furnished few members of the State judiciary.
Chancellors Harper and Carroll were of the best, as was Judge
Nott. No Columbian has sat upon the Supreme Court since the
Confederate War, with the exception of Judge A. C. Haskell, 1877-
78. The only Circuit Judges since Samuel W. Melton are Judge W.
H. Townsend, 1918-34, followed by Judge G. Duncan Bellinger.
The Richland County Court was the first in the state,[35] and was
presided over by Judge M. S. Whaley from its establishment in

[30] Brooks, *Bench and Bar,* I, 70-71.
[31] Stated to the writer by Mr. Reynolds.
[32] Brooks, *Bench and Bar,* I, 187-190.
[33] LeRoy F. Youmans in Brooks, *Bench and Bar,* I, 190.
[34] See "Memorial Exercises for Gen. LeRoy F. Youmans," 77 *S. C. Reports,* 563-601 (1906).
[35] See *Code of Laws of South Carolina,* 1932, I, Sec. 164.

1917 until 1934, when he was succeeded by Judge A. W. Holman. The present Solicitor for the Fifth Circuit is a Columbian, A. Fletcher Spigner. Judson Smith is Judge of the Richland County Probate Court. Judge Heyward Brockinton is City Recorder.

What is believed to be the only law journal ever published in this state, and certainly one of the earliest to appear in the entire country, was *The Carolina Law Journal,* edited by Abram Blanding and D. J. McCord.[36] The *Journal* was not a financial success, and ran for only one year, 1831. The lawyers of the state, and the students in the University Law School, would profit much were there a law journal here at the present time, devoted to legal matters of state interest.

After he went on the bench, Judge Nott delivered several series of lectures to young men studying law in Columbia. A note-book kept by Thomas Gaillard, who attended the lectures, was found recently by Prof. Emmet Kilpatrick, of the University of South Carolina, in the library of his father. Thirty-four lectures were given during the year 1810-11, covering practically all branches of the law. They follow, in general, Blackstone's treatment, but give the South Carolina law. The picture thus suggested of preparation for the bar in those days, reading law in the office of an older lawyer for perhaps a year, eagerly noting down "the law" as laid out in Euclid-like propositions in occasional lectures by judges or as found in the few available textbooks, chiefly Blackstone, forms an interesting contrast to the legal training obtained in the modern law school. Many of our finest lawyers have "read law" only, but the advantages of a law school are obvious. Three years are spent in study and discusion under specially trained professors, with the advantage of association with fellow students who are digging into the same problems. Thousands of reports of all the cases in all the common-law courts of the world are, or should be available, in addition to writings of legal scholars and commentators. It is now recognized that the law is not a body of fixed and definite rules of arithmetical exactness; conflicting rules are examined and evaluated in the light of results produced by either rule. Moot Court training provides some preparation for actual practise, though young lawyers must always continue to go through a period, out of law school, comparable to the doctor's interneship.

The only law school in the state is at the University of South Carolina, established in 1867. It has been headed by such distinguished

[36] *The Carolina Law Journal,* edited by A. Blanding and D. J. McCord, Columbia, 1831.

lawyers as Judge A. C. Haskell, Cyrus Davis Melton, Joseph Daniel
Pope, M. Herndon Moore, John P. Thomas, and J. Nelson Frier-
son.[37] The law school is of high rank, accredited by the American Bar Association and a member of the Association of American
Law Schools. Raising of standards for admission caused a decrease
in enrollment in 1925 to one hundred students, as compared with one
hundred fifty in preceding years. The enrollment has remained at
around one hundred to the present.[38] Members of the bar naturally
favor measures cutting down the number of those who will compete with them; but that is only an incidental result of raising standards of admission. The great good is the social advantage of in-
suring better equipped men at the bar, through higher requirements of training. The state is fortunate in having but a single law
school in its borders. In practically every other state there are numbers of night law schools, or day schools with low standards, putting out on society men sufficiently crammed to pass the bar examination, but poorly prepared as lawyers.

Since 1912, the state penitentiary in Columbia has been the place
of all legal executions in the State.[39] Prior to 1868 the execution
was by hanging, which might take place under any convenient tree.
Potter's Field was the favorite spot in Columbia.[40] From 1868 until
1912, the hangings took place in the county jail or jail yard.[41] The
whipping post was in use in Columbia for some time after the middle of the century. Williams, who came to Columbia in 1856, tells
of two men convicted of robbing a jewelry store, who were sen-
tenced to twelve months in jail and to be whipped thirty-nine lashes
every sales day, which was the first Monday in the month. They
broke jail and escaped after receiving the first installment of the
lashings.[42] Execution is now by electrocution.

Richland County has had three separate courthouse buildings,
the last of which is now being torn down to make way for a larger
and more suitably constructed building, erected with the aid of
Federal funds. All the buildings have been in the same square, the
first two facing on Main Street, the last on Washington. The first
courthouse, "a much handsomer building than the statehouse (the

---

[37] "Sketch of the Law School of South Carolina University," *supra*, n. p.
26, and writer's knowledge.
[38] See Bulletins, *Announcements of the School of Law, University of South
Carolina* for the years involved.
[39] *Statutes at Large*, Columbia, 1912, XXVII, 702.
[40] J. F. Williams, *Old and New Columbia*, Columbia, 1929, pp. 47, 48, 132.
[41] *Criminal Code of South Carolina*, Columbia, 1912, Sec. 946.
[42] Williams, *Old and New Columbia*, pp. 68, 69.

old one), being built of brick and two stories high," [43] was razed in 1850 to make place for one of more modern architecture. This building was destroyed in the burning of Columbia at the time of Sherman's invasion in 1865, practically all the records being destroyed except the wills, which were hidden in a country barn. As a result, abstracts of title to property in Richland County can seldom be car-

Interior of Courthouse, 1872-1935

ried back further than 1865. From 1868 to 1874, the upper part of Carolina Hall was used as a courthouse, the lower floor being occupied by the general merchandise establishment of James G. Gibbes. This was the hall used by the Wallace House in 1876. The present courthouse, on the corner of Washington and Sumter streets, was erected in 1874, at a cost of $30,000.00, and was described by Robbins in 1868 as "a handsome Corinthian style of Grecian architecture." [44] While this building is being demolished and the new one

[43] From an 1805 entry in the diary of Edward Hooker, quoted in Williams, *Old and New Columbia*, p. 24.

[44] D. P. Robbins, *Historical and Descriptive Sketch of Columbia, S. C.*, Columbia, 1888, p. 19. The Court of Appeals sat in the Richland County Court House during the first half of the century. Dr. James H. Carlisle, "The South Carolina Judge," lecture delivered in 1901, reprinted in *Addresses of J. H. Carlisle*, Columbia, 1910, pp. 164-178.

constructed, the Courts are being held in the Columbia Township Auditorium, but are dispossessed at intervals to make way for road shows and other entertainments, the colorful, if scanty, attire of the chorus ousting the sombre robes of the judiciary.[45]

---

[45] See *The Columbia Record,* November 30, 1935.

ART AND MUSIC

By Harriet Milledge Salley

MUSIC

A SURVEY of Columbia's musical activities for the past one hundred and fifty years, from the records that are available, reveals the fact that its citizens have enjoyed a surprisingly large number in proportion to the size of the city.

Even in its infancy, on August 30, 1799, a popular opera of the day, with the intriguing title of *The Devil To Pay,* by Hill, was presented by Messrs. Williamson and Jones,[1] managers of a theater in Charleston.[2] A few years later, in 1807, we find the South Carolina College including music on the program of its first graduating exercises. "The music was instrumental and very good, the performers being four or five of the best in the State." [3]

The issues of the *Columbia Telescope* for the year 1816 tell us that sheet music was being sold,[4] that a musical organization for the improvement of church and choral music called "The Uranian Society" was holding meetings regularly [5] and that Leverett H. Coe, formerly a teacher in the United States Army, proposed to establish a school to teach military music "in the most modern and approved manner on the most scientific principles." [6]

In the next group of newspapers, 1827 to 1831, there are indications that considerable development in music had taken place with the increase in population and wealth of the community. Columbia had evidently attracted some of the French musicians who were among those refugeeing to this country and particularly the South after the French Revolution and the negro insurrection in San Domingo.[7] In an advertisement of the Columbia Female Academy in the *South Carolina State Gazette* of January 20, 1827, the name of Mr. John LaTaste appears as "a gentleman highly respectable in his profession." According to Mills' *Statistics,* this institution in-

---

[1] O. G. Sonneck, *Early Opera in America,* Boston, 1915, p. 184.
[2] Eola Willis, *Charleston Stage of the Eighteenth Century,* Columbia, S. C., 1924, p. 416.
[3] Edwin L. Green, *A History of the University of S. C.,* Columbia, 1916, p. 320.
[4] *The Telescope,* Columbia, March 26, 1816.
[5] *Ibid.,* May 7.
[6] *The Telescope,* January 9, 1816.
[7] O. G. Sonneck, *Early Concert Life,* Leipzig, 1907, p. 133.

cluded music in its curriculum in 1826.[8] Subsequent newspaper notices indicate that music was taught there throughout its existence
till some years after the Confederate War.[9] Later we find Mr. La-
Taste teaching private classes.[10] In the notice of Mrs. Edmonds's
Female Seminary in the same paper for January 20, 1827, Miss
Hazard heads the music department. "Her qualifications are too
well known to require encomium!" The same issue announces a private class to be taught by Miss Duprey of Charleston.

The music department of Dr. Marks's South Carolina Female Institute from its establishment in 1828 [11] till after the Confederate
War was a strong factor in the musical life of Columbia. Any doubts
concerning the character of music taught, or instruction given,
are quickly dispelled by an examination of the records of Barhamville. As music was considered an essential part of a girl's education
in that day, the best teachers procurable were brought from the
North and Europe.[12]

The *South Carolina State Gazette* for April 21, 1827, contains an
advertisement of a musical instrument for sale called the "Grand
Harmonicon" or "Musical Glasses" and announces that for demonstration purposes a concert will be given, to which admission is
charged, the program consisting mainly of ballads and selections
from the classics.

These papers contain advertisements of a merchant, B. D. Plant,
offering for sale piano fortes, "first quality London make," Spanish
guitars, flageolets of all sizes, flutes, clarionets, tambourines, violins
of various qualities and sizes, violin strings, etc.,[13] and in other columns, notices of teachers and repairers of said instruments.[14] With
such an ample supply of instruments it is but natural that shortly
afterward we read in an account of the exercises attending the dedi-
cation of the monument to Dr. Jonathan Maxcy on the University
campus, on December 15, 1827, that a band, playing martial music,
accompanied the parade. The Euphradian Society paid twenty-two
dollars for this music.[15] In 1831, a military band was organized by
one Christian Stephan.[16] The magician, Mr. Dumilieu, varied the

---

[8] Robert Mills, *Statistics of South Carolina*, Charleston, S. C., 1826, p. 703.
[9] *The Daily Register*, July 31, 1879.
[10] *Carolina State Gazette*, Columbia, June 9, 1827.
[11] *Ibid.*, August 30, 1828.
[12] *Records of the S. C. Female Collegiate Institute* (Barhamville), owned
by Prof. Henry C. Davis.
[13] *Carolina State Gazette*, June 9, 1827.
[14] *Ibid.*, March 8, 1828.
[15] Pamphlet, *History of Euphradian Society* (Library of University of S.
C.).
[16] *Southern Times and State Gazette* (Columbia), January 10, 1831.

entertainment that he gave on March 13, 1829, with music by "Italian Troubadours who played on six instruments," [17] and a circus given on January 9, 1829, included songs and duets on its program.[18] In the *Southern Times and State Gazette* of January 26, 1831, there is a letter from a citizen praising the excellent music that had interspersed the programs of several theatrical performances that had

Barhamville School, about 1850

recently been given in the new theater and commenting on the singing, by Mlle. Heloise, of an aria from Auber's beautiful opera *Massaniello* "in a very pleasing style." The same company presented on one of its programs a sonata for three flutes.

At a celebration on August 16, 1828, of the Richland Volunteer Rifle Company we note "toasts were drank accompanied by appropriate music" [19] and at a celebration advertised June 16, 1827, to be held on July 4th by the Franklin Debating Club an ode composed for the occasion by one of its members was scheduled to be sung.[20]

In *The Chronicle* for April 21, 1841, is an account of a Grand Concert given by Mr. Braham "long a musical lion in Europe," assisted by Mr. and Mrs. Watson before a "large and fashionable audience!" They were greeted with "rounds of applause"; "Mrs.

[17] *Ibid.,* March 13, 1829.
[18] *Ibid.*
[19] *Carolina State Gazette.*
[20] *Ibid.*

Watson has a delightful voice and highly refined taste!" The same paper on October 23, 1844, contains an account of the opening of the theater for the season by John S. Potter with the promise of splendid musical attractions, Columbia having been connected with the Savannah, Macon, and Augusta theaters, thus enabling him to secure the best on the road. During the season of 1844-'45 there were Grand Concerts by a company of celebrated vocalists and orchestra, including artists from the Philadelphia, New York, New Orleans, Boston and Berlin theaters.[21] Other concerts noted were by Henry Phillips, a celebrated artist,[22] and one by Mr. Fallon assisted by flute, violin, and piano soloists.[23] In *The Chronicle* of April 30, 1845, is a notice of a Grand Concert by the Hughes Family assisted by Signor De Dio from San Carlo Opera House, Naples, "who has just arrived in this country" and another by The Orpheus Family "who have received great applause in New York, Philadelphia, etc." [24] The same paper for December 24, 1845, advertises that Mr. Thomas B. Neil of the South Carolina College will give instruction in sight singing to two separate classes—one male, one female. "Parents who are desirous of having their children lend a charm to the fireside or join in praises to their Maker" are urged to take advantage of these classes.

On May 3, 1847, mention is made of a German band furnishing the music on the occasion of Webster's visit to Columbia.[25]

The papers of the year 1849 fairly teem with announcements of musical activities. The Beethoven Association seems to meet regularly for rehearsals [26] and one issue says that there is "plenty of employment for the three good music teachers here." [27] In *The Telegraph* of May 3, 1849, we see that the Philharmonians, an orchestra headed by an excellent musician, Vincenz Czurda, formerly a member of the Steyermarkisch Band, who had settled in Columbia, furnished music for the exhibition of the senior class of the South Carolina College. A "Grand Concert" by a blind musician, Mr. Van Deusen, "who had given concerts over the whole Union" is mentioned in the issue of April 25, 1849. On May 4, 1849, "The Great Original Troupe of Sable Melodists", whose programs featured selections from the operas, gave a concert. "Their season of sixty-

[21] *The Chronicle,* November 20, 1844.
[22] *Ibid.,* December 25, 1844.
[23] *Ibid.,* January 1, 1845.
[24] *Ibid.,* May 7, 1845.
[25] *History of Euphradian Society.*
[26] *The Telegraph,* Columbia, April 23, 1849.
[27] *Ibid.,* April 27.

five nights in New Orleans was attended by the élite of the city and received with rapturous applause."

On May 7, 1849, a concert was given by Mr. Pucci, "the most celebrated performer on the harp in the United States," accompanied by vocal music. The season was climaxed by three performances by members of the New York Astor Place Opera Company. Signor Truffi, Signori Benedetti and Signor Rosi were among the celebrated artists rendering selections from favorite operas, *La Somnambula,* etc.

Among the records of Barhamville is mention of a piece of music composed by a member of the music department and published in 1854 by William Ramsay who kept a piano and music store. Three such stores are listed in the Columbia directory for 1860.

Many musical attractions are noted in the papers of 1856. A Grand Concert was given by Mlle. Parodi, distinguished vocalist of the day, assisted by Signor J. Leonardi under the direction of M. Strakosch with programs of classical, popular, and sacred music.[28] Mention is made of Mlle. Parodi's recent brilliant success in Charleston.[29] Tradition says that Adelina Patti, a child at the time, was with her relative, Mrs. Amalia Patti Strakosch, on this occasion, and was brought on the stage and presented. It is probably true as M. Strakosch was an early teacher of Patti.[30] Another concert given was by Miss Clara Kean, "celebrated Cantatrice and Pianist," who had recently been acclaimed in New York and Richmond.[31] On May 27, 1856, there was a concert given by a local artist, Miss Ellen Brennen, who, it is said, had a beautiful voice and afterwards married a prominent music teacher, Eugene Duvillieu. The couple taught music for many years afterwards. Their home at the corner of Bull and Washington streets afterward became the property of Colonel Wade H. Manning and is now being used as a medical building.[32]

Some time before the Confederate War a vocal teacher named Kimmerer came to the city for periods of weeks at a time, drilled large classes of young boys and girls and wound up his season with Grand Concerts.[33]

The musical activities of the city continued during the Confederate War to some extent, many benefit concerts being given by local

---

[28] *Daily Carolina Times,* March 13, 1856.
[29] *Ibid.,* March 26.
[30] W. S. Pratt, *New Encyclopedia of Music and Musicians, New York,* 1924, p. 781.
[31] *Daily Carolina Times,* April 16, 1856.
[32] Mrs. Legaré Inglesby.
[33] Personal recollections of Mrs. G. C. Harris.

musicians, a few visitors being included,[34] among them one by Madame Ruhl, a refugee from New Orleans.[35] A local choral union existed during this period, mention being made of this same organization as late as October 10, 1879. The Columbia Glee Club is mentioned in the *Tri-Weekly Carolinian* of August 27, 1864.

Title Page of Song Written and Published in Columbia During Confederate War

The Confederate War inspired the composition of several popular war songs by Columbians. One edition of "All Quiet Along the Potomac Tonight", by Lamar Fontaine, was published by Julian Selby of this city.[36] "Rock Me To Sleep, Mother", by Florence Percy, a Columbian, was another of Selby's publications.[37] "Chicora, Respectfully Dedicated to the Patriotic Ladies of the Southern Confederate States", with words by Dr. Marks and music by Prof. Hatschek, both of Barhamville, was published elsewhere.[38]

During the latter half of the nineteenth century Columbia produced many distinguished musicians.[39] The eminent teacher of piano and violin, August Koepper, who taught here for many years before and after the Confederate War numbered among his pupils Carl Feininger, who afterwards studied in Leipzig, returned to this country, gave many concerts en tour and filled responsible positions in New York, where he settled. His sister, Mrs. G. C. Harris, still, at an advanced age, a resident of this city, sang in New York and Co-

[34] *Ibid.*
[35] *Tri-Weekly Carolinian,* September 8, 1863.
[36] Item in book catalogue.
[37] *The Tri-Weekly Carolinian,* January 5, 1864.
[38] Collection of A. S. Salley.
[39] Harriet Milledge Salley, "Musicians of Columbia Forty Years Ago," *The State,* October 12, 1930.

lumbia at benefit concerts, in her girlhood. The Carri brothers, violinists and composers, attained fame in New York as did Alma Stolbrand, a Columbia pianist. Joseph Denck, pianist and composer, was said to be the greatest pianist ever produced in Columbia and probably the state. He studied abroad and upon his return gave concerts, taught, and for a year or two was accompanist for the great violinist, Ole Bull, who gave a concert here in the eighties. Denck gave several concerts in Columbia during the nineties, and his playing always received highest praise from the press. Miss Sally McCollough, pupil of Torriani, Italian teacher at Barhamville, became an opera singer and married a famous tenor of that day, Signor Brignoli, returning to Columbia to give a concert on March 8, 1870. Other well-known Columbia musicians of that period were William Orchard, Mr. Plate, Miss Sally Elmore, Mrs. Thomas Taylor, Miss Mamie Bryce, Mrs. Clark Waring, Miss Carrie LaVal, and Mr. Rawls, a violinist.

A Post Band gave a concert on November 9, 1869, and a band advertised with a circus performance on November 5, 1869, was said to be "the best in the world." The Silver Cornet Band, a Columbia organization mentioned in the issue of August 9, 1879, as giving park concerts, evidently figured for many years afterward, as Fitz Hugh Brown, formerly one of its members, organized early in the nineties the Columbia Orchestra and also a band. These organizations for many years furnished music on many occasions not only in Columbia but all over the state. This band also gave free concerts in the parks, to which the city contributed.

When the Gilbert and Sullivan operas were being acclaimed, there was a performance of *H. M. S. Pinafore* on September 12, 1879, by the Star Alliance Opera Company, of which Fay Templeton, born in Charleston, was a member. This production was followed by an amateur performance of the same opera, April 24, 1884, Miss Sawyer, now Mrs. Pringle Youmans, singing the rôle of Buttercup. The late Donald McQueen was also in it, as were Miss Francenia Brennen, now Mrs. J. Warren Allen, and John Bateman.

Later in the eighties, the Gilbert and Sullivan operas were given by the Herald Square Opera Company of New York. One of its members, J. D. Smithdeal, remained in Columbia, subsequently operating a music store and becoming leading violinist of Mr. Brown's orchestra.

The period of the nineties began auspiciously, through the establishment of the College for Women with an excellent music department, which was attended by many Columbia girls. The papers of that period contain many notices of musical activities at the College —recitals by visiting artists, etc., as well as by pupils and faculty.

There was a notice in *The State* of February 25, 1893, of the regular meeting of the Columbia Musical Club and in *The State* of April 21, 1894, is an account of a concert by the Columbia Choral Society assisted by a famous Austrian pianist, Schwarwenka. Mrs. Ida Folk was accompanist and the article comments on the remarkable stride Columbia had taken that year and the artistic development through the formation of the Choral Society. The love of good music in the community is mentioned and also that much of the success of the Society is due to the College for Women, the rehearsals being held there, and many from their music department being in the Society. The President was Ambrose E. Gonzales and the Director Prof. George McCoy of the College. The fine voices of both Mr. Gonzales and Herndon Moore are noted. These festivals, given in the State House for several years, increased in scope each season and brought famous orchestras and artists to the city. In 1901, Prof. George Kittredge of the College was Director and the Boston Festival Orchestra, Campanari, the great tenor, and other artists were featured.[40] Amateur companies gave *The Mascot* on January 14, 1895, and *The Pirates of Penzance* on October 3 of the same year.[41]

On February 19, 1896, is the startling headline, "Diavolo! Diavolo! His Satanic Majesty in Columbia last night!" "Ambrose Gonzales ideal bandit chief—voice sweet and powerful." [42] Next we read of the presentation in Spartanburg by the Columbia Operatic Association of *"Fra Diavolo!"* Other amateur productions were given over a period of several years, among them being *"The Mikado"* in 1905 with J. I. Sutphen and Leila Hamilton in leading rôles. Since the Town Theater was established several of the Gilbert and Sullivan operas have been given during Daniel Reed's and Belford Forrest's directorships.

To return to the nineties, concerts were given, among many others, by The McGibbeny Family on January 27, 1893, with a great band, splendid orchestra and ten soloists; by The Swedish Quartette Concert Company; Sousa's Band; Innes' Band and the Sherwood Concert Company, which presented scenes from grand operas, in costume; and by Hanna Rion Abell, formerly a student at the College for Women, who had become a concert pianist. Louis Blumenberg, world-famous violoncellist, assisted by distinguished artists, and the great Italian prima donna Moreska, on her first

---

[40] Personal recollections of Fitz Hugh Brown.
[41] *Ibid.*
[42] *Ibid.*

American tour, gave concerts. A number of light opera companies gave Gilbert and Sullivan operas and such operas as *The Bohemian Girl, Girofle-Girofla,* etc. Later these operas were supplanted by the popular comic operas and musical comedies of the day.

On April 27, 1897, was organized the Dertheck Music Club which lasted several years, meeting in private homes and carrying out programs by members of vocal and instrumental music as outlined in a manual by Mr. Dertheck of Chicago. Colonel A. C. Haskell, Dr. T. T. Moore, and Miss Swaffield were mentioned as entertaining the club.

After Fitz Hugh Brown became manager of the opera house, musical attractions followed in quick succession. Later, many concerts were given at the Township Auditorium and several at Camp Jackson. Among them were the Dresden Philharmonic Orchestra, Victor Herbert's Orchestra, the Cincinnati Symphony, New York Symphony, the Russian Symphony, the Metropolitan Orchestra, National Symphony, Damrosch's; concerts by Nordica, Gadski, Sembrich, Schumann-Heink, Calvé, Hempel, Farrar, Galli-Curci, Marion Talley, Zimbalist, Ysaye, Flonzaley Quartet, Paul Whiteman's Band, Kreisler, Paderewski, and several grand opera companies. A concert recently enjoyed was by Benjamin DeLoache, young South Carolina artist. These were supplemented by lyceum concerts and artists' series.

Following the College for Women, Chicora College contributed greatly to the musical life of the city. Dr. Henry H. Bellamann, pianist, teacher and composer, long the head of the music department and Mrs. Bellamann, vocal teacher, were very active when here with their associates, among whom were Miss Ruth Mayes, now Mrs. Richard I. Lane, Miss Patterson, now Mrs. Fred Parker, and Fred Parker, now head of the music department at Columbia College, Miss Warlick, now Mrs. D. A. Pressley and Mrs. Robert Earle who taught one season.

Columbia College has had an excellent music department for many years and its members have been most generous in participating in the musical activities of the city. For several years the College, with the co-operation of citizens of Columbia, presented a series of artists' concerts which have been in recent years supplanted by the Civic Music series given in the city. On May 22, 1904, mention is made in *The State* of the Columbia College Orchestra of twenty-five young ladies, under the direction of Prof. Utermohler, giving a concert with a chorus of college students. Some years later, Madame Felice de Horvath, head of the violin department of Columbia College, organized an orchestra which was supplemented by members from the city and furnished music on many occasions. Madame de Horvath now directs the violin department at the University of South Carolina and her orchestra, composed of violin students and musicians from the city, renders distinguished service to the community, with its delightful public concerts. Among others identified with Columbia College in recent years are Professor Frank Church, Professor and Mrs. Walter Golz, Miss Mary Chreitzberg, Mr. and Mrs. Fred Parker, Robert Lee, Miss Margaret Richards, Mrs. George Sumner, Miss Blundell and Mrs. Gilbert Barre.

Miss Katherine Bollinger was the music supervisor in the public schools for many years. E. T. Gavin has been in charge of this department since 1928, and, with his assistants, has greatly broadened the scope of the work.

The University of South Carolina organized a Glee Club on March 17, 1895, according to *The State* of that date and others followed, with Maurice Matteson becoming director in 1922. Other branches of music subsequently were included till students of the department now receive full credit for their work and the Glee Club, which has won national recognition on its tours, is now known by the name of "Carolina Folk Singers of the University of South Carolina." Mr. Matteson has published a book, *Beech Mountain Ballads,* and has given many lectures, telling of his experiences in gathering these ballads.

Berry Seay is president of the South Carolina College of Music and among his associates are Mrs. E. L. Crooks, Mr. and Mrs. Maurice Matteson, Miss Rachel Little and William Taylor. Edward T. Gavin heads the Major Conservatory of Music established this year and with him are associated Mrs. Gavin, Mrs. Julian Dendy, Walter Kreuger and others.

Miss Nell Mellichamp, teacher and composer, and Misses Julia Quattlebaum and Elise Currell, also prominent teachers, received their early instruction from Miss Rather of the College for Women, later studying in the North. Miss Edith Townsend taught at the College for Women, subsequently having private classes, and Mrs. Hal Dick and Miss Emily Dick were teachers for a number of years. Miss Evelyn C. Reed is a prominent piano teacher who studied in New York and Europe.

The Columbia Music Teachers' Association of Columbia was organized this fall with about thirty-five members, Mrs. Carl Summer being elected president.

The Afternoon Music Club, organized in 1905, has exerted a great influence on the musical activities of Columbia, having functioned for many years and being composed of the leading musicians in the city. Among its activities have been free public concerts, scholarships, and the organization, in 1922, by a committee from its membership, of a junior music club of fifty members, with Harriet Fishburne the first president. The following have served as presidents of the Afternoon Music Club: Mrs. Charles T. Lipscomb, Mrs. Henry F. Anderson, Miss Mattye Izard, Mrs. J. A. Cathcart, Mrs. R. W. Gibbes, Miss Mary Chreitzberg, Mrs. W. T. C. Bates, Mrs. Cora Cox Lucas, Mrs. Robert D. Earle, Mrs. Carl Summer, Mrs. Latimer Williams, Mrs. Lafayette Strasburger, Mrs. Percy Crown, Mrs. Robert Lafaye, Mrs. Henry Cappelmann, Mrs. Burwell D. Manning, and Mrs. Fred Parker.

Columbia musicians presented many programs for the entertainment of soldiers during their period of encampment at Camp Jackson.

Mrs. Robert D. Earle volunteered for the entertainment service of the Y. M. C. A. and in January, 1919, went to France where she, with other musicians, gave concerts in hospitals and camps.

The Evening Music Club of a hundred members has had the following presidents: T. I. Weston, Dr. Pinkney V. Mikell, R. Beverley Sloan, Morris C. Lumpkin, Asher P. Brown, John G. Prioleau, Joseph M. Bell, Henry W. Fair and John J. Seibels.

The State Federation of Music Clubs was organized in Columbia in 1920 with Mrs. Cora Cox Lucas as organizing president. Mrs. Carl Summer has also served as president of the State Federation. A number of Columbia musicians have held important offices in this organization, which has been a great factor in increasing musical activities all over the state.

Mrs. Theodore B. Hayne was organizing chairman of the music department of the Woman's Club of this city, having served for several years, and there are many other music clubs of various types.

The Shandon Choral Society, Mrs. James Y. Perry, president, and L. C. Moltz, director of the chorus, has done notable work, climaxed last spring with the presentation of the National Symphony Orchestra of Washington, D. C., in a concert at the Township Auditorium in conjunction with the chorus.

Among the musicians not already mentioned who have figured extensively in the city are Prof. Paul DeLaunay who went elsewhere to live some years ago, as did Henry F. Anderson and Miss Martha Dwight; Mrs. Christie Benet, D. A. Pressley, Miss Margaret Childs, Kenneth W. Baldwin, director of the Baldwin School of Music, Mrs. William J. Furtick, who was soprano soloist in Trinity Church choir for thirty years, Daniel Visanska, and Misses Florence and Bertha Visanska, W. A. Jaquins, Robert Lafaye, Edward P.

Hodges, Mrs. James Gooding, Mrs. Boyd Johnson, Mrs. J. W. Haltiwanger, Mrs. Curran Jones, Mrs. W. O. Sweeney, Mrs. Harry G. Kaminer, Mrs. J. L. Corzine, Mrs. Edwin Lucas, Misses Eliza Wardlaw, Nan Swearingen, and Dorothy Gilham, Mrs. Leila Caughman, Mr. and Mrs. Donald Ebaugh, William Boozer, and John Mc-Crea. Misses Mary Fishburne and Elizabeth Gaines hold important positions elsewhere.

Dr. Reed Smith's book of folk-ballads published some years ago is a distinct contribution to the music literature of the country.

With the presence of excellent teachers and artists in the city and the many musical organizations inspiring their members to keep up their music, there are musicians available for every type of entertainment, and most of the churches have splendid choirs. Many notable sacred concerts, including oratorios, have been given in the various churches.

The inventions of the graphophone and radio have given many, who would not otherwise have had the opportunity, the chance to become familiar with the world's best music, thereby increasing proportionately the number who appreciate it. With so many agencies conspiring in its favor, Columbia will continue to be a great musical center of the state.

ART

The record of art activities in Columbia from the earliest sources available to the present period is one of which its citizens may justly be proud. The population of the city, although small for many years after its establishment, was composed largely of people of wealth and culture. Its location in the midst of a rich agricultural section, its position as capital of the state and the fact that the South Carolina College and later other important institutions were here were factors that contributed largely to this condition. Naturally then, there has been from an early period in the history of the city a representative group, ever increasing with the city's growth, who have been deeply interested in the promotion of art in all its forms.

Unfortunately, the earliest Columbia newspaper files available are of the Columbia *Telescope* for the year 1816. These papers, however, indicate that their readers were interested in art by publishing art news of the day,[43] by advertising periodicals containing fine arts sections,[44] and in one instance devoting much space to an analysis of a Biblical painting by Washington Allston.[45]

---

[43] *The Telescope,* Columbia, S. C., January 23, 1816.
[44] *Ibid.,* September 16, 1816.
[45] *Ibid.,* May 14, 1816.

ART AND MUSIC   183

Although the files of the Columbia papers from 1816 to 1860 are
very incomplete, many of them contain quaintly worded advertisements of itinerant artists announcing their arrival in the city and
soliciting the patronage of the public.[46] Among those mentioned are
William Brown, "Engraver and Painter"; J. Marling, "Miniature
and Portrait Painter"; Mr. Leonard R. Hanna, "Portrait Painter
from Virginia"; W. K. Barckley, a Columbia artist and pupil of
Sully;[47] T. Wightman; "Mr. Masalon from Charleston";[48] James
McGibbon, portrait and landscape painter; W. G. Browne,[49] and
A. F. MacNeir,[50] portrait and historical painter. It is not known
whether William H. Brown, the silhouettist, worked here or not.
There is a silhouette of Dr. Thomas Cooper by Brown in his *Portrait Gallery*.[51] Freeland[52] and Maier[53] are other artists mentioned
and no doubt there were many more.

Mills' *Statistics*, published in 1826, in giving the curriculum of
the Columbia Female Academy, which it says, was established some
years before, includes art.[54] Mrs. Edmonds' Female Seminary advertises in the *South Carolina State Gazette* of January 20, 1827,
that drawing and perspective, velvet and satin painting are taught.
The Columbia Female Institute, Dr. Marks, president, established
in 1828,[55] and other private schools during this period for girls advertised art in their courses.[56] Among those teaching private classes
noted were Madame Manget[57] who had previously taught in several
cities and received her education in France, and Frederick Kissel-
stein, Jr., who taught drawing, map coloring, landscapes, flowers,
etc.[58] Mr. C. Zimmerman advertised that he would teach the rules
of perspective and drawing from nature.[59]

A distinguished early artist who figured extensively in Columbia
was James DeVeaux, born in Charleston, favorite pupil of Inman
in Philadelphia, and friend of Allston and Sully. During his stay

[46] Harriet Milledge Salley, "Early Art Activities in Columbia," *The State,*
Columbia, S. C., January 8, 1933.
[47] *The Chronicle,* Columbia, S. C., May 28, 1845.
[48] *Ibid.,* April 30, 1845.
[49] *Palmetto State Banner,* October 12, 1852.
[50] *Daily Carolina Times,* January 8, 1856.
[51] Wm. H. Brown, *Portrait Gallery of Distinguished American Citizens,*
new edition, New York, 1931.
[52] *The Telegraph,* March 28, 1849.
[53] *Ibid.,* October 3, 1850.
[54] Robert Mills, *Statistics of South Carolina,* Charleston, S. C., 1826, p. 703.
[55] *S. C. State Gazette & Columbia Advertiser,* August 30, 1828.
[56] *Ibid.,* June 23, 1827.
[57] *The Chronicle,* October 2, 1844.
[58] *The Telegraph,* March 28, 1849.
[59] *The Chronicle,* September 24, 1840.

here, from 1832 to 1835, he painted the portraits of many prominent men of the day, among whom were Hon. George McDuffie, Hon. Henry Deas, Dr. Thomas Cooper, Hon. F. W. Pickens, General J. B. Earle, and Hon. W. D. Martin. In 1838, after his return from Europe, he painted in New York a portrait of Colonel John L. Manning which pleased the latter so much that he invited him

to his home in Clarendon County where De-Veaux painted the likenesses of several of his f a m i l y. In 1840, he painted portraits of the family of General John S. Preston in Virginia. Later he was enabled to make a second trip to Europe through the generosity of Colonel Wade Hampton, Colonel Manning, Dr. R. W. Gibbes and Colonel John S. Preston. He was commissioned by these gentlemen to copy for them any of the works of the old masters that he cared to select. However, his p r e m a t u r e death in Rome in 1844 cut short his brilliant c a r e e r. From the time he began

Scarborough Portrait of Mrs. Thomas J. Goodwyn, Wearing Her Lafayette Ball Gown

painting in Columbia in 1832 to his last trip to Europe he painted two hundred and forty portraits.[60] It is thought that the portrait of Colonel Wade Hampton now in the possession of Mrs. Hagood Bostick is by DeVeaux.

William Harrison Scarborough, a noted portrait and miniature painter, born in Tennessee, made his home in Columbia from 1843 to 1871 except for short periods when he worked elsewhere. His studio was on the site of the present Wit Mary Apartments. Of the large number of his portraits that have been located, fifty-

---

[60] Robert W. Gibbes, M.D., *A Memoir of James DeVeaux,* Columbia, S. C., 1846.

seven are now owned by Columbians, most of the subjects being early citizens of Columbia and vicinity. Among them are
portraits of Dr. Thomas J. Goodwyn, mayor of Columbia when it
was burned, and Mrs. Goodwyn, owned by Keith Legare; James
S. Guignard, by Miss Mary Guignard; Dr. R. W. Gibbes, by his
grandson, Dr. R. W. Gibbes; William Glaze owned by Miss Mary
Lyles; Mrs. James G. Gibbes, by Mrs. D. A. Childs; John English
by Mrs. Beverly M. English; General William Hopkins by Dr.
T. J. Hopkins; John A. Crawford by Miss Harriet J. Clarkson;
Mrs. Artemus Darby, and Mrs. Wm. R. Thomson, by A. E.
Legare; Mrs. Fitz William McMaster and Mrs. James McFie,
by Miss Agnes McMaster; Mrs. John T. Seibels, by John J. Sei-
bels; Miss Elizabeth Shand, by Miss Mary Wright Shand; Mrs.
Richard Singleton, by Mrs. W. D. Simpson; Dr. Alex. N. Talley,
by Robert Moorman; Mr. and Mrs. Benj. F. Taylor, by Dr. Julius
H. Taylor; Dr. John P. Thomas, by John P. Thomas, Jr., Mrs.
Maximillian LaBorde, by J. C. LaBorde; Miss Sarah Walker, by
Mrs. Douglas McKay; Mrs. Elisha Hammond, by James H. Ham-
mond, Esq., Elias Kirkpatrick, by Mrs. C. O. Brown; Mrs. Sarah
Hopkins Clarkson, by Mrs. James H. Fowles; Frances Adams, by
Mrs. F. H. Weston; W. M. Lide, by D. R. Lide, and Mrs. Frances
Guignard Mayrant, owned by Miss Nilla Perry. Also Governor
James H. Adams, by the LeConte family, John M. Berrien, of
Georgia, by Mrs. F. D. Kendall; Mrs. James P. Carroll, by Miss
Ellen LaBorde, Colonel C. C. Tew, by C. M. Tew.[61] When the ex-
hibit of Charles Fraser's works was held in Charleston in 1857,
eight of the fourteen sent from Columbia were from the collection
of Dr. R. W. Gibbes and three pictures of game were lent by Colonel
Wade Hampton.[62]

During the Confederate War, John B. Irving, Jr., came from
Charleston and maintained a studio until after the war, when he
went to New York, where he settled.[63]

The burning of Columbia by Sherman destroyed many art treas-
ures that could never be replaced. Valuable paintings had been
brought to Columbia for safekeeping from other sections, in addition to those already here. The destruction of the collection of Dr.
R. W. Gibbes is but one instance of such loss. His gallery of about
two hundred paintings included works of Allston, Sully, Inman,

---

[61] Helen Kohn Hennig, "William H. Scarborough," *Art in America and Elsewhere*, October, 1934.
[62] Yates Snowden, "South Carolina Painters and Pictures," *The State,* June
9, 1912.
[63] *Ibid.,* June 9, 1912.

Fraser, DeVeaux and many originals and copies of European masters, also family portraits, busts, and portfolios of fine engravings, the last being a bequest of his friend Fraser.[64] According to a member of the family two Titians were among the number destroyed. A

Scarborough Portrait of Dr. Robert W. Gibbes

handsome marble bust of Dr. Gibbes by Hiram Powers and another of his small son DeVeaux by Brown, a New York sculptor, were the only things saved and are now owned by Dr. R. W. Gibbes.

After the desolation of the war, interest in art naturally suffered for some years, but with the restoration of white control, the indomitable spirit of Columbians soon asserted itself and gradually there was a revival of interest in such things.

Albert C. Guerry, a South Carolina artist who painted the fine portrait of General John B. Gordon and presented it to the state, worked here after the war, his studio being on the University campus, as did Williams Welch, another South Carolinian.

The annual State Fairs, from 1869 [65] to the present period, have done much to stimulate interest in art, by holding exhibits and offering premiums. Under the direction of Mrs. William Shand for the past ten years, this department has grown amazingly and aroused favorable comment.

The Columbia Female College, now Columbia College, has always had a strong art department. Among other activities was an exhibit

[64] Wm. Gilmore Simms, *Sack and Destruction of the City of Columbia,* Columbia, S. C., 1865.
[65] *Phoenix,* November 11, 1869.

from the Art Students' League of New York on January 20, 1900, according to *The State* of that date. Miss Mary Mayer is the present art teacher.

The art department of the College for Women during its existence exerted a great influence on art in Columbia, its excellent classes being attended by many Columbia girls. Among its art teachers were Misses Alice Springs, McRoberts, Meinke, Rinehart, Shattuck, Katherine B. Heyward, Sarah Cowan and Anna Taylor. In recent years Miss Cowan has returned to Columbia, exhibited her work, and has taken many orders for her charming miniatures. During Miss McClintock's administration as president of the college, she brought to the college exhibits of nationally known artists, including works of William H. Chase, R. Henri and G. Bellows, which were shown in a gallery provided for the purpose and attended by the public.

The city public schools in 1899 engaged Mrs. Annie I. Robertson, as teacher of drawing. This department has been under Sophie Wallace for several years and has done much to promote art appreciation among the young people of the city.

The University of South Carolina in 1925 established an art department, headed by Katherine B. Heyward, who completed her education in New York and Europe and formerly taught in the New York School of Applied Design for Women. Elizabeth White was the first assistant and May Marshall, formerly of Washington, D. C., is the present assistant. The work in this department has been notable, and an asset to the city and to the state. The classes are largely attended, full credit for the course is given, its exhibits highly praised and its graduates fill responsible positions in this state and elsewhere.

Although many Southern families have lost valuable works of art by the Confederate War, devastating fires and through their sale to parties and institutions outside of the state, there are to be found today in the main library and the two halls of the literary societies of the University of South Carolina, in the Senate, House of Representatives and Supreme Court room of the State House and in private homes of the city many handsome portraits, miniatures, and rare prints of a former day. At the University, among others, are portraits of men distinguished in the history of the University and of the state, by DeVeaux, Scarborough, John S. Cogdell, Williams Welch and in more recent years by Margaret Walker, G. B. Matthews, O. M. Branson, and James W. Pattison. Among those by unknown artists are excellent portraits of Thomas Jefferson and

James Madison.[66] At the State House, among the artists represented
are John Blake White, Albert C. Guerry, Scarborough, Esther
Edmunds, Caroline Carson, Williams Welch, P. P. Carter, Preston
Hix, L. Edmunds, and Clara Barrett Strait.[67]

Privately owned, besides the Scarboroughs mentioned, among
others are Sullys, by Mrs. William D. Melton, Mrs. Christie Benet
and Harry R. E. Hampton, who has one of William Elliott, author
of *Carolina Sports;* portraits by Gilbert Stuart, Sir Thomas
Lawrence and Sir Godfrey Kneller, owned by James H. Hammond,
Esq.; portraits by Jeremiah Theus, owned by Mrs. E. J. Brennen,
Jr., Mrs. Elias Cain, and Governor D. C. Heyward;[68] portrait of
Colonel Thomas Taylor by an unknown artist, owned by Thomas
Taylor, Jr.; and one of the Reverend Peter J. Shand, owned by
Miss Loulie Shand. Miniatures by Fraser and Malbone are owned by
Mrs. Yates Snowden, Mrs. Christopher FitzSimons, Mrs. J. J.
Pringle, Mrs. Hagood Bostick, Mrs. Legaré Inglesby, Mrs.
Wm. Elliott and others. One of Brown's silhouettes is owned
by Mrs. William Simpson. There is an Audubon set at the
University library, several Audubons in private homes, and the rare
print, "Charleston From Across Cooper's River," is owned by Dr.
William Weston. Paintings of the famous Hampton horses by Ed-
ward Troy, the eminent artist, are owned by the Hampton family.
At the University are many busts and replicas, most of which are by
unknown sculptors;[69] but the most valuable is the marble bust of
Colonel William C. Preston by Hiram Powers, presented by the latter
to the University. Powers was enabled to study in Italy, through the
assistance of Colonel John S. Preston and other citizens. At Colonel
Preston's home, now known as Chicora College property, Colonel
Preston had an exceedingly valuable art collection before the
Confederate War, among which were the celebrated statues, "Greek
Slave," and "Eve," executed and presented by Powers to Mrs.
Preston. The original "Greek Slave" is now owned by the Duke of
Cleveland in England, a replica being in the Corcoran Gallery in
Washington, and "Eve" was bought by A. T. Stewart, the New
York merchant.[70] A mantel and a fountain on this same property
were carved by Powers.

---

[66] Elizabeth D. English, *Caroliniana in the University of S. C. Library,*
edited by R. M. Kennedy, Columbia, S. C., 1923.
[67] J. Wilson Gibbes, *Legislative Manual,* Columbia, S. C., 1930.
[68] A. S. Salley, "Art in the Province of S. C.," *The State,* May 26, 1935.
[69] E. D. English, *Caroliniana.*
[70] Charles E. Fairman. *Art and Artists of the Capital of the U. S.,* Washington, D. C., 1927, p. 216.

Another eminent sculptor represented in the University library is Clark Mills.[71] A bronze bust of the late Congressman D. E. Finley in the State House is the work of P. Bryant Baker of New York.[72]

Edwin G. Seibels, at his home, "Laurel Hill," has a very valuable collection of paintings, among which are "Philip of Spain," by Velasquez, two landscapes by Aston Knight, works of Sir John Collier, Kasparides, Thomas Duncan, Da Silva, Le Sidaner, and water-color portraits of Mr. and Mrs. Seibels by the Russian artist, E. Shoumatoff.

Mrs. Ernest Sumner, who moved to Columbia from New York two years ago, has a number of paintings by distinguished artists among whom are Joseph Israels, Bosboom and Mesdag, Dutch artists; Constable, eminent English artist; Scherrewitz, James Maris, Van Soest, Weissenburgh and Ter Meulen.

An undated clipping from a Columbia newspaper, probably in the early nineties, contained in an old scrap book made by Mrs. T. C. Robertson, gives an account of an art club organized in Columbia with Mrs. W. K. Bachman, a prominent artist, as president, the object being to promote art studies.

Another clipping, dated March 15, 1895, in the scrap book, tells of the organization of the Columbia Ceramic Club, its object being the promotion of china painting. The members hoped to send an exhibit of hand-painted china to the woman's building of the Atlanta Exposition.

In *The State* of October 15, 1899, is an account of the organization of an Art League in Columbia with Mrs. Annie I. Robertson, president, the art directors being from the art departments of the College for Women and Columbia College, patronesses being Mesdames Julia Bachman, Clark Waring, E. W. Screven, A. C. Haskell, E. M. Brayton, Thomas Taylor, W. A. Clark and H. W. Richardson. Monthly meetings and teas were to be held at the Columbia Library and a number of activities were planned. The League functioned for several years.

In 1913, an art study club was organized by a group of young women. *The State* of February 13, 1916, gives an account of a splendid exhibit of etchings by nationally known artists, including some by Whistler, brought to Columbia by this club. Helen Hyde of Chicago, noted wood-block print exponent, came to arrange the exhibit and lectured before the club at the home of Mrs. E. W. Robertson, where she was a house guest.

---

[71] E. D. English, *Caroliniana*.
[72] J. Wilson Gibbes, *Mannual*, 1930.

A number of visiting portrait painters have practiced their profession in Columbia in recent years, among whom are George Barrett, Michael Rundolfus, a Russian, who painted portraits of Governor and Mrs. Richard I. Manning; Clara Barrett Strait, Margaret
Walker, Mrs. King Couper, Mrs. Jessie Voss Lewis, of Long Island,
Richard Lofton, and Leila Waring. Hannah Rhett, Annie C. Coles
and Frederick Weber are native Columbians, who, after their studies
abroad, attained eminence and have studios elsewhere but have
worked here in recent years. Anna H. Taylor, a former Columbian,
has a studio in Charleston and Blondelle Malone, another Columbian,
works in the north. Both have studied and traveled abroad extensively. Caroline Guignard has been prominent in Columbia art circles for a number of years, her exhibits having elicited praise both
in the north and south. Miss Guignard studied in Italy and has a
studio at her home "Still Hopes" where she has entertained many
visiting artists of note. Edna R. Whaley, well-known artist, is one of
the founders of the Southern States Art League and has exhibited
in the north as well as in the south.

Marion P. Ridgeway, Augusta R. Wittkowsky, Margaret R. Taylor, Margaret E. Manning, Catherine P. Rembert, Ruth Morse, and
Belle Quattlebaum are other local artists whose works have won
distinction. Most of the artists mentioned above are members of the
Sketch Club, the exhibits of which have won high praise by authorities. Before her death, Cornelia Earle was active in art circles, taught private classes and at one period headed the art department of Chicora College. On October 4, 1930, Henry P. Kendall of
Boston and Camden exhibited at the University Library an interesting and valuable collection of rare old maps and prints of South
Carolina, which attracted much attention.

With such a background of art activities it is but natural that
there should be a flourishing Art Association, established January
12, 1916, with Professor Yates Snowden as its first president.
Among its many activities, perhaps the most ambitious was the
exhibit from the Grand Central Galleries of New York held at the
Jefferson Hotel some years ago. Exhibits of paintings by Weyman
Adams and the late Ambrose Webster have been sponsored by the
Association, also of Alice R. Huger Smith and Mrs. Pettigrew Verner
of Charleston, and there are annual exhibits from the Southern
States Art League. It was during the administration of W. Bedford
Moore, Jr., as president, that the guest artist feature was inaugurated,
Frederick Weber being among the artists brought to the city. The
distinguished animal painter, George F. Morris, of Shrewsbury,
N. J., and Aiken, S. C., came while Edwin G. Seibels was president,

and William Elliott when president brought R. S. Sturtivant, landscape architect of Boston, and Huger Elliott, a director of the
Metropolitan Museum of Art in New York, for lectures. The present
president, Arthur W. Hamby, recently brought Margaret M. Walker
of Spartanburg for a lecture. One of the main objectives of the Art
Association has been to procure for the Columbia public a permanent
fireproof art museum where valuable paintings may be kept and
exhibited and a place provided for gifts of art that many public-
spirited citizens would offer were there such a place. The outlook is
favorable for securing such a building and with the cooperation of
the city and of art lovers, Columbia will be able to command the
position in the art world that it deserves.

LITERATURE AND THE THEATER

By Margaret Babcock Meriwether

LITERARY COLUMBIA

B Y WHAT yardstick does one measure the literary growth of a town, by what thermometer test the heat of its enthusiasm for letters from year to year? The answer is, of course, "by books," and in spite of the ravages of dust and fire, mice and men, we can still find most of the volumes which have made Columbia's book history. In this chapter they will speak for themselves, the books that have been written, published, bought and sold, incarcerated in and circulated by libraries, public and private. What they have meant to their readers must be found in other chapters, for the books themselves are only matches: the solitary candles, home hearths, and public bonfires they kindled make the whole, not the literary, history of our people.

Columbia began as a political theory, a city planned to revolve around the State House. It was inevitable that the first literary activity of the new town should be generated by its center, and we are not surprised to find that the first books printed here were legislative and legal reports from the press of D. and J. J. Faust, State Printers.[1] From 1802 till the current year, the mass of state publications has increased to match the multiplying functions of government. Reports of the governors, legislatures, treasurers, courts, charitable and penal institutions, boards of education and health, historical,[2] agricultural, forestry, and tax commissions, and the highway department, have kept the presses busy for many publishers since the Fausts (see appended list). By count of title and weight on the shelves these government works bulk larger than any other

---

[1] Separate editions of the legislative acts for 1791-1798 were published in Charleston. The earliest copy with a Columbia imprint in the library of the University of South Carolina is *Acts and Resolutions of The General Assembly of The State of South Carolina. Passed in 1800.* Columbia: Printed by Daniel & J. J. Faust, State Printers, Corner of Washington and Richardson Streets, 1801. In 1808 the Fausts reprinted the Acts of the Assembly "from February, 1791, to December, 1804," in two volumes.

[2] The publications of the Historical Commission have been edited, since its reorganization in 1905, by the secretary, A. S. Salley. He had previously edited the first nine volumes (1900-1908) of the *South Carolina Historical and Genealogical Magazine* in Charleston, and written a *History of Orangeburg County* (1898). Since coming to Columbia he has, in addition to his Commission editing, edited the valuable *Narratives of Early Carolina, 1650-1708* (1911), and written *Happy Hunting Ground* (1926).

part of Columbia's printed product. They form an invaluable collection of South Carolina literature, in the broadest sense of the term.

With the opening of the South Carolina College in 1805 a new focus was created for the literary life of the whole state and particularly for Columbia. In the early years of the century, the life of the town was in the State House and the College, and the breath of life in both was politics. Students were trained for public life, not by theorists, but by practical politicians. The politics of the time were planter politics, and political controversies raged around the necessities of the plantation system. But the spokesmen of the planters were the lawyers and professors who led public opinion by their oratory and by the series of remarkably well-written newspapers they controlled.

Dr. Thomas Cooper, Dr. Robert W. Gibbes, Dr. Francis Lieber, Professors Henry J. Nott, and Charles P. Pelham, with the brilliant legal group: Chancellors DeSaussure and Harper, James H. Hammond, David J. McCord, George McDuffie and William C. Preston, made the Columbia of the first half of the nineteenth century electric with the force of their political feeling. The mass of written work they have left in the files of newspapers, monthly and quarterly magazines, in pamphlets and books, still makes exciting reading. The political issues they fought over may be dead, but the vigor and venom of their style do not lose strength with the years.

The most illustrious names on the college faculty, before the Confederate War and since, are those of the expatriates, Thomas Cooper and Francis Lieber. Immigrants in search of American freedom for their liberal views, with political theories formed and reputations made abroad and in the north before they arrived in South Carolina, both men lived twenty years in the state and did an immense amount of writing here. But the parallel between them goes no further.

Cooper, the Englishman, was sixty when he came to Columbia in 1820. He had been a storm center of political and religious controversy all his life, and the gales of nullification, secession, and anti-clericalism that blew round him here until his death in 1839 were most congenial weather to the old agitator. Of his chief works during the South Carolina years Dumas Malone says *"Consolidation* (1824) and *On The Constitution* (1826) have greatest significance. His *Lectures on The Elements of Political Economy* (1826) served as a pioneer American text book . . . . Even his controversial works attest his notable scholarship, and his . . . *Statutes at Large of South Carolina* (5 vols., 1836-39) remain as monuments to his legal learning." [3]

Francis Lieber, political exile from Germany, had edited the first *Encyclopaedia Americana* in Boston, and engaged in educational schemes in Philadelphia before he came to South Carolina College in 1835, at the age of thirty-five. He succeeded Cooper as professor of political economy, but in no other way. In politics and in economics his views were anti-Southern. He was a brilliant teacher and conversationalist, personally beloved by students and older Southern friends. But he was not happy here and wrote in 1841 "with respect to culture and intellectual life and all that a man requires who takes part in the stirring movements of our time, I might as well be in Siberia. I am drying up." [4] "The days of my solitude are over," [5] he wrote in 1857 when he resigned and went to New York. There, at Columbia College, he wrote and taught in more congenial surroundings until his death in 1870, esteemed as one of the great liberal philosophers of the nineteenth century. His biographer says of his years in South Carolina: "Although he regarded himself as an exile, this period was decidedly fruitful, for in the course of it, Lieber produced the works which eventually made him famous. These were his *Manual of Political Ethics* (2 vols., 1838-39), *Legal and Political Hermeneutics* (1839) and on *Civil Liberty and Self Government* (2 vols., 1853)." [6]

Though political science was of first importance at the college, natural science came in for an increasing share of interest there as elsewhere, with the advance of the century. Dr. Cooper, Drs. R. W. and Lewis R. Gibbes, Oscar Lieber,[7] R. C. Brumby, James Wallace, and the brothers John and Joseph LeConte, made outstanding contributions to medicine, chemistry, biology and geology. Their work, like that of the political scientists, was not only theoretical but practical, and their knowledge was put to the plow for useful service in the railroad, canal-building, and agricultural developments that preceded the war, and later for the almost universal necessities of the blockaded Confederacy.

---

[3] *Dictionary of American Biography,* New York, 1930, IV, 415.
[4] Thomas Sergeant Perry, ed., *The Life and Letters of Francis Lieber,* Boston, 1882, p. 151.
[5] *Ibid.,* p. 179.
[6] *Dictionary of American Biography,* XI, 237.
[7] Oscar Lieber, state geologist, never taught at the college. He is included in the group because of his long residence on the campus in the house of his father, Francis Lieber.

The purely literary productions of the ante-bellum college rank below its contributions to practical fields. Professor Henry J. Nott was perhaps the most versatile of the men whose work lay wholly in what their contemporaries called Belles-Lettres. He wrote frequent scholarly articles for the *Southern Review* and amused his generation with his two-volume *Novellettes of a Traveller, or Odds and Ends from the Knapsack of Thomas Singularity* (1834). "It bears a close relation to Longstreet's 'Georgia Scenes' which it antedated." [8]

Georgia Scenes cannot be claimed as a Columbia product, since the genial author did not come here as president of the college until twenty years after its publication. His novel *Master William Mitten,* however, was written in part during his presidency and published elsewhere during the Confederate War. It did not attain the popularity of the *Scenes,* though it is full of lively pictures of South Carolina country life.[9]

Three other ante-bellum presidents of the college: Jonathan Maxcy, Robert Henry and James H. Thornwell, were primarily men of letters. All three were popular pulpit orators, and their published sermons and eulogies demonstrate the dignity and florid eloquence of the time. Dr. Thornwell was editor for the last year of its existence of the *Southern Quarterly Review.*

William J. Rivers, professor of Greek, and Maximilian LaBorde, professor of Logic and Belles-Lettres, are best remembered for their work on historical lines: Rivers for his *Sketch of the History of South Carolina to the Close of the Proprietary Period* (1856), and LaBorde for his *History of the South Carolina College* (1859).

Since the reorganization of the College after Reconstruction, and its development into the present-day University, a vast amount of writing and publishing has emanated from the campus. The favored science of the new century has been neither political nor natural, but the science of education. By far the greater part of the literary output has consisted of textbooks for schools and colleges, analyses of school problems, and surveys for and experiments in public education through the Extension Department. Notable work in these fields has been done by Drs. Edward S. Joynes, Patterson Wardlaw, George A. Wauchope, Reed Smith, Josiah Morse, W. H. Hand and J. A. Stoddard.[10]

---

[8] George Armstrong Wauchope, *Literary South Carolina,* Columbia, 1923, p. 31.

[9] Wauchope, *The Writers of South Carolina,* Columbia, 1910, p. 265.

[10] *Faculty Research and Productive Scholarship,* U. of S. C. Bulletin 211, part II, 1931.

Second in volume after the pedagogical works come the studies in local history and folklore: Professor E. L. Green's *History of the University of South Carolina* (1919) and *History of Richland County* (1934); R. M. Kennedy's *Historic Camden* (with J. J. Kirkland, 1905); Dr. G. A. Wauchope's *Writers of South Carolina* (1910), *Literary South Carolina* (1923) and numerous short biographies of literary Carolinians; Dr. Anne King Gregorie's *Thomas Sumter* (1931); Dr. Leah Townsend's *South Carolina Baptists 1670-1805* (1935); Professor S. M. Derrick's *Centennial History of the South Carolina Railroad* (1930) and shorter economic studies; Dean Reed Smith's *South Carolina Ballads, with a Study of the Traditional Ballad Today* (1928) and *Gullah* (1926); Elizabeth D. English's *Caroliniana in the Library of the University of South Carolina* (1923); and Professor Yates Snowden's many pamphlet studies of literary and historical South Carolina. Professor W. H. Calcott's *Church and State in Mexico* (1926) and *Liberalism in Mexico* (1931) are exceptions to the intensely local themes of most University historical research.

Work of a high order in pure science has been done by Professors J. E. Mills in chemistry and Stephen Taber in geology.

In the realm of pure literature, Professors Snowden and Wauchope take chief honors. Mr. Snowden, an easy and effective writer of prose, gave to his verse the care and precision of formal French artistry. Dr. Wauchope has retained, throughout his long teaching career, a remarkable balance between cherishing the old and welcoming the new in literary fashions.

The location of the Presbyterian Theological Seminary in Columbia in 1829 was of far-reaching influence in the intellectual life of the town. The church thereafter rivalled State House, Court and College in importance, and Calvinism became the fourth generator of books in Columbia. The Seminary faculty from the first included vigorous characters, fluent in spoken and written argument, who rapidly became leaders of the large Scotch-Irish element of up-country South Carolina. Presbyterian influence soon threatened to control Columbia's educational and cultural life to such a degree that a magazine, *The Reasoner,* was started here in 1831 to denounce it. But even the anonymous editor of *The Reasoner* did not foresee in his prophecy the long line of Presbyterian presidents and professors of the University, the outstanding Presbyterian publishers and publications, that were to give a decided tone of Edinburgh to this town set among Episcopal planters and German Lutheran farmers. The Seminary lost power in the materialistic development of the twentieth century city, but when it was moved to Georgia, after a hundred years on Blanding Street, an irreplaceable quality was lost from Columbia's civic personality.

The virtual founder of the Seminary, Dr. George Howe, author of the exhaustive *History of the Presbyterian Church in South Carolina* (2 vols., 1870, 1883) ; Dr. Thornwell, teacher in both college and seminary ; Dr. Benjamin Palmer, great teacher, preacher, and founder of *The Southern Presbyterian Review;* Dr. James Woodrow, editor of *The Review,* able publisher during the difficult Reconstruction era, and amazing arbitrator between evolution and orthodoxy ; Drs. James L. Girardeau, George A. Blackburn, Henry Alexander White and Thornton Whaling are famous names in Southern Presbyterian annals and in Columbia's literary history. Samuel Weir, R. L. Bryan, W. J. Duffie and James H. Woodrow have been notable denominational publishers.

No other church has had a cultural influence comparable to the Presbyterian. The Lutheran Seminary was moved here after the city had been industrialized, and the Lutheran press has been peacefully evangelical rather than controversial. The Methodists have had a girl's college and a press ; the Roman Catholics have had schools and convents here and the Baptists and Episcopalians have issued church periodicals. But none of them has been an intellectual dynamo like the old Seminary.

All the literary life of Columbia has not come from these institutional centers. The college has always attracted writers not directly connected with it. Edwin De Leon in his biography, *Thirty Years of My Life on Three Continents* (1890), recalled the Columbia of his boyhood from his London study with warm praise. His father had been a friend of Cooper, Lieber and their contemporaries "who constituted a select literary society, and gave an atmosphere to this country town very different from the ordinary one" [11] Louisa Cheves, the wife of Cooper's staunch supporter, David J. McCord, was a member of the college group.[12] She represented the best blue-stocking tradition, managing equably her family and plantation duties and a literary career which included lyric and dramatic poetry and numerous reviews and translations for the serious periodicals. Elizabeth F. L. Ellet, whose husband was professor of chemistry at the college from 1835-1848, is less generally known. Much of her literary work was done after her return to New York, but while in Columbia she published *The Characters of Schiller* (1839), *Scenes*

---

[11] London, 1890, p. 6.
[12] Jessie M. Fraser, *Louisa McCord,* U. of S. C. Bulletin 91, 1920.

in the Life of Joanna of Sicily (1840), and *Women of the American Revolution* (1848).[13] The third woman of letters in the college circle belongs to the present day: Frances Guignard Gibbes, wife of the late Professor Oscar L. Keith, of the French department. Her poetic dramas [14] have not only won the praise of critical readers but have been presented at the Town Theater in productions nicely suited to their dream quality.

Other Columbia schools have contributed writers. Dr. Marks of Barhamville condensed his educational theories in *Hints on Female Education* (1851), published a collection of poems in 1850, and a translation from Hippocrates in 1818.[15] Carlyle McKinley, later an influential Charleston newspaperman, began to write as a teacher in Captain Thompson's school during Reconstruction. Some of his best poems seem to belong to this period.[16]

The newspapers have fostered still another group of writers. The first nonpolitical book published in Columbia was Dr. James Davis' *Account of the Winter Epidemic of 1815-16* reprinted from its columns in pamphlet form and sold for twenty-five cents by the *Telescope* in 1816.[17] Columbia's second book, the anonymous *Flower Basket, A Miscellaneous Collection of Poems Mostly Original,* was advertised by the same press at the same price two months later.[18] Turner Bynum, whose verses had appeared in the newspapers, published a long poem in 1827: *Arlan or the Force of Feeling.* Howard Hayne Caldwell had written two volumes of verse and edited a literary magazine of his own—*The Courant*—when he died in 1858 at the age of twenty-seven.[19]

The most active newspaperman of early Columbia was likewise the most active general practioner of medicine, scientist, historian and collector.[20] The indefatigable Dr. Robert Wilson Gibbes is discussed elsewhere as doctor and publisher. His writings alone would have made his name memorable. They are: the three volume *Documentary History of South Carolina* "published" for the state in New York, but printed for Appleton on his own Banner Press in 1853; his scientific papers on a wide range of biological subjects; his travelogue, *Cuba for Invalids* (1860), and his biographies of his friends, the artists De Veaux (1846) and Fraser (1854).

[13] *Dictionary of American Biography,* VI, 98.
[14] *Jael* (1922), *The Stranger* (1923), *Hilda* (1923), *The Face* (1924), *Up There* (1932).
[15] Wauchope, *Writers,* p. 291.
[16] *Ibid.,* pp. 282-290.
[17] *Telescope,* April 16, 1816.
[18] *Ibid.,* June 4, 1816.
[19] Wauchope, *Writers,* p. 104; and Selby, *Memorabilia,* p. 191.
[20] Arney R. Childs, *Robert Wilson Gibbes,* U. of S. C. Bulletin 210, n. d.

Two of Dr. Gibbes' papers, *The South Carolinian,* and its post-Sherman successor, *The Daily Phoenix,* had on their editorial staff the most distinguished names in South Carolina literature. Felix G. De Fontaine was editor of *The South Carolinian,* an able writer himself and author of *Marginalia or Gleanings From an Army Note Book by "Personne"* (1864). But his associates outshone him. William Gilmore Simms was contributing editor [21] and Henry Timrod was associate.

Timrod's connection with Columbia is usually considered one of unrelieved sadness, but it began under the most cheerful circumstances. His editorial appointment gave him the wherewithal to be married in February, 1864, and *The South Carolinian* for the following day printed one of the most light-hearted accounts of a wedding

American Authors

Holmes, Hawthorne, Longfellow, Wells, Prescott, Irving, Paulding, Bryant, Kennedy, Simms, Hallech, Emerson, Cooper, Bancroft

that was ever written, the only one on record, probably, wholly concerned with the groom.[22] During the rest of the paper's existence Timrod's poems appeared regularly, as did those of his friend. Paul Hamilton Hayne. Was it Timrod's hand that added to an editorial on the high price of food "There never was a better time to live on

---

[21] *South Carolinian,* May 3, 1864.
[22] *Ibid.,* February 24, 1864.

poetry and flowers."?[23] Selby says that after the rest of the staff had left Columbia he and Timrod "remained and issued a 'thumb sheet' " while Sherman's "shells were dropping in the neighborhood."[24] The story of the next two years, with the poet's losing struggle against sorrow, disease, and poverty, is too well known to need repetition. Columbia gave him his first home for wife and child, work while he was able to work, and friends to the last. He has given Columbia the honor of a poet's grave, and the brightest name, thus far, of her literary history.

William Gilmore Simms seems to have been in Columbia off and on during the winter of '65. The old indomitable warrior who had hacked his way to fame and wealth with pen for sword, saw his wealth destroyed and fame tarnished by the war he had advocated so staunchly. He accepted the chance journalistic work that came his way, and after the burning of Columbia, assumed editorship of *The Columbia Phoenix* for several months. The outstanding productions of this brief Columbia episode of his long writing career were the famous pamphlet: *Sack and Destruction of Columbia, S. C.* (reprinted from the first twelve numbers of the *Phoenix*) and the account of the loss of his beloved low-country home "Woodlands" in a *Phoenix* editorial.[25]

Simms' pamphlet is the first and best of the almost inflammable little body of documents related to the burning of Columbia that has accumulated since 1865. The subject can scarcely be touched cooly. Plaintiff and accused must either smolder or flame, like the cotton in the streets on the unforgotten night of March seventeenth. Simms was followed in '66 by Dr. D. H. Trezevant's *Burning of Columbia, S. C., A Review of Northern Assertions and Southern Facts*. Other accounts were collected in Chancellor Carroll's *Report of the Committee to Collect Testimony in Relation to the Destruction of Columbia* (1893), James G. Gibbes' *Who Burnt Columbia?* (1902), Yates Snowden's *Marching with Sherman* (1929), and Cole L. Blease's *Destruction of Property in Columbia, S. C. by Sherman's Army* (1930).[26]

Columbia between 1861 and 1865 had enjoyed a high degree of literary activity despite the limitations of the blockade. Refugee publishers from Charleston increased the book-making resources of the town, and all were kept busy. Professor Snowden's papers on *Confederate Books* (1890), *South Carolina School Books* (1910),

[23] *Ibid.,* April 19, 1864.
[24] Selby, *Memorabilia*, p. 101.
[25] William P. Trent, *William Gilmore Simms*, Boston, 1895, pp. 279-283.
[26] Speech delivered in the Senate May 15, 1930, Washington, 1930.

and *War Time Publications* (1922) give a spirited account of the literary demands of the times. Manuals of cavalry and infantry tactics and of military surgery were grim necessities; school books, tracts, and soldiers' Bibles necessities less grim. But the Confederate novels were neither grim nor necessary. Through them, publisher and reader made a gallant gesture mocking hardship and defeat. Columbia's "most notable, one may say audacious, effort of this character," according to Mr. Snowden, was the republication in 1864, by Evans and Coggswell, of Thackeray's *Adventures of Philip* with "a really excellent lithographic portrait and . . . eleven atrocious illustrations." [27]

The Reconstruction period in Columbia was not conducive to writing or publishing. It is significant of the state of public affairs that most publications bore the imprint of either the Republican Publishing Company or the *Union Herald*. After 1876, the war recollections began to appear, and the glorification of the Old South in the pale romances of the '80s and '90s. Of exceptional local interest were the somewhat later novels of two Columbians: Mrs. Malvina S. Waring's *The Sand Hiller* (1904), and Mrs. O. Y. Owings' *Phoebe* (1912), and *David's Heritage* (1914).

Columbia's great, if unconscious, humorist flourished in the '90s. Though he was not a newspaperman, J. Gordon Coogler belongs to that fraternity, for his fame was a newspaper creation. His *Purely Original Verse* (1897) was tossed about the country from one editorial page to another, cherished and quoted gleefully for qualities unsuspected by the solemn versifier.

Columbia awoke from literary torpor in 1891 when *The State* was founded. This newspaper has been to the succeeding generation more than a purveyor of news and a vehicle of political opinion. It has set a high standard of daily literary fare and brought to its public the work of a remarkable family. N. G., Ambrose, William, and Robert Elliott Gonzales are treated elsewhere as journalists. That N. G. and R. E. Gonzales raised the daily grind to the plane of literature can be seen in the war notebook of the former: *In Darkest Cuba* (1922), and in the collected *Poems and Paragraphs* (1918) of the latter. "Captain Ambrose's" gullah stories: *Black Border* (1922), *Laguerre* (1923), *The Captain* (1924), and *With Aesop Along the Black Border* (1924)—have not only made a special niche for themselves in American humorous and local-color literature, but have brought about a renaissance in the treatment of the

---

[27] *War Time Publications*, Charleston, 1922, p. 24.

negro in fiction. Dr. E. C. L. Adams' *Congaree Sketches* (1927) and *Nigger to Nigger* (1928) are examples of the new realistic school.

A notable group of men has been associated with the Gonzaleses. W. W. Ball, long editor of *The State,* wrote much of his *The State That Forgot* (1933) in Columbia though the book did not appear until he had deserted his native up-country for Charleston. J. S. Reynolds was on the staff when he wrote *Reconstruction in South Carolina 1865-1877* (1905). Dr Stanhope Sams wrote with force

Cottage on Henderson Street where the Poet Timrod Died

and erudition himself and through the Quill Club encouraged almost a generation of aspirants to authorship. James Henry Rice, associated with the paper for many years *in absentia,* did much to bring about the present interest in the coast country and in the conservation of wild life. Dr. Henry Bellamann, formerly head of the Chicora College music department, after his return to New York, wrote a weekly page of literary criticism for *The State* that was for years a superlative feature of the paper. Dr. Bellaman had written during his Columbia years a volume of sensitive poems in the then "new manner": *Cups of Illusion* (1923). He and his wife have since written interesting novels. But he will probably be best remembered here as the teacher of Julia Peterkin, whose encouragement of her first efforts in negro character painting started her colorful progress through *Green Thursday* (1924), *Black April*

(1927), *Scarlet Sister Mary* (1929) and *Bright Skin* (1934) to secure artistic success.

This survey of Columbia's writers leaves out, perforce and regretfully, many names. Dr. J. W. Babcock's contributions to medical literature (1893-1917), Henry T. Thompson's *Ousting the Carpetbagger from South Carolina* (1926) and *Henry Timrod, Laureate of the Confederacy* (1928) and George Coffin Taylor's scholarly research into *Shakespere's Debt to Montaigne* (1924) should be added as examples of recent writing quite isolated from the city's habitual literary centers.

What names stand out most bravely in our three half centuries of writers? Timrod, Cooper, Lieber, Thornwell, and Ambrose Gonzales? What theme has been predominant in Columbia's writing history? Look back to the first publication by the State Printer; look at our present leading newspaper, and you have the answer: the state. The capital of the most passionate supporter of States' Rights has seldom gone beyond South Carolina's boundaries for her literary interests. The brand of our beloved triangle is burned deep in most that we have accomplished.

LIBRARIES

The first library in Columbia was in the State House. Separate appropriations of a thousand dollars each "for the purchase of a library for the use of the Legislature" were made in 1800, 1802, and 1803.[28] In 1805, Edward Hooker wrote in his diary "In the Senate Chamber is a Library for the use of the members of both houses. It appears to have on the shelves at present about one hundred and fifty volumes. . . . Mr. C. tells me there is a considerable number of books lost. . . . He says the legislature is very careless of the Library, doing very little more than to vote a supply of money occasionally to purchase books, which when purchased are often taken out without being charged, and retained for months and years without being demanded." [29] In 1814 an annual appropriation of five hundred dollars was made for the library,[30] which must have received better care since it contained "twenty-five thousand choice volumes" when it was "wholly destroyed in the old capitol" in 1865.[31] In 1888, when the new State House was being built, *A Historical and Descriptive Sketch of Columbia* says the collection

---

[28] Cooper and McCord, eds., *Statutes*, V, 396, 452, 475.
[29] *Diary of Edward Hooker 1805-1808* (from American Historical Association Report for 1896), Washington, 1897, p. 857.
[30] Cooper and McCord, *Statutes*, V, 724.
[31] [Simms], *Sack and Destruction*, p. 43.

of a new State library had succeeded so well that the librarian "has on hand forty-five cords of books that he is removing from place to place for security. If the work is ever completed the library will make a handsome showing." [32] The work was completed, and the collection does make a handsome showing. The Supreme Court has a law library, and at one time there was another law library in the Court House. [33]

Columbia's second library was connected with the South Carolina College. "The original plans called for a room over the chapel to be used as a library," but by 1835 "it was housed immediately over the chemical labratory." New appropriations made possible by 1840 its present fine old building, the first separate college library in the country. [34] Even before the removal, visitors to the town were taken to see the library as one of the sights. Hooker [35] commented rather unfavorably on the excessive modernity in the choice of its volumes —a direct contradiction to the humorous description of a collegian in 1816, who wrote that "in no part of the union can there be produced out of one room so great a quantity of antiquities in the Book way." [36] The legislature made a generous appropriation for the purchase of new books for many years before the war, as the catalogues show. The library was saved from Sherman's soldiers by the earnest efforts of the faculty, especially Professor W. J. Rivers. [37] Fire-proof wings were added to the building in 1928, but even with their increased shelf-room, there is serious overcrowding of the rich stores of South Carolina material as well as in the general departments of the library. The University used to have separate libraries in the rooms of the Clariosophic and Euphradian societies, but these have been turned over to the main collection within the last twenty five years. The Law Library in Desaussure College is the only independent one now on the campus.

The splendid theological library of the Presbyterian Seminary had been enriched by many bequests of both money and books. It was, of course, lost to Columbia on the removal of the Seminary. The Lutheran Seminary is now building up a good library, though it is still a small one. The other private colleges had and have libraries, and the public schools have worked hard with small means

[32] D. P. Robbins (compiler), *Historical and Descriptive Sketch of Columbia, S. C.,* Columbia, 1888, p. 15.
[33] *Columbia, S. C.,* etc., *Board of Trade,* Columbia, 1871, p. 59.
[34] *Library,* U. of S. C. Bulletin, VII, Columbia, 1906, pp. 1-2.
[35] *Diary,* p. 852.
[36] *Telescope,* May 14, 1816.
[37] [Simms], *Sack and Destruction,* pp. 42-43.

to supply their pupils with reading matter additional to their textbooks.

The question of reading for the general public was agitated in
Columbia for over a hundred years before it was settled in the
present Richland County Public Library. *The Carolina Telegraph*
for February 9, 1816,[38] carried an advertisement for establishing
"a Reading Room upon a liberal and improved plan." Mills in 1826
said that an "apprentices' library society is now organizing, and
promises great usefulness. Two circulating libraries are also to be
found here." [39] Two years later "An Apprentice" complained in the
Gazette that nothing had come of the library scheme.[40] The same
year appeared frequent advertisements of Marks' Porter and Relish
House, stating that "there is attached to the establishment a Reading
Room containing papers from different parts of the Union to which
gentlemen from the country as also members of the Legislature can
have free and uninterrupted access. Persons desirous of becoming
members to the Reading Room can do so for the small sum of 2
dollars for the year." [41]

The first Reading Room of real worth was the Athenaeum:
"Started through the liberality of Hon. William C. Preston, who
donated his valuable library to it, aided by other citizens who contributed until there was quite a respectable display of books. The
whole of the second story of the brick building on the southeast
corner of Main and Washington Streets . . . was secured for library
and exhibition purposes—the hall on the left and the library on
the right as you entered. Everything was moving along satisfactorily,
and additions of books and manuscripts were being constantly made
by purchase and donation," when just before the outbreak of the
Confederate War the treasurer absconded with the Athenaeum
funds.[42] In 1859 there were 2,600 volumes in the library, "leading
English and American magazines, and papers from the principal
cities." Proprietorship in the society cost $100, annual subscription
$5. The reading room was open daily 9-1, 3-5, 7-10.[43] The news-
papers of the '50s are full of advertisements of lectures and meetings
at the Athenaeum. There had never been anything like it in the town
before, nor has there been anything like it since. During the war,
Athenaeum Hall was pressed into service and became a manufactory

---

[38] Referred to in *Daily Telegraph,* March 24, 1849.
[39] Mills, *Statistics,* p. 707.
[40] *South Carolina State Gazette and Columbia Advertiser,* April 19, 1928.
[41] *Ibid.,* October 11, 1828.
[42] Selby, *Memorabilia,* pp. 45-46.
[43] *South Carolinian.* March 4, 1859.

for Confederate money,[44] before it was lost in the general con-flagration of '65.

The next effective move for a general library was made early in 1896 by the wife and sister-in-law of the manager of the Columbia Opera House, Mrs. Eugene Cramer and Mrs. M. W. Lovell. A report in *The State* on September 13, 1913, summarized the results of the movement during the intervening years. A Union for Practical Progress had been formed to raise funds for a free library; later in 1896 the Union was succeeded by the Columbia Library Associa-tion with Dr. J. H. Woodrow as President. Mrs. Cramer was li-brarian from the start, when the reading room was on the first floor of the City Hall. In the 1899 City Directory both the Columbia Li-brary Association and the Lend-a-Hand Library were listed at the address, 1528 Main Street, with Mrs. Cramer and Miss Ellen Elmore as librarians. When the Lend-a-Hand Library was burned, many books donated by General Hampton were lost.[45] After 1905 the directories give the organization its new title, The Timrod Library, with rooms on the second floor of the Loan and Exchange Bank Building, open from 10-1 and 4-7. Mrs. Cramer continued as libra-rian until 1922, when Miss Annie R. Locke took her place.

In 1924, the name was changed to The Columbia Public Library, the City Council and Chamber of Commerce assuming financial responsibility. In 1925 the old rooms were given up for others in the Sylvan building and an assistant engaged; the next year a second assistant joined the staff. The library moved to the second floor of 1534 Main Street in 1927 and received welcome assistance from the gift of the burned Broad River Bridge insurance. Its last move was made in 1929 to the Woodrow house, home of its first president and of the old Presbyterian Publishing Company. Miss Lucy Hampton (now Mrs. Hagood Bostick) has been librarian ever since the move, and under her guidance the library has become one of the most valuable of our civic assets. Since 1930 the county delega-tion has matched the appropriation from the Rosenwald Fund, giving the secure income which has tripled the number of volumes on the shelves and increased the circulation from 82,057 in 1929 to 449,855 in 1934. The legislature changed the name to Richland County Public Library in 1933, and the staff now includes twelve assistants, two of whom daily distribute books through the county by the "travelling library" motor truck.[46] The aggrieved apprentice

---

[44] J. F. Williams, *Old and New Columbia,* Columbia, 1929, p. 105.
[45] *The State,* October 30, 1899.
[46] Information from Mrs. Hagood Bostick.

of 1828 apparently went bookless, but no one need do so in Columbia in 1936.

PRIVATE LIBRARIES

Ante-bellum private libraries of especial value were in the possession of the Hamptons, Prestons, the Drs. O'Connell at St. Mary's school, Dr. M. H. De Leon, and most famous, Dr. Robert W. Gibbes. Fire has taken toll of or obliterated all these collections.

Since the war, the most notable Columbia book collectors have been B. F. Abney, whose large law and general libraries were bequeathed to the University; Professor Yates Snowden, whose superb collection of South Caroliniana was purchased by the University at his death; and August Kohn, whose daughter, Mrs. Julian Hennig, now owns his library and generously extends the use of it to students. Dr. J. W. Babcock was a great collector of books on many subjects, but he gave them away with day-by-day rather than post-mortem generosity, so that his collection was at no time so large as was generally thought. The late Charles Bruce owned very fine first editions and South Carolina books.

Mr. A. S. Salley has made a specialty of South Carolina magazines and the works of William Gilmore Simms, and Mr. W. S. Brown of books on Masonry and ancient religions. Drs. R. W. and J. H. Gibbes, Mr. John P. Thomas, Dr. R. E. Seibels, Mr. J. M. Bateman, and Mr. C. T. Graydon are among the present-day Columbians who have fine collections.

BOOKSTORES

Mills in his *Statistics* in 1826, said:

> It is worthy of record that in Columbia the first bookstore in the state (out of Charleston) was established. It originated with Messrs. Morgan and Guiry, and is the same now conducted by Joseph R. Arthur.
>
> The progress of literature in the upper country has been so rapid within a few years as to justify the establishment of another bookstore which is in successful operation.[47]

Morgan and Guiry's store was next door to Daniel Morgan's general mechandise business, and probably originated from it. At any rate it was well established ten years before Mills wrote of it and advertised a representative list of new books: Biography, Medicine, Law, and Novels.[48] The partnership was dissolved in 1816.[49] Joseph R. Arthur who succeeded in the business was a kinsman of Mr. Morgan.[50] He sold the stock of books to E. W. and A.

---

[47] Robert Mills, *Statistics of South Carolina*, Charleston, 1826, p. 707.
[48] *Telescope*, March 26, 1816.
[49] *Ibid.*, August 13, 1816.
[50] Edwin Scott, *Random Recollections of a Long Life*, Columbia, 1884, p. 37.

S. Johnston in 1827;[51] their partnership was dissolved and stock sold in 1830,[52] to J. R. and W. Cunningham. In 1839 the store was William Cunningham's alone,[53] and after his death, a firm of Charleston publishers, Allen and McCarter, bought the stock in 1844.[54] James L. McCarter's brother-in-law, Richard L. Bryan, came into the business, and the firm became R. L. Bryan when Mr. McCarter retired in 1853. From 1859-1866 Peter B. Glass advertised as "successor to R. L. Bryan." Like the rest of Main Street his store was burned in '65. Mr. Bryan returned to printing and bookselling after the war,[55] and on his retirement in 1882 left the business and firm name to his son and nephew T. S. and R. B. Bryan,[56] whose heirs still keep the name.

The R. L. Bryan Company, therefore, traces its trade ancestry back to Columbia's first bookstore. From its reopening after the war until its move in 1921 from the west to the east side of Main Street, its location was that of the second bookstore mentioned by Mills: B. D. Plant.[57] This bookseller advertised Mills' *Atlas* the next year.[58] In 1831 the firm name was changed to B. D. and T. H. Plant.[59] Before 1839 Samuel Weir had succeeded the Plants.[60] His estate was sold at auction in 1847, when A. S. Johnston appears again in business.[61] "Middelkauf and Calhoun opened up, but soon sold out to Townsend and North," [62] who were the leading booksellers through the '50s and '60s. Their store was burned in '65, as was the short-lived bookstore of Durham and Mason.[63]

Townsend and North, and Glass, both reopened stores on Plain Street after the burning, but did not last long.[64] In 1866 Townsend and North sold their stock to W. J. Duffie of Newberry,[65] whose bookselling and publishing business continued until Mr. Duffie's death in 1912.

Other booksellers listed in the city directories since the war have been E. R. Stokes (1875-80), W. T. Woodruff (1875), Glover

---

[51] *Gazette and Advertiser,* November 3, 1827.
[52] *Times and Gazette,* November 18, 1830.
[53] *South Carolinian,* August 23, 1839.
[54] *Ibid.,* June 20, 1844.
[55] *South Carolinian,* September 20, 1866.
[56] Robbins, *Sketch of Columbia,* p. 83.
[57] Scott, *Random Recollections,* p. 45.
[58] *Gazette and Advertiser,* December 1, 1827.
[59] *Times and Gazette,* May 14, 1831.
[60] *South Carolinian,* August 23, 1839.
[61] *Daily Telegraph,* October 20, 1847.
[62] Selby, *Memorabilia,* p. 141.
[63] [Simms], *Sack and Destruction,* list of property destroyed.
[64] See note 55.
[65] See note 56.

Wilson (1893-99), J. L. Berg (1893), W. Gibbes (1903), and Gonzales (1904) merging in the State Bookstore (1911 to the present). Lutheran and Baptist bookstores have been here since 1913, and since 1914 J. T. Gittman has presided over the most interesting and richly stocked of all Columbia's bookshops.

PERIODICALS

A survey of the periodicals which have been published here (see list, page 220), bears out the theory that Columbia is basically an institutional city. Long life has been the fortune of no magazine not supported by the strong arm of some religious or educational institution. Private efforts have not met with success, and even the agricultural papers have had to move elsewhere for support. Of the three purely literary magazines—*Whitaker's, The Southern Quarterly Review,* and *The Courant*—the two first were invalids in search of health when they reached Columbia, where they soon died without finding what they sought; the third (known only by contemporary reference) did not survive the death of its young founder. But the religious publications, especially those of Presbyterians, Lutherans, Methodists, and *The Way of Faith,* have made a fine record, and the teachers of the state have been served by an unbroken succession of ably edited journals.

THEATERS AND MANAGERS

When Columbia was being planned and built, no theater was included in its scheme of public buildings, for theatrical performances were forbidden in South Carolina by the Blue Law of 1787 by which actors were classed with "vagrants and other idle and disorderly persons." "All persons representing publicly for gain or reward, any play, comedy, tragedy, interlude or farce, or other entertainment of the stage, or any part thereof. . . ." were "liable to the penalties of this act"—which included imprisonment, hard labor, whipping, and expulsion from the district.[66] The second session of the legislature in the new capital in December, 1791, lifted the ban, however. Thereafter "magistrates throughout the state" might "permit and license persons to exhibit theatrical entertainments," the license costing each exhibitor one hundred pounds a year in Charleston and twenty-five pounds elsewhere.[67]

---

[66] Cooper and McCord, eds., *Statutes,* V, 41-43.
[67] *Ibid.,* p. 195.

What troupe of actors, tight-rope dancers, or performing bears first made use of the opportunity to earn Columbia's applause and shillings, has not been discovered. The earliest of the surviving newspapers list no performances, and the first definite reference to the drama appears in Scott's *Random Recollections*. Some time before 1822 he saw his first theatrical performance, "The Midnight Hour," in the "public hall and ball room" of John Suder "on Sumter Street, nearly opposite to Trinity Church." [68] A season or two later, "Charles Young's Theatrical Company after performing all winter" in the "back store" of Jacob Barrett, the general merchant to whom Scott had been apprenticed, were "preparing to leave Columbia" on January 21, 1822. The date was firmly fixed in the young apprentice's mind, for the day before he ran away from his master hoping to join the players. [69]

Apparently there was no theater here in 1822, if a back store was used for a season's engagement. Mills describing the town four years later says "a large edifice was built in Columbia some years ago, for a theater, which has occasionally been used for that purpose; but neither the population [4,000] nor habits of the place are of a description to countenance such an establishment." [70] Of this first theater, "situated on the northwestern corner of Assembly and Plain Streets," Selby says: "It was erected in the early twenties, I am informed, by a Dr. Harrison, and was originally a three-story building—the upper floor used as a ball-room; but it was thought to be unsafe, and the upper story was taken down." [71] Scott's account differs slightly: "Dr. B. J. Harris, a learned, eccentric and snappish little Englishman, had a drug store [on Main Street] and built a brick theater at the northwest corner of Plain and Assembly Streets." [72]

The first theater must have been built, therefore, between 1822 and 1826, and considered unsafe soon after. The *Telescope* for March 13 and November 20, 1829, carried advertisements for slight-of-hand performances to be given at "Appollo's Theater in Hillegas' Long Room," where there were seats in box and pit for fifty cents and in a "gallery for people of color" for twenty-five cents. The Long Rooms of hotels and taverns were primarily intended for dancing, so the disuse of the theater must have made it worth while

[68] Scott, *Random Recollections,* p. 66.
[69] *Ibid.,* p. 20.
[70] Mills, *Statistics,* p. 708.
[71] Selby, *Memorabilia,* p. 12.
[72] Scott, *Random Recollections,* p. 15.

for Mr. Hillegas to go to a good deal of expense to convert his dance hall into a substitute playhouse.

The *Telescope* for November 20, 1829, also announced, however, that "Mr. DeCamp respectfully informs the ladies and gentlemen of Columbia that at a considerable expense he has erected a theatre on Assembly Street opposite the Catholic Church. . . . The theatre will open on or about the 23rd inst. with a corps dramatique selected from the northern theatres." A brilliant season was enjoyed in 1829-30, and it is upsetting to find, the next autumn, Mr. DeCamp's announcement of "the rapidity with which the theatre advances to its completion . . . lowered one entire story and newly roofed," and his hope that "the prejudices which have existed to the building" will be removed.[73] We are left in a state of complete confusion about Mr. DeCamp's and Dr. Harris' theaters and their repairs and restorations. The building was probably carelessly constructed and subjected to rough usage by turbulent audiences, so that frequent refurbishing was necessary; this was easily translated by theatrical hyperbole into entire rebuilding. Mr. DeCamp enjoyed a brief career of great success. Selby says he was "a prominent actor from England," managed "Charleston, Savannah and Columbia theatres . . . had a coach and four, and traveled from city to city in grand style." He was popular in Columbia, but failed in business here and went to Mobile.[74]

The theater thereafter is referred to as "The new Theater," "Young's Theater," "Coleman's Theater," the "Brick Theater." Selby says it was last used for a "moving (dionamic-cosmorama, or an equally expressive term) representation of the funeral of Senator John C. Calhoun in Charleston," [75] which must have been after 1850. In 1849 it had been "thoroughly renovated . . . seats were reserved for the ladies and utmost decorum observed." [76] But it was found too small by one troupe who leased it and were obliged to "procure the old Circus on Beard's Lot where they have erected a Spacious Pavilion." [77]

The circus was apparently the theater's great rival. Performances took place in a permanent building, on the same block of Assembly Street, with the Roman Catholic Church between circus and theater: "Christ between the two thieves," as Selby says.[78]

---

73 *Times and Gazette,* October 21, 1930.
74 Selby, *Memorabilia,* pp. 12-13.
75 *Ibid.,* p. 18.
76 *Telegraph,* May 7, 1849.
77 *Ibid.,* May 10, 1849.
78 Selby, *Memorabilia,* p. 17.

"Circuses, menageries, and other road shows would remain from three days to a week." [79] The arena was also used for the exhibitions of fireworks which were a popular feature of all patriotic and political celebrations in the '30s, '40s, and '50s. "The building was finally converted into a ten-pin alley . . . then torn down." [80] The old theater and circus were also used as the starting point for balloon ascensions, which the public mind classed with fireworks as part of the glitter and daring of the stage.[81]

If we consider the Assembly Street building as one theater, often renovated, the title of second Columbia playhouse goes to the Town Hall built on the northwest corner of Main and Hampton Streets before the destruction of the old theater. In 1847-48, performances were advertised in the *Telegraph* for both stages, the strictly theatrical exhibitions, needing scenery, being at the theater; concerts, lectures, and "General Tom Thumb" at the Town Hall. After the brick theater had been torn down, alterations must have been made in the hall to make it the town's chief playhouse, for the Athenaeum Hall, Kinsler's Hall, Carolina Hall, and the hotel Assembly rooms during the '50s and '60s took over the concert and lecture engagements.

J. F. Williams included an architectural sketch of the City Hall in his *Old and New Columbia*. It must have been a handsome building, with its clock tower, open arcades below for the market, side stairway and entrance to the theater, which was on the second floor. It was burned, with the rest of Main Street, in '65—"as the clock struck 1, on the memorable February 17-18, the steeple fell and stopped the echoes summarily." [82]

The third Columbia theater was built on the same site during Reconstruction. Some of the ugliest political frauds of the era were grafted upon this unfortunate building, against which the angry tax payers petitioned in vain.[83] The financial tangle is most simply stated in Professor Means Davis' brief sketch of the city.[84] He says that more than $400,000 was bonded, less than $100,000 actually spent in the construction of the theater and City Hall. The City Directory for 1893 gives further details:

> When Mr. Eugene Cramer, a scenic artist from New York, was given the management of the Columbia Theater a dozen or more years since,

[79] *Ibid.*, p. 15.
[80] *Ibid.*, pp. 17-18.
[81] *Ibid.*, p. 10, and *Telescope,* November 20, 1829.
[82] *Ibid.*, p. 136.
[83] Scott, *Random Recollections,* pp. 206-7.
[84] In *Richland Almanac,* Spartanburg, 1904 (Professors J. A. Gamewell and D. D. Wallace, compilers).

he found the place a mere shell and at once set to work to make of it a first class stage and surroundings, which he has admirably accomplished. The seating capacity is about 700, but a thousand persons can witness a play, on pressure. . . . Mr. Cramer has earned a wide notoriety for his careful selections and good financial management, and his reputation as a scenic artist is not excelled by any in the South.[85]

When Mr. Cramer died in 1901, his obituary notice gave 1875 to 1899 as his years of "efficient and popular" managership of the theater. He was therefore, practically its sole manager, for the Opera House was burned in 1899.[86]

The northwest corner of Main and Hampton Streets, where two town halls and theaters had stood for more than half of the nineteenth century, was sold by the city, and the new City Hall and Opera House for the new century built opposite the State House on the northwest corner of Gervais and Main. Frank Milburn of Charlotte was the architect. Though in unfinished condition, the theater was opened on December 1, 1900, under the management of Fitzhugh L. Brown and J. D. Smithdeal.[87] It was remodelled six years later. Mr. Brown continued as manager alone, or with various partners, as long as the theater remained a legitimate playhouse. In 1919 it was turned over to vaudeville under E. B. Rawls for two seasons. Then Mr. Brown came back, in the Brown-Propst Amusement Company or alone, until 1931 (except in 1922 when J. T. Lester was manager; 1926 when the city directory lists no manager; and 1930 when City Council was in direct charge). Since 1931 the old Opera House, renamed the Carolina Theater, has been the first-run moving picture house of the city's group of movie theaters.

Moving pictures were first showed as a great treat, free, at the Merchants and Manufacturers Hall, in December, 1899.[88] Occasional moving picture programs were played for years thereafter at the Opera House. In 1910, there were three separate theaters for the new dramatic art: The Grand and The Lyric for white and the Majestic for colored patrons. Since that year there have always been from two to seven such houses for moving and talking pictures and vaudeville in Columbia. Their names: Dreamland, Bijou, Grand, Pastime, Strand, Ideal, Imperial, Rialto, Rivoli [89] have shifted with their managers, and their management has echoed the warfare waged between the syndicates and private owners all over the country.

---

[85] *Columbia City Directory,* 1893, pp. 59-60.
[86] *The State,* November 30, 1901.
[87] *The State,* December 2, 1900.
[88] *The State,* December 22, 1899.
[89] *Columbia City Directories,* 1903-1932.

Other places which have been used for theatrical exhibitions since the Civil War have been the University Chapel and the auditoriums of the women's colleges and the public schools, with the new Drayton Hall at the University offering the best equipment and acoustics; Parker's Hall, a second monument to Reconstruction graft;[90] Hyatt Park Casino; the Liberty Theater built during the World War at Camp Jackson and managed by F. L. Brown for several seasons; and the enormous Township Auditorium, memento of the ambitious "boom" years that preceded the financial depression of 1929.

PLAYS AND PLAYERS

It is possible in a short sketch to give only an approximate notion of the dramatic fare offered to Columbians since the first curtain rose on the first "comedy, tragedy interlude or farce" licensed by our magistrates. In the early years of the century, theatrical advertisements in the daily papers usually ended: "For Particulars see Bills." Popular prejudice against the theater may have kept newspapers from advertising; economy or old custom antedating newspapers may have inclined the managers to continue the practice of distributing advance programs in the form of handbills. Whatever the reason for their popularity, these cheap slips of paper carried the earliest theatrical news, and they have vanished completely.

The historian must depend on the newspapers and on reminiscences, both of which sources for Columbia are full of great gaps. Mr. Julian A. Selby whose *Memorabilia* has been so much used, was an enthusiastic theater-goer, but very casual in the matter of dates. Mr. Scott of the *Random Recollections* indeed began as a devotee of acting, but age cooled his ardor and he mentions no plays after 1822. Theatrical notices in the daily press depended entirely on the taste of the editor, and years when excellent companies performed in Columbia may appear now as a complete theatrical blank because the surviving newspapers for the period were published by straight-laced Calvinists who saw only the devil's grin in the theater's twin masks of Comedy and Tragedy.

A period when actors and critic were alike excellent is that of the early '30s. DeCamp's remodelled theater was open, his stock companies well trained, stars of the first American magnitude were not afraid of Southern travel, and James H. Hammond was editor of the *Southern Times.*[91] To Mr. Hammond the theater was an absorbing delight. Youthful plays of his composition, in the Hammond

---

[90] Selby, *Memorabilia*, p. 68.
[91] *Times and Gazette,* May 28, 1831.

Collection of the Library of the University of South Carolina, attest
his early dramatic enthusiasm. In the first issue of the *Times* he
took up the cudgels for the institution : "In all communities there is
a difference of opinion on this subject. . . . Some condemn without
ocular demonstration . . . others with enthusiasm applaud without
reflexion; and in both these extremes, much ensues to the disad-
vantage of the amusement." [92]

The customary "season" was made by the engagement, for two
months or more (usually during legislative session) of a stock
company with its manager. Thus, while it was DeCamp's theater
and he often acted, "Essender's Company," or "Charles Young's
Company" would be referred to. The companies had a repertory of
amazing length and range, for an evening's entertainment began at
seven and included a long play, a farce, a curtain raiser or interlude,
and often songs and dances by the hero and heroine of the long
piece, especially if the night was a benefit performance. A typical
bill was Shakespeare's Richard III; "at the end of the play a Scotch
Pas-Seul, followed by the farce *Rendez-vous, or All in an Uproar.*" [93]
Sometimes the stock leading man and woman played the important
rôles ; sometimes a traveling star appeared and the stock players took
second leads. The public thus got many interpretations of the great
parts in Shakespeare's, Sheridan's, and Goldsmith's stage classics,
as well as in the now forgotten romances, tragedies, French farces
and Italian musical plays of the long romantic period from 1800 to
the realistic reformation of the theater in the '90s.

An interesting pamphlet was published in Columbia in 1831 in
defense of one of these early stock companies, whose reputations
had been questioned by a Presbyterian editor in Charleston. A. H.
Pemberton, then an Augusta, though later a Columbia newspaperman, rushed into the fray with a stinging rebuke to the unco' guid:
Calumny Refuted or a Defense of The Drama.

The names of the actors of the '30s and '40s are faded memories
now but T. A. Cooper, Mr. and Mrs. Kean, Fred Brown, Clara
Fisher, Charles McCready, W. E. Burton, Mrs. Mowatt, the Forrests, Miss Rock, Mr. and Mrs. Hamblin, Mr. and Mrs. Blake, and
Maggie Mitchell—once drew discriminating audiences, north and
south.

A letter from an actress in Columbia to her husband at the Charleston theater gives a lively picture of 1840 conditions: "The theater is
worse than a barn, we dress without the luxury of a glass; have no

[92] *Southern Times,* January 29, 1830.
[93] *Times and Gazette,* November 23, 1830.

music, and I was obliged to sing a song last night without. I never
felt so contemptible in my life. . . . I was very well received and
dare say I shall get along very well. We had upwards of two hundred dollars in last night—all gentlemen, not one lady, which was
very disagreeable, I assure you. They are so noisy, they whoop and
yell like Indians." [94]

A more familiar name occurs in the next decade. Joseph Jefferson
and John Ellsler, "with their wives and an unusually good company
of comedians, played an engagement here in the winter and spring
of 1849-50. . . . They depended on their company and had no

Township Auditorium

'stars'." A more flattering compliment was never paid a theatrical
company than was paid by the town council to Ellsler and Jefferson.
As a token of appreciation, the license fees of ten dollars a day for
the entire season were refunded.[95]

Selby lists also the elder Booth, Dan Marble, William H. Crisp, C.
Toler Wolfe, Mr. and Mrs. W. C. Forbes, and Laura Keene as popular players in Columbia, but gives no dates of their engagements.[96]

Straight dramatic entertainment was varied by the performances
of individual magicians, musicians, jugglers, dancers and freaks who
would nowadays be banded together in vaudeville or in circus side
shows. In the '40s began the minstrels—called "Sable Harmonists"

[94] Mary Bunyie Smith, quoted in *News and Courier,* April 1, 1934.
[95] Selby, *Memorabilia,* p. 11.
[96] *Ibid.,* pp. 9-11.

and "Ethiopian Opera Troupes"—who were to enjoy popular favor until the talking and singing moving pictures crowded them out eighty years later. And through everything except the Civil War blockades, the circus has rumbled its heavy way and made its perennial appeal.

During the '60s, entertainment was of an almost wholly local character. Musical performances predominated, the majority of them given as benefits for the Ladies' Hospital Associations. Tableaux were also popular, appealing to one manly reporter, as "chaste, classical and exquisitely tasteful." [97]

The stock company system in Columbia did not long survive the war. It was replaced by "stars" playing one night stands with a new play each season instead of the oft-repeated and enjoyed repertory for several weeks or months. Manager Cramer's theater housed the leading lights of the last two decades of the nineteenth century, as did Manager Brown's for the first ten years of the twentieth. These were the great years of "the road," when a citizen of Columbia need never leave his home town to see the best that the American theater produced and imported. Broadway came to Main Street in the persons of: the Booths, the Forrests, the Sotherns, Joseph Jefferson, Sol Smith Russell, John Kellerd, Robert Edeson, Russ Whytal, Charles Coglan, James O'Neill, Denman Thompson, Augustin Daly, Lester Wallack, Richard Mansfield, John Drew, Nat Goodwin, Otis Skinner, David Warfield, Henry Dixey, William Gillette, James A. Herne, Stuart Robeson, William Collier, George M. Cohan, Robert Mantell, Louis James, Henry Miller, DeWolf Hopper, Ben Greet, James K. Hackett, the Barrymores, Ada Rehan, Sarah Bernhardt, Viola Allen, Elsie Leslie, Rose Coglan, Blanche Bates, May Irwin, Alla Nazimova, Blanche Ring, Lillian Russell, Edith Wynne Matheson, Julia Marlowe, Annie Russell, Mrs. Fiske, May Robeson, Henrietta Crosman, Olga Nethersole, Margaret Anglin, Billie Burke, and Maude Adams. Since the list must end, let it be with Miss Adams, whose return on New Year's Eve, 1931, after a retirement of fifteen years, reopened the theater for one night and revived memories of the whole bright era of travelling stars.[98]

Managerial strife in New York, and a growing tendenancy among younger actors to regard all territory beyond Manhattan as a savage wilderness, combined to kill "the road." Columbia, along with the rest of the provinces, was abandoned to the moving pictures. To fill

---

[97] *South Carolinian,* November 5, 1864.
[98] Dr. Stanhope Sams' dramatic criticisms in *The State* for this period (and afterward for outstanding moving pictures) are memorable.

the real need of many drama-loving communities thus marooned, the
little theater movement was started.

THE TOWN THEATER

Columbia was prepared for a share in the new dramatic development by long enjoyment of amateur theatricals. Older people remembered the benefits of the '60s and the home-talent plays of Mr.
and Mrs. Cramer's early years at the Theater. From 1905 to 1915 the
College for Women had contributed much pleasure to the town by
its out-door productions. The Drama Club and other reading groups
had found keen pleasure in the constantly growing supply of new
plays, particularly those in one act.

When the chances of war brought Daniel A. Reed to Camp Jackson, and thence to the notice of Columbia, "the time, the place and
the man" were set for a fortunate combination. Mr. Reed had had
years of experience in professional theaters, big and little. He was
eager to try his hand in a community enterprise, with amateurs acting under professional direction. When he left Camp Jackson in the

Town Theater
From a Watercolor by the late Harry Dodge Jenkins of Chicago

spring of 1919 plans were under way for the formation of the Stage Society, and when he returned with his wife, Isidora Bennett, in August, he found not only enthusiasm but financial backing ready for him.

The first season of the Stage Society's existence was a wandering one, making use of half a dozen different stages. The manufacture of scenery, the rehearsals, and the performances were accomplished with vigor and a new, surprising finish. The democracy of talent came to be recognized, and all sorts of people and their possessions found themselves enlisted. A wide variety of one-act and full length plays was given from October to June, in monthly programmes, and at the season's end a stock company was formed to buy or build a permanent theater.

The second season began in the first Town Theater, a remodelled house at 1012 Sumter Street. There, too, the third and fourth successful seasons were passed. In 1924 the present handsome little brick theater was built by the Columbia architect, Arthur W. Hamby. The Reeds continued with the theater until 1928, producing a long list of modern and classic plays and instituting the Junior Stage Society for children and a prize-play contest for South Carolina writers. To their remarkable gifts—idealism combined with plainest practicality, true sense of the theater, and wide friendliness—Columbia owes her most individual theatrical enterprise.

The Town Theater was directed for the two seasons of 1928-30 by an English actor, William Dean; then for two seasons by a young Columbian and his wife, trained by both Mr. Reed and Mr. Dean—Mr. and Mrs. Harry Davis. Since 1932 Belford Forrest, a second Englishman, has been director. The custom of giving a yearly Shakespeare production and closing each season with a Gilbert and Sullivan opera, seems firmly established and assured of state wide popularity. The prize-play contest has been dropped, but the children's work continues, and the choice of plays meets the test of unfailingly full houses.

No account of the Town Theater would be complete without mention of at least a few of the Columbia amateurs who have contributed to its success. Miss Martha Dwight, of *The State* staff (later business manager of the theater), launched the original plan and kept it afloat in the public mind by loyal publicity. Dr. and Mrs. Julius H. Taylor have been the theater's tireless friends for its sixteen years, as have the Visanska family (especially Morton Visanska and his nephew Lawrence Goodkind) and Dr. and Mrs. R. W. Gibbes. Mrs. William Farber, Mrs. J. J. Hope and Coleman Karesh are perhaps the most accomplished strictly amateur actors who have been developed. Fay Ball and Frank Woodruff moved on from the Town Theater to professional acting, while Harry and Leora Davis, Frank Durham and Wilbur Wertz have gone into professional directing and scenic designing. Ambrose Gonzales, Bedford Moore, James H. Hammond, and Charles H. Moorefield have been the theater's business advisors.

COLUMBIA PERIODICALS

(w, weekly; m, monthly; q, quarterly; *, file in U. of S. C. Library; +, active in 1936)

Date	Title	Editors and Publishers
1830–1831	Carolina Law Journal (q) *	.... Ed. E. A. Blanding, D. J. McCord
1831–1832	Reasoner: or, Anti-Clerical Politics *	.... Spencer J. McMorris
[1] 1834	Banner of the Cross	.... S. Weir
1834–1835	Southern Christian Herald (w)	* R. S. Gladney, S. Weir
[2] 1839–1851	South Carolina Temperance Advocate (w)	....
[3] 1840–1841	Carolina Planter (w)	.... R. W. Gibbes
[2] 1843–1848?	Christian Magazine of the South	
[4] 1844–1845	Carolina Planter (m)	.... State and Local Societies
1847–1885	Southern Presbyterian (Quarterly) Review *	.... { '49-'61 ed. by a Board '66-'85 ed. by Jas. Woodrow
[5] 1859–1861	Farmer and Planter Monthly *	.. R. M. Stokes
[6] 1848–1852	Illustrated Family Friend	...... Ed. Stuart A. Godman
[7] 1851–1852	Whitaker's (Southern) Magazine (m) *	.... Ed. D. K. & Mary S. Whitaker
1856–1857?	South Carolina Agriculturist (m) *	.... Ed. A. G. Summer
1855	Legislative Times*	.... E. H. Britton
[8] 1856–1857	Southern Quarterly Review, New Series *	.... E. H. Britton
[2] [6] 1858–1859	Courant: A Southern Literary Journal (w)	.... Ed. Howard H. Caldwell
[9] 1862–1865	Southern Lutheran (w)	.... Synod
[10] 1864	DeBow's Review (m) *	.... Ed. B. F. DeBow

[1] Times and Gazette, November 1, 1834.
[2] Gertrude C. Gilmer, Check List of Southern Periodicals to 1861. Boston, 1934.
[3] Arney R. Childs, Robert Wilson Gibbes, 1809-1866, Columbia, n. d., p. 26. Merged in Farmers' Register, Va. File in Library of Congress.
[4] Gilmer; file in Library of Congress.
[5] Published in Pendleton, 1850-1858.
[6] Julian A. Selby, Memorabilia, Columbia, 1905, p. 135.
[7] Vol. I, pub. in Charleston, 1850; N. S. Vol. I, in Columbia, May, 1851; Vol. I, Whitaker's Southern Magazine, Columbia, 1852.
[8] Frank Luther Mott, A History of American Magazines, 1741-1850, N. Y., 1930, pp. 722-727. Pub. in New Orleans, 1842; Charleston, 1843-1855; Columbia, October, 1854, because of epidemic in Charleston; then for 4 numbers, 1856-57, under editorship of James H. Thornwell.
[9] William P. Houseal, Columbia, S. C.
[10] Pub. 1846-1861 in New Orleans; 1861, moved to Charleston; 1864, July-August number in Columbia; 1866-70, Nashville, etc.

Date	Title	Editors and Publishers
[11] 1861–1865?	Portfolio: Weekly Record of the War....................	
[12] 1862–1865	Confederate Baptist (w).......	Ed. J. L. Reynolds, J. M. C. Breaker
[13] 1865–1893	Southern Presbyterian (w)*...	Ed. Dr. Jas. Woodrow
[14] 1868–1899	Christian Neighbor (w) (For peace) '....................	Rev. Sidi H. Browne
[15] 1868–1880	Lutheran (and) Visitor........	Synod
[10] 1869–1877	Working Christian (w) (Baptist)	C. M. McJunkin
1870–1874	Temperance Advocate*.........	C. M. McJunkin, J. A. Elkins
[16] 1877–1879?	Baptist Courier.................	J. A. Hoyt
1882–1888	Collegian (m) changed to*....	Students, S. C. College
1888–1933	Carolinian (m) *..............	Students, U. of S. C.
1883–1884	Temperance Worker (w) *.....	Temperance Societies
1884–1886	Carolina Teacher (m) *........	Teachers' Assn.
[17] 1887+	Southern Christian Advocate (w) (Methodist)............	
1890–1891	Palmetto School Journal*......	Teachers' Assn.
[18] 1890–1928	Way of Faith (w)............	Oliver Gospel Mission
[19] 1892–1895	Cotton Plant (w).............	Farmers' Alliance
[14] 1893–?	Soldier: In Support of the Sabbath	Rev. L. L. Pickett
[14] 1893–1899	Church Messenger (m)........	For Negro Episcopalians
[20] 1895–	Pythian Journal (w)..........	
1897–1898	Religious Outlook (m) *.......	Presbyterian
1897–1902	Carolina Teachers Journal (m) *.	State Teachers' Assn.
[22] 1898+	Criterion	Students, Columbia College
[23] 1898+	Epworth Orphanage Record (m) .	
[21] 1898–1919	Tidings (w) (Lutheran Sunday Schools)	Ed. Mrs. E. C. Cronk
1899	People's Recorder (w) (negro).	

[11] *South Carolinian,* February 25, 1864. Probably pub. by *South Carolinian* press.
[12] File in Library of American Baptist Historical Society, Chester, Pa., Winifred Gregory, ed. *Union List of Serials in the Libraries of the United States and Canada,* N. Y., 1927. (Hereinafter called *U. L. S.*)
[13] Pub. in Millegeville, Ga., from 1850-185?; then in Charleston till 1860; in Columbia thereafter except for a few months of 1865 in Augusta. D. P. Robbins, *Historical and Descriptive Sketch of Columbia, S. C.,* Columbia, 1888, p. 53.
[14] *Ibid.,* p. 56; *Columbia City Directory,* 1899.
[15] Pub. in Prosperity and Newberry, 1880-1903, then in Columbia again for a few months before being merged in *Lutheran Church Vititor* (q. v.) *History of the Evangelical Lutheran Synod of South Carolina, 1825-1925,* Columbia, n. d., Ch. V (by W. P. Houseal).
[16] Succeeded by *Baptist Courier.* Files of both in Library of American Baptist Historical Society, Chester, Pa. *U. L. S. Baptist Courier* pub. in Greenville, 1879+, though still listed in *Columbia City Directory,* 1880.
[17] Pub. 1887-95 in Columbia; 1895-98, in Greenville; 1899-1901, in Columbia; 1901-19, in Orangeburg; 1919-35, in Columbia—since 1921 by its own press. File at the *Advocate* office, Columbia.
[18] Founded and endowed by R. C. Oliver; ed. by L. L. Pick·tt and J. A. Porter till 1895; thereafter for 25 years by J. M. Pike, under whose editorship it became largest religious we·kly in south; moved to Asheville, N. C., then merged in *Pentecostal Herald,* Louisville, Ky. Files in N. Y. Public Library, and in possession of G. G. Pike, Columbia.
[19] Pub. as (m) in Florence from 1883; moved to Greenville, then to Orang·burg where it became (w) (*Columbia City Directory,* 1895); after 1904 merged in *Progressive Farmer,* pub. elsewhere. File in Dept. of Agriculture, Washington, *U. L. S.*
[20] *Columbia City Directory,* 1895.
[21] File in Congregational Library, Boston, *U. L. S.*
[22] Partial file in Columbia College Library.
[23] Partial file at Epworth Orphanage.

Date	Title	Editors and Publishers
1899	Standard (w) (negro)	
1899	Columbia Mirror (Business) . . .	C. C. Muller
[24] 1899–1913	Farmers' Union Sun (w)	Ed. H. A. Whitman, J. W. Reid
1901–1915?	Palmetto (m) *	Students, C. F. W.
1902–1904	Educational *	Ed. Zach McGhee, H. C. Davis
1903	Watchman (w) (negro)	
1904	Southern Home	Rev. Hugh R. Murchison
[25] 1904–1919	Lutheran Church Visitor	United Synod
[26] 1907–1922	South Carolina Pythian	
1908+	Gamecock (w) *	Students, U. of S. C.
1909–1925	South Carolina Odd Fellow (m) *	Ed. J. R. P. Neathery
1908–1910	Southern Plowman (negro)	Ed. Rev. Richard Carroll
1909–1917	Southern School News *	Ed. W. H. Jones
1912–1914	Pointers for Printers of the Carolinas *	C. C. Muller
[27] 1914–1920	American Lutheran Survey (w)	Ed. W. H. Greaver, J. W. Horine
[28] 1916–1921	Diocese (m) (Episcopal)	Diocese of S. C.
1916–1920	Southern Indicator (w) (negro)	Ed. J. A. Roach
1913-1915	Daily Index (Court Record) . .	J. S. Sloane
1916–1917	Industrial Record (w)	
1918	Carolina Farmer and Stock-man (m)	Ed. J. R. McGhee
1918–1920	South Carolina Baptist (negro)	Ed. J. C. White
[29] 1916–1931	South Carolina Christian (m) . .	S. C. Christian Missionary Soc.
1919	Labor Advocate and Trade Review *	Ed. C. S. Henry, E. C. DuPre
1919+	South Carolina Education (m) *.	'19-'25 Extension Dept., U. of S. C. / '25+ State Teachers' Assn.
[30] 1919	Jacksonian (Camp journal)	Lt. Mendenhall
1920–1921	Carolina Alumnus (q) *	Alumni, U. of S. C.
[31] 1910–1931	Columbian	Students, Columbia H. S.
1920–1922	South Carolina Association News *	Y. M. C. A.
[32] 1921–1933	Lutheran Messenger (m)	Synod

[24] Partial file in Dept. of Agriculture, Washington, U. L. S.
[25] File in Library, Lutheran Seminary, Columbia.
[26] File in possession of C. D. Brown, Abbeville.
[27] File at Augustana Seminary, Rock Island, Ill., U. L. S.
[28] Since there have been two dioceses, this paper has become the organ of the southern half of the state, with office at Charleston, and, later, at Georgetown.
[29] Founded by C. C. Ware at Greenwood in 1913, and printed by Connie Maxwell Orphanage Press until 1915, when it was moved to Ellenton. In 1916 it was moved to Columbia under editorship of the Rev. A. B. Reaves; later moved to Orangeburg, Batesburg and Sumter, then back to Columbia from 1927 to 1931, when publication was suspended. It was revived in 1932, and has since been published in Ellenton.
[30] Professor E. L. Green.
[31] Pub. quarterly 1910-1925; thereafter semi-annually. Partial file, High School Library.
[32] Pub. thereafter in Newberry, W. P. Houseal.

Date	Title	Editors and Publishers
[33] 1922+	Piedmont Churchman (m)	
	(Episcopal)	Diocese of Upper S. C.
1923–1924	Southern Farm and Dairy......	
[34] 1925+	Hi-Life (w).................	Students, Columbia H. S.
1927–1928	Spinner	Pacific Mills
1929+	Palmetto Leader (w) (negro)..	
1931–1934	The People (McMahan's Magazine) (m) *.........	Ed. John J. McMahan

TRANSACTIONS

Many associations and societies have had their annual, semi-annual, quarterly and occasional transactions published from offices, or by secretaries, in Columbia. Among them have been:

1819 The South Carolina Agricultural and Mechanical Society.
1885 The South Carolina Bar Association.
1888 The Board of Trade of Columbia.
1888 The South Carolina Pharmaceutical Association.
    The Daughters of the American Revolution.
    The United Daughters of the Confederacy.
1901 The South Carolina Bankers' Association.
1906 The South Carolina Cotton Seed Crushers' Association.
1906–1912 The South Carolina Live Stock Association.
1906 The South Carolina School Improvement Association.
1917 The Council of Defense.
1925 The Chamber of Commerce of Columbia.
1931 The South Carolina Historical Association.
    The South Carolina Federation of Labor.

COLUMBIA PUBLISHERS

This is a tentative list, compiled from the title pages of printed works in the University of South Carolina library. An attempt has been made to group together the names associated with newspapers, since editors or owners often published books from the news presses under several designations. Dates are not conclusive for a firm's duration, but refer simply to the first and last times found in print. State printers are indicated by an asterisk.

1792–1794 *D. Constable.[35]
1801–1830 *D. & J. J. Faust.
1818–1821   *D(aniel) Faust.
1824–1830   *D. & J. M. Faust.
1812–1825   State Gazette (Office) — pub. by the Fausts.
1817–   Cline & Hines.

---

[34] Partial file, High School Library.
[33] File in Bishop's office, Trinity Parish House, Columbia.
[35] E. L. Green, A History of Richland County, Columbia, 1932, p. 191.

1837–   B. D. & T. H. Plant.[36]
1824   Black & Kean.
1826   D. E. Sweeny.
1827   Sweeny and Sims.
1828–1834   *D(avid) W. Sims— ed. *Telescope.*
1816–1841   Telescope Office (or Press).
1832   Telescope and Times.
1830–1833   Times and Gazette Office.
1829–   McMorris & Wilson.
1830–1832   *S(pencer) J. McMorris— pub. { *Southern Times.* *Reasoner.*
1830–1834   (Southern) Times Office.
1832   *A(bner) Landrum— ed. *Hive.*
1831   Free Press and Hive Office.
1834   Hive Office.
1832   *Miller and Branthwait.
1833   Charles W. Miller.
1834   E. F. Branthwait.
1834   Christian Herald.
1834–1838   *S(amuel) Weir— ed. *Southern Chronicle.*
1834   J. R. & W. Cunningham.
1834–1852   *A. S. Johnston— ed. *Telescope.*
1836   Edw. W. Johnston.
1843   DuBose and Johnston— pub. *Telescope.*
1851–1872   Johnston and Cavis— ed. *South Carolinian.*
1855   Gibbes and Johnston.
1837–1858   *I(saac) C. Morgan [37]— ed. *Palmetto State Banner.*
1849   Palmetto State Banner.
1839–1845   *A. H. Pemberton— ed. *South Carolinian.*
1843–1851   (South) Carolinian Office or Press.
1845–1847   Allen, McCarter and Co. (from Charleston).
1846–1847   *Summer & Carroll.
1846–1848   *A. G. Summer— ed. *S. C. Agriculturist.*
1848–1849   John G. Bowman— ed. *Temperance Advocate.*
1853   T. F. Greneker (from Newberry).
1852–1863   *R. W. Gibbes— pub. and sometimes ed. { *South Carolinian.* *Columbia Banner.* *Phoenix.*
1853   Banner (Steam) Power Press, or Print.
1855   Gibbes and Johnston.
1864–1866   (South) Carolinian Steam Press.[3]
1865–1872   Daily Phoenix.
1855–1857   *E. H. Britton— ed. and pub. { *Southern Chronicle.* *Carolina Times.* *Legislative Times.* *Southern Quarterly Review.*
1855–1857   Carolina Times.
1856   R. M. Stokes— pub. *Farmer and Planter.*
1857–1859   R. L. Bryan.
1859–1861   P(eter) B. Glass,[37] "successors to R. L. Bryan."
1859–1870   Southern Guardian (Steam) Press.
1861–1864   *Charles P. Pelham— ed. *Southern Guardian.*
1862–1864   Townsend & North.[37]
1864–1867   *Julian A. Selby— associated with { *South Carolinian.* *Phoenix.*
1864–1867   *F. G. De Fontaine & Co.[37]— ed. *South Carolinian.*
1864   Evans and Coggeswell [37] (from Charleston).
1866   Southern Presbyterian Review.

[36] Note on B. D. & T. H. Plant: No books found for these booksellers, but Selby (*Memorabilia*, p. 141) says they published toy books with this date.
[37] Establishment destroyed by fire, 17 February, 1865.

1868–1870 *John W. Denny (from Charleston).
1869–1893 W. J. Duffie.
1870–1883   Duffie and Chapman.
1871   Carolina Printing Co.
1871–1876 *Republican Printing Co.
1873–1876 Daily Union Herald.
1873–1892 Presbyterian Publishing House.
1881–1889   *James Woodrow.
1889   *James H. Woodrow.
1878–1880 *Calvo & Patton   ⎱ pub. ⎰ *Columbia Register.*
1880–1893   *Charles A. Calvo, Jr. ⎰   ⎱ *Southern Christian Advocate.*
1898   Columbia Register Print.
1882–1897 William Sloane.
1885+   *R. L. Bryan & Co.
1891   J. L. Berg.
1891–19—   The Way of Faith.
1897   J. Gordon Coogler (at the printing office of D. A. Childs).
1897+   Epworth Orphanage Press.
1898–1922 *Gonzales and Bryan.
1901+   *The State Company.
1902   Columbia Printing Co.
1913–1923 University of South Carolina Press.
1913+   Lutheran Board of Publication.
1913–1916 DuPre Printing Co.
1917   Cary Printing Co.
1921–1925 McCaw.
1924-1931 Farrell Printing Company, Inc.

Special publications have been issued by temporary organizations such as:

1893—Centennial Publishing Company.
1915—Olympic Publishing Company.
1930—Carolina Biographical Association.
1935—Current Historical Association.

NEWSPAPERS

By J. Rion McKissick

Dean, School of Journalism, University of South Carolina

THE first newspaper in the capital apparently was the *Columbia Gazette,* although, as in the case of the first Charleston and first South Carolina newspaper, no copy is known to exist.[1] "On the 5th day of March, 1791, Robert Haswell and Richard Hatfield Homan, both of Columbia, entered into an agreement (Miscellaneous Records, A 176, office of South Carolina Historical Commission), whereby Robert Haswell was to print for Homan twice a week for one full year a paper on the same plan as the *Columbia Gazette,* 'which is now being published,' not to exceed 3,000 copies. Another volume in the same office known as 'Register of Accounts' contains the accounts of the November (1791) session of the legislature, in which (page 5) is record of payment to Robert Haswell for 250 copies of the *Columbia Gazette* furnished by him to the legislature. It would thus appear that Robert Haswell, who had been a printer in Charleston, published a paper, the *Columbia Gazette,* in Columbia from the beginning of 1791. His death occurred near January 1, 1792, for his will . . . was filed on January 2, 1792." [2] If Haswell printed a newspaper for Homan, there is no known further record of it.

The second newspaper seems to have been *The South Carolina Gazette,* first issued March 13, 1792. Number 18, the first now preserved, dated July 10, 1792, is in the library of the American Antiquarian Society, Worcester, Massachusetts. Daniel Constable, the editor, was state printer, postmaster, and deputy clerk of court. He seems to have ceased publication of the *Gazette* early in 1794.[3]

This paper passed into the hands of William P. Young and Daniel Faust under the name of *The Columbia Gazette.* The first copy under their control that has survived is dated March 28, 1794, and is Number 5, which indicates that the first issue was February 28.[4]

Without change of ownership or volume numbering, its name was altered to *The State Gazette.* The first issue located with this title is that of January 23, 1795, and the last that of February 27, 1795.

[1] Edwin L. Green, *A History of Richland County,* Columbia, 1932, p. 191; William L. King, *The Newspaper Press of Charleston, S. C.,* 1872, p. 9.
[2] Edwin L. Green, *A History of Richland County,* p. 191.
[3] *Ibid.,* pp. 191-193.
[4] *Ibid.,* p. 193.

Before June of that year the title was changed to *The South-Caro-lina State Gazette and General Advertiser*. It was issued weekly and, during the legislative sessions, semi-weekly. At some time between November 24, 1797, and April 27, 1798, the imprint of the pub-lishers was given as Daniel Faust and Company. With the issue of November 29, 1799, the title was again changed to *The South-Caro-lina Gazette and Columbian Advertiser*. Daniel Faust became the sole publisher. Some time between September, 1800, and January 9, 1801, Daniel and Jacob J. Faust became the publishers and al-tered the title to *The South-Carolina State Gazette and Columbian Advertiser*. At some time between 1811 and 1816 Daniel Faust be-came sole publisher, and the title was changed to *State Gazette and Columbian Advertiser*. In the winter of 1818–'19 the title was again changed to *South Carolina State Gazette and Columbian Advertiser*, and it was so continued until after 1820.[5] By 1827 the title had been altered to *South Carolina State Gazette and Columbia Advertiser*, a change of just one letter.[6] After more than thirty-six years' service as editor and publisher, Daniel Faust retired in 1830, "due to the in-firmities of age," and sold the paper to S. J. McMorris, publisher of the *Southern Times*.[7] The distinction of having on its staff the first Columbia newspaperwoman may have been the *Gazette's*. Ac-cording to Colonel T. G. White of Beaufort, "it was edited and con-ducted after the death of General Faust by my aunt and his wife who was a Miss White, and a sister of my late father John Blake White. Her name was Sarah A. Faust, née White, a strong-minded woman who wielded a powerful pen." [8] The inventory of General Jacob J. Faust's estate was made March 4, 1828, and Sarah C. W. Faust was appointed administratrix.[9]

The first paper to be established in Columbia in the new century was *The Telescope,* which began December 19, 1815. Its first editor was Thomas W. Lorrain who declared that, although William Har-per, afterward a famous chancellor, had "declined publication," his original plan for the paper would be followed as exactly as possible. The prospectus gives a general view of the contents not only of *The Telescope* but also of most ante-bellum Columbia newspapers:

[5] C. S. Brigham, "Bibliography of American Newspapers, 1690-1820," Part XVI, South Carolina, *Proceedings of the American Antiquarian Society,* 1924, n. p., pp. 292-94.
[6] *South Carolina State Gazette and Columbia Advertiser* (Columbia), Jan-uary 20, 1827.
[7] *Southern Times and State Gazette* (Columbia), July 8, 1830.
[8] Yates Snowden to John P. Thomas, March 31, 1896.
[9] Edwin L. Green, *A History of Richland County,* p. 288.

"The paper shall contain select specimens of the best modern literature in prose and verse; moral and religious apothegms and essays; detailed accounts of the various improvements and discoveries making in agriculture and the useful arts; lists of new publications, with some connected sketch of the progress of scientific and literary enquiry; selections of the most interesting foreign and American reviews of recent works; a summary, and when interesting, a detail of foreign and domestic news; sketches of the proceedings and debates of the National and South Carolina State Legislatures, and occasionally speeches of unusual interest in each will be given at length; important opinions and decisions of the Constitutional Court and Court of Appeals; prices current and rates of exchange in different commercial places, and various miscellaneous particulars." [10]

By 1829 the title had been changed to the *Columbia Telescope.* During the Nullification period a regular department was entitled "State Rights." [11] The paper continued publication until 1845. [12]

Next came the *Carolina Telegraph,* 1816–1818, [13] a "dingy little sheet, the size of a large bandanna handkerchief . . . mainly filled with items of foreign news." Its printer and publisher was David P. Hillhouse. [14]

The *Southern Times* first appeared January 29, 1830, its publishers having been S. J. McMorris and—Wilson. [15] After it absorbed the *South Carolina State Gazette and Columbia Advertiser,* the name of the paper was changed in a few months to *Southern Times and State Gazette.* [16] James H. Hammond began his striking political career by editing this paper. [17] He made it such an effective organ of the State Rights and Nullification cause that George McDuffie styled it "all-important in the present crisis" and "the ablest journal in the State." [18] In a nine-column editorial valedictory in 1831, Hammond, whose name had not been "appended to the paper" but had "never been concealed," proclaimed his conviction that the success of the cause he had been advocating was "absolutely necessary to the preservation of the Union." [19] The paper continued for

---

[10] *The Telescope* (Columbia), December 19, 1815.
[11] *Columbia Telescope,* January 2, 1829.
[12] John P. Thomas, manuscript list of Columbia newspapers.
[13] *Ibid.*
[14] *Daily Telegraph* (Columbia), March 24, 1849.
[15] *Southern Times* (Columbia), January 29, 1830.
[16] *Southern Times and State Gazette* (Columbia), July 8, 1830.
[17] Elizabeth Merritt, *James Henry Hammond,* Baltimore, 1923, p. 14.
[18] George McDuffie to J. H. Hammond, February 6, 1831.
[19] *Southern Times and State Gazette* (Columbia), May 28, 1831.

some time, and in 1832 had as its slogan, "Let South Carolina Do Her Duty and Leave the Consequences to God." [20]

The organ of the Union cause was the *Columbia Free Press and Hive* which began publication in February, 1831.[21] Its editor, Dr. Abner Landrum, had edited an anti-Nullification paper, *The Hive,* at Pottersville near Edgefield, and was brought to Columbia by a committee of the Union party.[22] In his proposals for his journal, he declared that one of the articles of his confession of faith was that "the famous doctrine of Nullification has neither the sanction of JEFFERSON nor MADISON, but is the watch-word of a party which would effect by stratagem what they dare not attempt in open day, *the dissolution of the Union."* [23] How long this paper continued is not known, but it was published for at least a year after its establishment.[24] About 1837 Doctor Landrum retired to the sand hills and spent his last years as a potter and planter.[25]

The South Carolinian was established in 1832 by A. H. and W. F. Pemberton, the former having been brought from Augusta by Democratic members of the legislature to edit a paper in support of their views.[26] Acquired by Dr. Robert W. Gibbes, it achieved a high literary standard.[27] It will be considered later as a Confederate newspaper.

Samuel Weir, "a fearless, independent and bitter partisan," [28] established the *Southern Chronicle,* a Whig paper, in 1840. It was discontinued at his death some time after 1845, but was revived by Edward H. Britton who published it for a year.[29]

The Palmetto State Banner was started in 1846 with I. C. Morgan, State printer, as its publisher and proprietor.[30] Between 1850 and 1852 it became the property of Dr. R. W. Gibbes [31] who continued it as the *Columbia Banner,* a weekly.[32]

[20] *Southern Times and South Carolina State Gazette,* May 25, 1832.
[21] *Southern Times and Southern Guardian* (Columbia), May 28, 1831.
[22] *Edgefield Advertiser,* April 13, 1859, quoted in Eleanor E. Mims, The Editors of the Edgefield Advertiser, MS, M.A. thesis, University of South Carolina, 1930.
[23] *Southern Times and State Gazette* (Columbia), February 5, 1831.
[24] John K. Aull to John P. Thomas, March 9, 1931.
[25] Eleanor E. Mims, The Editors of the Edgefield Advertiser.
[26] Julian A. Selby, *Memorabilia* . . ., Columbia, 1905, p. 135; E. J. Scott, *Random Recollections of a Long Life,* Columbia, 1884, p. 153.
[27] Arney R. Childs, *Robert Wilson Gibbes, 1809-1855,* Bulletin of the University of South Carolina No. 210, Columbia, n. d., p. 21.
[28] E. J. Scott, *Random Recollections,* p. 153.
[29] *Daily Telegraph* (Columbia), March 3, 1848.
[30] *Abbeville Banner,* September 16, 1846.
[31] Arney R. Childs, *Robert Wilson Gibbes,* p. 20.
[32] *Daily Telegraph,* April 26, 1851.

The city's first daily, as well as the first in the State outside of Charleston, was the *Columbia Daily Commercial Herald*. I. C. Morgan was the publisher. Apparently it was short lived, for Edward D. Sill, founder of the *Daily Telegraph,* claimed the latter was "the first and only successful attempt made to establish a daily paper in the interior of Carolina." [33] *The Telegraph* began publication October 18, 1847.[34] Edwin De Leon assumed editorial management and control the following year [35] and in 1849 bought Sill's interest in the paper.[36] In a prospectus published in 1848 the *Telegraph* promised that it would direct attention to what it thought "most concerned the South": improvement in agricultural methods and implements, railroad building, development of water power and manufactures.[37] Called to Washington to aid in editing the *Southern Press,* De Leon sold his interest in the *Telegraph* which was soon bought by the *Daily South Carolinian*.[38]

The Carolina Times was established in 1850.[39] About 1853 it was bought by E. H. Britton [40] who published it as the *Daily Carolina Times*.[41] Its distinctive feature consisted of verbatim reports of the debates and proceedings of the legislature made by a "legislative corps" of four reporters,[42] and a column entitled "The Paragraphist. Pen and Scissors," [43] possibly the earliest appearance of a column in a Columbia paper. *The Times* was sold in 1857 to T. S. Piggott of Columbia.[44]

Like some of the other ante-bellum Columbia journals, the *Commercial Transcript* was probably designed to be primarily a views paper. Started in 1851, early in its seemingly brief career it announced that it was "founded in the conviction that the questions now agitating the State, demand a more thorough and searching examination than they have yet received." While conceding the right of secession, this paper opposed it in the form of "immediate separate State action," favored cooperation or "united secession," ad-

---

[33] *Ibid.,* January 27, 1849.
[34] *Ibid.,* October 18, 1848.
[35] *Ibid.,* June 20, 1848.
[36] *Ibid.,* January 29, 1849.
[37] *Ibid.*
[38] Helen Kohn Hennig, Edwin De Leon, MS, M.A. thesis, University of South Carolina, p. 20.
[39] John P. Thomas, manuscript list of Columbia newspapers.
[40] W. L. King, *The Newspaper Press of Charleston, S. C.,* Charleston, 1872, p. 161.
[41] *The Daily Carolina Times,* January 2, 1856.
[42] *Ibid.*
[43] *Ibid.,* February 18, 1856.
[44] *Abbeville Press,* July 24, 1857.

vocated a Southern Confederacy.[45] The latest issue found is dated September 2, 1851.

Other Columbia newspapers of this period, copies of which have not been available for this study, were: *Southern Times and Democrat,* 1831–'32;[46] *Southern Light;*[47] *The States Rights Republican,* 1851;[48] *The New Era,* 1856;[49] *The New Daily,* 1857;[50] the *Columbia Bulletin,* 1859;[51] *Daily Legislative Reporter;*[52] *Daily American Patriot.*[53] Possibly some of these were periodicals rather than newspapers.

The Southern Guardian, daily, was established in 1858 by E. H. Britton.[54] A few months later it was bought by C. P. Pelham[55] who edited it until some time in 1865, the price of a year's subscription then having been $80.[56]

Apparently the only other Columbia newspaper which survived to the last year of the war for Southern independence was the *South Carolinian.*[57] Naturally, news and views of the war filled most of the space. Some of the constant captions were: "Blockade Goods";[58] "Our Army Correspondence";[59] "Notice to Conscripts";[60] "Recruits Wanted";[61] "Five Hundred Million Loan Non-Taxable Bonds";[62] "Seige of Charleston—550th Day."[63] Casualty lists and obituaries of soldiers appeared often. At one time seven wounded or disabled veterans were on the staff of the paper.[64] Telegraphic war news in Columbia newspapers was limited to 3,500 words a week, having been sent by the Associated Press of the Confederate States.[65] So great was the demand for the latest war news that a second edi-

---

[45] *Commercial Transcript* (Columbia), May 22, 1851.
[46] Volume of miscellaneous Columbia newspapers, "South Carolina Collection," University of South Carolina.
[47] Julian A. Selby, *The Daily Phoenix* (Columbia), August 23, 1874.
[48] *Daily Telegraph* (Columbia), May 13, 1851.
[49] *Carolina Times* (Columbia), February 28, 1856.
[50] *Abbeville Press,* September 11, 1851.
[51] Julian A. Selby, *The Daily Phoenix* (Columbia), August 23, 1874.
[52] *Ibid.*
[53] *Ibid.*
[54] *Abbeville Press,* April 9, 1858.
[55] *Ibid.,* October 22, 1858.
[56] *Daily Southern Guardian* (Columbia), January 2, 1865.
[57] *The Daily South Carolinian* (Columbia), November 20, 1864.
[58] *Ibid.,* May 28, 1864.
[59] *Ibid.,* April 19, 1864.
[60] *Ibid.,* May 6, 1864.
[61] *Ibid.,* March 5, 1863.
[62] *Ibid.,* August 27, 1864.
[63] *Ibid.,* January 12, 1865.
[64] *Ibid.,* December 11, 1864.
[65] *Ibid.,* October 15, 1864.

tion was published daily at 5 p. m.[66] Early in 1864 Dr. R. W. Gibbes, owner of the *South Carolinian,* sold it to F. G. DeFontaine, "widely known as 'Personne', graphic war correspondent of the *Charleston Courier."* In his valedictory Doctor Gibbes said: ". . . I recall with much satisfaction that the *South Carolinian* was the first paper in the South that suggested and urged its true position, to make the issue of resistance upon the election of a Black Republican President." [67] With the extraordinary adornment of pictures of the South Carolina and Confederate flags, a special supplement in 1864 bore the display headline: "Grand Demonstration/in Honor of/General Hampton's Troops/Stirring Speeches/by/Dr. Palmer, Gen. Hampton and Col. Gary/Banners, Booths and Beauty." The occasion was Hampton's parting from his immortal legion.[68] In an editorial printed less than a year before the burning of Columbia, the *South Carolinian* unconsciously prophesied the city's doom: ". . . The flames that encircle the dwellings of our fellow men light up the horizon around us, and the deep booming of cannon reminds us that the rancor against the 'nest of rebellion' is not yet allayed. Wherever that ruthless horde can penetrate, there they seek to pour out their cruel revenge. It is but idle mockery to speak of the safety of Columbia." [69] When Sherman burned Columbia, the building and much of the equipment of the *South Carolinian* were destroyed.[70]

The first newspaper to rise from the ashes of the city was appropriately named the *Columbia Phoenix.* William Gilmore Simms, its first editor, persuaded Julian A. Selby, veteran printer, to undertake the publication. "Paper, press, and type had to be procured from a distance, but after toilsome trips Selby succeeded in getting the necessary supplies and on March 21, 1865, the first number made its appearance." [71] It was only 7 x 8 inches, with six pages, folded in three parts.[72] In May its size was changed to 12 x 17.[73] The price was then $40 a month.[74] The following month the editor announced that he would exchange a month's subscription for any one of these commodities: 1 bushel corn; 1¼ bushels peas or potatoes; 5 pounds butter; 25 pounds flour; 7 pounds lard; 4 pounds candles; 7 pounds

[66] *Ibid.,* May 19, 1864.
[67] *Tri-Weekly South Carolinian* (Columbia), January 13, 1864.
[68] *Daily South Carolinian* (Columbia), April 23, 1864.
[69] *Ibid.,* August 13, 1864.
[70] Arney R. Childs, *Robert Wilson Gibbes,* p. 26.
[71] William P. Trent, *William Gilmore Simms,* Boston, 1892, p. 282.
[72] *Columbia Phoenix,* March 21, 1865.
[73] *Ibid.,* May 15, 1865.
[74] *Ibid.,* May 3, 1865.

This First Issue of a Newspaper in Columbia after the Burning of the City Carried William Gilmore Simms' Account of the Destruction

bacon; 9 quarts rice; 8 dozen eggs; or 4 head of chickens.[75] The paper expired in 1876.[76]

The short-lived yet valiant *South Carolinian* was established by John P. Thomas in 1872, but for lack of means ceased publication the next year.[77] An editorial on the first anniversary of the paper's

[75] *Ibid.*, June 5, 1865.
[76] John P. Thomas, manuscript list of Columbia newspapers.
[77] John P. Thomas, in circular in bound volume of the *South Carolinian* for 1873, "South Carolina Collection," University of South Carolina.

founding asserted that it had supplied the conservative citizens "with an honest, outspoken and fearless paper. . . ."[78] It constantly attacked Republican misgovernment. In his valedictory Colonel Thomas declared that his paper had not sought and had not accepted advertising patronage from Republican sources. He concluded: "With thanks for the support of its friends, with naught but calm defiance for its enemies and the enemies of the State, it yields the field—the whiteness of its soul unsullied and its standard undishonored."[79]

The two Republican organs, the *Union* and the *Herald,* were merged in 1873 under the title of the *Daily Union Herald.*[80] Its editor was L. Cass Carpenter who in 1877 was convicted of forgery in connection with the public printing.[81] In the campaign of 1876 it published false reports of division and demoralization in the Democratic ranks.[82] The paper "disappeared with the conditions which had produced and sustained it."[83]

The Columbia Register was established in 1875 by a cooperative company formed of workers on the defunct *Phoenix.*[84] In the campaign of 1876 it advocated a "straightout" fight for Hampton and the Democratic State ticket.[85] The outcome of that battle was heralded with this headline: " 'Our' Governor Hampton Inaugurated! The Light of Heaven Courted. No Bayonets Needed to Inaugurate the People's Choice. The Vast Multitude Rejoicing! His Inaugural Address. The State at Last Has a Ruler Worthy the Name!"[86] *The Register* opposed the candidacy of B. R. Tillman for the Democratic gubernatorial nomination in 1890, but supported him as the nominee against the independent candidacy of Colonel A. C. Haskell that year. For some time Tillman dictated the paper's policy. Under the editorship of George R. Koester, *The Register* in general supported the Reform movement, but often clashed with Tillman. It advocated Joseph H. Earle for United States Senator in 1896 against Governor John Gary Evans who had Tillman's support.

[78] *The South Carolinian,* January 25, 1873.
[79] John P. Thomas, in circular in bound volume of the *South Carolinian* for 1873.
[80] *The South Carolinian* (Columbia), May 24, 1873.
[81] Francis B. Simkins and Robert H. Woody, *South Carolina During Reconstruction,* Chapel Hill, 1932, p. 543; John S. Reynolds, *Reconstruction in South Carolina,* Columbia, 1905, p. 476.
[82] A. B. Williams, *Hampton and His Red Shirts,* Charleston, 1935, p. 135.
[83] Carlyle McKinley, Centennial Edition of the *News and Courier,* Charleston, 1903, p. 29.
[84] *Ibid.*
[85] *Columbia Register,* December 15, 1876.
[86] *Columbia Register,* December 15, 1876.

Earle was elected and "always gave *The Register* large credit for his success." [87] The paper went out in 1898.[88]

"Next to Charleston, Columbia is the biggest newspaper grave-yard in the State", Yates Snowden observed long ago.[89] Among those which appeared and disappeared in the period from 1865 to the present, in addition to those already named, were: *The Daily Sun;*[90] *The Carolina Times,* 1866—;[91] *The Palmetto Yeoman,* 1878–'84;[92] *The Daily Record,* 1885–'93;[93] *The Evening Journal,* 1893–'94;[94] *The Evening News,* 1895–'96;[95] the *South Carolina Gazette,* 1925–1930.[96] For lack of time and material, no additional informa-tion about these can be presented here.

The State, which has lived longer than any other Columbia news-paper, was founded by N. G. and Ambrose E. Gonzales, "ardent supporters of Judge A. C. Haskell in his campaign of protest against the unseating of certain legally elected 'straightout' delegates by the 'regular' Democratic convention of 1890." Nearly one hundred rep-resentative South Carolinians were associated with them in the for-mation of the State Company, the first president of which was Judge Haskell. "No other daily newspaper ever endured such hard-ships or survived such vicissitudes," Ambrose E. Gonzales, its first publisher, asserted.[97] It was a vigorous opponent of the Tillman ad-ministration.[98] Under the editorship of N. G. Gonzales, *The State* was "the first Southern newspaper to cry out against the cowardice and barbarity of lynching—the first to denounce lynchers as mur-derers and to denounce them here at home, where enemies are al-ways to be made . . . the first newspaper to advocate a Child Labor law for South Carolina"—and it waged a long fight for com-pulsory education.[99]

The present *Columbia Record* is not a continuation of the *Daily Record,* 1885-93, but was founded by George R. Koester in 1897. He published it individually until 1902 when he sold it to the Record

---

[87] George R. Koester to the author, November 30, 1905.
[88] John P. Thomas, manuscript list of Columbia newspapers.
[89] Yates Snowden to John P. Thomas, March 31, 1896.
[90] *The Daily Phoenix* (Columbia), August 23, 1874.
[91] *The Carolina Times,* October 17, 1866.
[92] *The Palmetto Yeoman,* March 29, 1854.
[93] John P. Thomas, manuscript list of Columbia newspapers.
[94] *Ibid.*
[95] *Ibid.*
[96] File, South Carolina Collection, University of South Carolina.
[97] Ambrose E. Gonzales on N. G. Gonzales, *In Darkest Cuba,* Columbia, 1922, p. 30.
[98] Francis B. Simkins, *The Tillman Movement in South Carolina,* Durham, 1926, p. 162.
[99] Ambrose E. Gonzales, *In Darkest Cuba,* p. 30.

Publishing Company which he organized and of which he retained control until he sold it to James A. Hoyt in 1909.[100] It will soon attain second place in longevity among all Columbia newspapers.

The weekly *Carolina Free Press* was founded in 1930 by Ben. E. Adams who continues as its editor and publisher.[101]

The long roster of Columbia newspapermen lists many who earned distinction in journalism and sometimes in other fields.

Among those in the ante-bellum period were: David J. McCord, one of the early reporters of the decisions of the higher State Courts; A. S. Johnson, author of "Memoirs of a Nullifier";[102] A. G. Summer, once editor of the *South Carolina Agriculturist;*[103] Edwin De Leon, Confederate and United States diplomat, author; Dr. Robert W. Gibbes, physician, scientist, historian, member of the South Carolina College faculty, surgeon general of the State during the war for Southern independence,[104] president of the Press Association of the Confederate States,[105] who, when denied the right to attend and report a session of the city council and ejected forcibly from the council chamber, established that right in court and so won a noteworthy victory for the freedom of the press;[106] James H. Hammond, Governor, United States senator, one of the foremost American political figures of his day.

In the war and reconstruction eras Columbia newspapers were served by several distinguished men. Henry Timrod, the poet, joined the staff of the *South Carolinian* as associate editor in 1864,[107] wrote stirring editorials[108] until the paper was destroyed in the burning of Columbia.[109] William Gilmore Simms was the first editor of the *Phoenix.* A caustic editorial about General Hartwell, commander of the Federal army department, caused his arrest, but the latter was so charmed by the gifted South Carolinian that he dismissed the case and had Simms as his dinner guest. Afterward the general remarked that, if Simms were a specimen of the South Carolina gentleman, he would never again enter into a tilt with one of them,

[100] George R. Koester to the author, November 30, 1935.
[101] *Carolina Free Press* (Columbia), November 15, 1935.
[102] E. J. Scott, *Random Recollections,* p. 155.
[103] *The Carolina Times* (Columbia), May 8, 1856.
[104] Robert Lathan, *Proceedings of the Thirty-Seventh Annual Meeting of the South Carolina Press Association, 1911,* n. p., p. 35.
[105] *The Daily South Carolinian,* April 19, 1864.
[106] Arney R. Childs, *Robert Wilson Gibbes,* pp. 21-25.
[107] *Tri-Weekly South Carolinian,* January 13, 1864.
[108] Henry T. Thompson, *Henry Timrod, Laureate of the Confederacy,* Columbia, 1928, p. 36.
[109] *Ibid.,* p. 38.

because "he out-talked me, out-drank me, and very clearly and politely showed me that I lacked respect for the aged." [110] F. G. De Fontaine was a celebrated war correspondent under the nom de plume "Personne" before he edited the *South Carolinian*.[111] Charles P. Pelham, once a member of the South Carolina College faculty, an editor whose service began before the war and extended through reconstruction, after his death was lauded by the South Carolina Press Association in a resolution which declared that "his thoroughly rich and cultivated mind has done much to elevate and refine journalism in the State" and that his "unflinching devotion and untiring zeal contributed . . . much to the success of the recent campaign and the redemption of South Carolina." [112] Colonel James Hoyt, editor of the *Register* in the later '70s, founded the *Baptist Courier,* edited the *Greenville Mountaineer,* and led the prohibition forces of the state.[113] R. Means Davis, famous professor of history in the South Carolina College and in the University of South Carolina, wrote a bit for the *Phoenix* when it was on its last legs and later contributed editorials to the *Register*.[114] Julian A. Selby, founder of the *Phoenix,* who devoted many years to publishing, possessed "comprehension of all the multifarious details which are met with in his Sisyphean task." [115] W. H. McCaw, after editing the second *South Carolinian,* rapidly added to his reputation by his correspondence for the Charleston *News and Courier*,[116] but soon afterward was burned to death in his office.[117] Miles B. McSweeney, later Governor, worked on the *Phoenix*.[118] John P. Thomas, founder of the second *South Carolinian,* served successively as superintendent of three military schools, the Arsenal Academy, the Carolina Military Institute, and The Citadel.[119]

One of the ablest groups in the annals of local journalism consisted of the managers and correspondents of the Columbia Bureau of the *News and Courier* which was regarded as "almost as

[110] Julian A. Selby, *Memorabilia,* Columbia, 1905, pp. 24-25.
[111] Henry T. Thompson, *Henry Timrod, Laureate of the Confederacy,* Columbia, 1928, pp. 36-37.
[112] *Minutes of the South Carolina Press Association from 1877 to 1888,* Newberry, 1903, p. 14.
[113] J. C. Garlington, *Men of the Time,* Spartanburg, 1902, pp. 212-14.
[114] Prof. Henry C. Davis, memorandum to author, 1935.
[115] William L. King, *The Newspaper Press of Charleston, S. C.,* p. 156.
[116] R. Means Davis to Sallie E. LeConte, July 20, 1873.
[117] *Ibid.,* March 28, 1874.
[118] Carlyle McKinley, Centennial Edition of the *News and Courier,* Charleston, 1903, p. 29.
[119] John P. Thomas, *The History of the South Carolina Military Academy,* Charleston, 1893, pp. 331, 527.

much a Columbia paper as a Charleston publication." [120] Among them
were Carlyle McKinley, later a brilliant *News and Courier* editorial
writer, poet, author; N. G. Gonzales and J. C. Hemphill, who were to
become nationally known editors;[121] Matthew F. Tighe, who, "though
on an opposition newspaper, frequently scored beats on inside Reform party news," [122] and, as a Washington reporter for the *New
York Journal* scooped the world on the news of Dewey's victory at
Manila Bay in the Spanish-American War;[123] August Kohn, one of
the most capable and prolific reporters and correspondents the Palmetto State has known, whose long service was marked by a series
of extraordinary journalistic achievements.[124]

Three brothers stand out among Columbia newspapermen of the
last half century: N. G., Ambrose E., and William E. Gonzales.
The first, a master of militant journalism for the common good,
"never sold the truth to serve the hour." An editor probably un-
rivalled in all the two centuries of South Carolina newspapers for
vigor, courage, and force, he was a martyr to the cause of the freedom of the press. Ambrose Gonzales, termed "altogether . . . the
most important and greatest South Carolinian since Hampton," [125]
aided substantially in upbuilding South Carolina, did more to encourage developments of its own literature than any other man, and
in his Gullah stories made enduring contribution to American letters.
William E. Gonzales, editor of *The State* for a generation, served
in the Wilson administrations as ambassador to Cuba and Peru.

The narrow limits of this article exclude mention of the numerous
Columbia newspapermen of note who are still living.

Other noteworthy newspapermen of the period were Paul M.
Brice of the *Columbia Record,* "one of the strongest and most
vigorous editorial writers;" [126] John S. Reynolds, uncommonly able
editorial writer for *The State,* who made the supreme sacrifice in
action in France; James Henry Rice, Jr., editor of the short-lived
Evening News, whose work was characterized by great charm and
felicity of style; J. Wilson Gibbes, probably the most efficient clerk
the South Carolina House of Representatives has ever had, origi-
nator of the Legislative Manual, useful annual compendium of

[120] Paul M. Brice, Centennial Edition of the *News and Courier,* Charleston, 1893, p. 26.
[121] *Ibid.*
[122] George R. Koester to the author, November 30, 1935.
[123] Newspaper tradition.
[124] Paul M. Brice, Centennial Edition of the *News and Courier,* p. 26.
[125] W. W. Ball, *The State That Forgot,* Indianapolis, 1932, p. 138.
[126] Elbert H. Aull, *Proceedings of the Thirty-Sixth Annual Meeting of the
South Carolina Press Association,* 1910, n. p., p. 59.

information about the State Government; E. J. Watson, afterward Commissioner of Agriculture, Immigration, and Labor, who was by himself "the reportorial staff of *The State* in its earlier years," who had "a prodigious capacity for work and frequently turned out more local copy than the average staff of 2 or 3 men would accomplish;" [127] William Banks of *The State* and the *Record,* an adept in writing stories full of human interest and color; W. W. Price, *Journal and Register* reporter, "afterward very successful as a Washington newspaperman," [128] who taught the press corps of the national capital a new and highly effective method of gathering White House news;[129] Dr. Stanhope Sams, editorial writer on *The State,* ripe scholar whose knowledge was veritably encylopedic; and Robert E. Gonzales, whose brilliant editorial paragraphs won national recognition, who, while in his country's service on the Mexican border died in 1916, "ending at 28 an earthly career so full of achievement that its promise was immeasurable." [130] He was the brightest star of his generation of South Carolina newspapermen.

LIST OF COLUMBIA NEWSPAPERS

This list is incomplete and doubtless inaccurate in some particulars. In many cases the dates merely indicate the first or last copy found, and not necessarily the dates which begin or end the period of publication. The author is deeply indebted to John P. Thomas, Jr., for use of his manuscript list of Columbia newspapers which has been freely utilized.

Abbreviations after titles of papers: w, weekly; sw, semi-weekly; swdl, semi-weekly during legislative session; tw, tri-weekly; d, daily; ddl, daily during legislative session.

Title	Editor	Period of Publication
Columbia Gazette	Robert Haswell(?)	1791
The South Carolina Gazette (w)	Daniel Constable	1792–94
The Columbia Gazette	Wm. P. Young(?) Daniel Faust(?)	} 1794–
State Gazette (w, swdl)	" "	1795
The South-Carolina State Gazette and General Advertiser (w, swdl)		1795–99
The South-Carolina Gazette and Columbia Advertiser	Daniel Faust(?)	1799–01
The South-Carolina State Gazette and Columbian Advertiser	Daniel and J. J. Faust	1800–16

---

[127] George R. Koester to the author, November 30, 1935.
[128] *Ibid.*
[129] Editorial, *Greenville News,* n. d.
[130] Ambrose E. Gonzales in *Poems and Paragraphs by Robert Elliott Gonzales,* Columbia, 1918, p. 3.

Title	Editor	Period of Publication
State Gazette and Columbian Advertiser	Daniel Faust(?)	1811–19
South Carolina State Gazette and Columbian Advertiser (w, swdl)	Daniel Faust (?)	1818–2–
South Carolina State Gazette and Columbia Advertiser	Daniel Faust(?) Sarah A. Faust(?)	} 182—30
The Telescope (w, swdl)	Thomas W. Lorrain William Cline and Hines David W. Sims(?)	
Columbia Telescope	A. S. Johnston D. J. McCord	} 1815–45?
Carolina Telegraph (w)	David P. Hillhouse(?)	1816–18
Southern Times (w, sw)	S. J. McMorris	
Southern Times and State Gazette (w, sw, ddl)	J. H. Hammond Samuel Weir	} 1830–38
Southern Times and South Carolina State Gazette	John Ramsay Davis	
Southern Times and Democrat		1831–32
Columbia Free Press and Hive (w)	Abner Landrum	1831–3–
The South Carolinian (w, sw, tw, d)	A. H. Pemberton A. G. Summer B. R. Carroll	
Columbia Banner (w)	W. B. Johnston R. W. Gibbes	} 1832–65
Portfolio (w)	Franklin Gaillard F. G. DeFontaine Henry Timrod	
The Southern Chronicle (w, d)	Samuel Weir H. Raiford E. H. Britton	} 1840–48
Temperance Advocate		
South Carolina Temperance Advocate and Register of Agriculture and General Literature	John G. Bowman William Martin Julius J. DuBose E. J. Arthur	} 1840–54
South Carolina Temperance Advocate		
Palmetto State Banner	I. C. Morgan John G. Bowman E. J. Arthur(?) R. W. Gibbes	} 1846–52
Columbia Daily Commercial Herald	I. C. Morgan(?)	1847–
The Telegraph (d, tw)	Edward Sill John Stubbs(?) Edwin De Leon W. B. Carlisle	} 1847–51
The Southern Light		1849
Carolina Times (d, w, tw)	James H. Giles E. H. Britton(?) John G. Bowman	} 1850–60
The States Rights Republican	James C. Carroll	1851
Commercial Transcript (d, tw)	S. Olin Talley	1851
The New Era	J. H. Curtis(?)	1856
The New Daily		1857
The Southern Guardian (w, tw, d)	E. H. Britton(?) Charles P. Pelham	} 1858–65
The Columbia Bulletin	E. H. Britton(?)	1859

Title	Editor	Period of Publication
Daily Legislative Reporter	E. H. Britton	
Daily American Patriot	E. H. Britton(?)	
Columbia Phoenix (w, d, tw)	Wm. Gilmore Simms W. B. Johnston Frank Elmore John P. Thomas	} 1865–76
Weekly Gleaner (w)	W. H. McCaw Charles P. Pelham H. Judge Moore	
Southern Guardian	W. H. McCaw	186 –
The Carolina Times		1866
Columbia Daily Union (d, w)	L. Cass Carpenter	1869–73
The South Carolinian	John P. Thomas W. H. McCaw	} 1872–73
Daily Evening Herald (d)	E. C. Northrop E. W. Everson	} 1873
Daily Union Herald	James G. Thompson Walter R. Jones(?) L. Cass Carpenter	} 1873–76
Daily Sun		
Columbia Register (w, tw, d)	H. N. Emlyn Charles P. Pelham Jos. Daniel Pope J. W. R. Pope J. P. Thomas C. M. Douglas R. Means Davis Charles A. Calvo, Jr. C. A. G. Jackson T. Larry Gantt George R. Koester Thomas Addison John S. Reynolds	} 1875–98
The Palmetto Yeoman	H. Judge Moore	1878–84
The Daily Record (d)	Arthur C. Moore John S. Reynolds Fitz Hugh McMaster O. N. Flanders A. M. Clayton(?)	} 1885–93
The State (d)	N. G. Gonzales A. E. Gonzales W. W. Ball W. E. Gonzales	} 1891+
The Evening Journal	John G. Capers John S. Reynolds W. W. Ball	} 1893–94
The Evening News	James Henry Rice, Jr.	1895–96
The Columbia Record (d)	George R. Koester Paul M. Brice James A. Hoyt James H. Moore William Banks R. Charlton Wright Fitz Hugh McMaster G. A. Buchanan, Jr.	} 1897+
The South Carolina Gazette (w)	Walter E. Duncan	1925–30
The Carolina Free Press (w)	Ben E. Adams	1930+

SOCIETY

By Mary Reynolds Forbes

IN A CITY carved from a plantation, as Columbia was, there is not an immediate arising of any formal society. There was no doubt a continuance of customs that prevailed in this sparsely settled part of the back-country. But the new capital leaped to life. By 1790 there was a village with the State House near enough to completion to allow the constitutional convention to meet there.[1] And inevitably there was the village neighborliness from which grows what is called society.

By 1791 there were formal events, as witness the dinner in the State House for President Washington, with more than a hundred and fifty guests. This banquet shared a condition common to all early American parties which women of today can but look upon with envy: the overwhelming stag line—perhaps a hundred men to fifty or sixty ladies.[2]

Presidents did not drop in every day, and the village grew peacefully on. By 1802 there were two hundred houses and ten or twelve stores, so whatever else was lacking in amusements, there was shopping; and there were visits by traders of the up-country who did not care to go on to Charleston.[3]

In a town of this character, those connected with state institutions formed an important element of life. The South Carolina College, opened in 1805, brought to the city as members of the faculty men valuable socially and intellectually.

In 1805, Edward Hooker, a young instructor down from Connecticut, wrote of customs here. With New England conscience he noted with satisfaction that women's dresses were not so immodestly cut as those of Northern fashionables.

> Ruffles are more in use, both at the bosom and the hands . . . Vehicles are peculiar in their construction . . . Chairs designed for horse—most of them without any spring . . . All made without tops and furnished in very plain manner . . . cost about one hundred dollars. The harnesses are made in corresponding style. I don't believe there is a top chaise or a silver-plated harness in the whole town.[4]

---

[1] A. S. Salley, *President Washington's Tour Through South Carolina*, Columbia, 1932, p. 26.

[2] Washington's *Diary*, Boston, 1925, May 23, 1791.

[3] F. A. Michaux, *Travels*, London, 1805, pp. 327-328.

[4] "Diary of Edward Hooker, 1805-1808," *Report of Historical Manuscripts Commission for 1897*, J. Franklin Jamieson, ed., p. 856.

One doubts that young Hooker took any Columbia girls, for all their modest dress, to drive in such vehicles, for there was no room for chaperones.

Simple and plain, ordinary life must have been in the young capital on the Congaree; that is, in between grand affairs like balls and dinners for visitors and commencement festivities. Early Columbia, even its best circles, ate peas with a knife. Good reason there was for this: the new-fangled two and three-tined "split spoons",[5] ancestors of today's array of forks for everything from oysters to ice cream, which had entered society here in the early 1800's, were scant help to sturdy appetites.

Of course there were no steam engines, no telegraph, no telephone; travel was by stage coach and boat. Business and social communications were hand-written notes. There were no buggies, only high two-wheeled gigs and sulkies. Water, even in the town, was from pumps at widely scattered locations. There was no kerosene and no matches.[6]

But if customs were simple, hospitality was generous.[7]

A critical, not to say catty, British visitor in 1828, entertained at a dinner and a military ball here in February of that year, says the Yeomanry and the Volunteers wore their uniforms with colonial gaucherie. The ladies had the appearance of wearing "cast-off finery . . . such fabrications of silver muslin and tinsel, such feathers and flowers, it would require the pen of a poet or the pencil of a painter to do justice to it."[8]

This visitor, complaining that she found the American woman too much the housekeeper and not the cultivated hostess, did not consider that Columbia women were many months from Paris and London, many weeks from New York, and many days from Charleston, their own style center. "Cast-off finery" was doubtless treasured from year to year for lack of facilities for obtaining new material.

In 1825, a gallant Frenchman saw the Lafayette ball as "distinguished for the beauty of the ladies and the good taste which presided over the arrangements."[9]

[5] Edwin J. Scott, *Random Recollections of a Long Life, 1806-1876,* Columbia, 1884, p. 33; Mrs. Basil Hall, *The Aristocratic Journey,* Una Pope, ed., New York, 1831, p. 208.
[6] Scott, *Random Recollections,* p. 33.
[7] Mrs. Hall, *Aristocratic Journey,* p. 208, "The people here are very hospitable which is indeed the character of all the Southern States. The Coopers wished us to make their house our home and Chancellor de Saussure sent his carriage for me this morning to make what use I pleased of it the whole day."
[8] *Ibid.,* p. 209.
[9] A. Levasseur, *Lafayette in America,* New York, 1829, II, 51.

On the occasion of the ball for Captain and Mrs. Hall, much of the best society of Columbia was in Charleston for the races.[10] There was racing in Charleston, in Augusta, in Camden and later in Columbia. Gentlemen and horses were inseparably associated in this section. "To maintain his character as a gentleman", says Scott of a man wealthy but socially an upstart, "he kept racehorses and made a match of four heats for $5,000.00 or $10,000.00 a side . . . at Augusta. He went to Augusta in a coach and four." [11] Of racing here at a somewhat later date, Selby says: "Columbia formerly had one of the finest race tracks, or two I might say—the Columbia Jockey Club, a portion of the present Epworth grounds, and Hampton's . . . on the South Carolina Railroad, a few miles below the town. Such names as Hampton, Singleton, and the other gentlemen of like ilk managed the racing. Some of the finest stock in the country would run there." [12]

Mrs. Hall could hardly have found fault with the finery of a certain Columbia dandy of that day. He wore

> a bottle green cassimere coatee, buff Marseillese vest, loose pantaloons of finest white linen [direct sartorial ancestor of Columbia's white linen and cotton-clad males of today in summer], with a ruffled shirt, a bell-crowned beaver hat, and around his neck a black silk Barcelona handkerchief showing a double bow-knot in front. On his feet white silk socks and low-quartered pumps.[13]

Ladies then wore for best dresses, gowns of black silk, and of changeable silks, white with blue, yellow or pink. White dresses were of muslin or cambric. Bombazine and bombazette, light weight silk and silk-and-worsted materials, in dark colors were popular. Canton crepe in black or white with wide floral borders at the skirt's edge made an effective fashion, as witness a male observer's comment: "To my eye the black Canton crepe, which clung close to the body, on a tall, well-shaped woman, was the most becoming garment ever worn." [14] Fashions in a century have changed mightily, men but little!

From the racing, the four-horse coach and the richness of attire, it is seen that life was steadily becoming more elegant in the state capital. Visitors reported delightful and in some cases lavish entertainment among Columbia's leading families. A German professor in 1844 found his stay something to write home about: "Dined with

---

[10] Mrs. Hall, *Aristicratic Journey,* p. 210.
[11] Scott, *Random Recollections,* p. 23.
[12] Julian A. Selby, *Memorabilia and Anecdotal Reminiscences of Columbia, South Carolina . . . ",* Columbia, 1905, pp. 132-133.
[13] Scott, *Random Recollections,* p. 40.
[14] *Ibid.,* p. 80.

an agreeable party at the house of Colonel P. [Preston]. After dinner
we had a very interesting conversation on Shakespeare and the
Greek tragedians." [15] Daniel Webster in 1847 found Colonel Hampton's "establishment very handsome, and his family very well educated and agreeable."[16] This Colonel Wade Hampton, second of that
illustrious name, was active in political as well as military life. Following a vigorous campaign in behalf of Governor William Aiken
(1844-46), Colonel Hampton gave at Millwood what Governor
B. F. Perry termed "the most elegant and elaborate entertainment"
he ever witnessed anywhere.

> When we reached the avenue leading from the public road to his house,
> we saw on both sides of it, huge lighted torches of pine, making the road
> as bright as if it were mid-day. The supper was most luxurious and very
> handsomely decorated. The ladies were all young and beautiful and
> dressed with a taste and elegance which I never saw surpassed in Wash-
> ington, New York or Boston." [17]

This is a far cry from the split spoons and the brave but dowdy
ladies as recorded by Mrs. Basil Hall's sharp pen and acid ink.

Columbia, having early become a college town, its social customs
have been affected by the mingling of Town and Gown. Commencement at the South Carolina College, in the early days held on the first
Monday in December,[18] included a grand procession of state and
academic officials, the supreme court and the legislature, a great
deal of oratory, and a commencement ball.[19] This commencement
ball, on the evening of graduation day, was at first danced in the
State House. Boys being boys, and students even more so, an Act
of 1814 forbade the use of the building for this purpose on account
of danger to the building and records.[20] Before the War of Secession,
a young lady was not considered "out" in society until she had attended the grand commencement ball.[21]

Professors at the university and other educational institutions in
the city, together with their families, have formed a nucleus of intellectual and cultivated people. In 1857 when Joseph LeConte came
to the then South Carolina College, he found in Columbia what he

[15] Extract from letter of Fred von Raumer, University of Berlin, May 13, 1844.
[16] Extract from letter of Daniel Webster, May, 1847.
[17] B. F. Perry, *Reminiscences of Public Men,* Greenville, 1889, p. 110.
[18] Edwin L. Green, *A Short History of the University of South Carolina,* Columbia, 1816, p. 206.
[19] Mrs. A. I. Robertson, "Columbia, A Short History", *The New South,* Nashville, Tennessee, 1889, p. 45.
[20] Green, *History of the University of South Carolina,* p. 209.
[21] Mrs. Robertson, "Columbia", p. 45.

described as the most cultivated and refined society he had ever known.[22]

Into the midst of this agreeable society varying from the baronial to the academic, came the war that ended forever the social system built up through two hundred years and more of life in Southern states and colonies.

War struck Columbia quickly and hard. Here the Secession Convention brought its fever heat of state pride. Here families saw sons, husbands, and finally father and boys in the 'teens drawn into military service. Here pillage and torch swept. Here those who stayed at home made their contribution to the cause of the Confederacy. Women scraped lint and made bandages for the wounded; and men unable to bear arms organized under the Relief Association to collect supplies for the soldiers.[23]

Pleasures were necessarily simple at this time. All that could be spared in the way of supplies went to the front. That those at home learned to enjoy what was available is shown in this touching little description of Columbia society on a spring day in 1864:

> One of the loveliest walks or rides in Columbia is Sidney Park and its vicinity, about the hour of 5 p. m. Nature is donning herself in her spring attire, the birds make music, the children prattle with their nurses, the young ladies enjoy flirtations with their gallants, and altogether the associations of the place are perfect, save in a single respect, music. Twice a week at least there should be music and twice a week the community should turn out for an airing in the flower-embroidered basin of Sidney Park.[24]

Now, look in on a benefit concert of about the same time to see the courageous citizens of a war-wrecked town enjoying themselves for an hour or two:

> The ladies of Columbia have a peculiar habit of never doing anything unless they do it well. And when we say that the amateur concert last night was, like its predecessor, a great success, it embodies the strongest compliment that can be uttered. The Athenaeum was crowded to overflowing, the body of the hall being a bed of full-blown roses, the aisles a fringe of soldier shrubs. Beauty, wit and fashion, rank and file, stars and bars, the hero in his homely suit of gray, scarred with wounds, and the civilian in his suit of black, all had representatives present, and all alike entered with zest into the rational enjoyment of the evening.[25]

In the spring of 1864 a great barbecue for Confederate troops in Columbia was given. Some 3,000 soldiers were entertained at tables almost large enough to seat a regiment. These tables were decorated

---

[22] Joseph LeConte, *Autobiography,* William Dallam Armes, ed., New York, 1903, p. 172.

[23] Scott, *Random Recollections,* pp. 169-172.

[24] *Daily South Carolinian* (Columbia), April 22, 1864.

[25] *Daily South Carolinian,* April 21, 1864.

View of Sidney Park—1905

with "garlands, wreaths, mottoes and all the et cetera which woman's fancy can conceive and woman's ingenuity execute." [26]

Finally, the weary war was over and even a defeated people welcomed its end. In Columbia people took heart and faced problems of the new day as bravely as they had the years of conflict. There was a natural rebound of cheer at the coming of peace. Dr. LeConte says he never observed such genuine social enjoyment in Columbia as in the years 1866-67. Gatherings were extreme in simplicity. The hostess furnished lemonade and cake, and the young men provided music, usually by a negro fiddler.[27] The good doctor with his kindly outlook saw beauty in the plain homespun gowns that Columbia girls and women wore to these entertainments.[28]

Students at the re-opened South Carolina College and graduates and former students living on the campus in this time of sparse lodging places resulting from the destruction of many homes during the war, also enjoyed Columbia society, writes one of these young men:

> Fresh from a long deprivation of female society we were naturally eager to make the most of our new opportunities . . . Young ladies had . . . undergone a similar isolation and were perhaps as glad to participate in dances as we, and to receive visits and make them . . .

---

[26] *Ibid.*, April 30, 1864.
[27] LeConte, *Autobiography*, p. 236.
[28] *Ibid.*, p. 230.

seldom have any three years (1866-67-68) passed in the history of any
university as full of unalloyed delight. We were all too poor to think
about dress or refreshments. We met simply for the pleasure of being
together. The young ladies were less of social butterflies than they had
ever been at like age. The young men had had an experience that had
made them more manly than is usual at their age; they sometimes talked
sense to girls.[29]

Columbia society, too, was enriched by the addition of a number of
Charleston families who had refugeed here during the bombardment
of "the city," and remained afterwards, "adding much to the charm
of our various social circles." [30]

This breathing spell in the new-found peace was rudely ended by
the horrors of Reconstruction. The years from 1865 to 1876 were
marked by determined efforts of Northern Republicans, backed by
the United States government, to impose an association of the races
entirely repugnant to all ideals of Southern civilization. Carpet-
bagger and scalawag staged the spectacle, hideous to Columbians, of
mingling publicly with negroes and of entertaining them in their
homes.[31]

From the oppression of the white citizens there grew a social organization which was to exert great influence upon the state, first
by its efforts to remedy demoralized social conditions of the Reconstruction era; and, perhaps more important, by bringing together in
Columbia year after year from its founding in 1870 [32] to its quiet
passing out of the picture in 1918, many of the best people from all
sections of the state to enjoy an evening of pleasure. This was the
South Carolina Club.

Its first ball, danced on the evening of November 13, 1870,
from 9:00 to 3:00, made front page copy for even the Charleston
papers:

> It is at least ten years since Columbia has seen so fine a gather-
> ing . . . The great feature of course was the ladies . . . The dancing
> was the usual alternation of quadrille, galop, waltz and lancers . . .
> Supper, McKenzie's best and served in best style. Both larder and
> cellar furnished quotas befitting the occasion; so that all—guests, danc-
> ing, music, supper, wine and management were of the first . . . The
> South Carolina Club is an association designed to embody the best
> elements of society, furnishing yearly a ball which is to take the place
> of the old Commencement balls. This affair demonstrates the success of
> the establishment of a social club . . . on a basis permanent, elevated
> and prospective of many reunions of the elite of our people.

[29] Letter of Charles Woodward Hutson, August 29, 1909, published in Green,
History of the University, pp. 395-402.
[30] *Ibid.,* p. 398.
[31] John S. Reynolds, *Reconstruction in South Carolina, 1865-77,* Columbia,
1905, pp. 501-502.
[32] *The State* (Columbia), October 25, 1917.

A Grand Ball, Just Before the Confederate War

There were about 250 guests.[33]

After the government of the state was restored to its own people, the State Ball was danced in the hall of the House of Representatives, desks being removed and special floor laid for the occasion.[34] The ball became the climax of social activities for the state as a whole. Here distinguished guests were introduced and debutantes presented to South Carolina's best society.

For a few years, 1891-1896 inclusive, the ball was not allowed in the State House.[35] The ball of 1892, held in the old Agricultural Hall,[36] showed much of the glories of society in the nineties, both in the entertainment and in the reporting thereof.[37] Poor the people still were, but they left poverty behind on this evening when the ball was danced amid a setting of rose-colored lights, festoons of moss, and garlands of bunting. Carriages rolled up in long procession and discharged elegantly clothed ladies and gentlemen.

Fortunately this was before the days of dieting; note the supper made up of the following light snack:

> Turkey and cranberry sauce, boned turkey, aspic jelly a la mayonnaise, sandwiches a la Baltimore, crabs, deviled, oysters fried, olives, pickles, celery, oranges, bananas, Malaga grapes, Isabella grapes, wine jelly, charlotte russe, vanilla and chocolate ice cream, meringues,

[33] *Charleston Daily News* (Charleston), November 14, 1870.
[34] *The State,* November 12, 1897.
[35] *Ibid.,* November 1, 1897.
[36] Building on west side Main street, No. 1209. Thompson, *Ousting the Carpetbagger,* Columbia, 1926, p. 82.
[37] *The State,* November 18, 1892.

> chocolate cake, spice cake, raspberry jelly cake, citron cake, pound cake, fancy cakes; coffee, Manzanilla wine and Lewis Roederer champagne.[38]

Small wonder guests lingered two hours at supper,

> Where the popping of bonbon crackers and the Roederer corks replaced the music of the band . . . When spirits were high and wine was low, they returned to the ballroom for the german, which was led most acceptably by Mr. Edwin Grenville Seibels . . . New figures were introduced and the accomplished leader added new laurels to those already won on slippery floors of a hundred ballrooms.

A delightful feature of the ball of 1897, danced in the hall of the House of Representatives, dined and wined in the Senate chamber, was the absence of wallflowers. The ball of 1905 marked the omission of all square dances and the dinner by this time was a mere six-course affair.

In 1917 the State Ball, danced at the Jefferson hotel, while the nation was at war, was dedicated to liberty. Youth on this occasion was preponderantly khaki-clad and fully half the flying feet were booted. A "conservation menu" was served and a military band provided music.

Born from the disturbed conditions following the Confederate war, the South Carolina Club had "joined the years with its chain of entertainments until it . . . reached another great war and added another historical link."

Meanwhile, Columbia men and women were reorganizing their local society along definite lines. In 1884 there was formed the Columbia Club, with John Peter Richardson as first president. Columbia, then a town of 4,000 or 6,000 white inhabitants, had no men's club. The need was apparent,

> for Columbia then, as now, was the meeting place of gentlemen of South Carolina. They came to the Legislature, the Supreme Court, to the State ball and the fair, and to the political conventions, and they were a rarely delightful and accomplished kind of gentlemen—they that flourished in those days and fixed the standards of conduct . . . The older men had been Confederate soldiers (officers most of them).[39]

In the minds of the founders was the thought that a "center might be organized that would tend to preserve and strengthen the best social traditions of the State,"[40] giving to gentlemen of Columbia rooms where they might gather to spend their leisure and extend to friends outside the city and state,

> a cordial if not sumptuous hospitality . . . For it must be borne in mind that the spirit of hospitality was in that day far livelier than

---

[38] Descriptions of this and subsequent State balls, from *The State,* in issues of November 18, 1892, November 12, 1897, October 28, 1905, October 25, 1917.

[39] W. W. Ball, *Constitution of Columbia Club . . .,* Columbia, 1913, pp. 6-7.

[40] *Ibid.,* p. 6.

the means to manifest it . . . Perhaps it would not be going too far to
say that the forming of the club was a natural sequel of the winning
back of the State from aliens . . . by the strong and good men who had
learned to know and trust one another as only men who have suffered
for a common cause and triumphed.[41]

After several moves, the Columbia Club obtained, in 1887, rooms
in the DesPortes building,[42] southwest corner Main and Hampton
streets. It was here that the club grew up, and

gained its character as a South Carolina institution, where the splendid
old men of a generation that has almost vanished, found a home in
Columbia, and where a group of brilliant and noble spirits, with story
and jest created an atmosphere that survives and makes the Columbia
Club the honored institution that it is.[43]

There was a non-resident membership of influential citizens of
the state. Later the club moved into the "skyscraper" (National
Loan and Exchange Bank Building). Like the
South Carolina Club it served to knit city and
state together, as well as providing rare and
charming entertainment to the ladies of the
city.[44] Like the South Carolina Club, too, it
seemed to have served its purpose largely in
the day before the World War. This war, like
the War of Secession, worked a social up-
heaval, and after it many old institutions
passed away, the Columbia Club among them.

A club for men opened September 1, 1935,
in the Jerome hotel, bearing the same name as
this older club, and carrying on its lists some,
at least, of those who knew the old Columbia
Club.[45]

*Loan and Exchange
Bank Building. One-
time Home of Co-
lumbia Club*

Responsibility for preserving the social
amenities was not left to gentlemen of Columbia alone. In 1889, a group of women organized the Assembly, its purpose to set up and
maintain a standard of dignity and graciousness in Columbia society.[46] The balls of the Assembly, though its membership has grown
from less than fifty to about 125, have been kept as private as possible. There is no such thing as "crashing" the Assembly. Formerly
young women attending its balls always went with chaperones. Card
dancing is still its custom.

[41] *Ibid.*, p. 8.
[42] *Ibid.*, p. 11.
[43] W. W. Ball, *Columbia Club, Historical Sketch*, pp. 11-12.
[44] *The State*, February 15, 1893.
[45] *The State*, September 2, 1935.

In early days members of the Assembly prepared the supper at home and sent it to the hall. Gallons of coffee were made by a member gifted in coffee-making; a brand new wash-tub of chicken salad made by the combined efforts of cooks and members; and a punch bowl of sorts. On one occasion, it is related, the mixers of punch, seeking to be decorative, painted the tub from which the liquid refreshment was to be served. As spirits and paint mingled only too well, male guests became strangely shy of the festive bowl that night.

But simplicity, wooden tubs and homemade suppers never kept the Assembly balls from achieving a special dignity and charm all their own. For a while two balls were given each year, one in the fall, usually in the State House; one in the spring, at Clark's Hall. Since the discontinuance of the State Ball, the annual Assembly given in early December has become the social event of first rank, where Columbia girls are formally introduced to society.

The Assembly, now setting a beautiful table, uses its own silver. The ball of 1917 was marked by the presence of military guests and by the absence of supper. Funds which would have furnished refreshments bought Liberty bonds. Later when these matured, the money was used to purchase silver. Of this service, the handsome tray is engraved with the names of the charter members. Mrs. Mary Preston was the first president. The Assembly ball is now usually held at the Jefferson Hotel.

Not to be outdone by the feminine contingent, a group of Columbia gentlemen in 1890 organized the Cotillion Club.[47] This club, which originally gave four dances a year, sent out engraved invitations and had the best music to be obtained. The dances were first held at Clark's Hall, and some have been held at Craven Hall.[48] The club now gives two dances a season.

This club, like the Assembly, is conservative. When the "new

[46] Information about the Assembly from Mrs. Allen Jones, Mrs. J. M. Bell, Major Arthur Metts, in conversations during October and November, 1935. Also incidentally from other members earlier, Mrs. T. T. Talley, and the late Mrs. Albert R. Heyward, Sr. Further information from a sketch by Leonie D. Harvin published in Columbia Record, January, 1927, and various newspaper accounts in The State and The Record.

[47] Data furnished by Joseph M. Bell, now and for many years Secy.-Treas. of Columbia Cotillion Club.

[48] Clark's Hall, on present site of Central Union Bank Building. Craven Hall, a large dancing hall at the rear of the Berkeley apartments on south side of 1300 block of Washington Street.

dances" under such weird names as "bunny-hug," and the like appeared in Columbia about the second decade of the twentieth century both these clubs held out for the old dances and admitted the new only when they had tamed to a proper degree of respectability. The Cotillion club now has a membership of two hundred and it, too, is difficult to "crash." It has given many beautiful balls, and the champagne served at its post-repeal dances is only a part of its sparkle in Columbia society.

From the early eighties until about 1910 was the famed horse-and-buggy era. Young Columbians, following the Confederate war, were entirely too poor to have horses and buggies; but there were livery stables, and few were the sweet courtings of that day not speeded up by a Sunday drive in a hired rig, vulgarly but truthfully termed the "hug-me-tight."

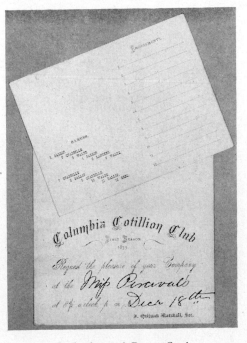

Invitation and Dance Card,
In First Season of the Club

Other amusements were Sunday school picnics with caravans of wagons filled with shouting children; strawrides on moonlight nights to the old canal locks, and bicycle rides. Excited the shirt-waist girl, in wide Gibson straw hat, plump rounded pompadour, who went riding on a tandem affair. The scuppernong arbor on Mr. John Sloan's farm was a popular resort for cyclists and buggy-riders, particularly in the fall when free refreshment could be secured fresh from the vines.

There were, too, candy-pullings, spelling-matches, and charades. There were romantic young college boys who serenaded town girls and girls at the College for Women. These latter could not acknowledge by speech the presence of singers, but they had a system of lighting matches in the windows for signals that made serenades as full of heart interest as the warmer "dates" of today.[49]

The trolley-car age overlapped the horse-and-buggy era. The electric car line to Shandon opened in 1894, the Belt Line a year later.[50] At Shandon was a wooden pavilion where on all summer Friday evenings were held the Shandon dances of fond recollections. There was Pinckney's band on the platform, long rows of benches around the wall, and a fine array of chaperones.

It was an unhappy young girl of this age who did not have a pressing engagement every Friday afternoon in summer, to make smooth and ready her beruffled flowered muslin or her blue lawn shirtwaist and stiffly starched white duck skirt; and in the evening catch the Shandon car either in company with her beau (girls had "beaux" then, not "dates") or her father. After an evening of wild two-stepping and slow waltzing, the dances ended at eleven o'clock. Even those who went with chaperones were usually allowed to return on the trolley, provided they would promise not to get off on Main street for an ice cream soda at Thomas' drugstore.[51]

Other evenings, girls, young matrons, parents and children rode "around the belt," a circuit made by the trolley through Main street, out through the wilds of Waverly and Shandon and back again, all for five cents.

In this age, declares a man who was in the thick of it himself, a boy could ask a girl to walk to a college dance, carrying her slippers in a bag; could take her to Shandon dances on the trolley, could get by with a "hack" for some of the Clark's hall dances; but the Assembly and the State Ball rated a "slam-door." [52]

Now, the slam-door was a closed, two-horse carriage, the driver outside, similar to old family carriages of elegance. Almost no one in Columbia owned one after the war. Livery stables kept them for funerals, weddings, state occasions at the University, and for the big balls. Often two young men shared a carriage for an occasion, but deepest devotion was indicated by providing a whole slam-door for one couple.

---

[49] Information on these informal amusements of the day obtained from varied sources, letters of R. Means Davis; recollections of H. C. Davis; from Mrs. J. M. Bell, from Mrs. Berrien Brooks, and others, and from personal recollections.

[50] *The State,* March 8, 1894, May, 1895.

[51] Personal recollections of Mrs. J. M. Bell.

[52] Hack, a one-horse public conveyance, carrying four, or in emergency, five passengers. Usually driven by negroes. Price 25c a trip. There were no telephones, so one usually got word to his favorite hack-driver by walking uptown the day before the hack-ride was needed, and finding the driver at his regular hack-stand at some particular corner.

While men played whist at their clubs, women and girls played euchre. Euchre clubs that met weekly flourished. And there was also creeping in that strange thing known as the woman's club.

There had always been church societies for women, among them the Ladies' Benevolent Society, founded in 1832;[53] and the Society for Orphan and Destitute Female Children, organized in 1839,[54] both still functioning. Historic and patriotic societies had also arisen; but this movement was a new creature—women's clubs.

In 1896 five or six young girls formed the Book Club;[55] in 1901 a group of young married women organized the New Century Club,[56] the oldest of the literary clubs in the city affiliated with the State Federation of Women's Clubs. These were forerunners of an almost uncounted array of women's clubs. More literary and reading clubs, civic clubs, clubs for sociological study, home and garden clubs, music clubs, drama clubs, and others sprang up. About this time the telephone came into common use. Without it one doubts that the woman's club as a general and active movement could have been sustained!

The Woman's Club, founded in 1923, embodies the broad principle that any woman of good character wishing to affiliate with a club may join this and under one or more of its various departments develop her special interests.[57]

A branch of the Junior League, nationally organized groups of girls and young matrons drawn from that portion of young American womanhood prepared by education, social and cultural background to help the less fortunate, entered the field in Columbia in 1923, also.

A charter group of twenty-five young women has expanded to one hundred twenty, who on a regularly planned schedule of hours of work, render co-operation with the city's organized welfare agencies.[58]

Other clubs which hold high rank in Columbia's social life are bridge clubs and golf clubs. Bridge whist, brought home by adventurers to Northern cities and summer resorts between 1900 and 1905, spread like wildfire. Classes were set up and clubs formed. Through changes to auction and contract, the popularity of the game persists, and bridge clubs today, formal and informal

[53] *Columbia Record,* December 7, 1935.

[54] Original minutes of the society, furnished by Mrs. H. C. Davis, Secretary.

[55] Data supplied by Mrs. Jos. M. Bell, long a member.

[56] From program of the New Century Club, 1935-36, and from original minutes of the club.

[57] Data furnished by Mrs. Fletcher Spigner, one-time president.

[58] Data furnished by Mrs. Burwell Manning, who as Katherine Heath, was one of the organizers of the Junior League here.

gatherings of players of both sexes, form an important part of the
social fabric.

Following the trolley-car age, arrived very noisily and a bit
haltingly, the automobile age. Daring souls had the strange machines
almost at the turn of the century. Buck McMaster was a pioneer,
and the writer remembers yet the gathering about midnight of
practically the entire population of the 1400 block of Pendleton
street to see if his new automobile could be made to go on up the
hill where it had stalled half-way, and was making terrific noises.
The kindly Miss Alice Sloan and her witty sister, Miss Ponie,
came out to hold a kerosene lamp for him, and men put their
shoulders to the wheel and pushed.

The coming of the motor car brought the day of the country club.
Columbia's first country club was Ridgewood, on the hills to the
north of the city, and at the end of a trolley line. The clubhouse
was opened November 1, 1904.[59] Only men were members of this
club, the main attraction of which was the golf course. Women
were invited to dances and receptions held here, and later were
admitted to privileges of membership.

Forest Lake country club, fed by no trolley line, was possible
only after the automobile became common. This club, a few miles
to the east of the city, opened about twenty years later than Ridgewood, offers a lake for water sports in addition to golf.

Fraternal organizations have long played a part in the life of
Columbia. Even before there was Columbia, there was in 1785 a
chapter of Ancient York Masons at Saxe-Gotha.[60] This was the
first lodge hereabouts and became Richland No. 39 after the Ancient
York and the "modern" or Free and Accepted Masons in South
Carolina united.[61] This lodge, with a membership of about 250,
is not only the oldest but also the largest in the city. It owns and
occupies the large building on Lady and Sumter streets, where it
holds its own meetings and also houses the office of the Grand
Secretary of the South Carolina Grand Lodge.

Other lodges added more men to Masonic ranks in Columbia.
These are Acacia No. 94, founded in 1859, Pacific, No. 325, in
1919; Columbia No. 326 in 1919, and Eau Claire No. 344 in 1925.[62]

The Independent Order of Odd Fellows has been in Columbia
since May 18, 1842, and now has three lodges, Palmetto, Congaree

[59] *The State*, November 2, 1904.
[60] Albert G. Mackey, *History of Freemasonry in South Carolina*, Columbia,
1861, p. 152.
[61] *Ibid.*, pp. 256-257.
[62] Information furnished by the Grand Secretary, November, 1935.

and Wade Hampton, and the woman's organization, the Re-bekahs.[63]

Myrtle Lodge, No. 3, of the Knights of Pythias was founded in Columbia in 1882, and is the oldest existing lodge of this order in the state.[64]

The Benevolent and Protective Order of Elks came to Columbia shortly after 1900. The Columbia Lodge of this order now owns and uses for its meetings and other activities, a large house on Hampton street.

The fraternal spirit on which these and other similar organizations in Columbia is based, has been exemplified again and again in the life of the city. Shortly after the Confederate War, according to minutes of Acacia Lodge No. 94, Masons from several Northern lodges were elected to honorary membership in that lodge in appreciation of their "true Masonic spirit in their presentation to Columbia No. 108 (Richland No. 39) meeting in the same lodge rooms, a beautiful set of officers' jewels in behalf of their respective lodges." [65]

Rather definitely the World War did something to Columbia society. While it lasted all attention was concentrated on the conflict. It was a unifying and democratizing influence. People of all classes worked in patriotic drives together, in the American Red Cross and in the Women's Service League and other organizations for soldier welfare.

Homes and clubs were wide open to soldiers at Camp Jackson and others passing through the city. The Community Club, in its rooms in the building on the northeast corner of Main and Taylor streets, fed thousands of soldiers, probably dispensed millions of meals. Churches and non-denominational agencies co-operated.

The streets were thronged with khaki-clad men. Great parades thrilled citizens who lined the streets by thousands to see them.

Girls were in much demand. Groups formed to promote social welfare of service men both in Columbia and at the cantonment, were constantly giving entertainments, parties of all sorts, and carloads of girls, truck-loads of them, were transported to the camp and to various halls in the city almost every evening. Girls for the soldiers! Girls and eats! These were the cries that went up.

---

[63] Certificate of membership of Edwin DeLeon, on July 8, 1842, in possession of Mrs. Julian Hennig.

[64] Data supplied by Alva M. Lumpkin.

[65] Original of resolution and reply in Grand Secretary's office, Columbia.

Natural result, pretty weddings with uniformed grooms and sparkling-eyed brides marching under crossed swords. Many Columbia girls were carried to other parts of the country by marriages with men who came to Camp Jackson. Also Columbia gained a number of valuable citizens who married here or who just liked it here anyhow.

Of course, not all our girls found soldier husbands. There is the classic example of a Columbia mother with several daughters who remarked that Camp Jackson took a lot of girls, to be sure, but ninety thousand soldiers passed her girls up.

After the war came the same rebound of society as noted at the close of the Confederate War, a mad resurgency of joy and a determination to get all the pleasure possible out of life. After the World War, too, there was prosperity, the means to spread a little. Here, as all over America, people felt the same expanding influence. The usual institutions of dance and country club, of social and literary groups continued, but scarcely one did not take on added frills. The automobile came more and more to have a place in social life. The craze (here it amounted to that) for swimming in ponds in and out of town, was perhaps one of the most wholesome developments of the time. An afternoon swim became almost necessary to the happiness of the young, the middle-aged, and a few brave elderly ones.

Social life, too, at the University, took on new features. Co-eds, already there since the early nineties, increased in numbers and in influence. A girls' dancing club was added to the old German club. Fraternities returned, sororities came in, both bringing added social activities.

Back about 1820 Edwin Scott recorded that it took about five and a half yards of cloth to make a woman's dress.[66] A century later it took two yards, perhaps, for a tall girl, two and a half. The peak of the amazing short-skirt fashion was reached about 1928 and 1929. Limbs had become legs, knees something to have pretty dimples in, not to pray on.

National prohibition brought changes in, rather than the abolition of drinking customs. The hip-flask in the automobile, at the dance, at the football game took the place of or was added to the custom of social drinking as practiced in many Columbia homes throughout the 150 years of the city's life.

Of the 1930's there is little comment that can be made now. The economic situation of these years has brought trials and changes

---

[66] *Random Recollections,* p. 80.

again. Shrinking incomes have forced simpler entertaining. The loss of wealth by some, the reduction to real poverty by others has lined up our people on a similar battlefront to that after the Confederate War, the battle of genteel poverty. This struggle has been for the most part bravely met, and 1936 finds the people facing better days, and perhaps somewhat the wiser for their experiences of the past fifteen years.

In the brief compass of this one chapter no attempt has been made to list all social, fraternal and patriotic organizations that have existed or now exist in the city. Rather, the intention has been to show the place and influence of typical organizations in and on the city's social life.

Columbia, with an estimated population of city and suburbs of about 60,000 to 70,000, is not the close-knit body socially it was in the eighties and nineties, or even in the 1900's. It is a society of diverse interests. It is honeycombed with organizations, circle within circle, overlapping circles, a society based of course somewhat on the old idea of ancestry, more on a general rule of good breeding, and rather slightly influenced by wealth. A society that welcomes outsiders of congenial mind; and yet from year to year seems to revive more and more of its old traditions of social life.

FAMOUS VISITORS TO COLUMBIA

By Elizabeth Finley Moore

MANY visitors have come to Columbia; they have admired her broad tree-shaded streets, her beautiful public buildings, her charming homes and have enjoyed the generous hospitality of her citizens.

One of the first and most famous visitors to Columbia was George Washington, who, while President, made a tour of the South in 1791. To quote from his diary, entry for Sunday, May 22: "Beyond Granby 4 miles I was met by sevl. Gentlemen of that place & Wynnsborough; and on the banks of the River on the W. side by a number of others, who escorted me to Columbia."

There is no doubt but that President Washington was escorted to the capital in the best style the little town could afford and that he was given the most comfortable place to stay but it is not known at what house he was entertained while here, as the writers of reminiscences of early Columbia are silent on the subject and it is quite certain that the house is not still standing, the business section of that day having been totally destroyed by Sherman's army in 1865.[1] In his diary President Washington gives the following account of the entertainment given him while in Columbia: "Monday, May 23rd, Dined at a public dinner in the State house with a number of Gentlemen & Ladies of the Town of Columbia & Country round about to the amt. of more than 150, of which 50 or 60 were of the latter."

Of the dinner Henderson has this to say:

> On Monday, 23rd, the President held a huge reception at noon—to accomodate the very large number of gentlemen of Columbia, Granby, Winnsborough, Camden, Statesburgh, Bellville, Orangeburgh, and their vicinity who had assembled to pay him their respects. After this fatiguing ceremony was over, the President was conducted to the Assembly Room of the Representatives in the State House, where were assembled "sixty ladies who upon his entering the room arose and made an elegant appearance, to whom he was individually introduced. The ladies were then led by the gentlemen (there being present 153) to the Senate Room, where they sat down together in a well conceived arrangement to a farmer's dinner, where plenty abounded, and from the satisfaction visibly expressed on each countenance it is but just to conclude, that concord and true hilarity presided!" Memorable among the toasts were; one to

---

[1] A. S. Salley, Bulletins of the Historical Commission of South Carolina, No. 12, *President Washington's Tour Through South Carolina in 1791*, Columbia, 1932, p. 26.

the National Assembly; . . . one to the memory of Justice Henry
Pendleton, through whose vigorous efforts the capital of South Carolina
had been removed from Charleston to Columbia; one to Miss Assumption;
. . . and—most extraordinary and comical of all—one likening Washington to a gorgeous flower!

To continue: "At eight O'clock that evening, the President returned
to the Assembly Room, where a grand ball was held which lasted
until eleven o'clock."[2] The President has this further to say of Columbia in his diary:

> Tuesday, May 24th. The condition of my foundered horse obliged me
> to remain at this place, contrary to my intention, this day also. Columbia
> is laid out upon a large scale; but in my opinion, had better been placed
> on the River below the falls.—It is now an uncleared wood, with very
> few houses in it, and those all wooden ones.—The State House (which
> is also of wood) is a large and commodious building, but unfinished.—
> The Town is on dry, but cannot be called high ground, and though
> surrounded by Piney and Sandy land is, itself good. The State House
> is near two miles from the River, at the confluence of the Broad and
> Saluda. . . .[3]

Dr. F. A. Michaux, a visitor to Columbia in early days, writes:

> Columbia . . . has been built fifteen or eighteen years. . . .
> The number of its houses does not exceed two hundred. They are almost
> all constructed of planks, and painted grey or yellow; and although there
> are very few of them raised more than two stories, on the whole they
> have a very agreeable appearance.[4]

From Edward Hooker's diary, 1805-1808, we get a picture of the
little town with perhaps the first description of the trees which have
always been a distinguishing feature of Columbia.

> Monday, Nov. 11th.—The Township of Columbia is not large; being
> two miles square. This territory is laid out into lots and streets; but not
> more than one third of the streets are yet opened; and of those which are
> opened, several have not more than two or three buildings, upon them.
> The State House is placed on an eminence directly in the center of the
> township, though very far from the center of the buildings. . . .
> Richardson Street and some others are lined in part, with a beautiful
> tree called the Pride of India. In some few places a native pine is left
> standing, though they are every day diminishing in number. . . .
> Around the State House are left standing some lofty forest oaks which
> afford a grateful shade and give the scenery a rural and charming cast.[5]

In 1824 Lafayette came at the invitation of the United States
government to visit America; his tour was one series of ovations and

[2] Archibald Henderson, *Washington's Southern Tour, 1791*, Boston and
New York, 1923, pp. 254-257.
[3] A. S. Salley, Bull. 12, Historical Commission of S. C., p. 26.
[4] *Columbia, South Carolina, Chronicle and Comments*, 1786-1913, Published
by the Columbia Chamber of Commerce upon the Occasion of the Meeting of
the American Historical Association, December 31, 1913, p. 6.
[5] *Ibid.*, pp. 7-8.

it was March, 1825, before he reached South Carolina. Great preparations were made to entertain the distinguished guest in Columbia and the legislature made a handsome appropriation to defray the expenses of a proper reception. The city was crowded; visitors poured in from all over the state and hotels and private homes were filled to overflowing.[6] The students at the South Carolina college were given a week's holiday and a reception was held on the campus.[7] Columbia was gaily decorated; Main Street was spanned with arches of evergreens and flowers; on one of these arches was displayed a banner on which was written in letters of gold "Lafayette, DeKalb, Pulaski,"[8] and another arch was ornamented with yellow flannel balls resembling oranges, as Lafayette was a native of Orange in the south of France.[9]

One of Columbia's patriotic citizens, Richard O'Neale, loaned the city 1,800 bales of cotton to be used in decoration. These bales were piled into pyramids at the intersection of Main and the principal streets.[10] Mr. O'Neale was a marshal in

GENERAL LA FAYETTE was born at Auvergne, in France, in the year 1757. At the age of 19, he embarked in a ship furnished at his own expense, and arrived in America, in January, 1777, to join in the glorious contest for LIBERTY in the colonies of America. He entered the American army as a volunteer, and on the 31st of July, same year, he was commissioned a Major General. He was in many battles—At Brandywine, when wounded, he refused to quit the field of battle. The American army being in want, this distinguished patriot supplied it from his private purse to the amount of 10,000 dollars, at one time, for clothing. He continued in the service until the war closed—saw our Independence sealed, and our country free and happy. In 1784 he embarked for France, loaded with honours and the gratitude of the American people. Throughout his illustrious life, he has been the constant advocate of LIBERTY and the RIGHTS OF MAN. Having lately expressed a wish to visit America once more, and this fact having reached the Congress of the United States, that body in 1824, unanimously passed a resolution inviting him to our shores, and offering a national vessel for his conveyance, but he declined this honour, and arrived in the ship Cadmus, Captain Allyn, on Sunday, the 15th of August, accompanied by his son George Washington La Fayette.   1824.

Badge Worn by Officials upon Occasion of Lafayette's Visit to Columbia

[6] Dr. Maurice A. Moore, *Reminiscences of York,* Yorkville, S. C., n. d., p. 64.
[7] *The State,* "At the University," January 26, 1913.
[8] A. Levasseur, *Lafayette in America,* N. Y., 1929, II, 51.
[9] *The State,* March 25, 1901.
[10] Authority of Mrs. A. S. Gaillard, Columbia, October 18, 1935.

the parade that day and wore a badge of narrow white satin ribbon with a picture of the hero and the inscription, "Welcome Lafayette, The Nation's Guest," printed upon it. That bit of faded ribbon is today treasured by Mr. O'Neale's decendants.[11]

Lafayette came to Columbia from Camden, being escorted by a brigade of horse under General Bradley of Chester.[12] About a mile out of Columbia the military companies were halted and Governor R. I. Manning with his staff [13] waited to receive the gallant Frenchman. William C. Preston as chief aid to Governor Manning, had been assigned command of the military escort sent ahead to receive Lafayette at the North Carolina line and conduct him to Columbia.[14]

When Lafayette appeared he was greeted by shouts and cries of welcome. He was handed into an elegant open barouche, attended by servants in livery. By the hero's side rode Colonel Thomas Taylor, himself a Revolutionary hero—both uncovered. The military display was imposing. Among the companies was one under Captain Meyer (Mayer) of Newberry, who had 125 men, each one mounted on a white horse and all handsomely uniformed and caparisoned. Afterward this company had the special honor of escorting Lafayette from Columbia to Charleston.[15] As the procession moved toward the city it was greeted by glad hurrahs from the crowds of people who lined the way. Lafayette, beaming with pleasure, bowed low again and again from side to side. After the procession had passed down Main Street it halted at Main and Gervais; here the Mayor made his speech of welcome, the orator of the day delivered his address; and the military companies dismounting, the men formed a double line down Gervais Street to the house of Isaac Randolph (Rudolph) which had been fitted up for the use of Lefayette while he was in Columbia. Cut glass and silver in profusion had been loaned for use on this momentous occasion and generous citizens had sent their most accomplished house servants to attend the guest. To Francis K. Huger, in recognition of his efforts to free Lafayette from imprisonment at Olmutz, was accorded the honor of walking by Lafayette's side down this living avenue of soldiers to his temporary residence.[16]

---

[11] *Ibid.*

[12] Moore, *Reminiscences of York*, p. 66.

[13] On Governor Manning's staff were Col. Wade Hampton, Capt. Franklin Elmore and others. *The State,* March 25, 1901.

[14] Minnie Clare Yarborough, *The Reminiscences of William C. Preston,* Chapel Hill, 1933, p. 61.

[15] Moore, *Reminiscences of York,* p. 66.

[16] *Ibid.,* p. 66.

"Little girls,[17] in holiday attire threw bouquets under his feet, thus literally strewing his path with flowers. Behind him came the dignitaries of state and city, two and two, arm in arm, a most imposing spectacle." [18] At this point an amusing incident occurred. At a cross street some mischievous boy threw in an old gander; there was no outlet for the intruder between the ranks of soldiers and so he led the procession poking out his neck from side to side and stopping now and then to give a hiss at the men. Dr. James Davis and Professor Henry Nott who had been assigned the duty of going about twenty paces in front to clear the path could only wait his movements, now and then venturing a mild "shew! shew!" and giving a gentle flourish with their hats. The gander would give a "quaw! quaw!" in return not improving his pace at all and so he led the way to the end of the line.[19]

At the Randolph house Lafayette held a reception and here a touching incident occured. An old African, neatly dressed, came to the front door and started in but was stopped by the guards. Brushing them aside, he came straight up to Lafayette and asked him if he knew who he was, to which Lafayette replied: "Yes, stop, don't tell me your name. Ah! I have it. Pompey,[20] belonging to Colonel Buchanan, the first servant who waited on me when I came to America."

The kindly Frenchman then called for a glass of champagne with Pompey which that worthy took with great dignity and then saying goodbye he went out, mounted his pony and started for his home near Winnsboro.[21]

Governor Manning addressed Lafayette in the presence of the people "in the place where the Congress of South Carolina hold their sessions and the evening as well as the morning was devoted to public rejoicings." [22] On the 12th a grand ball was held, according to one narrator, in the basement of the State House.[23] Levasseur

[17] Sarah Briggs, Elizabeth Clark, Gabriella DeSaussure, Katherine Hampton, Sarah Taylor, Jane Wallace and Grace Anne Sternes are names of some of the young girls who strewed flowers in Lafayette's path. This is given on family tradition of the first six named and for the last named see Selby's *Memorabilia*, p. 124.
[18] Moore, *Reminiscences of York*, p. 66.
[19] *Ibid.*, p. 66.
[20] Pompey's name was really Fortune. He was servant to Capt. John Buchanan of Winnsboro, who gave the old negro a piece of land as reward for his services. This land, about one mile from Winnsboro has recently been made into a recreational park called "Fortune Spring Park." Authority Mr. Fitz Hugh McMaster, November 27, 1935.
[21] Moore, *Reminiscences of York*, p. 68.
[22] Levasseur, *Lafayette in America*, N. Y., 1929, II, 51.
[23] E. J. Scott, *Random Recollections of a Long Life*, Columbia, 1884, p. 137. Also *The State*, November 18, 1931.

records that the ball was "much distinguished by the beauty of the
ladies who attended it and by the good taste which presided over the
arrangements." Owing to the uncertainty of travel in that day, the
invitation to the ball which was dated March 1, said by way of post
script: "It is expected General Lafayette will be in Columbia about
the 12th inst." [24]

One of the young ladies presented to Lafayette wore a miniature
of her father on a ribbon around her neck.[25] When she was presented
to Lafayette he recognized the picture as that of Major Cadwallader

House in which Lafayette was Guest

Jones, aide de camp on his staff during the Revolution, and he kissed
the daughter of his old friend on both cheeks in true French fashion.
It was said the young lady was afterwards loath to apply soap and
water to the sacred spot.[26]

There is in the Clearwater Collection of Early American Silver
in the Metropolitan Museum of Art, New York, a beautiful silver
map case which was presented to Lafayette while in Columbia
March 11-14, 1825. It bears on one side the following inscription:
"Presented by Richard I. Manning, Governor of South Carolina, In

[24] *The State,* March 13, 1932.
[25] This was Mrs. Allen Jones Green, daughter of Maj. Cadwallader Jones,
aide de camp to Lafayette.
[26] Col. Cadwallader Jones, *A Geneological History,* Columbia, 1900.

the name of the State, to General LaFayette, whilst at Columbia in
March 1825. In tracing your route through our Territory every in-
habited spot will recall to your memory the devotion and affection
of a grateful people."[27]

In 1827 Captain Basil Hall, a retired English naval officer, came
to America accompanied by his wife. Captain Hall travelled for
fourteen months in the United States and later published a book,
"Travels in North America." [28] The Halls came to South Carolina
in February, 1828, spending two days in Columbia. Captain Hall
makes his observations of life in America "in a tolerant and kindly
manner." [29] Mrs. Hall, however, was not as sympathetic or appreciative as her husband. While in America she wrote a series of
letters to her sister, Jane, back home in Edinburgh, and with no
thought of their ever being published she described men and manners
as they appeared to an elegant lady of fashion placed suddenly in
a society for which she had no preparation and for which she
showed little sympathy or understanding.

> February 22:—It was our intention to have set out today for Charles-
> ton, and we were actually packed and ready, but it occurred to us early
> this morning that we were running away from the capital of the state
> with rather too little ceremony, and that we ought to bestow another
> day upon it. This has been the most perfectly beautiful day that I have
> seen for months, serene and clear with a bright, warm sun. We went by
> appointment at ten o'clock to call at Dr. Cooper's, the President of the
> College; . . . the Coopers wished us to make their house our home
> and Chancellor de Saussure sent his carriage to me. . . . After
> sitting an hour with Dr. and Mrs. Cooper, they took us to see the College
> and the Lunatic Asylum, which is just finished, but is yet untenanted.
> . . . We were asked to dine at the Governor's, Mr. Taylor's, to a
> military ball by some officers, and to a party at Judge de Saussure's. All
> this we were resolved to accomplish as well as we could. To the dinner
> we went at half past four. . . . I was fortunately well placed next
> an exceedingly agreeable old man, Judge de Saussure, a most gentleman-
> like person. On the other side I had one of the young ladies of the
> house, for ladies in America have a vile custom of crowding all together
> at dinner tables and leave the gentlemen likewise to herd by themselves.
> We had neither tea nor coffee after dinner, and at seven o'clock went
> off to the ball, but if the dinner was queer, what was the ball! . . .
> An hour of this was, you will believe, enough, and we were glad to
> exchange the ball for a party at Judge de Saussure's where I had as
> tough an argument regarding slavery with some ladies as ever Basil had

[27] Letter to the writer containing the above inscription from Jos. E. Hart,
Jr., assistant librarian, Columbia University Library, March, 1935. Mr. Hart
copied the inscription from the map case on exhibit in the museum at that date.
[28] Basil Hall, *Travels in North America,* 1830, III, 133-34.
[29] J. Rion McKissick, "Some Observations of Travelers in South Carolina,
1800-1860," *The Proceedings of the South Carolina Historical Association 1932,*
Columbia, 1932, p. 46.

on any subject with gentlemen, and by ten o'clock we were at home. . . . We crossed the Congaree River this evening on leaving Columbia by a covered bridge which is not yet finished overhead.[30]

Mrs. Anne Royall was perhaps one of the earliest women journalists to visit Columbia. Travelling from the north through the south in the spring of 1831 she spent two days in Columbia and was shown so much attention and kindness by the citizens that she regretted she could not stay longer.[31] She stopped at the United States Hotel which she described as being handsomely furnished and well conducted. "From Boston to Columbia I never saw a more splendidly furnished tavern. . . . More costly or more highly finished furniture I never at any time saw in a public house, and it is the first time I ever found the owner and house equally matched, and a third remark is no less due, the barkeeper was equally accomplished." [32] She appears disappointed that Dr. Thomas Cooper did not call upon her; she writes: "doubtless he was better employed . . . it might be he is a woman hater." She evidently did not even see Dr. Cooper—"but I saw his poney, next thing to himself; it was saddled and bridled, about the size of a stout goat."

Mrs. Royall's visitors consisted entirely of gentlemen for she writes:

> I saw no ladies, I suspect they were at church. . . . I was however, sufficiently honored and highly gratified in Columbia; the hospitality and kindness I received there was not surpassed by any town in the south, though by association I was more attached to Camden. . . . The Lunatic Asylum is superior to anything of the kind. It leaves that of Philadelphia a long way behind for beauty and convenience and one, if not the handsomest buildings in the United States except the U. S. Bank at Philadelphia, and cost $100,000. . . . The bridge over the Congaree is very handsome, and cost $86,000, the workmanship is very fine. . . Columbia is a very flourishing town, and one of the handsomest in the United States; and the citizens are industrious, polite and hospitable.[33]

In May, 1847, Daniel Webster came to Columbia and was extensively entertained as shown by his letters written while he was here; he gives a pleasing picture of the capital city:

> The situations and the town are very beautiful. The College was established 40 or 50 years ago and is flourishing; here is the seat of

---

[30] Mrs. Basil Hall, *The Aristocratic Journey, Being the Outspoken Letters of Mrs. Basil Hall Written During a Fourteen Months Sojourn in America, 1827-1828.* Prefaced and edited by Una Pope Hennessy, New York, 1931, pp. 207-210.

[31] Mrs. Anne Royall, *Southern Tour or Second Series of the Black Book,* Washington, 1831, II, 57.

[32] *Ibid.,* p. 57.

[33] *Ibid.,* pp. 62-64.

government, and here sit the principle courts. Great care was taken early
to plant ornamental trees in the squares and along the streets, so that
the town is now one of the handsomest and nicest looking of our little
inland cities. It contains, I suppose, five or six thousand people. . . .

We arrived last evening by railroad, at six o'clock, and were received
with all kinds and degrees of hospitality. The college buildings were
illuminated in the evening, and the boys made a torchlight procession
through the college campus or square. Mrs. Preston had a little party.
The governor and all the judges, and the people of the town and the
professors, etc., all present. . . .

Today we all go to dine at Col. Hampton's, he not being at home;
but his daughters doing honors of the house. He has a great and profitable cotton plantation. We mean to go over it, and examine it, and
see exactly what a cotton plantation is. Tomorrow we dine with the
governor, Mr. Johnson. Here, of course, is Dr. Leiber, and here we
meet Mr. and Mrs. Poinsett. . . .[34]

While in Columbia Mr. Webster addressed the Euphradian Literary
Society of the South Carolina College, of which he had been elected
an honorary member, and the story goes that the student who introduced the distinguished guest made a better speech than did the
famous statesman.[35]

A fine picture of the capital city in ante-bellum days is given by
A. K. McClure, the publisher, writing in 1886:

Columbia was the favored city of the South before the War. It was
the special pride of South Carolina and South Carolina was the special
pride of the whole Southern Sentiment.

It was a vast village of old-time planters' houses, with their heart-
some shades, large verandas, wide halls, climbing flowers and vines, and
with the live-oak to cool the streets and the ever-blossoming magnolia to
perfume the atmosphere. Its broad avenues, excepting on one short business street, are almost forests of green shade in summer, and winter is
softened into our Northern spring.[36]

The great number of handsome homes in Columbia in ante-bellum
times were often scenes of lavish hospitality and brilliant entertainments. One of these was the Hall-Hampton-Preston mansion still
standing on Blanding Street, its beautiful gardens covering a city
block. To quote: "Some of those entertained in the Preston home

[34] Columbia, S. C., *Chronicle and Comments,* 1786-1913. Published by the
Columbia Chamber of Commerce upon the Occasion of the Meeting of the
American Historical Association, December 31, 1913, pp. 10-11.

[35] This is told by Dr. D. D. Wallace of Wofford College, described to him
by Dr. Carlisle, a student and a member of the Euphradian Society at the
time of Webster's visit. *The Clariosophic and Euphradian Societies, 1806-
1931, 125th Anniversary Celebration,* Columbia, 1931, p. 42.

[36] A. K. McClure, *The South, Its Industrial, Financial and Political Condition* (Philadelphia 1886), p. 40. Columbia, S. C., *Chronicle and Comments,*
1786-1913, Columbia, 1913, pp. 16-17.

were Winfield Scott, Daniel Webster, Henry Clay, Millard Fillmore and Franklin Pierce." [37]

When a young man, traveling abroad 1817-1819, William C. Preston, later United States Senator and President of the South Carolina College, met Washington Irving and a warm friendship sprang up between them. In 1832 Washington Irving visited Preston in Columbia.[38]

Dr. Robert W. Gibbes of Columbia was identified with the great scientists of his day, Agassiz, Audubon, Morten, etc. One of Audubon's letters tells of an evening spent in Dr. Gibbes' home and it is believed that Agassiz obtained many of his specimens from the collection of Dr. Gibbes.[39]

From the pen of James Burrill Angell, the distinguished president of the University of Michigan, we have an account of a visit paid to Columbia in 1850. Young Angell and his friend Rowland Hazard, who was travelling south for his health's sake, came on horseback to Columbia and as the legislature was in session, they found it hard to secure lodgings, but finally were received at a boarding house.

> The next day being Sunday, we had the good fortune to hear Rev. Dr. Thornwell, one of the most distinguished preachers in the South, deliver the baccalaureate sermon to the graduating class of the University of South Carolina. It was a discourse of great power. On the next day we attended the commencement exercises. The governor (Seabrook), the President of the Senate, the Speaker of the House, and a group of prominent citizens occupied the stage. . . .
> We thought the students' speeches only moderately good. The President's address to them was solely an appeal to them to abide by the State in the dissolution of the Union which he regarded as inevitable. He exhorted them to fight and conquer or fall beneath the Palmetto banner. Several of the students' speeches referred to the secession of the State as certain to come. . . . It will be remembered that this was nearly nine years before the attack on Fort Sumter.[40]

In May, 1858, General John A. Quitman came to Columbia to address the Palmetto Association (the survivors of the famous Palmetto regiment) at their anniversary meeting. General Quitman was proud of the regiment and it was closely associated with his own career. He arrived May 3rd and was met at the railroad station by the entire population of the city and was welcomed by

[37] H. K. Leiding, *Historic Homes of South Carolina,* Philadelphia and London, 1921, p. 264.
[38] M. C. Yarborough, ed., *Reminiscences of W. C. Preston,* Chapel Hill, 1933, pp. 32, 134.
[39] A. R. Childs, *Robert Wilson Gibbes, 1809-1866,* Columbia, n. d., pp. 14-15.
[40] J. B. Angell, *The Reminiscences of James B. Angell,* N. Y., 1912, p. 55.

Captain W. B. Stanley, chairman of the committee and himself a gallant soldier, as "the general of their pride, affection and veneration." General Quitman was entertained at the home of his friend Colonel A. J. Green; on the 4th he was escorted to College Hall by a large parade composed of the military and civil organizations of the city, the students and faculty of the college and the Palmetto Association, sixty-eight in number. The battle flags of Fairfield, Chester and Newberry companies were borne in the procession and placed on the platform in College Hall. The opening prayer was made by Dr. Thornwell, two odes, "Welcome to the Chief" by W. Gilmore Simms, and another written for the occasion by H. H. Caldwell, were sung in full choir and General Quitman delivered his address before a large audience.[41] At the grand ball and supper given that night one of the table ornaments was a model of the Castle of Chapultepec, "which was attacked and demolished in a shorter time than the Palmetto and New York regiments did the original; the other eatables suffered a similar fate." [42]

Secession was the talk of the hour and patriotism was at high tide in 1860 when a group of college students from the north spent a month's vacation in South Carolina in the spring of that year.[43] Twenty-four years later, E. G. Mason, one of the group, recalls the experiences of that visit, with appreciation of the courtesy shown to him and his friends. However, he observes, "South Carolinians feel themselves to be vastly superior to the citizens of other states and their self confidence is boundless." [44]

Young Mason and his party attended the state convention in the State House; visited Millwood, the beautiful country home of Wade Hampton, and spent much time at the University of South Carolina.

> We met many bright and agreeable young fellows, and enjoyed their society exceedingly, save that we wearied of the talk about secession. . . . They had recently resolved to show their patriotism by wearing clothing made of South Carolina fabrics, and the sudden demand had severely taxed the limited manufacturing resources of the State. A small supply of shoddy blue cloth, woven at one mill for the use of the poor whites in its neighborhood, was exhausted before one quarter of the students had been supplied, and the rest went to the most reckless extreme.
>
> The only other dry goods actually manufactured in the State were some cheap and gaudy calicoes, intended for negro wear; and of these the crazy youngsters ordered whole suits of clothes. The effect was actually astounding. Here would go one youth, striped like a barber's

---

[41] J. F. H. Claiborne, *Life and Correspondence of John A. Quitman,* N. Y., 1860, II, 277-283.

[42] J. A. Selby, *Memorabilia,* Columbia, 1905, p. 81.

[43] E. G. Mason, "A Visit to South Carolina in 1860," *Atlantic Monthly,* February, 1884.

[44] *Ibid.*

pole, and glowing like a meteor in his fiery red and yellow garb; there, another, completely covered with bright green leaves upon an intensely blue ground; yonder, two abreast, clad in patterns of gigantic vines and flowers; then a whole company, arrayed from head to foot in the most startling colors, diversified with the most singular figures. . . .[45]

When the President of the Confederacy came to Columbia in 1864, the following account appeared in a local paper:

> President Davis arrived in this city yesterday morning on his way to Richmond, and was during the day the guest of General Chestnut. . . . The hospitalities of the city were tendered to the President by our worthy Mayor, Dr. Goodwin, in a brief and appropriate speech, whereupon Mr. Davis, in response to the evident desire of the large assemblage, made an excellent address.[46]

General R. E. Lee passed through Columbia on the train March 30, 1870. His brief stop here was the inspiration of a tender little poem written by Dr. Henry Mazyck Clarkson, a native Columbian. It is called "Lee's Welcome" and is included in Dr. Clarkson's published works.[47]

September 22, 1868, a committee of citizens consisting of Wade Hampton, Jos. Daniel Pope, F. W. McMaster and W. B. Stanley wrote a letter to John Quincy Adams of Boston urging him in strong terms to come to Columbia and address a mass meeting. Mr. Adams accepted the invitation and came; he spoke in Carolina Hall to a large gathering of people and was frequently applauded.[48]

The following are his closing remarks:

> I am deeply and seriously impressed with the difficulties under which you labor and the dangers which threaten our system of government. I have spoken seriously because I felt seriously. Whatever shall come of it, I shall feel amply rewarded if, by any chance, I may have turned one heart to a calm, patient, earnest, honest effort to forward, so far as in it lies, the restoration of the Constitution and the Union.[49]

During the stirring days of Reconstruction there were visitors to Columbia who came to help the citizens rescue the state from Radical rule. One of these was General John B. Gordon who came in 1876 to aid his friend Wade Hampton in his race for governor. The story goes that a reception was given the General at Wright's Hotel and that the dashing officer kissed all the pretty girls who came.[50]

---

[45] *Ibid.*
[46] *Tri-Weekly South Carolinian,* Columbia, October 6, 1864.
[47] Dr. Henry M. Clarkson, *Songs of Love and War,* Manassas, Va., 1898, p. 89.
[48] *The Phoenix,* Columbia, October 11, 1868.
[49] *Ibid.,* October 13, 1868.
[50] Authority Miss Harriet Clarkson, Columbia, November, 1935.

It is recalled by a valued resident of Columbia, that Ex-President Rutherford B. Hayes addressed the young ladies of the Winthrop Training School a few years after it had been organized in Columbia in 1886.[51]

Thomas Nelson Page, the Southern author and humorist, pleased a large and representative audience of Columbians when he appeared in the Opera House January 6, 1893, under the auspices of the Y. M. C. A. His recitations were rendered with his usual polished and finished style.[52]

When Susan B. Anthony was in Columbia in February, 1895, a reception was given her by her friends on the afternoon of the 13th and was well attended.[53]

Booker T. Washington spoke at Calvary Baptist Church September 7, 1898.[54] He also paid a visit to Columbia March 15, 1909, and spent the entire day in the city. That evening he addressed an audience of several hundred negroes at the Columbia Theatre, retiring later to the Colonia Hotel, where he conferred with Robert C. Ogden of New York, president of the Southern Conference for Education.[55]

President William McKinley stopped in passing through Columbia December 19, 1898. He made a brief speech from the platform of his train at the Blanding Street station to about four hundred people assembled there to greet him.[56]

Two ladies living in Columbia today recall that about 1895, Mrs. Stonewall Jackson was a visitor in Columbia and was given a morning reception at the home of Mayor and Mrs. T. J. Lipscomb, 930 Richland Street. They were among a group of young girls invited to serve at the reception.[57]

William Jennings Bryan passed through Columbia September 21, 1898, on his way to Washington. When it was known he was at the depot many citizens rushed down to catch a glimpse of the Great Commoner.[58]

In 1900 Mr. Bryan was invited to speak in Columbia and he arrived February 15th. After taking a brief rest at the home of Colonel Wilie Jones, Mr. Bryan was taken to the University of South Carolina and addressed the students in the chapel. The whole

---

[51] Authority Mrs. L. D. Yarborough, Columbia, November, 1935.
[52] *The State,* January 7, 1893.
[53] *Ibid.,* February 14, 1895.
[54] *Ibid.,* September 8, 1898.
[55] *Ibid.,* March 16, 1909.
[56] *The State,* December 20, 1898.
[57] Mrs. Gadsden Shand and Miss Harriett Clarkson, Columbia, November. 1935.
[58] *The State,* September 22, 1898.

audience rose as the great man walked up the aisle and the old chapel rang and rang again with cheers. At one o'clock Mr. Bryan spoke from a stand erected in front of the State House to a great throng of people; special trains had brought many visitors from all parts of the state. The day was ideal, clear and balmy. Lieutenant Governor Scarborough, Speaker Gary and members of the legislature occupied places in the stand. Speaker Gary introduced Mr. Bryan who rose to speak amid deafening cheers.[59]

To quote from a newspaper account: "Without any 'taffying'; not a single reference being made to South Carolina's glorious history, the enthusiasm touch button of every visiting speaker, Mr. Bryan commanded the breathless attention of his great audience of thousands of representative people from start to finish." [60]

As the new Secretary of State in President Wilson's cabinet Mr. Bryan's visit to Columbia in 1913 was of special interest when he delivered his famous lecture "The Signs of the Times" to a large audience, coming under the auspices of the Y. M. C. A.[61]

Theodore Roosevelt attended the South Carolina and West Indian Exposition at Charleston April 8-10, 1902, and on his return trip his train stopped for twenty minutes on the 11th in Columbia at the Union Station, and he spoke from the platform to a crowd of about 5,000 people. He was greeted by Mayor and Mrs. Earle; the college boys cheered and many in the crowd took pictures. Someone sent up to Mr. Roosevelt a box of crabapple blossoms, dogwood and yellow jessamine from the grounds of the old Barhamville school which the President's mother had attended. He was very much pleased by this attention.[62]

Captain Richmond Pearson Hobson, Spanish-American war hero, addressed a large audience at the Columbia Theatre on the evening of October 18, 1906. With the speaker on the stage were the followin: Major Micah Jenkins, General Wilie Jones, and General John D. Frost. General Frost introduced Captain Hobson who spoke upon the American Navy and its glorious achievements.[63]

On November 7, 1906, Captain Hobson again came to Columbia as a speaker at the Missionary Conference held in Trinity Church.[64]

Dr. Charles W. Elliot, retiring president of Harvard, came to Columbia accompanied by Mrs. Eliot, March 19, 1909, as the guest of the University. Acting President A. C. Moore met the guests at

[59] *Ibid.,* February 16, 1900.
[60] *Ibid.,* February 16, 1900.
[61] *Ibid.,* March 2, 1913.
[62] *The Columbia Record,* October 12, 1935.
[63] *The State,* October 19, 1906.
[64] *Ibid.,* November 8, 1906.

the train and conducted them to his home on the campus where they were entertained at luncheon. During the afternoon a drive was made about the city and at 6:30 Dr. and Mrs. George A. Wauchope entertained the distinguished visitors at tea. At 8 o'clock Dr. Eliot addressed a large and appreciative audience in the House of Representatives, the hall being crowded to capacity. During his visit, while making a tour of the State House grounds in company with Dr. J. W. Babcock, a Harvard alumnus, Dr. Eliot paused before the Confederate monument and asked Dr. Babcock to read the inscription to him. After Dr. Babcock had finished, the stirring beauty of those words caused Dr. Eliot to remark: "I have traveled throughout this grand country of ours. Thank God manhood is the same everywhere." [65]

October 24, 1911, Alfred Tennyson Dickens came to Columbia under the auspices of the College for Women and Columbia College and delivered a lecture in the chapel of the former institution on "My Father's Life and Works." Mr. Dickens was introduced by Dr. E. O. Watson and after the lecture members of the audience enjoyed meeting and talking to the oldest living member of the great novelist's family.[66]

For the first time since George Washington's visit in 1791, a President of the United States was entertained in the capital city when President William Howard Taft spent the day of November 6, 1909, in Columbia as the guest of the people of South Carolina.

The program included an address at the Fair Grounds; a ride over the city; a luncheon at the State House and a review of school children and college students on the University campus. It was a gala day and the arrangements for the reception of the President were admirable and adequate. The luncheon began at 3 o'clock. The hall of the House of Representatives had been beautifully and tastefully decorated; the state and national colors were in evidence; the place cards were unusually attractive; ferns and greens were lavishly used and on the tables were American Beauty roses. Seated at the President's table were: Governor Ansel, Chief Justice Ira B. Jones, Senator E. D. Smith, Captain W. E. Gonzales, Dr. S. C. Mitchell, Dr. Samuel M. Smith, Judge W. H. Brawley, Honorable A. F. Lever, Honorable D. E. Finley, Mayor W. S. Reamer, Captain Archibald Butt, the president's aide, and Dr. J. J. Richardson, the president's physician. About three hundred other guests were seated at small tables, which radiated from the President's table like the spokes of

[65] *The State,* March 20, 1909.
[66] *Ibid.,* October 25, 1911.

a wheel. The gallery was filled with ladies, a feature which pleased
Mr. Taft and on which he remarked. The President was introduced
by Governor Martin F. Ansel and the spirit of his greeting was the
spirit of the whole day; the respect, the acknowledgment of the
people in a wholesome manner that South Carolina knows no
political lines in extending a welcome to the President. Mr. Taft's
speech was a very happy one and created quite a favorable impression.[67]

*President Taft, Arriving at Speaker's Stand with Governor Ansel, Mayor
Reamer, Colonel Archie Butt, and Dr. E. M. Whaley (driving) in car
belonging to Mr. E. W. Robertson. Messrs. Edward Finley and
Frank Lever standing immediately behind President Taft*

During his term of office as governor of New Jersey, Woodrow
Wilson was the guest and principal speaker at a meeting of the
South Carolina Press Association in Columbia June 2, 1911.[68]

He was introduced by Mr. August Kohn, retiring president of the
Press Association, as the "Democratic Hope." When Governor
Wilson rose to speak he was enthusiastically cheered and was
frequently interrupted by prolonged applause during his address.

[67] *Ibid.*, November 7, 1909.
[68] *Ibid.*, June 3, 1911.

Seated with Governor Wilson on the stage were about a hundred men of prominence in various circles in the state. The evening's entertainment concluded with a reception in the beautiful gardens of the College for Women where hundreds of lights burned among the trees and rose arbors. Governor Wilson with Miss Euphemia McClintock, president of the college, and other members of the receiving party greeted the guests in the handsome west drawing room but soon all repaired to the cool gardens.[69]

Guests invited to meet Woodrow Wilson, June 2, 1911. Seated, left to right: J. L. Sims, Mayor W. H. Gibbes, Woodrow Wilson, H. L. Watson. Others in the picture: Dr. J. C. Mace, E. H. Aull, James A. Hoyt, August Kohn, G. M. Berry, A. W. Knight, William Banks, Clarence Poe, Ed. DeCamp, Dr. S. C. Mitchell, W. E. Gonzales, W. R. Bradley, Dr. J. J. Watson, Ambrose E. Gonzales, B. F. Taylor, George L. Baker, A. H. Seats, C. O. Hearon, J. L. Mimnaugh, W. D. Melton, Phil D. Kohn, F. N. Brunson, W. F. Caldwell, Robt. L. Lathan, Thomas Waring, J. L. Mims, John J. Earle, B. L. Abney, Dr. J. W. Babcock, R. E. L. Freeman, W. D. Guist. The two boys are August Kohn, Jr., and Theodore Kohn.

The first day of Governor Wilson's visit of two days in Columbia, he delivered the principal address at the laying of the cornerstone of the Y. M. C. A. building on Sumter Street. Several hundred Columbians were present at 6 o'clock when the exercises began. They were under the direction of Mr. T. S. Bryan, president of the association, who welcomed Mr. Wilson back home and referred to him as the next Democratic president. He then introduced Mrs.

---

[69] *Ibid.*, June 3, 1911.

James Woodrow, aunt of Governor Wilson, who had given the site for the building. Mrs. Woodrow laid her hand upon the granite block and it swung into position.[70]

The first speaker was Dr. D. B. Johnson, president of Winthrop College and first president of the Y. M. C. A. Rain interrupted the exercises and they were concluded in the First Baptist Church where Captain W. E. Gonzales introduced Governor Wilson. Mr. Wilson's address was short and impressive; he said he was glad to be in

Boyhood Home of Woodrow Wilson

Columbia and that the site of the new building was a loved spot to him; it was his old playground and the thought brought back sweet memories of his boyhood days.[71]

On Friday June 2, Mr. August Kohn entertained in honor of Governor Wilson with an elegant luncheon at his home on Gervais Street.

At 6 o'clock Friday evening a dinner was given by the Messrs. Gonzales at their home on Senate Street in honor of Governor Wilson, who was their house guest during his visit. A group of prominent men, some of them old schoolmates of the visitor, were invited to meet Governor Wilson.

Besides these formal affairs Mr. Wilson was welcomed informally by many friends in the city. He called upon his aunt, Mrs. James

---

[70] *Ibid.,* June 2, 1911.
[71] *Ibid.,* June 2, 1911.

Woodrow, and upon the McMaster family who were his closest boyhood friends. He was entertained at tea at this hospitable home the evening of his arrival in Columbia.[72]

During his term of office as President of the United States, Mr. Wilson came back to Columbia, September 18, 1916, to attend the funeral of his only sister, Mrs. Annie Josephine Howe, wife of Dr. George Howe.[73]

As the chief speaker in a Founder's Day program at the University of South Carolina, Charles Francis Adams came to Columbia January 16, 1913. President of the Massachusetts Historical Society, direct descendant of two presidents of the United States and himself one of the most distinguished men of his time, Mr. Adams was well qualified to address an audience on the subject " 'Tis Sixty Years Since." He was introduced by Judge W. H. Brawley of Charleston and at the conclusion of his address presented with flowers. Later a smoker was given in Flinn Hall.[74]

Walter Hines Page, then editor of *World's Work,* and later, during the World War ambassador to the Court of St. James, delivered the principal address on Friday January 31, 1913, at the Corn Exposition in Columbia. Friday was National Education Day and Mr. Page made a brief and informal address, laying stress on the value of country life.[75]

The chapel of the University of South Carolina was crowded March 29, 1913, when Dr. George Lyman Kittredge, professor of English at Harvard University, and a rare combination of finished scholar and successful teacher, gave his famous lecture on Macbeth. At the conclusion of the program a smoker was given in Flinn Hall, Professor Reed Smith, with the aid of The Scribes, a literary student organization, acting as host.[76]

Members of the class of 1885 of Yale University came to Columbia in April, 1913, as the guests of E. W. Robertson. On April 9th they gathered together with members of the faculty and students of the University to hear an address by Dr. Wilbur L. Cross, head of the English department at Yale. Others on the program were: Rev. C. L. Corbart, George C. Woodruff and Dr. G. A. Wauchope who introduced Dr. Cross in a short and witty speech. Dr. Cross spoke on "Yale and South Carolina." Afterward a smoker was given in Flinn Hall by Richland County alumni.[77]

---

[72] *Ibid.,* June 3, 1911.
[73] *Ibid.,* September 19, 1916.
[74] *Ibid.,* January 17, 1913.
[75] *Ibid.,* February 1, 1913.
[76] *Ibid.,* March 30, 1913.
[77] *Ibid.,* April 10, 1913.

The American Historical Association met in Charleston in December, 1913, and during the meeting the members came to Columbia for one day's visit.

The feature of the day was a beautiful luncheon in honor of the distinguished guests and at each plate was a copy of a pamphlet "Columbia, South Carolina, Chronicle and Comments 1786-1913" which was published for the occasion by the Columbia Chamber of Commerce. The luncheon with its attractive place cards drew forth this comment from President Dunning of the Association: "You call this a luncheon! I would like to attend a dinner."[78]

The period of the World War brought many persons of note to Columbia. Only a few may be mentioned here. Major General Leonard Wood, commander of the Southeastern department, paid his first official visit to Columbia June 6-7, 1917. The reception of General Wood included a visit at 9 o'clock to the site of Columbia's cantonment, 6 miles east of the city; an address to the negroes of Columbia at Allen University at 12:30; a parade in which thousands participated: military companies, school children, civic organizations, independent military companies and others—the parade ending at the State House where General Wood spoke from the steps. The day ended with a banquet at the Jefferson Hotel.

General Wood expressed himself as being highly pleased with the site chosen for the cantonment.[79]

Major C. E. Kilbourne visited Columbia on July 10, 1917, and inspected the Columbia cantonment. He expressed himself as highly pleased with the progress made. Major Kilbourne had selected the camp site several months before so he was particularly interested in its development.[80]

Newton D. Baker, Secretary of War, came to Columbia December 2, 1917, and reviewed the troops stationed here. Mr. Baker was the guest of Governor R. I. Manning while in the city. He was entertained at luncheon by General Barth and his staff at the camp and in the afternoon made a stirring address to Columbians at the Ideal Theatre.[81]

Many important men and women were brought to Columbia as speakers on Preparedness programs and to assist in Liberty Loan drives. Among these may be mentioned W. J. McAdoo, Charlie

[78] Authority of Mr. A. S. Salley, Columbia, November, 1935.
[79] *The State,* June 7, 8, 1917.
[80] *Ibid.,* July 11, 1917.
[81] *Ibid.,* December 2, 3, 1917.

Chaplin, and Mrs. Anna Shaw, pioneer suffragist and chairman of the Woman's Committee of National Defense.[82]

Will Rogers, America's loved humorist, came to Columbia on two occasions. April 2, 1926, he appeared at the Columbia Theatre with the De Reszke Singers and kept the audience in a continual uproar. He praised Columbia and said that the Carolinas seem to *have* "what California and Florida are advertising." [83] On February 14, 1927, Will Rogers gave a typical performance at the Columbia Theatre, and later addressed the members of the House of Representatives. He was entertained at dinner at Ridgewood Club by a group of *The Columbia Record* staff and others, R. Charlton Wright, editor of *The Record,* being chairman of the committee on arrangements. Will's wit was in rare form that evening at the theatre where he kept a large audience laughing for over two hours, and later poked fun at the members of the House.[84]

Columbia and South Carolina gave a warm welcome to Governor Albert C. Richie of Maryland, when he came to the city March 4th, 1932, to inaugurate local observance of the George Washington Bi-Centennial. He was welcomed at the train by Mayor L. B. Owens, W. Bedford Moore, Jr., chairman of the George Washington Bi-Centennial, Brigadier James C. Dozier, and other state and city officials. He was conducted to the State House where he was welcomed by Governor Blackwood and then he addressed the joint session of the legislature. From the State House he headed a large and colorful parade, given in his honor up Main Street to his hotel. That evening he was the chief speaker at the public celebration in the Columbia Township Auditorium when a pageant especially prepared for the occasion and entitled "Turning Back the Pages of History" was given as a prologue to his address. He was the guest of honor at several private functions, was tendered a luncheon at the Governor's mansion by Governor Blackwood and was honor guest at a special banquet given him at the Jefferson Hotel by citizens of Columbia.[85]

The following is a list of a few of many other visitors to Columbia; lack of time and space prevents more than a mere mention of their names: Richard Burton, George Pearce Baker, Eamon De Valera, John Temple Graves, John W. Davis, James M. Beck, Clarence Darrow, Senator Thos. J. Walsh, James J. Davis, Dr.

---

[82] Recollection of Columbia citizens, November, 1935.
[83] *The State,* April 3, 1926.
[84] *The Columbia Record,* August 17, 1935.
[85] *The State,* March 5, 1932.

Wilfred Grenfel, Marquis James, William Allen White, Governor Harry F. Byrd, Senator Royal S. Copeland, General Charles P. Summeral, Billy Sunday, Aimee Semple McPherson, Huey Long, the flying Mollisons and Amelia Earhart Putnam.[86]

---

[86] Information furnished the writer by citizens of Columbia.

MILITARY ORGANIZATIONS

By John M. Bateman

FROM THE earliest times settlers on the outposts of civilization have found it necessary to familiarize themselves with the use of firearms, for the protection of their families as well as for procuring hides and furs for domestic use and for barter. For mutual assistance they have naturally grouped themselves into bands of a more or less military nature. Such was the case in South Carolina.

On the tenth of May, 1751, Captain John Fairchild of Fairchildsboro, on the north side of the Congaree, wrote the Governor: "It is my duty to inform you that several distressed families have been driven from their habitations and living on the Little Saluda, and have, with great difficulty, retreated down to the Congaree, to escape the Indians . . . our corner of the country is not in a condition to defend itself. . . . We would, therefore, be most thankful to your Excellency for a supply of ammunition and warlike accoutrements; many among us are really poor and distressed—objects of compassion—and not able to purchase them for themselves. Having command of a company on this side of the river, for our better defence, I have divided it into parties, some of whom I keep constantly scouting through the country; while the rest are employed in building a fort." [1]

Among the first settlers on the east side of the Congaree River were Colonel Thomas Taylor and his brothers, Captain James Taylor and John Taylor. When hostilities commenced in the War of the Revolution Thomas Taylor was commissioned colonel of a regiment. John Taylor died in the war. [2] James Taylor raised a company for his brother's regiment. "Their command was composed of their friends with but few exceptions. Captain James Taylor was with his company in Charleston during the siege, and after its surrender went home on parole, under the terms of the capitulation. But when he found that the British authorities were violating those terms . . . he concluded that the British having violated those terms, had virtually relieved him from their obligation. He broke his parole and joined General Sumter. [3]

[1] John H. Logan, *History of the Upper Country of S. C.,* Charleston, 1859, I, 437.
[2] E. L. Green, *History of Richland County,* Columbia, 1932, p. 88.
[3] Joseph Johnson, *Tradition and Reminiscences of the American Revolution,* Charleston, 1851, p. 536.

In the war of 1812 with Great Britain "except the grand finale at New Orleans all the main engagements were along the Canadian border, and there is little that appeals to patriotic ardor or the pride of country until Harrison, Winfield Scott and Andrew Jackson took charge. The state, however, made preparations for invasion. Fortifications were raised in and around Charleston, and such places along the coast as were available for the landing of the enemy were put in a condition for defense and manned with troops." [4] The British made several descents upon the coast, none of which had any effect upon the result of the war. We may be sure that the young town of Columbia, then twenty-six years old, was well represented among the defenders.

Now we come to the organization in Columbia of a militia company with a long and honorable record. The Richland Volunteer Rifle Company was organized August 8, 1813.[5] The first recorded active service of the company was in the campaign against the Seminole Indians, in Florida, over their removal beyond the Mississippi River. The war began in 1835 and lasted nearly eight years. It resulted in the practical expatriation of the tribe at the cost of the lives of nearly 1,500 Americans.[6]

The Richland Volunteer Rifle Company left Columbia February 11, 1836, and marched to Granby where it took passage on the steamer *James Boatright*. The *Boatright* went down the river to the sea, reaching Charleston three days later. At Charleston the only casualty of the campaign occurred. One of the men fell overboard and was drowned. Captain B. F. Elmore was in command. The company was encamped near St. Augustine for several months and returned to Columbia in the early summer of 1837 without having been engaged in battle.[7] Columbians came out of this affair unscathed; not so a few years later when the gates of Janus were again open.

"A high-toned martial spirit has always characterized South Carolina. The great battles of the War of Independence were within her territory. The death of Jasper, the martyrdom of Hayne, the victims of the prison ships, the imprisonment of Laurens, the forays of Tarleton, the enormities of the Tories, the brilliant partisanship of Sumpter, the *coups de main* of Marion, and the patriotic spirit of her daughters, are incidents never to be forgotten. Her habitual chivalry of character may be traced mainly to those glorious recol-

---

[4] Yates Snowden, ed. *History of S. C.,* Chicago and New York, 1920, I, 537.

[5] So claimed and conceded during the life of the company.

[6] F. W. Hodge, ed. *Handbook of American Indians,* Washington, 1910, Pt. 2, pp. 500-501.

[7] J. B. Morrison, *The State* (Columbia), January 20, 1901.

lections. . . . This military spirit had not been extinguished when the war with Mexico commenced." [8]

As the war was seen to be approaching, another of Columbia's famous militia companies was organized. December 19, 1843, the General Assembly of South Carolina granted a charter to the Governor's Guards upon the petition of W. W. Eaton,[9] M. R. Clark, Asher Palmer, James Cooper and Elias Pollock. James D. Tradewell was elected captain.[10]

Upon the outbreak of the war the president called for 50,000 volunteers. One regiment was accepted from South Carolina—the Palmetto Regiment. It was commanded successively by P. M. Butler,[11] J. P. Dickinson and A. H. Gladden.[12] H Company of this regi-

Squad of the Governor's Guards Who Won the Drill for the Barrett Cup, September 28, 1886. Reading from left: Captain Jones, Brennan, Bateman, Berry, Martin, Summers, Boyne, Platt, Southgate

ment was organized of men in and around Columbia of whom, as might be expected, many were from the existing militia companies— Richland Volunteer Rifle Company and Governor's Guards. The officers elected were Wm. Davie DeSaussure,[13] captain; Wm. B. Stanley,[14] first lieutenant; E. W. Moye and M. R. Clark, second lieutenants. Captain DeSaussure was, or had been, captain of the

[8] J. F. H. Claiborne, *Life and Correspondence of John A. Quitman*, New York, 1860, II, 311.
[9] Later U. S. Senator from Connecticut.
[10] Mayor of Columbia, 1857-58.
[11] Governor of South Carolina, 1836-38.
[12] Intendant of Columbia, 1851-52.
[13] Later colonel of 15th S. C. regiment, killed at Gettysburg, 1863, Monument First Presbyterian Churchyard.
[14] Intendant of Columbia 1845-46, Mayor 1878.

Richland Rifle company, and M. R. Clark was first lieutenant of the Governor's Guards. Upon his election as lieutenant of H company the Governor's Guards presented a sword to Lieutenant Clark. He carried it through the war. At the battle of Chapultepec, while acting as adjutant of the regiment, he was wounded in the hand, the shot also carrying away a part of the pearl grip of the sword. About 1880 Lieutenant Clark returned the sword to the Governor's Guards and it is now deposited in the relic room at the State capitol.

The Palmetto Regiment was received into the service of the United States in the fall of 1846. It rendezvoused at Charleston; from there it moved to Atlanta by rail, from Atlanta to a point on the Alabama River, whence it took steamer to Mobile, and from there the bark *Florida* carried it to the island of Lobos, off the Mexican coast. There General Scott's army was organized for attack on Vera Cruz.[15] The regiment took part in the battles of Vera Cruz, Contreras, Churubusco, Chapultepec and the Garita de Belin.

Of the fighting at the Belin gate, General Quitman, the division commander, said: "Before the smoke had ceased to curl over the heads of the brave victors, the Palmetto flag, the flag of your gallant regiment, was seen floating over the conquered walls, the first American flag within the city of Mexico. . . . This occurred in the presence of more than five hundred witnesses, and leaves no doubt of the fact that the flag of the Palmetto Regiment is entitled to the honor of being the first American banner victoriously unfurled within the walls of the city of Mexico." [16]

A celebration of the homecoming of the regiment was held on the campus of the South Carolina College, July 27, 1848. Swords were presented to Colonel Gladden, who had succeeded to the command upon the deaths of Colonel Butler and Lieutenant Colonel Dickinson, and to each of the officers of H Company. Also, a medal to Sergeant Patrick Leonard, who had carried the flag of the regiment after the fall of Lieutenant Colonel Dickinson, who was bearing it, leading the regiment.[17]

After the Mexican war "there existed a nominal militia in the State and numbered by battalions and regiments. These met every three months by companies and made some feeble attempts at drilling, or 'mustering' as it was called.

"To the militia was intrusted the care of internal police of the State. Each company was divided into squads, with a captain, whose duties were to do the policing of the neighborhood, called 'patrol-

---

[15] J. M. Bateman, *Sketch of Governor's Guards,* Columbia, S. C., n. d., p. 8.
[16] Claiborne, *Life and Correspondence of John A. Quitman,* II, 377.
[17] *The State,* March 26, 1919.

ling.' They would patrol the country during Sundays, and occasionally at nights, to prevent illegal assemblies of negroes and also to prevent them from being at large without permission of their masters. But the system had dwindled down to a farce, and was only engaged in by some of the youngsters, more in a spirit of fun and frolic than to keep order in the neighborhood. The real duties of the militia of the State consisted of an annual 'battalion muster' and 'general muster.' This occasioned a lively turnout of the people, both ladies and gentlemen, not connected with the troops, to witness the display of officers' uniforms, and bright caparisoned steeds, the stately tread of the 'muster men,' listen to the rattle of the drums and inspiring strains of the fifes, and horns of the rural bands." [18] The Columbia muster ground was the area within and around the present city block bounded by Elmwood Ave., Assembly, Calhoun and Park Streets. [19]

The Lightwood Knot Springs near Columbia had a history "first as a summer resort of some note, and again as the muster ground of the old time South Carolina militia, and again as the camp of instruction for the raw Confederate States soldiers in the early days of the War between the Sections. It was here that the soldiers that were to be trained for the battlefield went into camp in 1861 followed by others from time to time during the first year of the war. . . . A portion of Sherman's army camped there for a day and a night after they left Columbia in 1865. It would seem that there was a hotel at one of the largest springs about one-half mile to the right of the railroad opposite the six-mile post" (near the present State Park station on Southern Railway). The camp of instruction was laid out on a level plot of land of about one hundred acres. [20]

There was also at the Springs a school and [21] in 1830 Mrs. Mary Hillegas advertised the opening of a tavern at Lightwood Knot Springs and the days on which a stage would be operated. [22]

In 1860 the long roll sounded again. After the death of Brigadier General Maxcy Gregg, Governor Pickens, writing to his sister Dec. 28, 1862, said "I felt the deepest responsibility on the night of the 28th of December, 1860, when I sent for your brother, who was then a member of the Convention. I told him it was clear we would have to fight and I wanted him to command a picked regiment

[18] D. Augustus Dickert, *History of Kershaw's Brigade,* Newberry, S. C., 1899, p. 15.
[19] Information from Maj. John Meighan, 1910.
[20] Jas. L. Anderson, *The State,* July 6, 1909.
[21] E. L. Green, *The State,* November 14, 1909.
[22] *Ibid.,* February 12, 1934.

for immediate action and authorized him to pick his companies in the State and order them down" to Charleston.[23]

On January 7, 1861, the Governor notified the Senate of South Carolina that this regiment, authorized by the convention, had been raised and enlisted for a period of six months [24] and submitted for its approval the names of Maxcy Gregg for colonel, A. H. Gladden for lieutenant colonel and D. H. Hamilton for major. These officers were promptly confirmed by the Senate and the regiment became known as the First (Gregg's) Regiment, S. C. V. One of the companies was the Richland Volunteer Rifle Company of Columbia, commanded by D. B. Miller.[25]

The companies composing this regiment were of various origin, some of them being volunteer militia companies of long standing. They rendezvoused at various dates in Charleston whence they were distributed on Sullivan's and Morris Islands and had all assembled by February 1, 1861. Nothing occurred to vary the monotony of drill and picket duty until the bombardment of Fort Sumter by the Confederate forces, April 12th. A portion of the regiment was under fire of artillery during that engagement but no casualties occurred.[26]

In the month of May, 1861, the regiment was called upon to transfer to the service of the Confederate States. The greater portion agreed to the transfer and were ordered to Richmond early in June. They became a part of Bonham's Brigade,[27] the other regiments being the 2nd, 3rd, and 8th South Carolina regiments. Without having been seriously engaged the regiment was disbanded early in July, its term of service having expired. The field officers were continued in commission and authorized to reorganize the regiment under the former name. Several of the old companies were reorganized and some new ones raised, forming the regiment. They rendezvoused partly at Lightwood Knot Springs, near Columbia, and partly at Richmond.[28] The Richland Volunteer Rifle Company became C company, volunteering for the Confederate service at Columbia, July 29, 1861, and being mustered in at Richmond August 30, under command of John Cordero.[29]

---

[23] J. F. J. Caldwell, *History of a Brigade of South Carolinians Known First as Gregg's and Subsequently as McGowan's Brigade,* Philadelphia, 1866 Ms. appendix to copy in library of University of South Carolina.
[24] A. S. Salley, Jr., ed. *South Carolina Troops in the Confederate Service,* Columbia, 1913, I, 212.
[25] *Rivers Account of the Raising of Troops in S. C. for State and Confederate Service,* J. P. Thomas Ed., Columbia, 1899.
[26] *Ibid.,* p. 213.
[27] M. L. Bonham, Governor of South Carolina, 1862-64.
[28] Salley, *South Carolina Troops in the Confederate Service,* I, 213.
[29] *Ibid.,* p. 252.

From that time until the end of the war its history is merged with that of the regiment.

The twelfth, thirteenth and a portion of the fourteenth South Carolina regiments were already in camp near Richmond. Gregg's regiment and Orr's First S. C. Rifles joined them there, forming a brigade "which continued without interruption (except for perhaps one month) during the remainder of the war." [30]

Now, leaving the "Richland Volunteers" for the present we turn to the Governor's Guards.

After the Mexican War Colonel A. H. Gladden [31] took command of the company. He was succeeded by John Meighan,[32] who became major of the volunteer battalion of the twenty-third South Carolina regiment of militia, and F. W. McMaster,[33] followed by A. D. Goodwin.[34]

When Governor Pickens, under authority of an act of the Legislature, ordered the organization of ten regiments for duty around Charleston harbor, the Governor's Guards volunteered, and April 9, 1861, it was mustered into the second regiment, commanded by Colonel J. B. Kershaw,[35] for twelve months' service within the State. During the bombardment of Fort Sumter it was stationed on Morris Island. After the fall of Sumter, when the troops were invited to transfer the unexpired term of their enlistment to the service of the Confederate States, fifty-four men volunteered to make the change. At that time the company was commanded by Captain W. H. Casson.[36] It was ordered to Richmond April 23 and was mustered into the service of the Confederate States May 22, 1861, as A Company of the 2nd Regiment of S. C. V.[37]

Mustered in at the same time were Columbia Grays, C Company; Sumter Volunteers, D Company; Camden Volunteers, E Company. These four companies formed a battalion of which Captain Casson was made major, and was the nucleus upon which the 2nd S. C. was formed. At the first battle of Bull Run the regiment was in Bonham's Brigade.[38]

In the Peninsular Campaign and the Seven Days Battles the brigade had become Kershaw's, and formed part of McLaws's Divi-

---

[30] Caldwell, *Hist. of a Brigade of S. C.*, pp. 11-12.
[31] Later Brigadier-General, killed at Shiloh.
[32] Later, Major S. C. Cavalry.
[33] Later, Colonel 17th S. C. Regiment.
[34] Later, Lieut.-Col. 2nd S. C. Regiment.
[35] Later, Maj.-General.
[36] Later, Major 2nd S. C. Regiment.
[37] Salley, *S. C. Troops in Confederate Service, Columbia*, II, 3.
[38] In this battle Colonel McMaster, who had been captain of the Governor's Guards, served in the ranks of his old company.

sion. It served through the Maryland Campaign and at Fredericksburg, Chancellorsville, Gettysburg, Chickamauga and Knoxville in
the same division. Upon the opening of Grant's campaign against
Richmond the division had become Kershaw's. Then followed The
Wilderness, Spottsylvania, North Anna and the siege of Petersburg.

The brigade took part in the battles of Winchester and Cedar
Creek. At the close of 1864 it was on duty around Richmond, commanded at that time by Colonel J. D. Kennedy of the 2 S. C. One
regiment of the brigade was commanded by a major, four regiments
by captains, and one regiment by a lieutenant.[39] Such had been the
casualties of war!

The Columbia Grays
was organized January
7, 1861, under the com-
mand of Captain Wm.
Wallace.[40] It was sta-
tioned at Wappoo Cut
during the bombardment
of Fort Sumter, mus-
tered into the Confed-
erate service near Rich-
mond May 23, 1861,[41]
and became C Company
of the 2 S. C. V. Its
history is merged with
that of the regiment. It
does not appear to have
been reorganized after
the war.

Early in the war
Colonel Wade Hamp-
ton [42] received authority
from the war depart-
ment of the Confederate
States to organize a
mixed force, composed
of infantry, artillery and
cavalry, with the idea of

Wade Hampton, From Harper's Weekly,
November 11, 1865

operating as a sort of independent command. It consisted of eight
companies of infantry, four troops of cavalry and two bat-

---

[39] J. M. Bateman, *History of the Governor's Guards,* Columbia, n. d., p. 11.
[40] Afterward Colonel 2nd Regiment.
[41] Salley, *S. C. Troops in Confederate Service,* Columbia, II, 62.
[42] Afterward Lieut.-General.

teries of artillery.[43] Captain Langdon Cheves McCord organized the Columbia Zouaves [44] which became H Company. Later in the war another company from Richland County was organized under Captain D. B. Miller, which was also attached to the Legion.[43]

After General Lee took command of the Army of Northern Virginia the troops were brigaded according to their different arms, all independent commands were done away with. The infantry of the legion was brigaded with the infantry, the cavalry with the cavalry and the artillery with the artillery of the army.[45]

A troop of cavalry, under command of Captain Thomas Taylor was also a part of the legion, being D Troop. This was probably a successor to the Richland Light Dragoons, who "had the first parade in full uniform on June 26, 1841,[46] Alexander Taylor, captain." "Light horse, under Col. Kershaw, completely accoutred" were in evidence on the occasion of General Washington's visit to Columbia, 1791.[47]

The Columbia Artillery was one of the first militia companies organized in Columbia. Col. J. P. Thomas discovered in the Capitol at Columbia a manuscript roll of the organization, bearing the date of May 28, 1803, James S. Guignard, captain. In an old newspaper the Columbia artillery was notified that there would be a parade the following February, 1806 [48] or 1807.

In 1855 the Columbia Flying Artillery [49] attended a celebration of an anniversary of the battle of King's Mountain. On that occasion Major John Meighan commanded the Columbia contingent.[50]

Under the command of Captain Allen J. Green the Columbia Flying Artillery was stationed on Morris Island during the bombardment of Fort Sumter.

The students of the South Carolina College organized a company in 1860, under the command of John H. Gary. It was furnished with arms and accoutrements by the state. When the firing on Fort Sumter began the company tendered its services to the Governor. It was ordered to remain in readiness. Discouraged, the company was disbanded and another company formed with the determination to go without orders. This it did, without arms. Arms were furnished

---

[43] J. P. Thomas, ed. *River's Account of the Raising of Troops.*
[44] Monument in Elmwood cemetery.
[45] T. G. Barker, *The State,* May 20, 1906.
[46] E. L. Green, *The State,* November 28, 1929.
[47] Archibald Henderson, *Washington's Southern Tour,* Boston and New York, 1923, p. 252.
[48] E. L. Green, *The State,* October 17, 1909.
[49] Under command of Captain Frank Hampton.
[50] W. H. Manning, *The State,* November 21, 1909.

in Charleston from the State Armory. The company was taken to Morris Island and witnessed the bombardment of Fort Sumter. About three weeks later it was ordered to return to Columbia. During the latter part of June another company was formed and its services tendered to the Governor. The Governor expressed the thought that the students would be of more service scattered about in different organizations. When the college again opened in October a third attempt was made. Another company was organized, but failed to get anywhere, and many of the number joined commands already in the service.[51]

Toward the close of the war a company of sixteen-year-old boys was organized with Lawrence Taylor in command. They did duty in Florence, S. C., guarding prisoners.[52]

From time to time there have been in Columbia militia companies other than those mentioned, of whose history little or nothing is known. Chicora Rifles, Emmet Guards, Carolina Blues, Harper Rifles, Republican Light Infantry (1827), are among them.

Defeat and demoralization extinguished all military enthusiasm for some years after the war of 1861–1865. At length, for the protection of their homes and families and of civilization in the South, "rifle clubs" began to be formed. July 13, 1874, a meeting was held in Columbia for the purpose of organizing such a "club." It was necessary that the military nature of the club should not be avowed as military companies not connected with the National Guard were outlawed and the National Guard were allied with the carpet-bag régime which was then in control of the State government. The club took the name of Richland Rifle Club (not Richland Volunteer Rifle Club), and elected Hugh S. Thompson,[53] president. Enthusiasm ran high within the club and among the friends of its members. Drills, dances, suppers, and barbecues followed each other in quick succession.[54]

The Richland Volunteer Rifle Club was reorganized about the same time, but a little later than the R. R. C., under the command of Captain Richard O'Neale.

By the authority of the General Assembly the Richland Rifle Club took over the name and organization of the Governor's Guards in 1877.

---

[51] Bulletin of University of South Carolina No. VIII, Part 2, *War Records,* Columbia, 1907.

[52] J. G. Williams, *Columbia Old and New,* 1929, pp. 115-116.

[53] Governor of South Carolina 1882-1886. Assistant Secretary of the Treasury of the United States 1886.

[54] See manuscript minutes of the Governor's Guards in the library of the University of South Carolina.

The story of one of these old organizations, the R. V. R. C. and the G. G., is typical of each of them. They furnished their own arms and ammunition as well as their own uniforms. They paid their own running expenses, and when they visited other cities on gala occasions, they paid for their own transportation and subsistence.

The Governor's Guards attended the first inauguration of President Cleveland and was the only company from South Carolina in the inaugural parade. It also attended the inaugural centennial at New York, the constitutional centennial at Philadelphia and the unveiling of the Lee monument at Richmond, and other smaller affairs.

General M. L. Bonham, Jr., Adjutant and Inspector General of South Carolina, in making his annual report for 1887 said: "The centennial of the adoption of the Constitution of the United States was fittingly celebrated at Philadelphia. The ceremonies included a parade of troops from the U. S. army and navy and nearly all of the States. Several of the States made ample provision to defray the expenses of their civic and military representatives. It was eminently proper that South Carolina, one of the 'old thirteen' should be represented upon this occasion of national interest. . . . The State was handsomely represented by the Governor's Guards, Captain Wilie Jones commanding and the Butler Guards, Captain J. C. Boyd commanding. These two fine companies sustained with credit the reputation and fame of the State, and attracted to themselves much favorable comment by their fine appearance and drill."

In the autumn of 1897 a few officers of the Columbia militia conceived the idea of having a military demonstration at the State Fair. The plan which they outlined met with general approval and the result was a parade of two full regiments of infantry, one battery of artillery, two troops of cavalry and a company of cadets, on November 11 of that year. "Beside bringing a large crowd of soldiers and their friends to the city, the second object of the committee was to assemble a large number of soldiers, uniformed alike and organized into battalions and regiments as provided for in the United States Army Drill Regulations for Infantry. They achieved both these objects; the second in greater measure than their highest expectations. Not more than one-third of the number of men in our parade have been assembled in this State, in one uniform, since 1865." [55]

Another assemblage of State troops took place when the city celebrated her centennial anniversary May 13-15 1891.

---

[55] Report. John M. Bateman, Jos. K. Alston, John D. Frost, Jr., Committee. Privately printed, n. d.

In April, 1898, our country found herself in a state of war with Spain. South Carolina was called upon to furnish one regiment and one battalion of infantry and one battery of heavy artillery. The Columbia Zouaves had been reorganized in 1890. That company combined with the R. V. R. C. and volunteered under the command of Captain Chas. Newnham, becoming I Company of the 1st .S. C. Regiment U. S. V. The Governor's Guards divided into two companies. One remained in the State militia and the other under the command of Captain B. B. McCreery, Jr., volunteered, becoming K Company, 1st S C. Regiment, U. S. V. The regiment under Colonel Jos. K. Alston left home June 6 for Chickamauga Park where it was encamped seven or eight weeks when it was moved to Jacksonville. It remained in Jacksonville a few months, until it was ordered back to Columbia and mustered out November 10, 1928.[56]

The first organization completed for the Spanish-American War in South Carolina was the Independent Battalion, Henry T. Thompson, Major, William E. Gonzales, Adjutant. It was held in Columbia. One company was taken from it by authority of War Department, to complete the first Regiment. The Independent Battalion promptly recruited another company to complete its quota of four companies. It was still held in Columbia. After the "second call" for troops, War Department authority was given to form the Second Regiment with the Independent Battalion constituting the first four companies, with Major Thompson becoming Lieutenant Colonel. By requirement of the Adjutant General of the army a captaincy was given the adjutant of the Independent Battalion, and men for *his* command furnished him by other captains of regiment.

There were no units from Columbia in the 2nd S. C. Regiment, U. S. V. That regiment, under Colonel Wilie Jones, was mustered into the service of the United States August 23, 1898. It was first moved to camp at Jacksonville, then to Savannah, whence it sailed for Habana January 3, 1899. After being encamped near that city for about three months it returned to Tampa, then to Augusta, where it was mustered out April 10, 1899.

The Richland Volunteer Rifle Company, after many years of service to the State, was separated from the service about 1901.

When orders were issued in 1916 for the mobilization of troops on the Mexican border, the quota of this state was two regiments of infantry, one troop of cavalry and one sanitary company. They were assembled at Styx, Lexington County. The Governor's Guards

---

[56] Bateman, *History of Governor's Guards,* p. 32.

were included. The troops left the mobilization point August 9. Governor Manning said to them: "I know that you will be true to your State, true to yourselves and true to your God. May God bless you. I wish you well." [57] After about six months' service on the border the troops returned about the middle of March and were mustered out March 21, 1917.[58] A machine gun company, which had been recently organized by Captain E. B. Cantey and attached to the 2nd S. C. Regiment served with the regiment on the border. When the regiment, in the World War, became the 105th Ammunition Train, the machine gun company was also mustered into the Federal service, and when the regiment was moved to Camp Sevier and the troops reorganized to conform to Federal requirements, the machine gun company became D Company of the 114th Machine Gun Battalion. At the close of the war it was mustered out at Camp Jackson.

When the United States entered the World War the 2nd S. C. Regiment rendezvoused at Camp Jackson. The first battalion, composed of Charleston troops, became the motor section of the 105th Ammunition Train. The second battalion, composed of the Governor's Guards, W. M. Carter, captain, Brookland Light Infantry and Darlington Guards, became the wagon company of the train. The third battalion was broken up and the men assigned to various companies.

These companies went into camp at Camp Jackson August 20, 1917. In the middle of the month of September the Governor's Guards and the Brookland Company were consolidated, and were moved to Camp Sevier, Greenville. May 26, they reached Montreal, Canada. From Montreal they went down the St. Lawrence River, arriving at Halifax, N. S., five days later. June 1, with a fleet of thirteen transports, convoyed by a British cruiser, they sailed from Halifax. On nearing England the fleet was met by submarine chasers and destroyers and conducted to Liverpool where they landed. Ten days later the troops crossed the English Channel to Havre France.

The train served in the St. Mihiel offensive, Argonne Forest, Verdun-Meuse, and the Woevere offensive.[59]

The ammunition train embarked for home March 14, 1918, on U. S. S. Mercury. It landed at Charleston, and on April 1, the men were discharged at Camp Jackson.

The Governor's Guards suffered two casualties, both from pneumonia.

[57] *The State,* August 8, 1916.
[58] *History of 55th F. A. Brigade,* Nashville, n. d., p. 107.
[59] *History of 55th Artillery Brig.,* Nashville, n. d., B. M. Gilbert. *The State,* January 19, 1919.

The militia of the present day is a very different body from the militia of former years. Previous to the war of 1861-1865, a roster of the divisions and regiments into which the citizens were organized would make it appear that South Carolina maintained a standing army. But, in the larger towns, only, was there a company uniformed and armed. When war came there were volunteers a-plenty and they made as good soldiers as ever carried arms, but a newspaper correspondent thus describes a regiment arriving in Charleston in 1861: "It was a tangled compound of frock coats, working clothes and Sunday suits, with a liberal sprinkling of shirt sleeves. There were trousers of every hue and shape from gay cassimere to the patched emblems of better days, the nether extremities lost in the tops of boots or snugly gathered within the stockings. The headgear consisted of slouched hats, caps, stovepipes and last year's old straw hats that on parade presented an outline indescribably ragged. A blanket or patched bed quilt, a home-made knapsack and a canvas bag in which the rations were carried completed the outfit." [60]

Poor fellows! "Constant in their love for the State" many of them "died in the performance of their duty."

In 1902, the Adjutant and Inspector General of South Carolina reported "The disorganization following the Spanish-American War had caused an apathy and waning of enthusiasm for the State volunteer service, that resulted in the depletion and disbandment of organizations all over the State . . . the one over-topping reason that from year to year gradually provoked the decline of sentiment was the lack of interest and support given her Volunteers by the State through her law-making body." [61]

Chapel, World War Memorial Building

[60] F. G. deFontaine, *Army Letters,* Columbia, 1896, I, No. 1, p. 20.
[61] *Report,* Columbia, 1902, p. 7.

This was the condition of the militia when the Spanish-American War came. The experience of the national government in creating an army at that time showed that the militia system needed reorganization.

In January, 1903, the Congress passed a bill making larger appropriations for the militia, at the same time requiring more interest and effort on the part of the States.

This brought about a change, such a change as to permit the Adjutant and Inspector General of South Carolina to report in 1907: "I believe the National Guard of this State is more efficient today, considered as a military organization, than at any period of its existence." [62]

That comment might be repeated with equal truth today.

----

[62] *Ibid.*, Columbia, 1907, p. 4.

OUTDOOR SPORTS IN COLUMBIA

By Robert Moorman

HORSE racing was the major sport of earliest Columbians. One of the principal and first race tracks here was owned by Thomas Puryear and was located between Woodrow Street and the Garners Ferry Road.

Tournaments were rather frequently held here in the early history of Columbia. Most of the gentlemen of that time owned one or more fine saddle horses and almost every man in this section was a good rider. These tournaments were big social events with numerous spectators, and the occasions were graced by the presence of the most beautiful and fashionable ladies of that day. The successful knight won the great privilege of crowning his favorite belle as queen of love and beauty. Those knights winning second and third and even fourth places in the tournament were granted the appreciated privilege of naming the maids of honor to the queen.

Sun-Beau, Famous Race Horse Trained in Columbia

Usually these tournaments were followed by a ball in the evening of the tournament day.

Elmwood was the parade ground of the military companies, and the cavalry company used to have its tournaments there. It was also the place for gander pullings. This was a brutal sport. They would take a gander and pick his neck and grease it, then tie him up by the feet.

The contestants on horseback, going as fast as they could, would try to pull his head off. The one who succeeded got the prize.[1]

Hunting and fishing have always been popular sports and the people of ancient, medieval and modern Columbia have in considerable proportions followed their natural impulses to so indulge. Our illustrious citizen, the late General Wade Hampton, was a devotee of these sports, as were his fathers before him. He had the reputation of being an excellent shot. On a deer hunt in 1879, in Congaree Swamps, he met with an accident that eventually caused the amputation of one of his legs. If General Hampton had not been a man of powerful physical strength and will power he probably would not have survived this accident.

Besides shooting quail, duck, geese, doves and other birds, fox hunting was enjoyed by many Columbians.

In the olden days Dent's Pond was a great fishing place. This place is known as Forest Lake and is a popular bathing resort. Forest Lake Country Club is situated on the bank of Dent's Pond.

Our famous Lake Murray furnishes an excellent fishing place for hundreds of Columbians.

> Deer, wild turkeys and smaller game were abundant in the swamps and sand hills, and every winter wild pigeons came in numbers numberless. Where they roosted at night, on the trees and bushes in Congaree Creek Swamp, parties went with sticks and killed them by hundreds. On their departure in the spring I happened one morning to be on the hill above the village, commanding a view of six or eight miles to the South and two or three both East and West, where for nearly an hour the whole horizon in every direction was filled with them as they passed in rapid flight toward the South (North?). Considering the number that must have been in sight at one time and the short period in which they were replaced by others, the aggregate would seem to be simply incalculable.

> Fire hunting for deer was not uncommon, one carrying a torch of fire, which reflected the light in the eyes of the game and showed the marksman where to direct his aim. Old Mr. Wilson on one occasion took three fair cracks at the moon, which he mistook for deer's eyes, as she rose through the bushes.[2]

> Just above the Congaree bridge were two rows of fish traps belonging to Mrs. Mayrant. I have seen a cart load of shad caught there at one time and any quantity of sturgeon, some of them weighing five or six hundred pounds, but all of that is gone.[3]

---

[1] J. F. Williams, *Old and New Columbia*, Columbia, 1929, p. 53.
[2] Edwin J. Scott, *Random Recollections of a Long Life,* Columbia, 1884, p. 97.
[3] Williams, *Old and New Columbia,* p. 54.

FOOTBALL

The earliest organized football in Columbia was at the University of South Carolina. Certainly as early as 1888 football was played at Carolina on what was then known as "Gibbes Green"—a vacant plot of land bounded by Pendleton, Pickens, Green and Bull Streets. Now this land is occupied by Davis, Le Conte and Sloan Colleges of the University. The athletic field of the University of today is known as Melton Field, but big games are played at our stadium, where the seating capacity is about 16,000.

Amongst the students at Carolina in 1888-1889 who were conspicuously good football players were Thomas J. Kinard of Ninety Six; Rawlins Lowndes and Dan Hanckel of Charleston.

The first football team at Carolina to engage in an intercollegiate football match was organized in the fall of 1891. During the Christmas holidays of that year this team played Furman College at Charleston. Amongst the men on that team were Ed Parker of Columbia; Mack James of Cheraw; George Laney of Chesterfield; William Wannamaker of Orangeburg; Albert Hane of Fort Motte; Stead Shand, Bob Shand, Melton Clark, Wardlaw Moorman, William H. Lipscomb and Robert Moorman of Columbia. There were two or three others, whose names the writer does not recall. We suffered overwhelming defeat, about 42 to 0.

In 1896 Carolina played its first football game against Clemson, and Carolina won 12 to 6. These teams have met in contest every year since 1896, except a few years. Clemson won over Carolina every season after 1896 until 1902. In 1902 Carolina defeated Clemson 12 to 6, and during the evening of the day that game was played a very serious fight between Carolina and Clemson students was narrowly averted. The result was that the teams severed athletic relations for several years thereafter. All of the Carolina-Clemson football games have been played at the Fair Grounds during the State Fair, and this annual contest has become the football classic of South Carolina. The writer has the record of having witnessed every game ever played between Carolina and Clemson—not always the pleasure, because he is a Carolina man and Clemson has humiliated us too often. The first coach in football that Carolina had was Dick Whaley, in 1896. The personnel of the Carolina teams and coaches changed so much it would require too much space to name many of them. Some of the greatest football players at Carolina in the old days, under a coach, were Christie Benet, Frank Haskell, Billie Shand, Sid Smith, Eugene Oliver, Douglas McKay, Ralph Foster, Luke Hill, Jim Guignard, Irvin Belser, Jim Verner,

Heyward Gibbes, Barnie Heyward; and in later years "Brue" Boineau, "Monk" Shand, "Red" Fulmer, Harold Mauney, Harry Lightsey, Julian and Carlisle Beall, and others too numerous to mention.

Football teams at Columbia High School have been remarkably successful, having won the state championship many times. Columbia is very proud of her high school teams, and supports them generously and enthusiastically. Our high school teams always play a good game.

An Exciting Moment in a Football Game on Melton Field

BASEBALL

Baseball was popular in Columbia as early as 1870. The Union soldiers stationed here at that time played this game almost daily when the seasons permitted. The young men of our town then organized a team, and had many contests with the team of the soldiers. Amongst the early good players in Columbia were T. Hasell Gibbes, G. Powell Miller, Samuel W. Melton, Jr., F. Sumter Earle, Warren Scruggs.

Samuel W. Melton, Jr., introduced pitching of curved balls in Columbia.

The most famous players and best organized of the early baseball teams in Columbia were the Mechanics. This team was composed of men connected with the railway shops. It was a winning team and had some excellent players. Amongst its best players were Jack

Fetner, pitcher, and Frank Fetner, catcher—well known as the "Fetner Brothers Battery." Some of the others connected with this team were Will Waites, Bob McDougal, Louis Forde, Will McDougal, Bob Waites, Alex McDougal, Tom Dunn, Hamp Swygert, Doc Kraft and Arthur Williamson. The Mechanics were organized about 1883. Their enthusiastic manager was James T. Rideout.

About 1886 there was formed here a wonderful nine of youths in their 'teens under the name of "Midgets." At its best this nine was composed of Jimmie Campbell, pitcher; William McGregor, catcher; George McAuley, first base; Talley Tarrer, second base; George B. Radcliffe, third base; Ed Clarke, shortstop; Mack Dick, left field; Jimmie Sloan, center field, and Bill Lindsay, right field. This organization lasted at least eight seasons. This was one of the best youngster teams in this part of the country, for they won nearly every game they played.

In the late eighties or early nineties there were several other good baseball teams in our city, namely, the South Carolina College team and the Columbia Athletes, and amongst the younger men or "kids" were the Athenians, Spartans, GGs and Pickard's Favorites. Many well-known Columbians of today, now comparatively old men, played on these various teams.

Amongst the best of the old Carolina players were James Henry Rice, Maner Rice, Otis Withers, Frank Elmore and Mack James, as pitchers; Ossie Westfield, Bob Shand, Wardlaw Moorman and Allie Webster, as catchers; "Bunny" Rhett, Aiken Rhett, Marion Hannahan, George Legare, George Laney, Bob Moorman, Harry Edmunds, Herman Spahr, Dick Carwile, Ed and Irvine Belser and Stead Shand. Mack James became a famous pitcher in the big leagues.

The first professional baseball team in Columbia was organized in 1889 or 1890. This team played in a league composed of Winston-Salem, Charlotte, Charleston and Columbia. The league lasted only a few months.

Columbia joined the South Atlantic League in 1902. For many years Columbia had a team in this league, and in several seasons won the pennant, under the management of Zinn Beck.

Boating was not very popular with Columbians until Lake Murray was completed. However, there have been a few pleasure boats on the Congaree River. There is some boating at the bathing resorts near Columbia, such as Forest Lake. At Lake Murray there are hundreds of motor boats and sail boats.

Up to a few years ago there was always horse racing at the

State Fair, both running and trotting. Training stables were established in Columbia about five years ago by Buxton Brothers, from the north. These training stables have grown into a big enterprise and some of the most famous horses of our country have been and are being trained here. "Cavalcade" was trained here, and sport-loving Columbians are very proud of his fine record.

About 1890 there existed a famous rifle team in Columbia, composed of William E. Gonzales, Frank Hampton, F. W. Huseman and William Lykes. Trap-shooting, and its recent development skeet-shooting, have been popular.

For thirty-five years golf has been played in Columbia and has become more and more popular here. In or near Columbia there are now at least seven golf courses. Eugene McCarthy was the first professional golfer in Columbia. Perhaps Columbia's most widely known golf player is young Kathryn Hemphill. She has contested with success in many tournaments in and out of the state. Her many admirers entertain the ambition that she will be amongst the nation's best women golfers.

The climate and well-drained soil of Columbia make tennis a year-round sport. The game first became popular on the courts of the Columbia Seminary. Dr. Reed Smith, Dean of the University Graduate School, who has been associated with South Carolina tennis for more than forty years, started playing with the Seminary set in the late '90's. He was champion of the Carolinas for a number of years, and has conducted the city and state tournaments, usually held on the excellent courts of Ridgewood Club. Outstanding Columbia players beside Dr. Smith have been Dick Reed, Elmer and Wingate Waring, and—most famous—Wilmer Hines, who is this year the ninth ranking player in the United States Lawn Tennis Association. Inter-collegiate tennis has brought out fine University teams, and Columbia High School teams have included Wilmer Hines, Bill Ellis, Heyward Belser and Marion Hunt. Excellent women players have been Mrs. Don Dial (Marjorie Robertson), Mrs. Victor Barringer (Gertrude Hampton), Miss Sarah Currell, Mrs. T. J. Robertson, Mrs. William Melton, Jr., and Mrs. T. B. Spigner.

It can be said without disparagement that Columbians are lovers of good sport and have always been. Many of the most popular and influential men in Columbia have been conspicuously good athletes at various colleges and universities in and out of the state. In the opinion of the writer a good athlete is nearly always a good sportsman, and makes an unusually good citizen—for example, Dr. Henry D. Phillips, Louis Guion, Christie Benet, and hundreds of others.

NEGROES

By C. A. Johnson
Supervising Principal of Colored Schools

SINCE the subject, negroes of Columbia, is inclusive, the writer has decided to limit the article to those negroes who have made some contributions to the city of Columbia or have in some way rendered valuable services. There were many honest, hardworking, law-abiding negroes whose contributions and services were never recorded. However, our dependence on the record of those who lived before us makes it necessary to mention only those whose achievements were perpetuated in the main by a written record. This will be especially true in two divisions of the article, namely: negroes of Columbia before 1865 and during reconstruction; negroes in Columbia since reconstruction—many present day negroes being mentioned.

I

NEGROES OF COLUMBIA BEFORE 1865

During the seventy-nine years between 1786 and 1865 the negroes' greatest contribution to Columbia was a desirable and a much needed type of labor. To the average person this perhaps seems very small in importance, but when one considers that there were few, if any, labor-saving devices, and that there was a great deal of work to be done to build the struggling little village at Taylor's Hill near Granby into a city that South Carolina would be proud to call its capital, this service looms large. Streets had to be built; houses needed to be erected; homes had to be cared for; errands had to be run; trees had to be planted. All of the money in South Carolina and all of the planning of the architects could not make these things possible without the labor which the negro helped to furnish. This service looms even larger when we consider that this was entirely slave labor.

Just above the Congaree bridge were two rows of fish traps belonging to Mrs. Mayrant. She had a negro named Dick who sold the fish for her. After the war he became a politician and was made an alderman. His name was Richard Young.[1]

Another negro who performed an important service was Joe Randals, an outstanding free negro. He was a bandmaster and a re-

---

[1] J. F. Williams, *Old and New Columbia,* Columbia, 1929, pp. 54-55.

markable musician, serving not only Columbia but other cities as well. His home was on the west side of Assembly Street, just back of the filling station on Gervais and Assembly Streets and is still standing and occupied. There was another free negro who was a member of the band—Bill Simmons. He lived on the northeast corner of Marion and Richland Streets. There was no white band then and the negro band played for all occasions.[2]

All of the barbers were negroes. They were: C. R. (Capt.) Carrol, who later became county superintendent of education; Alonzo Reese, Chris Haynsworth and Sam Glover.[3]

Ben Delane, while a slave, hired his time and bought two boats, which he ran on the river, commanding one himself and employing hands to work the other. His character for industry and integrity was beyond reproach and he could get credit for all asked.[4]

Jaggers' Home

Another remarkable Columbia negro was Alfred Parr, an African by birth, who came to this country at an early age. He had more than ordinary intelligence as to public matters and preserved many records of long past events.[5]

---

[2] *Ibid.*, p. 67.
[3] *Ibid.*, p. 71.
[4] Edwin J. Scott, *Random Recollections,* Columbia, 1884, p. 57.
[5] *Ibid.*, p. 67.

There were no negro churches in Columbia at this time. Most of the white churches had galleries and the negroes attended there. Two negro Methodist ministers were used to bury the negroes. Their names were Sancho Taylor and Peter Cooper. Both were very old and dignified and had the respect of the community.[6]

J. F. Williams, a Columbian, author of *Old and New Columbia,* made the following statement concerning the negroes during the War of Secession: "Be it said to the credit of the Negroes, they were faithful to their masters while they were in the army. They were at home raising food for them and their families. The whole country was practically at their mercy but they remained faithful."

NEGROES OF COLUMBIA DURING RECONSTRUCTION

Unfortunately, it was during this period (1865-1876) that the negro was most misunderstood. He is pictured by many historians as a lazy individual who wanted to get away from the dirty tasks and get white collar jobs. While this is not true of the majority of negroes, even those who did look for political jobs did only what any other racial group suddenly emancipated would have done. It is human nature to try out your wings when released from a cage in which you have been confined for a long period of time.

Another erroneous impression obtained of the negro during this period was that all of the negro office holders were ignorant, incompetent and dishonest. A number of them were intelligent and well educated. This is evidenced by their contribution to the Constitutional Convention of 1868 in which the negroes were in the majority. The negroes in Columbia were no exception. C. M. Wilder, W. B. Nash and S. B. Thompson[7] were Columbia negroes who were delegates to this convention. The competency of the negro politicians can be best judged by considering the system of free public instruction which they made possible from this Constitutional Convention of 1868. As to the dishonesty, most of it is traceable to the work of the carpet-baggers and scalawags.[8]

During reconstruction most of the city's aldermen were negroes. At one time all of the police force except the chief were negroes.[9] One of the aldermen was named Israel Smith,[10] and Charles M. Wilder was postmaster for approximately sixteen years.[11]

---

[6] Williams, *Old and New Columbia,* p. 59.

[7] *Ibid.,* p. 120.

[8] Alrutheus Ambush Taylor, *The Negro in South Carolina During Reconstruction,* Washington, 1924, p. 128.

[9] Williams, *Old and New Columbia,* p. 137.

[10] Julian A. Selby, *Memorabilia,* Columbia, 1905, p. 78.

[11] *Ibid.,* p. 73.

Speaking of economic adjustment, A. A. Taylor, author of *The Negro In South Carolina During Reconstruction,* says: "Columbia, the capital, moreover, may also be called an exception, for the Negroes there easily grounded themselves in things economic during the reconstruction régime and lived in conformity to a standard superior to that of many well-to-do white families in the North. Among the most prominent of these were Joseph Taylor, William Taylor, Junius S. Mobley, and Augustus Cooper. William Taylor had such a large grocery business that he had to call in the police on Saturday to handle the crowd." [12]

Although not a Columbian, Richard T. Greener, the first negro graduate of Harvard College, won from the University of South Carolina a degree in law and served as Professor of Mental and Moral Philosophy, completed a catalogue of the library and prepared a list of the rare books which it contained. This list was sent to Washington for the government report on libraries.[13]

NEGROES IN COLUMBIA SINCE RECONSTRUCTION

To the negroes in this period (1876-1936), goes most of the praise, because, in the first two periods, the other groups labored under abnormal conditions. From 1786 to 1865 they were slaves and could not follow the occupations or professions of their choice because of certain inhibitions. From 1865 to 1876 they held their positions through force. The troops from the Union army and the cunning of those who wished to benefit by the spoils of a mismanaged government were largely responsible for the part the negro played during reconstruction days. But in this last period the negro was left to himself and in many ways was worse off than he had been before because he had lost the care of his master and protection of the Union army and had to contend with a hatred and prejudice that would not accept him as a citizen. We are fortunate that in Columbia this condition has been reduced to a minimum and mutual good will exists between the two races. With two exceptions there has been no visible check placed on the advancement of negroes in business and other vocations. The two blots on Columbia's record are the denial to the negro of the plumber's license and of the privilege of voting in the democratic primary.

For some time after the city government was restored to the local group, a negro fire company and two troops of the National Guards

[12] Taylor, *The Negro in South Carolina During Reconstruction,* p. 68.
[13] Minutes of Board of Trustees, University of South Carolina, MS, October 10, 1873.

served Columbia and the State of South Carolina. The name of the negro company was the Vigilant and it was housed on Assembly and Taylor streets. Captain John R. Nowell was in charge of the Capital City Guards. Captain John Lark commanded the Carolina Guards.[14]

NEGRO TRADESMAN

There was one negro who deserves special mention—Page Ellington. He was a bricklayer and an architect and very reliable in every respect. Much credit is given to him for playing such a large part in building the State Hospital for the Insane. He was a member of Bethel Church and later of Ladson Presbyterian Church—serving as superintendent of the Sunday school for thirty-three years.[15] Every one who knew him respected him. James Patterson was a highly respected carpenter and Andrew Wallace was a greatly esteemed bricklayer.[16]

There are some buildings in Columbia which were erected almost entirely by negro masons and carpenters—the Jefferson Hotel and the Palmetto National Bank Building. James James was the foreman of the group which built the Jefferson Hotel. Henry Champion was also an excellent brick mason and foreman on many of Columbia's important buildings.[17]

An interesting character is James A. Harper. He is so quiet and unassuming that few people know of the record he has made at the Southern Railway shops. He has worked there for fifty-four years and his job is to put brake shoes on the engines. He is said to be a skillful mechanic.[18]

NEGRO BUSINESS MEN

R. J. Palmer conducted a business as a merchant tailor on Main Street opposite the old postoffice. He once owned the property on Main Street where the Woolworth building is located.[19]

Another negro merchant who was located on Main Street was Irving Miller. His store was on the corner of Taylor and Main

---

[14] In March, 1838, a Sunday School for colored children was organized under the auspices of the First Presbyterian Church. In 1846 it was given the use of a part of a building owned by the church which stood about where Ladson Presbyterian Church now stands. From this beginning developed the Ladson Church. George Howe, *History of the Presbyterian Church in South Carolina,* Columbia, 1870-1883, II, 500.

[15] This and other statements following as to contemporary negroes for which no references are given are made on the writer's personal information.

[16] Williams, *Old and New Columbia,* p. 67.

[17] Selby, *Memorabilia,* pp. 72-73.

[18] Statement of J. B. Lewie, Columbia, November 25, 1935.

[19] Statement of J. A. Harper, Jr., Columbia, November 24, 1935.

Streets where the Bon Marche was. It is said that he had the best home of any negro of his time and that his was the first negro home to have gas in it.[20]

A very remarkable negro was Thomas H. Pinckney. He started his business career by selling old rags, watermelon rinds, and fish until he accumulated enough captial to open a barber shop. From this he obtained enough money to make a trip to New York to learn embalming and later to open up an undertaking establishment in Columbia. He trained quite a few younger negro barbers and musicians and gave employment to many negroes in his business.[21]

Another enterprising negro engaged in the undertaking business is Willis C. Johnson. When quite a young man he learned the business under E. W. Biggs in Greenville, South Carolina, and came back to his home, and with two other partners went into business for himself. Due to his sagacity and good business sense the firm has steadily grown until now the Johnson-Bradley Funeral Home is one of the best in the state. Mr. Johnson is very active in all civic and uplift movements and offers training and employment to deserving negro youths. His business is twenty years old.

William Manigault has made a great contribution to the business of Columbia by manufacturing caskets.

An enviable record has been made by John Cornwell. He has been in the barbering business in Columbia for forty-six years and has been in one place—1629 Main Street—for forty-four years. Many governors and other important state and city officials have been served by him. Two other negroes had barber shops on Main Street —David Means and William Sumter. The latter still conducts his shop and has good trade.

R. H. Paul, a tailor, has served Columbia for eighteen years. Other business men who should be included in this group are: W. H. Harvey, district manager of the North Carolina Mutual Insurance Company, and George Hampton, who for twelve years has edited the *Palmetto Leader,* the only negro newspaper in the city, and the best in the state.

NEGRO MINISTERS

Richard Carroll developed an unusual gift of eloquence in public speech and distinguished himself by his interest in all that contributed to the welfare of his race and in bringing about a more helpful understanding between the races in the South. He became

---

[20] I. E. Lowery, *Life on the Old Plantation,* Columbia, 1911, p. 141.
[21] Statement of M. G. Johnson, Columbia, November 23, 1935.

a Baptist minister and developed in Columbia a home for negro orphans and delinquents. During the Spanish-American War he was a chaplain in the army. In 1908 Rev. Carroll organized a race conference in South Carolina which met annually for some years afterwards. He was the editor of *The Plowman* for a number of years and in 1913 he accepted a position as evangelist to negroes of the South.

An outstanding Methodist minister was the Rev. W. D. Chappelle. In 1900 he was elected Secretary-Treasurer of the Sunday School Union with headquarters in Nashville, Tennessee, and edited the Sunday school literature of the A. M. E. Church for eight years. He built for the A. M. E. Church one of the best negro printing houses in the country. In 1898 and 1899 he served as president of Allen University and was re-elected president of Allen in 1908 and served until 1912 when he was elected bishop of his church.

The Rev. A. P. Dunbar served as pastor of the Second Calvary Baptist Church for almost ten years and was the founder of the Mutual Benevolent Insurance Company which is still in existence. This same church was also fortunate in having as its pastor the Rev. P. P. Watson, a highly respected minister, who travelled throughout the state delivering inspiring messages and conducting revivals.[22]

The minister who served the longest number of years in one church was the Rev. M. G. Johnson. He served the Ladson Presbyterian Church for forty-four years and was greatly admired and respected for his sterling character.

The most unique character of all the Columbia ministers was the Rev. Charles Jaggers. He had very little education but he was overpowered with a great desire to help people less fortunate than he. He started what is known as the "Jaggers Old Folks Home" which still exists. He supported this home for the aged by asking his white friends for contributions. In all Columbia there was not a negro of whom they thought more. On the day of his funeral many of the merchants closed their stores at twelve o'clock because of their high regard for him. He usually preached from one text: "Let the same mind be in you that was also in Christ Jesus our Lord."

The Rev. R. M. Myers has been serving Columbia churches for thirty-two years. During his lifetime he has built eight churches, one of them the tabernacle in which Billy Sunday conducted a special

[22] A. E. Asmond, Columbia, November 25, 1935.

service. He also played a large part in helping Columbia get its first negro bank, the Victory Savings Bank.[23]

EDUCATION AND EDUCATORS

In the years immediately preceding and during the War between the States there was a spirit of great unrest in both master and slave, in and around Columbia. The masters kept themselves posted on important matters by reading the few newspapers then to be had, with an occasional letter from a distant friend. The slaves knew from the strained look on the faces of the masters and by their nervous actions that something serious was about to happen. What it was he could not tell. If, sometimes by eavesdropping, a maid or carriage man or butler was lucky enough to catch a word or so of a whispered conversation, it was immediately broadcast with numerous additions by means of the grapevine telephone.

Realizing how much they were handicapped by not being able to read or write, these Columbia negroes vowed if they were ever freed they would leave no stone unturned to get an education for themselves and their children.

Allen University

Among the first acts of the freedmen was to establish churches where they could praise and thank God for deliverance from bondage. Their next thoughts were of schools.[24]

Northerners who flocked in were colored as well as whites. Both brought some good along with the bad. While the bad were preying

[23] Statement of R. M. Myers, Columbia, November 23, 1935.
[24] C. G. Garrett, *Reminiscences,* MS, Columbia, 1933.

on the credulity and the ignorance of the negroes just loose from slavery, the good were establishing schools. Many schools were taught by white and black men and women. These private schools were always crowded, some having as many as three different groups of students daily. (These private schools were attended in large numbers because many negroes of the early days disdained the idea of free schools, having gotten the idea from their former masters. A few of our own white folk joined the ranks of teachers of negroes.)

As churches of different denominations were established, each church maintained a school for its adherents. In many instances both adults and children were taught to read and write while attending Sunday school.

> Bethel A. M. E. Church on Sumter Street played an important part in the work of the education of negroes. Being one of the leading churches in this connection, only educated ministers were acceptable, thus these ministers were preachers and teachers. Among them was a Rev. Porter who with his wife taught a church school on Sumter Street between Laurel and Richland which proved to be the beginning of Allen University in Columbia.
>
> The following are a few of the places where early schools for negroes were held: J. E. Bingham conducted a school over the fire engine house on lower Main Street. A. D. Forest's school was upstairs in a frame building where the Red Cross Society now is. Rev. Salters, brother of Bishop Salters, had a school upstairs in the McCreery building where the J. C. Penney store is. Mrs. Hunter's school was on Marion Street just north of the Medical Building. A Mrs. Harris and her daughter taught a school in a small building on the Arsenal Hill.[25]
>
> Columbia like Charleston made a good beginning in negro education. Schools numbering one to nine were established in rapid succession. These schools were in the main taught by northern ladies with the assistance of the few colored who were competent to render this service. Howard School, the Columbia background of secondary education, had its beginning in the fall of 1867 and at the close of the school year (1868) it had an attendance of six hundred.[26]

For forty-nine years (1867-1916), Howard School was the only public school in Columbia for negroes. The Booker Washington school was erected in 1916 as an elementary school, but became the high school two years later—1918. Columbia now has seven modern schools for negroes with an enrollment of 5,000. The Booker Washington School is the only public high school in the state accredited by the Southern Association of Colleges and Secondary Schools.

[25] *Ibid.*
[26] J. Andrew Simmons, *Professional and Cultural Background of Teachers in South Carolina High Schools for Negroes,* Columbia University, 1935 (Master's Thesis), p. 4.

Booker Washington High School

Payne Institute, at Cokesbury, South Carolina, established by the A. M. E. Church, was moved to Columbia in 1880 and the name changed to Allen University. The Right Reverend W. F. Dickerson, who was instrumental in locating the school in Columbia, insisted that it should be called "Allen University." He said, "Let the school catch up with the name." "This institution has given to the state and the nation many of its outstanding negro leaders." [27]

Benedict College, established 65 years ago (1870) by the American Baptist Home Mission Society, was made possible through the gifts of Mrs. Bathsheba Benedict of Pawtucket, Rhode Island. It would seem that she must have given some $40,000 or more during her life time. Eighty acres of land, including the present campus, were purchased for the prospective school. On this land was the plantation home which stood where Morgan Hall now stands. The first pupil was a colored preacher sixty-six years old—Rev. Edmond Green. The first year was prosperous and closed with nine boarders and thirty day scholars. [28]

Benedict College has a splendid history, being regarded as one of the leading colleges for negro men and women in the state. During the administration of Dr. J. J. Starks, the first negro president, the college has had remarkable physical development.

William Dart, an early graduate of Howard University, Washington, D. C., was the first principal of Howard School, and J. E. Wallace served in the same position for twenty years. The most remarkable record of all the negro educators in Columbia was made by Mrs. Celia Dial Saxon. She gave fifty-seven years of her life to the Columbia public schools and had a record for attendance that is laudable—never tardy and absent only three days. In all of her teaching she always taught right living and good manners. Everyone who was ever taught by her realized that she instilled something a little deeper than mere subject-matter. In addition to her school work, to which she was very faithful, she always en-

[27] Garrett, *Reminiscences.*
[28] Statement of T. G. Brownson, Benedict College Library, 1909.

Benedict University

gaged in civic affairs which had as their purpose the welfare of humanity. She founded the Y. W. C. A. on the corner of Park and Hampton Streets and was one of the founders of Fairwold—a home for delinquent girls.

Another enviable record is that of Thomas J. Greggory, who has taught the same one-teacher rural school in Richland County for more than fifty years. Some years ago he refused the principalship of a five-teacher school because he wanted to round out his life in his little school. He lives in Columbia and has commuted back and forth to Gadsden for almost his entire life.[29]

NEGROES IN PROFESSIONS

N. J. Frederick, who at one time served as principal of the Howard high school, is the outstanding negro lawyer in the state. He became nationally famous when he defended the Lowmans in the celebrated Lowman case of Aiken, South Carolina. He has been practicing law in Columbia for more than twenty years and has the respect of both races.

The first negro physician to practice in Columbia was Dr. C. C. Johnson, a graduate of the medical school of Howard University. He began his practice here in 1890 and maintained his home and office on the northeast corner of Hampton and Assembly Streets.

One of Columbia's most noted physicians was Dr. Matilda A. Evans. She was actively engaged in the medical profession here for

---

[29] Garrett, *Reminiscences.*

thirty-seven years, and in addition to her practice, she conducted a clinic where the poorer colored children of the city were given free treatment. The Taylor Lane Hospital—the first negro hospital ever located in Columbia—was founded by her. A number of Columbia's leading surgeons did their first surgical work at this hospital. She also founded the South Carolina Good Health Association.[30]

Dr. J. G. Stuart is the first and only negro specialist in the city—specializing in the ear, eye, nose and throat. He studied at Freedman's Hospital in Washington, D. C. Two other physicians who, from the standpoint of length of service, should be mentioned here are: Dr. N. A. Jenkins, who founded the Waverley Hospital, and Dr. Frank Johnson, one of Columbia's pioneers in the medical profession.

GOVERNMENT EMPLOYEES

Quite a few negroes have made splendid records in the Columbia post office. J. B. Lewie, who is now retired, worked there thirty-five years. Robert Jackson, the oldest clerk in the office, has been employed there for thirty-two years. There are three other Columbians who have given more than thirty years of service to the department, namely: F. K. Butler, railway clerk, H. N. Vincent, letter carrier, and W. H. Corley, clerk,[31] and N. P. Russell, letter carrier.

Thus we see that the negro has been serving Columbia for one hundred and fifty years. Let us hope that those who are in authority will broaden their opportunities for service so that when the next history of negroes of Columbia is written the contributions of negroes will have greatly increased.

---

[30] *Palmetto Leader,* Columbia, November 23, 1935.
[31] Statement of J. B. Lewie, Columbia, November 25, 1935.

COMMERCE AND MANUFACTURING

By Benjamin F. Taylor

I T WAS inevitable that a city of importance should be established where Columbia now is. It lies at the head of navigation of the greatest river system in the state and practically in the center of the state. In early days it was the meeting point for trade with the Indians and Up Country and Charles Town traders. In 1718 a fort and trading point was established at "the Congarees" to which the Indians and traders resorted for carrying on their business. For thirty years there was no interruption of this peaceful commerce but the French and Indian War necessitated the rebuilding of the fort in 1748 and an expedition into the Indian country. With peace the trading was resumed and thousands of Virginians and Pensylvanians settled in our Up Country. "The Congarees" grew in importance and eventually a town was built near-by, known as Granby.[1]

Granby continued to be the trading place for the Up Country until Columbia grew into a town of some importance.

In 1792 the white population of Columbia was 2,479 and the negroes numbered 1,451. Only 596 of the white population were males over sixteen years of age. Manufacturing in the whole Up Country was entirely in the household stage excepting metals, hides, shoes, glass and liquors.[2] The stores of Kershaw and Chesnut, James Taylor and others at Granby brought from Charleston, cloth, sugar, salt, spices, tea, soap, and other articles that could not be made at home. They bought the produce of the plantations to be transported to Charleston by wagons or boats for resale.[3] There was but little currency and the merchants had to keep running accounts which were settled once a year.

The Catawba Indians peddled bows and arrows, moccasins, earthenware pots and pans of their own manufacture, and Yankee peddlers supplied families with tinware and other light goods.

The completion of the Santee Canal and the other canals and locks on the Broad and Saluda rivers gave great impetus to the trade of young Columbia. Before that boats could go only as far as George-

---

[1] "Dr. Thornton Whaling Tells of Granby . . .," *The State,* April 28, 1930.

[2] D. D. Wallace, *The History of South Carolina,* New York, 1934, II, 87, 365.

[3] John Drayton, *A View of South Carolina* . . ., Charleston, 1802, pp. 210-211.

town, a place of comparatively little importance, and most of the goods had to be hauled by wagons to Charleston. So difficult and slow was water transportation that the boats were often sold as lumber when they reached the ports.

By 1800 the commerce of Columbia was well on its way. Boats of 70 tons burden departed for Charleston loaded with tobacco, cotton, ropes, corn, beeswax, and other articles, returning with salt and such merchandise as the wants of the country required. Castor oil and cottonseed oil were being manufactured; Stephen Brown had a rope walk which promoted the cultivation of hemp and made 80 tons of cordage, rope, and cables in a year. The hemp was raised mostly in the Dutch Fork. He furnished the first rigging of the

Log-Cart and Fine Pine Log

John Adams, a war vessel of 32 guns built near Charleston in 1799.[4] A number of grist mills were in operation and saw mills were turning out millions of feet of lumber for export—such lumber as we shall never see again. I have seen solid boards of heart pine, with not a strip of sapwood on them, three feet wide, in a wing of Colonel Thomas Taylor's home. A tan yard was in operation and the owner, Benjamin Waring, was the first to use circular saws for disintegrating the oak bark instead of grinding it as had been done before.[5] William Edward Hayne the son of the martyr and John G. Brown, a son-in-law of Governor John Taylor, were operating saw mills.[6]

[4] *Ibid.*
[5] J. M. Bateman, *A Columbia Scrap Book,* 1701-1842, Columbia, 1915, p. 31.
[6] E. L. Green, "Columbia in 1806," *The State,* Oct. 17, 1909.

George Henesay was making coaches; C. Hochstrasser, hats; Boatwright and Matthews, cotton gins;[7] and blacksmiths, iron implements, nails, hinges and other metal articles.

Cattle were driven to Charleston in herds.[8] And be it known, the first settler of Richland District established cow pens just above Columbia on Crane Creek. The will of John Taylor, father of Colonel Thomas Taylor, mentions fifty head of black cattle (1766) so it would appear that our planters were not unaware of good breeds of cattle if these were in fact the black Angus cattle of Scotland.

The records do not show that beef was packed in casks for export but salt pork and bacon were cured at Columbia for export and for sale to the plantations.[9] Scott says that prior to the organization of the bank of the state in 1812, the drovers sold their cattle in Charleston for Spanish silver coin which composed almost the entire currency; that goods were hauled by wagons and upon the rivers, and freights on heavy articles like iron and salt were enormously high. For safety and company the wagons went together in large numbers, and it was not unusual to see a dozen or more in a gang.

Mills, in his *Statistics of South Carolina* published in 1826, from notes taken in the field while making his survey of the state, and which, therefore, may refer to conditions several years prior to that publication, says that much of the trade of Charleston had been taken by Columbia and several Charleston merchants had moved to Columbia. The population of the town was 4,000. There were four stage coaches a week to Charleston leaving three times a week; one to Augusta three times a week; one to Camden three times a week, and one to Greenville once a week.

The planters of Columbia, unlike those in the Low Country, had not abandoned their merchandising. Merchants were not looked upon as socially below the planters and many marriages between the planter and merchant families occurred.[10] In 1790 James Taylor owned 170 slaves, but he continued to conduct his store until about 1806 and died soon after.

Adequate and prompt transportation is essential to trade and manufacturing. While the Santee Canal improved trade in Columbia it was still a slow and expensive method, particularly as to the trip up the rivers to the city. It took from three weeks to a month to

[7] E. L. Green, "Columbia, Her Beginning as a City," *The State*, November 14, 1909.
[8] E. G. Scott, *Random Recollections of a Long Life*, 1806-1876, Columbia, p. 10.
[9] Alexander Gregg, *History of the Old Cheraws*, Columbia, 1925, p. 10.
[10] Wallace, *History of South Carolina*, II, 363-364.

pole the boats up stream, and at least a week to float them down.
As many as fifteen men were required for each boat of large size
and few of the boats were equipped with sails. Salt could be bought
at 75c per bushel in Charleston and the freight cost was $1.50.
Many other articles cost less than the amount of the transportation
charges.

In the decade, 1820-30, Charleston declined in trade. The improvement of transportation by water and by the state road, completed in 1829, was having its effect. Columbia and other fall line
towns were growing in importance. Still the freight rates were
enormously high. The tolls for using the state road from Charleston
to Columbia amounted to $9.00 for the round trip for four horse
wagons.[11] The South Carolina Canal and Railroad Company was
chartered in 1827 to build a road from Charleston to Aiken in order
to draw some of the business to Charleston that was going to
Augusta from the Up Country. That line was completed in 1830 but
not until 1842 did it carry 60,000 bales of cotton a year. In soliciting
subscriptions not a share was taken at Columbia. A line was later
run from Branchville to Columbia.[12]

In 1821 the steamboat, *City of Columbia*, ascended the Santee
and Congaree to Columbia. A bridge across the Congaree at the
foot of Gervais street was completed in 1827, and one over the
Saluda in 1829.[13]

In 1822 John McLean owned a street railroad, worked by horse
power, which ran from Cotton Town (Elmwood Avenue and Main
street) through the middle of Main street and Gervais street to
the basin on the canal, where Alexander Herbemont kept a warehouse for storage of goods.[14] When an excavation was being made
at the corner of Main and Taylor streets a number of years ago the
writer saw a section of this tram road uncovered showing the cross
ties and rails. It was some four feet below the then surface of the
street.

At that time the city had developed into a considerable market for
cotton, tobacco and other country produce. This trade was concentrated at Cotton Town. Later Richard O'Neal, James Cathcart,
P. P. Chambers and Amzie Neely were the cotton merchants. Cotton
was brought down the Saluda and Broad in boats to the basin at the
foot of Elmwood Avenue and hauled to Cotton Town and there

---

[11] *Ibid.*, p. 402.
[12] *Ibid.*
[13] Green, "Columbia, Her Beginning as a City," *The State*, November 14,
1909.
[14] Scott, *Random Recollections*, p. 22.

Columbia Curb Market, 1935

disposed of. Much of it was hauled in by wagons from the surrounding country.[15] Hogs were driven from Tennessee and Gabe Starling butchered them and cured the meat at Butcher Town on Main street above Elmwood Avenue.

Tobacco had been from early days an important article of trade. There were state inspectors at Granby and Charleston. Williams states that in his day the tobacco was packed in large hogsheads, to the ends of which were fixed axles, and to these, shafts for hitching a horse so that they could be rolled along.[16]

The manufacture of cotton gins was far behind the demand for many years after Whitney's invention. The production of cotton was growing by leaps and bounds. In 1806 James Boatwright and Middleton Glaze, William Manson and James Young had factories at Columbia.[17] In 1856 James M. Elliott was manufacturing the "Campbell Gin." [18] In addition to gins, cotton presses were necessary. The early press consisted of a box at the bottom into which the bags were put to hold the cotton. Into this box, what might be called the "screw" was forced down upon the cotton by mule power. The screw was made by cutting a large thread in a heart pine log about a foot in diameter. It ran through a block in which grooves were cut to fit the screw. At the top of the screw two long levers were extended

15 J. F. Williams, *Old and New Columbia,* Columbia, 1929, p. 44.
16 *Ibid.,* p. 43.
17 Green, "Columbia in 1806," *The State,* October 17, 1909.
18 Advertisement of James M. Elliott, *South Carolina Agriculturist,* Columbia, July, 1856.

Old Style Cotton Press and Gin, 1825

to about three feet from the ground, and to the ends of these two mules were hitched who walked around in a circle, gradually pressing down on the cotton in the box until the required density was reached. The screw was lubricated to lessen the friction, nevertheless the screeching of these presses could be heard for quite a distance. As late as 1880 one of these presses stood on Major Tom Taylor's place a mile or two from the city.

The manufacturers of gins also made these presses, but they were abandoned with the invention of the steam press.

Cooperage was a necessity from early days. The cooper shops made hogsheads, barrels for molasses and whiskey, well buckets, water buckets and milk piggins. As late as 1856 Henry Hennies had a shop in the city.

The grinding of wheat and corn was coeval with every settlement. Practically every creek around Columbia had its grist mill. They used burstone for the grinders. In the early days of the city there was a grist mill on the branch which ran from Sidney Park to the river, and later one on the canal operated by Jacob Geiger. The Fishers had one on Rocky Branch and Dr. Fred Green one on the canal. "Water Ground Meal" still has its advocates. The application of steam and electric power and the use of steel disc mills (about 1890) instead of the rock grinders has greatly reduced the cost of milling.

In 1934 the investment in grain mills in the city was $275,500.00 and the value of annual output $746,461.00. Wages paid were $49,768.00.[19]

Man must eat to live. There were few bakeries, at first, since every family and plantation made its own bread. There was little chance of going beyond the confines of the city to dispose of bakery products because transportation was slow and servants' hire, or maintainance cheap. In 1826 servants' wages were from six to ten dollars a month. Before the War of Secession bakeries were established and for a time served only the community. In 1860 there were five bakeries in the city.[20] By 1880 several bakeries were operating successfully. I recall that Mrs. Stieglitz conducted one for many years. The quickening of rail and express service and the advent of the auto-truck have made the city an important center for bakery products. The Claussen Bakery has on several occasions taken the prize for the best loaf of bread in the contests of the Bakers' Association of the United States.

In 1934 the bakery business of the city had $209,577.00 invested; an annual value of product of $548,273.00; and paid in wages $128,-554.00. In number there were seven.

Prior to 1826 Mr. Abram Blanding established a water system for the city. It was located in Sidney Park and drew its water from the cold spring at the bottom of the hill. It was pumped by a steam engine which also provided the power for grinding wheat and corn.[21]

In 1867 Professor Holmes of Charleston discovered phosphate rock. A plant was erected at Charleston for making acid phosphate, which is most important as a fertilizer for crops.

In 1889 the Columbia Phosphate Company was organized by Dr. T. C. Robertson. Two years later he built the Globe Phosphate Works. These were followed by the F. S. Royster Guano Company, The Congaree Fertilizer Company, and The American Agricultural Chemical Company and the Swift and Armour plants.

These plants have a greater distribution territory at lower cost of freight than the port plants. In volume of business the fertilizer plants rank very high in the city.

In 1934 the Year Book of the Commissioner of Agriculture, Manufacture and Labor gives the invested captial in four plants as $478,474.00; the value of annual product $1,440,607.00; and wages $85,825.00.

---

[19] J. Roy Jones, *Twenty-Seventh Annual Report of the Commissioner of Agriculture, Labor Division,* Columbia, 1933-34.
[20] Williams, *Old and New Columbia,* p. 75.
[21] Robert Mills, *Statistics of South Carolina,* Charleston, 1826, p. 706.

The reduction in the consumption of fertilizer in the state has caused the abandonment of three of the plants that were once here. The peak of production and sale of fertilizers within the state was in 1920 when 1,106,941 tons were sold within the state. Comparatively low prices for cotton, and more recently, the production curtailment program reduced fertilizer sale to 613,620 tons in 1934.

The census report gives the production of cotton in South Carolina in 1920 as 1,652,177 bales and in 1934, 682,000 bales.

Furniture was, of course, made at home in the early days. Those planters who had their trained carpenters and cabinet makers supplied their own needs, and even the poorer people made their "split bottom" oak and hickory chairs and rude tables and beds.

My search of the records in the newspapers has not been by any means thorough, but I find our old and respected citizen M. H. Berry advertising in *The Farmer and Planter Advertiser,* in June, 1859, that he was "prepared to make with steam and machinery, furniture in the best style."

Back in the eighties the Bentwood Furniture Factory was operating at the penitentiary but for some reason discontinued. The Fibercraft Chair Company is now operating at the same place. Its investment is $50,000.00; annual product $240,000.00, and wages paid $50,732.00.[22]

We have spoken of lumber as being one of the principal products manufactured in the early days. Most of the lumber was cut at water mills. At one time Congaree creek on the Lexington side of the river was diverted by a dam and canal that ran near Granby graveyard, and timber was floated down the canal to be sawed at the river bank. The old Charleston road crosses this canal just below Cayce, and remains of the old dam are still evident in Congaree creek swamp. It was not long after the steam engine and circular saws were invented that practically all the timber near the city was exhausted. There were no large saw mills near the city in my boyhood. Since the war I think four lines of railroads have entered the city and points along these were closer to the timber and therefore most of the cutting of lumber was outside the city.

In my lifetime the forests have become somewhat re-established and portable saw mills have cut many millions of feet of lumber. There are now two mills operating at Cayce that bring in the logs by rail and by truck to be sawn.

---

[22] Jones, *Twenty-Seventh Annual Report of the Commissioner of Agriculture,* 1935.

Within the city the lumber business is still considerable but it is brought in for retail sales, and for manufacturing dressed lumber; doors, blinds, paneling, sashes and other building supplies. The investment in these enterprises is $91,800.00 and the annual output is $186,729.00. Wages paid amount to $54,790.00.[23]

Iron working in the early days of the town was a prime necessity. The blacksmiths made everything from nails to strap hinges. Horses and mules and even oxen had to be shod. The wagon wheels had to have iron tires. The multitude of iron implements needed on the farms and all the axles for wagons were made at home.

On December 15th, 1806, William Edward Hayne advertised that

> The Aetna Furnace (in York District) is now blowing, and will continue so during the winter and ensuing spring. All kinds of machinery, hollow and other castings, will be furnished on the shortest notice, delivered in any part of the State on the most reasonable terms. * * * For further particulars apply to Messrs. Waring and Hayne in Charleston, Messrs. John Schultz & Co. in Columbia, Mr. Willie Vaughan in Camden, Mr. Thomas Barrett in Augusta, or at the Furnace.

There were at least nine iron furnaces in the state at one time but they were all finally abandoned. The state bears the distinction of being the only one in the Union which has abandoned the smelting of iron ore.

Coaches and wagons were recorded as being made early in the nineteenth century. In 1850 the Palmetto Armory was built by Glaze & Boatwright, one of our early manufacturing concerns, for converting old arms to more modern types and Mr. Geo. A. Shields, who in his day was one of our most respected and successful citizens, came to work for that concern July 4, 1850. Was this preparation for war?

In 1859 Boatwright was still making cotton gins; S. F. Moore was making wagons. John Alexander & Company making sugar cane mills, iron and brass castings, steam engines, mill gearing, wagons, and saw mills.[24]

J. F. Williams in *Old and New Columbia* records that in 1860 there were four carriage manufacturies, five blacksmiths and wheelwrights,[25] and Scott records the manufacture of nails, copper working, bayonets, files and swords.

In 1871 there were four iron works, and the car shops of the Charlotte, Columbia & Augusta Railroad, now Southern Railway.[26]

---

[23] *Ibid.*
[24] *The Farmer and Planter,* Columbia, June, 1859.
[25] Williams, *Old and New Columbia,* p. 75.
[26] J. D. Caldwell, *The Future Manufacturing and Commercial Center of the South,* Columbia, 1871.

Parr Shoals Power Plant

This shop built and repaired box cars and passenger coaches and kept the locomotives in running order. Many of our best mechanics served their apprenticeship there. I recall at the moment S. B. Mc-Master, Christopher Atkinson, and Laurence Taylor.

In 1888 D. P. Robbins lists the Dial Engine Works, Palmetto Iron Works, and Congaree Iron Works. Tozer and Dial made the best portable engine of their time. They also repaired and built locomotives and manufactured saw mills and agricultural implements. With the advent of the cotton mills the Palmetto Iron Works (Geo. A. Shields, proprieter), did a thriving business making castings for many of them.[27]

The first gas plant was established in Columbia in 1852.[28] I remember well the lamp-lighter who drove from lamp-post to

---

[27] At present (1934) the machine shops of the city have invested $229,877.00. The value of annual output is $799,366.00, and they paid out in wages $592,369.00. See Jones, *Twenty-Seventh Annual Report of the Commissioner of Agriculture.*
[28] D. P. Robbins, *Descriptive Sketch of Columbia, S. C.,* Columbia, 1888, p. 59.

lamp-post and lit the burners, and often wonder how he got around in time. I suspect there is not a single pipe of the old distribution lines in service today for the growth of the city has necessitated the enlargement and extension of the lines several times in the eighty-three years since the first plant was built.[29]

The first electric light plant was built in 1891 on Gates street between Gervais and Lady streets. Mr. A. F. McKissick was in charge of the plant but soon afterwards left it to become a professor at Auburn, Alabama. Mr. Alfred Wallace had charge of this plant from 1892 to 1893 when power was taken from the canal and the Columbia Street Railway Light and Power Company was organized. This company and its successors became eventually the Broad River Power Company which still supplies lights to the city.

At some later date the gas plant was acquired by the Broad River Light and Power Company.

The first street railway was built in 1882 and was operated by horse power,[30] but on March 8, 1894, it was converted into an electric line,[31] and consolidated with the electric lighting plant in 1896.

The Columbia Canal was completed December 11, 1891, official announcement being made January 11, 1892, by Bryon Holly. In 1893 electricity was being generated from it, but the demand for power was greater than the production from the canal when the cotton mills began to operate so a ten thousand horse power steam auxiliary plant had to be built. Still there was not enough power, so the Broad River Power Company built the dam on the Broad river at Parr Shoals and later added a large powdered coal auxiliary plant there.

The Lexington Power Company was organized by Mr. T. C. Williams and W. S. Barstow Company and completed the development at Lake Murray on the Saluda river in 1930. The cost of this development was given at $20,000,000.00 and the electric horse power as 222,600.[32]

---

[29] Columbia has $3,054,272.00 invested in gas plants and equipment with a yearly production of $315,899.00, and pays $74,601.00 wages yearly in this industry. See Jones, *Twenty-Seventh Annual Report of the Commissioner of Agriculture.*

[30] Robbins, *Sketch of Columbia,* p. 62; *The News and Courier,* Charleston, December 19, 1886.

[31] *The State,* March 8, 1894.

[32] Wallace, *History of South Carolina,* III, 481. Electric production in and near Columbia is enormous. The investments are given as $48,283,556.00; the annual output, $4,656.075.00; and the annual wages paid are $347,466.00. See Jones, *Twenty-Seventh Annual Report of the Commissioner of Agriculture.*

Small industries such as confections, coffins, mattresses, soft drinks, monument and stone cutting, paints, medicines and tobacco are reported as having a combined investment of $131,041.00 with an annual output of $673,068.00 and pay annually in wages $124,204.00. See Jones, *Twenty-Seventh Annual Report of the Commissioner of Agriculture.*

Between 1830 and 1840 ice was cut on Dents Pond by my grand-father and kept until July of each year by which time it was used up or had melted. I have seen the old ice house in my day. I recall the

Highway Across Lake Murray Dam

Bateman's ice house which stood where the Berkeley Apartments now are. The ice was shipped to Columbia from the north and kept in a large pit filled with sawdust. Many and many a time I have gone there after ice. A string was always supplied to tie around the ice so we could carry it in our little hands without freezing them. There were no ice delivery wagons.

Mr. John A. Seegers was the first to install an artificial ice machine in connection with his brewery beyond the State Hospital. It made two tons of ice a day and was imported from Germany. Later Seegers and Habenicht made ice at their plant between Main and Assembly streets on Taylor in 1880.

I believe Messrs. W. S. Reamer and George L. Baker erected the first plant for making ice only in the city. It was located on the Atlantic Coast Line Rairoad between Gervais and Senate streets. Later it was moved and enlarged and put on the Southern Railway at Laurel street. This was followed by the Columbia Ice and Fuel Company and the Reamer ice and fuel plants, in Seaboard Park.

The amount invested in ice plants is $166,208.00; the annual value of product is $176,172.00; and the wages paid $55,634.00.

The first commercial daguerrotypes were made in the city in 1844 by Libolt.[33] Zealy was making ambrotypes and photographs in 1859.[34] There are now five photographic studios in the city.

---

[33] "Columbia in the Early Forties," *The State,* November 28, 1909.
[34] In June, 1859, Zealy advertised in the *Farmer and Planter Advertiser.*

Schmidt was operating a steam laundry in 1888 at the corner of Green and Main streets. There are now six laundries in the city.

The first message over a telephone was completed in 1876. Four years later the Bell Telephone Company was in operation in Columbia with 62 subscribers. The first manager at Columbia was Mr. W. R. Cathcart.[35] He was succeeded in 1892 by W. H. Galloway. Mr. S. T. Lucas succeeded him in 1899. Then came A. C. Hobson in 1910, Fred Marshall in 1915, and Tom Crouch in 1919.

Messrs. Miller and Melton operated a long distance telephone system for a while but this was acquired by the Bell Company very soon. The name of this company was the South Carolina Long Distance Telephone Company.

The dial system was installed in Columbia in 1922 and the number of subscribers in the city is now 9,447.[36]

It may be of interest to know that the Columbia Commercial Association was founded in the city in May, 1844.[37] Its successors have preserved the commercial history of the city in their reports and prospectuses and they afford a mine of information for the student to draw material from.

COTTON

Since early days cotton has been most important in the commerce of the city. Unfortunately there are but few sources of information available to give a full history of the cotton business so far as Columbia is concerned.

In 1823 Robert Mills found that not less than 30,000 bales weighing about 330 pounds each were handled at Columbia. The value was 15c per pound. The freight from Columbia to Charleston was $4.00 per bale. He stated that the price of cotton was very low at that time.[38]

Nearly all the cotton was bought at Cotton Town, as we have stated elsewhere, and stored in brick warehouses to await shipment by boats to Charleston. Some of these warehouses are still standing.

Between 1830 and 1837 Columbia cotton merchants were handling 130,000 bales of cotton but the coming of the railroads diverted most of this to other railroad points.

[35] *Southern Telephone News,* August, 1926; *The State,* June 24, 1926.
[36] Statement by Thomas Crouch, manager.
[37] Green, "Columbia in the Early Forties," *The State,* November 28, 1909.
[38] Mills, *Statistics of South Carolina,* p. 708; Scott, *Random Recollections,* p. 78.

From 1818 to 1821 cotton sold for from 16c to 19c; in 1825 it
went up to 27c. In 1846 it sold for about 9.1c; in 1847 about 9c; in
1857 about 14.3c; and in 1862 about $1.07.[39] Cotton culture re-
covered rapidly after 1865, prices holding generally above 28c
through 1869.[40] It dropped steadily from 8.1c in January, 1894, to
5.12c in November and December and after partially recovering from
late 1895 to September, 1897, sank to 5.1 and 5.8 during 1898. Not

A Modern Cotton Warehouse

until 1900 did New York pay 10 cents, after which prices ranged
for three years between 8.6 and 12.12c a pound.

The average price of cotton from 1909 to 1914 inclusive was
12.4c per pound. This, under the agricultural adjustment Act was
taken as the parity price on which benefit payments were calculated.[41]

---

[39] "Leitzsey Account Book," *The State,* October 7, 1935.
[40] Wallace, *History of South Carolina,* III, 232.
[41] The following were the prices of cotton for the years 1923-1932 and
represent its value on the market free from any governmental interference:

Year	Cents Per Pound
1923	28.7
1924	22.9
1925	19.6
1926	12.5
1927	20.2
1928	18.0
1929	16.8
1930	9.5
1931	5.7
1932	6.5

The prices of cotton mentioned by authorities quoted cannot be compared
with the reports of prices published by the Census Bureau because yearly
average prices only are reported by the Government. And for the years 1910
to 1933, inclusive, the average price received by the growers is given; for earlier
years it is the average price of the grade marketed in New Orleans (1902-
1909). For the years 1890 to 1901 it is the average price of middling cotton

From 1868 to 1895 the cotton buyers depended almost entirely upon the local deliveries of cotton in Columbia. There were no mills in the city and most of the cotton was shipped to the ports for export or for supplying the New England mills. Among the buyers were Mr. Richard O'Neal and John A. Crawford & Sons. The cotton was bought on Gervais street near the Atlantic Coast Line and Southern freight depots.

In 1887 the Columbia Compress Company was organized for the compression and storage of cotton. Their compress had a capacity of 100 bales an hour. Of recent years the compression of cotton has been discontinued and the warehouse is now used for storage of cotton. It can take care of 35,000 bales.

As has been noted elsewhere, the building of the large cotton mills between 1895 and 1900 created a much larger demand for cotton than the surrounding country could supply. New cotton merchants opened offices in the city and extended their operations all over the state. The late M. C. Heath built up a large business and was succeeded by Joseph Walker and Company. At present Anderson Clayton and Company, P. A. Lowry and Company, and John F. Maybank and Company are, with Walker, the leading cotton merchants of the city.

The city has become a concentration point for export and domestic supplies of cotton. The mills consume about 50,000 bales and the merchants handle about 200,000 bales.

The Columbia Compress has a storage capacity of 35,000 bales, the Standard Warehouse organized in 1905 a capacity of 40,000 bales, and the Palmetto Compress and Warehouse Company a capacity of 60,000 bales, and in connection with the warehouses, a compress with capacity of 100 bales per hour of high density or 125 of standard density.

COTTON MILLS

When Columbia had its birth commerce with Charleston and Virginia was already taking its first steps. One of the chief articles of trade was cloth. Our people had passed the frontier age and its buckskin garments, and linen and woolen goods were in demand. Nearly every poor family had its spinning wheel and loom and raised its "patch" of cotton which they harvested, and while sitting by their light-wood fires at night separated the seed from the lint. They

on the New Orleans Exchange; and for the years 1790 to 1889 from reports of the Department of Agriculture.

carded the fiber by hand and spun and wove it into sheets and cloth for making clothes.

The slave owning families had their negroes to do this manufacturing of cloth, both woolen and cotton, because it was cheaper than having to buy the cloth from merchants. They seldom, if ever, made more than what was required for family or plantation. As early as 1777 Daniel Heyward writes his son Thomas Heyward, Jr., that he could make as much as 6,000 yards of cotton cloth on his looms.[42]

The invention of the cotton gin made it possible to increase greatly the use of cotton. In 1801 the state of South Carolina purchased from Messrs. Miller and Whitney the right to use the Whitney gin and it is recorded that General Wade Hampton purchased before that, three gins in Georgia which he brought to Columbia. These were said to be the first power gins used in the state. His cotton crop for that year was worth about $90,000.00.[43] Very soon several concerns began to manufacture gins in Columbia and the manufacture of cotton goods gained great impetus. James Boatwright and Middleton Glaze were probably the first to engage in this business of making gins in Columbia, but in 1806 William Manson and James Young were also making them.[44] For a time the demand was greater than they could supply.

I have before me the following letter dated Columbia, March 28th, 1809, from Colonel Thomas Taylor to his son, Henry P. Taylor in Charleston.

> Dear Son
> This will Serve to tell you we are all well and to request you to try and get me a flying Shuttell and send it up by your brother John. By applying to Mr. frenow Expect you will hear where they are to be got as he told me they are making them Sum where in town. We are going on well with the Common Shutell But my Irish man Says we will do doubell if wee had the flying Shutell. Gasgard weaves me 12 yds a day 1½ yds wide of as good Bagging as ever was packed i have 325 lbs of cotton put into 4 3/4 yds of cloth not one bag has a singel thred gave way & are the nicest bags I ever Saw all made out of the infearer yellow cotton i began in febuary & have got 1600 yards ready which is suficient for the balance of my present crop I nevar Shall purchis another Cotton bag nor Negro Clothing Sheats nor Counterpins Were I a young man

---

[42] August Kohn, *The Cotton Mills of South Carolina*, Charleston, 1907, pp. 7-8, quoting from Governor Glen, in his answers to the Lords of Trade (1748), reprinted in P. C. T. Weston, *Documents Connected with South Carolina*, London, 1856, p. 86.

[43] Wallace, *History of South Carolina*, II, 381-382, quoting from D. A. Thompkins, *The Cotton Gin; The History of its Invention*, Charlotte, 1901, p. 57. See also Green, *History of Richland County*, p. 139.

[44] Green, "Columbia in 1806," *The State*, August 17, 1909.

the Expearance of that wise meashure of the Imbargo that our gover-
ment first took, and to live as long as i have done I Should more than
doubell the fortune i have made by this mode of Saving

  Am with due respects your well wishing father

  Mr. Henry Taylor.   THOMAS TAYLOR

(Pinned to the letter are samples of the sheeting and cotton
bagging.)

The mere fact that a dependable and adequate supply of cotton
was at hand could not in a few years convert the community into a
manufacturing town. The extent of its manufacturing was at first
only to supply the
immediate a n d
personal needs of
the people. There
w a s no thought
of p l a c i n g its
g o o d s on the
markets of t h e
world. The lack
of transportation
h a d forced the
people to econom-
ic s e l f suffici-
ency.[45]

In 1810 govern-
ment reports show
that all manufac-
turing plants to-
gether made less
than one million
y a r d s of cloth,
while plantations
a n d individuals
made f o r family
use more than fif-
teen m i l l i o n
yards.[46] However,
that valuable and
enterprising citi-

Sheeting Made in Columbia, 1809

zen of Columbia, Benjamin Waring, promoted and operated a fully
equipped cotton mill near Stateburg in 1790.

---

[45] Wallace, *History of South Carolina*, II, 384.
[46] Kohn, *Cotton Mills of South Carolina*, p. 7.

Edward and John Fisher established the first real cotton factory at Sand Creek (now Gill Creek) and the old building still stands just below the dam at Dents Pond. It was operated by negro labor and continued until they bought the Saluda factory from Ewart and Blanding who built it in 1832.[47] The Saluda factory was operated largely by slave labor until the close of the war, when it was

Where Cotton Goods were Manufactured as Early as 1809, Originally Built by Thomas Taylor

operated by white labor. Hammond states that one white overseer was in charge of ninety negro slaves as operatives and that these slaves were "capable of learning within reasonable limits." In 1847 this factory had 5,000 spindles and 120 looms on brown shirtings and southern stripes.[48]

> The evolution of the Cotton Mills in South Carolina has been exceedingly slow; partly because of slave labor being regarded as more profitable when employed in growing cotton, and because white labor was not available to any extent for mill purposes." [49]

In the *Farmer and Planter,* published June, 1859, is quoted a letter published in *Dr. Bow's Review* condemning the mechanical training of slaves, contending that this competition would drag down the white mechanic and was calculated to breed discontent and hatred on the part of the white mechanic and make him an enemy to an institution which should be the means of promoting the interests of the very pursuit in which he is engaged. It would create a spirit of antagonism between the rich and the poor, from the fact that the rich arrayed capital against labor and elevated the negro at the expense of the poor white mechanic.

---

[47] Scott, *Random Recollections,* pp. 44-45; Kohn, *Cotton Mills of South Carolina,* pp. 44-45.
[48] *Ibid.,* p. 16.
[49] *Ibid.,* p. 20.

Gregg in 1855 said about the operatives who were contributing to the success of the Graniteville mills, "We may really regard ourselves as the pioneer in developing the real character of the poor people of South Carolina. Graniteville is truly the home of the poor widow and helpless children, or for a family brought to ruin by a drunken, worthless father." [50]

Columbia Mills, Where Electricity First Applied as Motive Power for Cotton Mill

"Even under the unfavorable influence of slavery, cotton manufacturing was struggling toward its natural place. In 1820, South Carolina had 588 spindles; . . . in 1860, 30,890 in 17 mills; . . . and in 1931, 5,689,642 (spindles) in 239 mills, employing 73,559 people, and supporting a village population of 187,305 people." [51]

As to the value of slave labor: In 1841 some rice planters entered into a contract to build a dyke for their mutual protection on the Savannah River and engaged to pay their respective shares in cash or in slave labor at the rate of one dollar per day per head. In 1862 Nathaniel Heyward supplied 50 slaves to the Confederate States for building military defenses around Charleston at the rate of thirty

---

[50] *Ibid.,* p. 21.
[51] Wallace, *History of South Carolina,* III, 479-480.

dollars per month per head.[52] As late as 1917 the average daily wage for negro labor at Columbia was one dollar per day. This probably was not increased until 1932 when the National Recovery Act and the President's agreement were put into effect as to rates and hours for labor. White labor has always commanded better wages than negro labor, and so those white persons wanting work have drifted naturally into the textile plants where they can work side by side with their own race.

Section 1272 of the Code of South Carolina provides for the separation of the races in textile plants, and permits employment of negro labor only for scrubbers, firemen, carpenters, brick-layers, pipe-fitters, and as laborers engaged in repairing and erection of buildings and machinery.

In 1860 there were but three cotton mills in the state, one of them at Columbia. There was also a small plant in the city making yarns for knitting stockings, and carded cotton for quilting and mattresses. After the war there was no progress in cotton manufacturing in the city until 1880, when the Columbia canal was sold to Thompson and Nagle. This firm advertised sites along the side of the canal for cotton mills and other manufacturing plants, but they got into financial difficulties and sold the canal before it was completed. Their

Olympia Mill, 110,000 Spindles Under One Roof

successors completed it about 1895. The engineers of the Columbia mills, then about to be built, urged that the mill be placed on the

[52] Nathaniel Heyward Papers, MS University of S. C. Library.

hill above the canal instead of on the river side and be operated by electricity, generated at the wheels and transmitted to motors in the mill. After much discussion and considerable doubt it was decided to install the electric drive.

This was the first time electricity was used for driving a cotton mill and the almost limitless use of transmitted power ensued.[53]

About this time Mr. W. B. Smith Whaley and his associate, Mr. G. E. Shand, successfully introduced and applied the electric motor at the Granby and Olympia mills in Columbia.[54] These large mills, the Olympia having 110,000 spindles under one roof, were soon followed by the Richland, the Capital City and the Glencoe Cotton Mills. All of these are operating at this time. In addition to these the Coltex Fabrics, Inc., has a plant operating for making hair cloth for use in oil mills, and the Southern Aseptic Laboratories make absorbent cotton, and cotton pads.[55]

Some one has said where one's family is buried, there is his home. The mill people of Columbia who came here uneducated, sickly, and impoverished forty years ago, are today indistinguishable from the rest of the white population in appearance, dress, or education. No one can see any difference between a "mill hand" and any other working person. Many of the sons and daughters born in the mill villages have sought other work and have been successful in other pursuits. We are informed by the manager of one of the large mills that labor turnover in his plant is negligible. This is because the mill population consider this their home. Their families are here, their friends are here and so are their dead. Their boys served across the seas and some were left there.

The efficiency of operations in the mills at Columbia has caused the concentration of orders for cloth here rather than at affiliated mills elsewhere, and has had much to do with having Columbia recorded as having "good business conditions" all through the depression from which the country is now emerging.

-----

[53] Kohn, *The Water Powers of South Carolina,* Charleston, 1910, p. 17.
[54] *Ibid.*
[55] The report of the Commissioner of Agriculture, Commerce and Labor for the year 1934 gives the following data concerning the textile plants at Columbia:

Capital invested, $2,929,272.00; value of annual product, $7,221,848.00; number days operated, 234; number salaried employees, 41; number persons employed, 2,943; total wages, not including salaries of managers, $1,853,576.00; number of spindles, 257,052; number of looms, 5,129; number of bales of cotton, 50,129; tons of coal consumed, 6,418; village population, 5,800; electric horse power consumed, 10,225. See Jones, *Twenty-Seventh Annual Report of the Commissioner of Agriculture.*

COTTONSEED OIL MILLS

Cottonseed oil and seed cake was produced many centuries before the Christian era in India and China. The seed from the West Indies and English colonies was crushed in England to a limited extent before the Revolution, but the crush was limited because of the difficulty of separating the lint from the seed. Exports from South Carolina did not amount to much until the Whitney gin came into use.

One of the early settlers of Columbia was Benjamin Waring, a decendant of Governor Thomas Smith. He was treasurer of the state and one of the commissioners appointed to sell the lots of the newly formed city.[56] As early as 1790 he was associated with others in the establishment of a cotton mill at Stateburg on or near his plantation there.[57] Before 1801 he had been operating a mill for making castor oil at Columbia and some time before 1801 had crushed cottonseed in this mill producing half a gallon of oil from a bushel of seed.[58] This was the first known attempt to manufacture oil from cottonseed in the United States.

How long he continued the experiment is not known but the successful operation of oil mills in this country at that time was practically impossible because of lack of adequate transportation and lack of a market for the oil. At any rate the potential value of the oil and cake was known. In 1808 Mr. John Palmer of St. Stephen's wrote Dr. David Ramsay that "he had wonderful corn by putting a pint of cottonseed around each hole," showing that the value of the seed as a fertilizer was also known.[59]

The next recorded attempt to manufacture cottonseed oil was by Governor David R. Williams at Society Hill about 1826. He, as Waring had done, was making castor oil and probably used the same kind of machinery for producing cotton oil.[60]

In 1869 General E. P. Alexander, then a resident of Columbia, established an oil mill in Columbia which produced 3,000 gallons of oil a week. The company refined its own oil, making one grade said to have been as good as olive oil, and for cooking better than lard, and a third cheaper; another grade destined to supersede linseed oil. The cake was stated to be the best stock food in the market.

---

[56] A letter from him in the possession of the writer.
[57] Kohn, *Cotton Mills of South Carolina*, p. 9.
[58] Drayton, *View of South Carolina*, p. 212.
[59] Letter in Charleston Library quoted by Wallace, *History of South Carolina*, II, 377.
[60] Wallace, *History of South Carolina*, II, 407; *The Southern Agriculturist*, December 1829, p. 563.

The hulls were used as fuel and the ashes for fertilizer. This mill continued in operation for several years but was closed because, as Dr. A. N. Talley, one of the stockholders, said, the price of oil was too low and the price of seed was too high.[61] At that time the English exporters were free buyers of cottonseed, but preferred the sea-island variety because it was less liable to heat aboard ship than the upland variety. As late as 1905 these exporters continued to harass the oil mills by keeping the cost of cottonseed too high.

Mr. H. M. Gibson and his son-in-law Mr. W. C. Mikell established a small mill at Columbia about 1880 which continued in operation for several years but was finally driven out of the market by competition from the two large mills built in the city.

The Oliver Oil Mill was built at Columbia in 1885 and soon after was merged with The American Cotton Oil Company. Not long after that the Olivers withdrew from the company on account of a disagreement with the president, Mr. Urquhart, and organized the Southern Cotton Oil Company. One of its mills was built in Columbia in 1887 under the management of Mr. Stirling Price. Soon after, Mr. Christopher FitzSimons was made manager and continued in that capacity until his death.

It is not the purpose of this history to dwell too much upon the men we mention but we must record the fact that the city has had in all its history no finer men and citizens than Christopher FitzSimons and George L. Baker. These two, managing competing oil mills, were life-long friends, public-spirited citizens, and accomplished gentlemen.

In 1904 the Taylor Manufacturing Company was built and in 1911 was sold to Swift and Company. It continues to be operated under the management of Mr. W. T. Mikell, a grandson of Mr. H. M. Gibson who built an oil mill in the city in 1878.

The American Cotton Oil Company's mill was abandoned and sold some years ago when that company was liquidated.

And so, Columbia, the pioneer city of oil milling, still does its part in feeding both man and live stock. It still supplies the material for comfortable sleep; for soft pads for the wounded and sick; for fine clothing, and in time of war for explosives.[62]

---

[61] L. A. Ransom quoting John D. Caldwell.

[62] Commissioner of Agriculture, Manufactures and Labor report on cotton-seed oil mills—year 1934:

Capital invested, $275,000.00; value of products, $569,625.00; days operated, 168; salaried employees, 11; average number of employees, 72; wages, not including salaries of managers, $26,931.00. See Jones, *Twenty-Seventh Annual Report of the Commissioner of Agriculture.*

MINING

Columbia lies on the last outcrop of granite in the Santee drainage area. Strange as it may seem it was not until 1856 that any attempt was made to use this excellent building material. The State House is the first structure in the city made of this stone. A quarry was opened on the river where Granby Lane ran down to the landing and where a ferry was once operated. The stone was of most excellent quality and the great monolithic columns on the front and back porches of the State House testify as to its fine grain and beauty.

In order to carry the stone from the quarry to the site of the building a tram road was built which ran down Main street to the corner of College street and thence to the west through the woods and through the present Olympia village to the quarry. The immense stones, weighing tons, were put on the trams and hauled up the hill by oxen to the building and there sawn, dressed, and carved. The elevation was about 200 feet.

There seem to have been no native-born stone masons, for the stone cutters were all Irish or Americans from the north.

With the exception of some rough granite work in chimneys, fire places and foundations this excellent stone has been little used for outside facing of buildings in the city; but large quantities have been mined for construction of jetties in the harbors on the coast and in the rivers. The so called Belgian blocks have been shipped to pave the streets of many cities, and the more recent paving of roads and streets in the state has taken thousands upon thousands of tons of crushed stone from Columbia quarries.

The sand pits near the city supply excellent material for mortar and cement work.

There has been some mining of kaolin near the city, notably at Horrell Hill and Edmunds, in Lexington County.

Large quantities of clay have been used in the surfacing of the sand-clay roads of the country.[63]

BRICK, TILE AND POTTERY

Closely allied to mining is the manufacture of clay products. Near Columbia are admirable deposits of brick clay, and shale. Long

---

[63] The report of the Commissioner of Agriculture, Commerce and Labor for 1934 gives the following statistics concerning mines and mining for Columbia: Capital invested, $475,300.00; value of output, $242,615.00; days operated, 320; salaried employees, 19; other employees, 167; wages, not including salaries of managers, $138,217.00. See Jones, *Twenty-Seventh Annual Report of the Commissioner of Agriculture.*

persons directed in their wills that their personal estates be sold and that slaves be bought and held until their minor children became of age.

The commercial needs of Columbia demanded banking facilities at home, so in 1831 the Commercial Bank of Columbia was chartered. Its stockholders were cotton buyers, merchants, and professional men.[75] This bank weathered the panic of 1837 but went under in 1865 because like all other banks in the state it had bought Confederate and State bonds against which they issued currency and had accepted the fiat money in circulation during the war. Its other assets also became, for the most part, worthless. In 1857 its statement showed discounts of $672,800.00; deposits $140,772.00; specie $78,650.00; and circulation $299,940.00. This bank during its existence had but two presidents, Abram Blanding and John A. Crawford.[76]

In 1852 the Exchange Bank of Columbia was organized but its banking house on Main street was destroyed in 1865 by Sherman and it was then closed.[77] The Bank of the State of South Carolina continued its existence until 1867. Its last manager was John Fisher. It became the prey of the dishonest officials of the state who soon thereafter came into power.[78]

These early banks issued currency secured by their assets as the needs of the people required and the system was good, for they did not fail until the conditions of the War of Secession compelled them. They weathered the panic of 1837 brought about by President Jackson's determination to destroy the Bank of the United States. He withdrew the government deposits in specie and made it necessary for all other banks to suspend specie payment. This caused lack of confidence in all banks and forced the General Assembly to pass a bill imposing impossible penalties on banking.[79] Cotton fell from 18c in February to 8c in May and negroes from $1,500,00 to $400.00 Specie payments were suspended to keep the banks in the state from being drained by the North from May, 1837, to September, 1838, and again from October, 1839, to July, 1840.[80]

As a means of financing the War of Secession Congress passed the act providing for national banks. Circulation notes could be issued when secured by United States bonds and if not secured by them,

[75] Ibid.
[76] Ibid., p. 233.
[77] Ibid., pp. 233-234.
[78] Ibid.; Wallace, History of South Carolina, II, 396.
[79] Clark, Banking Institutions of South Carolina, p. 233.
[80] Wallace, History of South Carolina, II, 481.

there was a tax of 10%. This greatly hampered the issuance of currency and it has only been since 1914, when the Federal Reserve Act was passed, that other securities than bonds could be used as a basis for circulation notes.

Before the war the banking capital of Columbia had been about $2,300,000.00. In 1872 it was reduced to $605,000.00.[81]

During the panic of 1873 the national banks in Columbia suspended payment for sums exceeding $100.00, and the Citizens' Savings Bank went into bankruptcy.[82] It was impossible to raise money. All the banks had ceased to discount notes even upon the best collateral. They had out every dollar they could spare with safety and borrowers offering 2% per month with good security went begging.[83]

George W. Williams of Charleston, who had amassed a fortune during the war by buying sterling exchange in 1861 with Confederate money at 103 which he sold at 225 in 1865, and who had his brokers in New York to sell $600,000.00 sterling exchanges for him, and invest in U. S. Government 7% bonds at less than par, was able to establish the National Bank of Charleston immediately after the war. He furnished $10,000.00 to his partner E. J. Scott in 1866 to establish a bank in Columbia and two years later a profit of $8,000.00 was divided. Scott with a capital of $75,000.00 made a profit of $25,000.00, or more, during 1870-72 without dealing harshly or illiberally with any customer.[84] At that time there were no penalties for usury, the law having been repealed in 1866.

On May 11, 1868, the Carolina National Bank was chartered and Colonel L. D. Childs was elected president. It had a capital of $100,000.00. The demand for money was so great that the capital was increased to $200,000.00 in June, 1869, and to $300,000.00 by January, 1874.

The bank advertised in 1868 that it was "now ready for business and would make loans upon the following collaterals, viz: gold coin, United States bonds and State bonds". Money was in great demand and the rate of interest meant nothing to the borrower, so the bank was tempted to depart from the original conservative policy adopted. The rates of interest on good security were 1% a month for no longer than 60 days, renewals at the rate of 1½% per month. Un-

[81] Simkins and Woody, *South Carolina during Reconstruction,* Chapel Hill, 1932, p. 271.
[82] Scott, *Random Recollections,* p. 208.
[83] Simkins and Woody, *South Carolina during Reconstruction,* p. 273.
[84] Scott, *Random Recollections,* pp. 199, 207-208.

der this influence very questionable collateral was taken and the bank was well nigh ruined.

Then came the great panic of 1873, which threatened failure for every bank in the city. The national banks alone survived. The Citizen's Saving Bank went into the hands of a receiver; the South Carolina Bank and Trust Company went into the hands of a receiver in 1874 costing the state about $400,000.00. Scott, Williams and Company, who had been crippled by a robbery in April, 1870, also made an assignment in June, 1877.[85]

The Central National Bank, organized in 1871, survived the panic of 1873. It was at a subsequent day absorbed by the Loan and Exchange Bank organized in 1886 under a State charter. It later became a national bank.

In 1881 the Carolina National Bank found, after its many losses, that reorganization was necessary and Mr. W. A. Clark was elected president. The capital stock was reduced to $100,000.00 and on February 11, 1881, its resources were $320,139.11. In 1918 its resources had increased to $3,014,795.42 and its capital to $300,000.00.

The Carolina National made it possible for the city to complete the Columbia Canal when it was abandoned by the State as worthless. The building of the cotton mills promoted by W. B. S. Whaley could not have succeeded without the aid of this bank. It was also the financial stay of the electric street railway and the electric light company, and other enterprises in the city.

During the year 1892 the Canal Dimes Savings Bank, the Farmers and Merchants Bank, and the Bank of Columbia were organized in Columbia. Apparently the panic of 1893 had little effect on any of the banks in the city, for little foreign money had been invested here.[86]

The Canal Dime Savings Bank bought the Central National Bank and soon after that it bought the Loan and Exchange Bank of South Carolina and nationalized under the name of the National Loan and Exchange Bank.

The Farmers and Merchants Bank eventually became the Palmetto Bank and Trust Company and then the Palmetto National Bank, which encountering difficulties, was reorganized as the Columbia National Bank and was in a year or two consolidated with the Central Union Bank.

The Union National Bank and the Peoples National Bank consolidated and became the Liberty National Bank.

---

[85] *Ibid.*, pp. 208-209.
[86] *The State*, March 9, 1892; April 1, 1892; June 29, 1892.

In 1907 there was a money panic all over the country. It was almost impossible to get currency or specie, so the clearing house of Columbia issued clearing house certificates to meet the situation. At that time currency circulation was restricted and there was considerable discussion as to what changes should be made in the laws relating to circulating notes. As a result the Aldrich-Vreeland Act

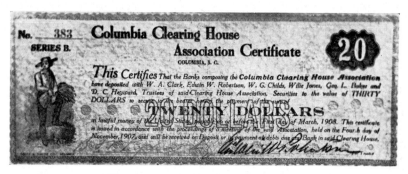

Clearing House Certificate, 1907 Panic

was passed that provided for issuance of currency against securities at a progressive rate of interest. This was followed by the Federal Reserve Act of 1914. At the breaking out of war in 1914 currency became scarce and cotton fell about 7c per pound and the clearing house had again to issue certificates to provide currency to move the crops.

In the period from 1900 to 1914 many banks were organized in the state and Columbia had more than its proportion. The bank examiner in his report for 1910, said:

> Since November, 1901, forty-one new banks were organized. Where will the formation of new banks end? A limit should be placed upon the formation of new banks because they are a menace to existing banks. They compete in unfair ways, break down at critical moments, and threaten the solvency of others.

It was soon to be seen that he was right. When the pressure came bank after bank was consolidated in Columbia. However, under the agreement for mutual assistance, made through the Columbia clearing house, in no case did the depositors lose a cent until the failure of the American Bank and Trust Company, which was not a member of the clearing house.

In 1914 the total deposits of the state banks amounted to about $43,500,000.00 with resources of $79,250,000.00. The last call for

1919 showed deposits $151,500,000.00 and resources $188,994,760.00. In one year from November 1, 1918, to November 17, 1919, there had been an increase of $52,250,000.00 in deposits.

During the war the government had called for greater and greater production on farms and in factories. If the people did not have the money, the War Finance Board would furnish it. If a person did not have the money to buy Liberty Bonds, the banks were begged to lend it with the assurance that payment could be made in installments.

Then the severest test was put on the banks in the state and nation. The Federal Reserve Bank was determined upon deflation, and all loans on agricultural products were called. Banks were called for their loans. People who had borrowed money to pay for Liberty Bonds on the assurance that they would be given time to pay were called and the Liberty Bonds held by the banks as collateral would bring no more than 80% of their face value.

The banks sustained millions upon millions of dollars in losses and were left with notes and real estate mortgages of comparatively little value.

In the face of this the boll weevil infested the cotton fields and reduced the cotton crop enormously in the state, and the banks could not collect their farm notes. In 1920 The Bank of Columbia failed and was liquidated through the clearing house.

The report of the State Bank Examiner for the year 1923 states "that the number of banks closed during the year was perhaps the worst in the history of banking since the establishment of the department. There were closed during the year, twenty-eight banks. The failures were due to the pre-existing conditions." The Federal Reserve Bank had insisted upon deflation. Loans were called on cotton and all agricultural products, bringing about forced sales and county banks were "called" for their loans, and in turn they had to insist upon payment of loans made by them. In Columbia the Merchants Bank was closed. During the following year 25 more banks were closed. But at Columbia The American Bank & Trust Company was organized, giving the city five state banks. Again the year 1924 broke the record for failures. Thirty-seven banks were closed, nine merged or were absorbed without loss to depositors and twelve were reorganized. The American Bank and Trust Company was closed in June, 1926, on account of irregularities on the part of officers and one of them was convicted and fined. The depositors, however, recovered about 80% of their money. During the previous year the Columbia Savings Bank and Trust Company had gone into liquidation. In 1928 the Peoples Bank of Columbia was opened as a branch of the Peoples Bank of Charleston. During 1932 the Peoples State Bank of South Carolina failed with 44 branches; two of these were in Columbia.

On March 9, 1933, the legislature passed an act providing that the governor should appoint a board of bank control, and in April an act was passed abolishing the office of State Bank Examiner and authorizing the Board of Bank Control to assume the duties of that office. This legislation grew out of the widespread banking troubles in the middle west in February, 1933, which culminated in the closing, on March 4, 1933, of all banks in the Second Federal Reserve District and was followed on March 6th by the closing of all banks in the United States.

The Central Union Bank was ordered to liquidate June 19, 1933. The South Carolina State Bank, a branch of the Charleston Bank of same name, was reopened March 27, 1933.

STATEMENT OF COLUMBIA BANKS DECEMBER, 1934

	Deposits	Resources
Homestead	$ 436,232.32	$ 497,028.79
Lower Main Street	870,487.64	1,001,188.15
Victory	30,923.55	68,455.92
South Carolina State	3,961,649.40	6,099,400.03
First National	4,066,778.90	4,395.177.98

At the same time the State Banks had deposits of $49,600,000.00 and resources of $64,215,000.00. The loss in resources since 1914 was $15,000,000.00.

The First National Bank was organized by the depositors and stockholders of the National Loan and Exchange Bank which had been closed in 1933. This bank had been of great benefit to the community by financing the electric plants in and near the city, and other enterprises.

In 1935 the Citizens and Southern Bank of Columbia was given a charter.

After the longest period of depression the country has ever known confidence has been restored in our banks, and we are on the way to recover the tremendous losses which were occasioned. In all the history of Columbia, since the days of carpet-bag rule, but once has a banker been charged with dishonesty, and in no other case has the failure of a bank been attributed to the officers. They may have been too liberal in making loans, or have lacked judgment, but conditions they could not control have been responsible in the main.

SOME INDUSTRIES THAT HAVE DIED

The causes for discontinuance of the manufacture of articles are various. The most usual are distance from raw materials, loss of markets, transportation, lower prices of competitors, lack of skilled labor and in some cases legislation and lack of capital.

It was inevitable that coach and wagon manufacture in the city should be discontinued; nails, and manufactured iron products and machines moved nearer the iron and steel plants; tobacco moved to the eastern part of the state where the lands were better suited to its culture, and where better grades could be grown. Cooper shops moved to the oil refineries, turpentine stills, and nearer to the forests where the staves were cut, and now, for the most part, wooden containers have been replaced with glass jars, iron drums and tank cars.

The manufacture of leather goods on a large scale has passed largely to the north and there are no longer any shoemakers in these parts who will make a pair of shoes or boots to order. The breweries were legislated out of business. The match factory, powder plant, shoe and hat factory, sword and bayonet plant, soap factory, were no longer needed when the War of Secession ended. The glass factory that was built in 1903 to supply the dispensary with bottles passed away with the repeal of the dispensary law; so did the Richland Distilling Company, and while there have been thousands of gallons of liquor made near the city since then, it has been of the illicit variety.

In the early days candles, soap, and many household necessities were made at home but the manufacture of better articles at cheaper cost together with lower rates of freight, caused the discontinuance of their home manufacture.

The cutting of the forests destroyed the turpentine and rosin business, and the manufacture of tar and charcoal. The last turpentine and rosin dealer in Columbia was Mr. W. J. Keenan who amassed a considerable fortune. A few tons of charcoal are now made, principally to keep the smoothing-irons of the tailors hot. And bundles of "light wood" for starting fires in the homes are still to be seen on our "curb market." [87]

SOME THINGS WE SHOULD MANUFACTURE

We have deposits of clays from which all sorts of china articles can be made. Included would be china tubes and switches for

---

[87] At present Columbia handles on the average 3,400 barrels of turpentine and 11,500 barrels of resin. If the size of trees to be boxed is limited there will be a reduction in production for some time.

electric wiring. The millions of yards of fine cloth made at Columbia would suggest the manufacture of garments. Our ample supply of fine water and linters, abundance of labor, and healthful climate make the city or its environs suitable for the manufacture of rayon and cellophane. The proximity of marl containing as high as 90% of calcium carbonate and brick clay suggests the manufacture of portland cement.

There are ample supplies of hard woods in the river swamps which are being used in North Carolina, Illinois, and New York for making high grade furniture. With an abundance of hydro-electric power at cheap rates there is no reason why we could not compete with any furniture manufacturing center.

There is a large demand in the state for mixed feeds for poultry, hogs and cattle which could be partly supplied from Columbia. One large mixer at Spartanburg does business from Florida to Maine, and Columbia is as well located as any city, from every standpoint.

The Coastal Water Way has been completed from Georgetown to Charleston giving Columbia water connection to that port and the Santee development, when completed, will give a shorter route. It remains only to clear the Santee and Congaree rivers of obstructions to make water transportation practical. If there were a line of boats put on the route it would naturally lower the freight rates on such commodities as could be handled by water.

TRANSPORTATION

By Samuel M. Derrick

COLUMBIA owes its existence to the fact that it was located at the head of navigation on a large river, giving it access to the outside world, and that it possessed a supporting tributary area around and behind it.[1] The up-country of South Carolina—that is, the portion of the state lying above the "fall line"—did not become permanently settled until about 1750. For several decades thereafter the area maintained a self-sufficing economic order. However, with farmers becoming more firmly established and better equipped, larger and larger amounts of grain and livestock were produced. Thus there arose a surplus and a consequent demand for a market. Such a potential market existed in the lowlands, for the planters of that area were buying these same commodities from out of the state at high prices. To develop that market the upland farmer brought his surplus products to the head of navigation to be shipped down the river. Here was the beginning of Columbia.

But Columbia did not become a market of great importance until after 1800. Soon after the invention of the cotton gin it was found that the up-country was well suited for cotton production. The crop was cultivated with vigor. With cotton came the negro slave and the plantation system.[2]

To what extent this change was made is indicated by the increase in the number of slaves in the up-country districts. Abbeville, which had only 2,962 slaves in 1800, boasted of 30,861 in 1830. In Laurens the number increased from 1,919 to 7,343, in Newberry from 2,204 to 8,316, and in Union from 1,697 to 7,165. No such marked increases were made in white population.[3]

The problem of the up-country now was that of getting the cotton to seaport to be exported and of securing from seaports necessary supplies for the plantation and some of the comforts of life for which the new economic order created a demand.

In response to this need Columbia became an established market.[4] It was in Columbia that the central South Carolina farmer sold his

[1] U. B. Phillips, *Transportation in the Eastern Cotton Belt,* New York, 1908, p. 6.
[2] William A. Schaper, "Sectionalism and Representation in South Carolina." *Annual Report of American Historical Association,* Washington, 1900, I, 323.
[3] United States Census of 1830.
[4] Other towns likewise established were Augusta on the Savannah River, Camden on the Wateree River, and Cheraw on the Peedee River.

cotton and there he also bought his plantation supplies. The cotton was shipped from Columbia to the coast and supplies were brought back.

WATER TRANSPORTATION

Some of the earliest efforts to develop transportation facilities to serve Columbia were directed to water routes. In 1786 a private company was formed to build the Santee Canal, connecting the Santee and Cooper rivers in order to form a water route between Charleston and the up-country. The canal, completed in 1800, served a useful purpose, both in providing inland navigation to Charleston and in keeping down the rates of land carriage. But it was unfortunately located, and its passage therefore uncertain and hazardous.[5]

In 1815, a system of canals, sluices and locks was begun at Columbia on the Congaree and above Columbia on the Broad and Saluda rivers.[6] This work was done by the state under a board of public works at first and later under a superintendent of public works. The Columbia Canal was completed in January, 1824, and the locks and sluices higher up the Saluda river were completed in 1825. It was then possible for a boat laden with forty bales of cotton to descend from Cambridge, near Abbeville, all the way to Charleston.[7] At about the same time Broad river was made navigable for small boats above Lockhart to Kings creek.[8]

Unquestionably, the Columbia Canal and the other water routes greatly aided the development of Columbia in its early history. As early as 1796, before the completion of the canal, it is reported that as many as twenty freight boats were plying between Charleston and the Congaree,[9] while Trenholm states that for the year ending September 30, 1827, the cotton shipped through the Columbia Canal amounted to 45,612 bales. In addition, 10,000 bales were shipped from Granby, the old head of navigation.[10] In some years the canal carried over 60,000 bales of cotton.[11] Two steamboats, besides a number of bay and canal boats, were used to transport the cotton and

---

[5] W. L. Trenholm, "Transportation in South Carolina," *South Carolina Handbook,* Charleston, 1883, p. 623; Phillips, *Transportation,* pp. 35-43; *Southern Review* (Charleston), VII, 187.

[6] Phillips, *Transportation,* p. 42.

[7] *Ibid.,* pp. 88–89; August Kohn, *Water Powers of South Carolina,* Charleston, 1910, pp. 13–14.

[8] Robert Mills, *Statistics of South Carolina,* Charleston, 1826, pp. 157-158.

[9] David Duncan Wallace, *History of South Carolina,* New York, 1934, II, 401.

[10] Trenholm, "Transportation," p. 627.

[11] Wallace, *History of South Carolina,* II, 400-401.

return with full freight, the amount of which was equal to 5,000 tons.[12]

However, it appears clear that early water transportation to and from Columbia was slow and costly. Flat boats carrying cotton from Columbia to Charleston usually consumed twenty-four days in the round trip. The tolls on the Santee Canal were $40.00 on each boat per round trip. The freight was $1.00 per bale, or $7.00 per ton.[13] Mills, writing in 1821, states that the water route was so hazardous that shippers preferred wagons at a cost of $3.00 per bale, or $21.00 per ton.[14] The introduction of the steamboat proved helpful, but it was not altogether satisfactory. To show its maximum efficiency, Phillips quotes the following from the *Charleston City Gazette* of April 9, 1822: [15]

> "The steam boat Carolina, Captain Harvey, arrived yesterday morning at 9 o'clock, in the extraordinary short passage of 4 days and a half from Granby, with tow boats carrying nearly 900 bales of cotton."

The Columbia Canal served Columbia as an important route of transportation for about twenty years. With the coming of the railroads during the decade 1840-1850 it was practically abandoned for navigation.[16]

Since the coming of the railroad to Columbia, the matter of using the Congaree river and the Columbia Canal for the transportation of freight to the coast has been periodically agitated. In 1904, the Chamber of Commerce took definite action in that direction, with the result that navigation was established between Columbia and Georgetown. The whole purpose behind the movement at that time was to secure cheaper freight rates for the city.[17]

EARLY ROADS AND BRIDGES

During the early history of Columbia the chief routes of transportation were the dirt roads that radiated in every direction from the city. Robert Mills' *Atlas of South Carolina* shows that in 1826 no less than ten roads led into the town. The most important was the "State Road" leading from the Piedmont area down Enoree and

[12] Mills, *Statistics,* p. 708.
[13] Trenholm, "Transportation," p. 627.
[14] *Inland Navigation,* Columbia, 1821.
[15] *Transportation,* p. 42.
[16] Columbia Railway, Gas and Electric Company, *The Columbia Canal,* Columbia, 1914, p. 6.
[17] *The State* (Columbia), January 9, 11, February 2, and September 28, 1904.

Broad rivers to Columbia and then on to Charleston through the Orangeburg district. The "State Road" was joined a few miles below Columbia by a road from Barnwell. From the west came a road from Augusta through Edgefield and Lexington; and from the northwest came the road from Newberry down the north side of Saluda River. This route was known locally as the "River Road." From the north and northeast came four routes leading from Jenkinsville and Monticello; from Chester and Winnsboro; from Camden and Cheraw; and from the country lying between Camden and Winnsboro. From the east and southeast two entered Columbia: one from the direction of Stateburg and the other up the north side of Congaree river.

Boat, "City of Columbia," on Columbia Canal

Note should be made of the distinctive nature of the "State Road." This project, undertaken by South Carolina, was to be a turnpike for most of the distance with numerous causeways, culverts and embankments. It was presumably completed in 1829. It was a toll road and on the section from Charleston to Columbia there were to be eight toll-gates. The charge for a four-horse wagon for the round trip between these two points was $9.00. The road was never a success. It seems never to have been in prime condition, and due to the relatively heavy charges the free roads of the area were used.[18]

The two rivers, Congaree and Broad, offered serious handicaps to overland transportation into Columbia. For some years ferry boats were the only means of crossing these streams. In 1771 Wade Hampton built a bridge across the Congaree at Granby. It was soon destroyed by a freshet. A second bridge was built, but it was destroyed in 1796. The ferry boat was used until 1827, when the Columbia Bridge Company constructed a bridge across the river at

---

[18] U. B. Phillips, *Transportation*, pp. 90-94.

the foot of Gervais Street. The Broad river bridge was built two
years later, 1829.[19] Both of the bridges remained toll bridges until
1912.[20]

The condition of these early roads leading into Columbia was not
good as measured in the light of the needs of that period. They were
full of "sand-beds, mud holes, and crude corduroy patches." Below
the city there were swamps and streams requiring causeways, bridges
and ferries which were dangerous for want of repairs and for carelessness in management; in the sandhills there were great depths
of sand, heavy and hot; in the uplands there was the frequent wash-
ing of gullies in the hillside roads.[21]

But in spite of this condition, a considerable amount of wagon
trade came to Columbia from long distances. Moreover, there must
have been an appreciable amount of passenger travel over the roads.
In 1826 four stage coaches ran from Columbia to four points in
the state: one to Charleston three times a week; one to Camden
three times a week; one to Augusta three times a week; and one
to Greenville once a week.[22]

THE COMING OF RAILROADS

Efforts to build canals and turnpikes ceased with the coming of
railroads. After about 1830 and down to 1900 Columbia's activities
in transportation were concerned in the main with securing railroads
to every part of the state.

The railroad from Charleston to Hamburg was completed in
1833 by the South Carolina Canal and Railroad Company, chartered
in 1827. Under terms of the charter, this company was given the
exclusive right to build a road to Columbia, but due to the lack of
funds it could not exercise its right immediately. It suggested,
however, to a group of Columbia inhabitants that a separate company
be organized to construct a line from Branchville, on the Charleston-
Hamburg line, to Columbia. Accordingly, the Columbia Railroad
Company was chartered in December, 1833. Under rights granted by
the older company, a committee was appointed early in 1834 to make
a survey of the route. The route that the road was to take and the
probable cost of construction and operation were given in the report of the survey made in September. The conclusion of the committee was that the road would cause an increase in the business

---

[19] E. L. Green, *History of Richland County*, Columbia, 1932, I, 120; Wallace, *History of S. C.*, II, 403.
[20] Details given in later section of this chapter.
[21] Phillips, *Transportation*, p. 94.
[22] Mills, *Statistics*, p. 710.

of Columbia and a decided increase in real estate values. Indeed, it was the settled conviction of the committee that the road was "indispensably necessary, not merely to the prosperity of Columbia, but to save it from decay and ruin."

This was about as far as the Columbia group went in the matter. It was seemingly unable to meet certain conditions imposed by the charter. However, the idea of building the road was not abandoned. It was agitated by both Orangeburg and Columbia, but nothing definite was done until the latter part of 1837, when the Louisville, Cincinnati and Charleston Railroad Company bought the stock of the South Carolina Company and the right to build the road from Branchville to Columbia. This line was to be the first section of the ambitious scheme of the Louisville, Cincinnati and Charleston Company to build a trunk line from Charleston to Cincinnati.

Early in 1838 contracts were let for preparing the road bed for the section between Columbia and the Congaree River, and construction was immediately begun. By September, 1839, all of the road had been put under contract. After a number of delays, occasioned by financial difficulties and weather conditions, the line was completed in 1842. Passenger trains entered Columbia on June 20 and freight trains on July 1. The total cost of constructing the road was $2,274,906.21.

The arrival of the first trains in Columbia was fittingly celebrated with elaborate ceremonies on June 28. There was much speaking, no little eating and drinking, and the usual display of military pomp. At the barbecue of "Congaree mutton, Berkshire pigs and Durham veal" a number of appropriate toasts were offered. *The City of Charleston* was offered by Wade Hampton:

> "The pride of our state. The efficient aid which she has rendered in the projection and accomplishment of the great lines of railroad to Hamburg and Columbia are worthy of her position. May she reap the rich reward which she so justly merits."

The Mayor of Charleston, *The Town of Columbia*:

> "This day honorably allied to the household of Charleston, and now mutually identified with her interest, her fame and her prosperity."

The Intendant of Columbia (William M. Myers), *Charleston and Columbia*:

> "The metropolis and the capital: What man has magnificently joined together, surely God will protect against the ravage of time and the wars of the elements."

Thus entered the first railroad into Columbia.[23] By it Columbia now had direct connection with Charleston and indirect connection by way of Branchville, with Hamburg across the Savannah River from Augusta.

At about the time the Branchville-Columbia road was completed, a definite movement was under way to build a line from Camden to connect with this road at some point on the east side of the Congaree river. The citizens of Camden prevailed upon the South Carolina Railroad Company, the successor of the Louisville, Cincinnati and Charleston Company, to build the branch, and accordingly the actual work of construction was begun in 1845. Great difficulty was experienced in building the four miles of necessary trestle work in the Wateree swamp. This, together with the frequent flooding of the swamp area, caused delay and Camden was not reached until the last of October, 1848. Connection with the Branchville-Columbia section was made at Kingville.[24]

A few years after the completion of this line Columbia was given connection with the Peedee section of the state by the construction of a road extending from Wilmington, N. C., through Marion and Florence to Manchester, a station on the Camden branch. The work of construction was begun in 1850 and was completed in 1853. The length of the road was 158 miles. Originally known as the Wilmington and Manchester Railroad,[25] it later came to be known as the Wilmington, Columbia and Augusta railroad. As such it built its own line into Columbia from Sumter, reaching Columbia in December, 1871.[26]

The next railroad services secured for Columbia were with Greenville and Anderson, Charlotte and Spartanburg. In 1846 the Greenville and Columbia Railroad Company was chartered to build a road between Columbia and Greenville. After much jockeying with local interests as to the towns through which the road was to pass, track-laying was begun from the Columbia end in 1849. Newberry was reached in 1851; Greenwood, in July, 1852; Anderson in June, 1853, and Greenville in the following December.[27] The road was extended from Anderson to a point beyond Pendleton in

---

[23] S. M. Derrick, *Centennial History of South Carolina Railroad*, Columbia, 1930, Ch. XII. A detailed account is given in this chapter.
[24] *Ibid.*, Ch. XIII.
[25] Phillips, *Transportation*, pp. 352-353.
[26] *Reports and Resolutions of the General Assembly of South Carolina*, Columbia, 1886, pp. 900-901. These reports contain the annual reports of the South Carolina Railroad Commission. The author has found them indispensable in tracing the development of railroads after 1880.
[27] Phillips, *Transportation*, pp. 343-344.

1856 and 1857, and later on to Walhalla. This was the work of the Blue Ridge Railroad Company, which was to build a road across the mountains to connect Charleston with the golden west.[28]

The route of this road swung around the direct line to Greenville through Laurens; hence, Laurens had no railroad until two years later. The Laurens Railroad Company was chartered, and in 1855 completed thirty-two miles of road from Laurens to Newberry, there joining the Greenville-Columbia road.[29] A final connection was made with the Greenville-Columbia road by the building of a line, sixty miles in length, from Spartanburg through Union to Alston. The work was done by the Spartanburg and Union Railroad Company, chartered in 1847. The road was completed in 1859.[30]

The Charlotte and South Carolina Railroad Company was chartered in 1846 with its purpose, in the beginning, to build a road from Charlotte to Camden. However, because of the larger subscription of stock taken by Columbia, the southern terminus was placed at that point. In October, 1850, thirty miles of the road was finished, and in November, 1852, Charlotte was reached.[31] Three years later a road from York to Chester was built to connect with the Columbia-Charlotte line.[32]

These lines constituted the extent of railroad developments prior to the Civil War. But even at that relatively early date Columbia had superior transportation facilities to the more important parts of the state.

Following the war period, the first railroad building was a direct road from Columbia to Augusta. Prior to this time traffic between these two points had to go by way of Branchville. As early as 1853 the Columbia and Hamburg Railroad Company was chartered to build the road from Columbia to Augusta.[33] It was rechartered in 1858,[34] but apparently could not raise the funds necessary to do the work. In 1863 another organization, the Columbia and Augusta Railroad Company, was chartered.[35] It began work of construction in Columbia in 1867.[36] The road was completed in 1868, and one year later was consolidated with the Columbia-Charlotte road.[37]

[28] *Ibid.*, pp. 375-380.
[29] *Ibid.*, p. 347.
[30] *Ibid.*, pp. 345-348.
[31] *Ibid.*, pp. 338-340.
[32] *Ibid.*, p. 346.
[33] *Statutes at Large of South Carolina,* XII, 283.
[34] *Ibid.*, p. 696.
[35] *Ibid.*, XIII, 200.
[36] Derrick, *S. C. Railroad,* pp. 245-247.
[37] *Reports and Resolutions, 1880,* p. 751.

No additional railroad entered Columbia until 1890, when the Columbia, Newberry and Laurens Railroad Company, chartered in 1885, built the line up through the middle of the area lying between the Broad and Saluda rivers. The road was opened to Prosperity, June 30, 1890; and to Newberry, October 27 of the same year. In 1891 it was completed to Dover Junction, and in 1896 the Company bought from the Laurens Railroad Company the line from Dover Junction to Laurens, completing the 75 miles of road.[38] This railroad gave Columbia access to an important and rapidly developing territory which had for years been without railroad service.

In 1891 another railroad tapping a new territory entered Columbia. It was the old South Bound Railroad extending from Savannah. In September of that year fifty-six miles of the road was opened from Savannah to Denmark; in October, the forty-four miles from Denmark to Columbia was completed; and on November 2 trains were authorized. The road stopped at Cayce and connected there with the road from Columbia to Augusta.[39]

Columbia gained access to more new territory in 1899, when the Southern Railway Company built a road from Cayce to Perry, thirty-one miles, to connect with the Carolina Midland Railroad at Perry.[40] This formed another direct line between Savannah and Columbia.

The final railroad to enter Columbia was the Seaboard from Cheraw. It was under construction in 1899;[41] and on February 20, 1900, the first train came over the road from Camden. The engine could come only as far as Smith's branch, just beyond the incorporated limits of Columbia, but it was reported to have arrived with blasts from its whistle and with many people to welcome it.[42] The line entered Columbia in May.[43] It opened up a large territory between Cheraw and Columbia, hitherto isolated from the markets of the state. It also reduced passenger and freight rates between Columbia and the territory about Camden and Cheraw.[44]

The completion of the Seaboard road from Cheraw gave Columbia nine separate and distinct railroads of seventy-five miles or more in length entering the city. This constituted transportation facilities

---

[38] Statement of Mr. J. P. Taylor, President of the Columbia, Newberry and Laurens Railroad Company; *Reports and Resolutions, 1890,* p. 297, 1891, p. 291.

[39] *Reports and Resolutions, 1891,* pp. 290-291.

[40] *Ibid., 1899,* p. 7.

[41] *Ibid.*

[42] *The State,* Feb. 22, 1900.

[43] *Reports and Resolutions, 1901,* p. 1219.

[44] *Ibid.*

unsurpassed by any other city in the state of South Carolina. Indeed, Columbia was the railroad center of the state.

Throughout the whole period of railroad building the matter of passenger and freight rates was of the deepest concern to Columbia. Unquestionably, the rates charged by the early railroads were extremely high as measured by present-day standards. For example, in 1838 the passenger rates on the old South Carolina road were fixed by legislative act at seven and a half cents a mile. In 1859 it is claimed it cost a dollar and twenty-five cents to carry to Laurens a sack of salt bought for seventy-five cents in Charleston.[45] Constant complaint was expressed by farmers and shippers throughout the state. After 1865, rates were materially reduced by the keen competition of the various roads entering the city, but even as late as 1887 passenger rates were as high as four and a half cents a mile.[46] A survey of the reports of the South Carolina Railroad Commission indicates that the forcing down of rates for both passengers and freight was a constant struggle.

An important factor in facilitating transportation through Columbia was the standardization of the gauge of railroads in 1886. Prior to that time the distance between the rails was not uniform. Consequently the transfer of cars from one road to another had to be accomplished by changing the trucks under the cars. The change to a uniform gauge was accomplished in the last days of May and the first part of June, 1886.[47]

Another change in railroad facilities that greatly aided passenger travel was the construction of Union Station in 1902. Before that time two passenger stations were maintained on opposite sides of the city, one on Blanding Street to accommodate the Charlotte, Columbia and Augusta Railroad and the other on Gervais street to accommodate the other lines. As early as 1880 City Council requested Railroad Commissioner M. L. Bonham to endeavor to get the four roads then leading into Columbia to unite in erecting a union depot.[48] Commissioner Bonham wrote in his report of 1880 that

> it is not creditable to the roads concerned that there is neither at the Wilmington, Columbia and Augusta, the Greenville and Columbia, nor the South Carolina depots in this city, even a shelter to protect the traveling public from exposure, and a very inadequate one at the Charlotte, Columbia and Augusta depot.

The question was agitated for the next twenty years. In 1899

[45] *The Farmer and Planter* (Columbia), June, 1859, p. 180.
[46] *Reports and Resolutions, 1887,* p. 553.
[47] *Ibid.,* 1886; Derrick, *S. C. Railroad,* pp. 263-264.
[48] *Reports and Resolutions, 1880,* p. 676.

the Southern Railroad and the Atlantic Coast Line agreed to build a union station on lower Main Street. The plans were approved by both the South Carolina Railroad Commissioner and the Columbia City Council.[49] Grading on the project was started in 1900 and after some delay work was completed early in 1902. The station was opened on January 14 of that year.[50]

STREET RAILWAY [51]

The first street cars to run in Columbia were horse drawn affairs. In 1886 the Columbia Street Railway Company was organized with a capital stock of $50,000.00. At that time six cars and twenty-five to thirty horses were used. The lines then established began at the union station on Gervais Street. The car barn was located where the Columbia Supply Company now operates. The road with its branches measured four miles in length. A double track ran up Main Street from the State House to the old post office on Laurel Street. Here it branched into two single tracks; one continued up Main Street to Elmwood Avenue and out by the old fair ground to the cemetery; the other went out Laurel Street to Barnwell, then to Blanding and then east to the Charlotte, Columbia and Augusta railroad depot. From Laurel Street a branch ran up Pickens Street to the State Hospital. The number of passengers carried daily in 1888 was estimated at 800.[52]

This mode of street transportation continued until 1893, when electric cars were placed on the line. At that time six cars were put in use. The only extension of the system during that year was a line from Blanding Street to Gregg and south to Taylor and east to Heidt Street, and then south on Heidt to Gervais Street. In 1895 an extension was made from Gervais to the Shandon Pavilion near what is now Valley Park. In addition, a line was run off Elmwood Avenue south on Gadsden Street to Richland and then east to Main.

In 1896 the line was extended from Shandon Pavilion north on Harden Street to Gervais and then west to Main. This construction formed what was known as the "belt line." It is reported that a ride over the "belt line" was a popular form of recreation for all ages at that time. It was particularly attractive to children. Mr. Alfred

---

49 *Ibid., 1900,* p. 44
50 *The State* (Columbia), Jan. 6, 16, 1902.
51 The author is indebted to Mr. Alfred Wallace and Mr. J. W. Spence, long connected with the street railway in Columbia, for most of the material in this section. Except where otherwise stated, they were the main source of information.
52 D. P. Robbins, *Historical and Descriptive Sketch of Columbia, S. C.,* Columbia, 1888, p. 62.

Wallace, for years superintendent of transportation, narrates that on many occasions when the cars broke down he would take a "hack" to go around to collect the children and bring them home. Close within the city the only other important street railway that was laid was a track off Gervais Street up Pickens to Hampton, and then by the Colonia Hotel to Gregg Street and up Gregg to Taylor Street. This construction was completed in 1915.

The line to Hyatt Park from Scott's alley, just north of Elmwood Avenue, was constructed in 1896, being completed about June 15. It was built by a separate corporation, the Columbia and Eau Claire Electric Railway Company, of which F. H. Hyatt was president and treasurer.[53] One year later it was leased to the regular company operating in Columbia. The Hyatt Park line was of more than passing significance in that it was the first to connect the city proper with outlying territory. In 1907 it was extended to Ridgewood; one year later, to College Place; and in 1912 to Arden.

Another important suburban connection was formed in 1898. It was then that the line was extended from the Shandon Pavilion out Divine Street to Maple and then to the Garner's Ferry road. Two important branches were constructed from this stem: the Shandon Annex line leaving Divine Street at King, completed in 1911; and the line to Camp Jackson, built in 1917.

Street car service to the south of the State House was not provided until about 1900, when the line from Gervais Street to the Granby mill was built. In 1908-1909 the branch from this line to the Fair Grounds was completed.

The track down Gervais Street was extended to the Congaree River in 1904. The following year from this line at Huger Street a branch was built to the penitentiary and water works. The only other additions to the system were the construction of the lines to Colonial Heights in 1912, and to Wales Gardens in 1915.

Beginning about 1920 came the private automobile and taxis, and later the bus. With them the street railway ceased to be a major means of transportation in Columbia.

LATER DEVELOPMENTS

The most significant improvements in transportation facilities in Columbia came with the automobile. It was then that interest became active in paving streets and in developing highways to and from the city.

---

[53] *The State*, May 26, 1896.

The commissioners who laid out the city in 1786 provided ample space for travel, making the streets 100 to 150 feet in width. But for years these streets were relatively poorly kept, being characterized by dust in summer and mud holes in winter. The first surfacing of streets in Columbia was done in 1908, when blocks were laid on Main Street between Rice and Wheat streets. The following year Main Street was paved from Wheat Street to Scott.[54]

The following years, that is, from 1909 through 1915, the paving of streets was confined largely to the area adjoining Main Street from Gervais northward. The only noteworthy exceptions is that in 1914 nearly three and a half miles of pavement was laid in Wales Gardens. From 1915 to 1919 no paving whatever was undertaken in Columbia, but beginning in 1919 and continuing through 1925 the area out in the residential section received greater attention. The greatest amount of paving was accomplished during the four years 1927-1930. During this period approximately thirteen miles of streets were paved. At the present time Columbia has 152 miles of streets, of which 40.9 miles are paved.

From the standpoint of Columbia's development as a state and sectional market, the greatest influence has been in the building of highways radiating in every direction from the city. In 1910 Columbia business men, appreciating the part that highways were to play in developing the city, started a movement to free the two toll bridges across Congaree and Broad rivers.[55] In 1912 the Congaree bridge was purchased by Richland County in co-operation with Lexington,[56] and the Broad River bridge was freed when a portion of "Dutch Fork" was annexed to Richland County.[57] Following this development some improvement was realized in dirt roads, but it was not until 1920 that a great deal of progress was made. In that year the Richland legislative delegation had passed by the General Assembly an act authorizing the issuance of two million dollars in bonds for the purpose of paving the four main roads of the county leading into Columbia.[58] Under the direction of a road commissioner and an engineer the work of building the roads was immediately begun and completed by 1923. This was the first county-wide bond issue in South Carolina for the purpose of paving highways.

---

[54] The data on street paving was supplied by reports on file in the office of City Engineer W. S. Tomlinson.

[55] *The State,* March 29, 1910.

[56] *Acts of General Assembly of South Carolina,* 1912, p. 887.

[57] *Ibid.,* p. 821.

[58] The author is indebted to Mr. Thos. B. Pearce, then Richland Senator, for information on this topic. For the bond act, see *Acts of General Assembly of South Carolina,* 1920, p. 1628.

For a number of years Columbia had no outlet to Sumter and the Peedee section except by the long route through Camden. The great Wateree swamp had for years been a trade barrier, but it was traversed in 1923 when Richland and Sumter counties, aided by the Federal government, built a bridge across the Wateree River. The bridge was opened for traffic on May 9.[59]

Following the lead of Richland, other counties and districts began the building of hard surface highways, until finally the state highway system was established. Roads were built connecting Columbia with every part of the state, making it the trade as well as the governmental center of South Carolina.

---

[59] *The State,* May 8, 1923.

PHYSICAL GROWTH

By A. S. Salley

THE GROWTH of Columbia during its early years was slow.
From 1786 to 1790, while the State House was being slowly
constructed, with the proceeds of sales of town lots, there was
little to bring inhabitants or business to the legislative created town.
With the arrival of the public officials from Charleston and the occupation of the then unfinished State House at the close of 1789, and
the meeting of the General Assembly here in January following, zest
was added to the development.

While on his visit to Columbia in May, 1791, President Washington entered in his diary for May 24th:

"Columbia is laid out upon a large scale. . . . It is now an un-
cleared wood, with very few houses in it, and those all wooden ones
—the State House (which is also of wood) is a large and commodi-
ous building, but unfinished."

In 1799 Richland District was established from a part of Kershaw
District and Columbia was made the district seat,[1] and soon thereafter the district courthouse was built in the town. This added governmental function materially aided the growth of the town. The
opening of the South Carolina College in January, 1805, and the incorporation of Columbia as a town, December 19, 1805, also contributed to its growth. No figures of the censuses of the United
States prior to 1830 are available. A writer in *The Telescope,* a
weekly paper then published in Columbia, for May 14, 1816, stated
that the town contained 250 houses and 1,000 inhabitants, white and
black. He said the town contained a nail factory and a paper mill, to
contribute to its support, and Baptist, Episcopal, Methodist and
Presbyterian churches (all of wood), to contribute to its spiritual
welfare.

The census of 1830 shows a population of 3,310. The census of
1840 shows a population of 4,340, an increase of 1,030, or a percentage increase of 31.1.

The census of 1850 shows a population of 6,060, an increase of
1,720, or a percentage increase of 39.6.

The population in 1860 was 8,052, an increase of 1,992, or a percentage increase of 32.9.

---

[1] *Statutes at Large of South Carolina,* VII, 290.

The population of 1870 was 9,298, an increase of 1,246, or 15.5 per cent increase.

The population of 1880 was 10,036, an increase of but 738, or a percentage increase of 7.9.

The population of 1890 was 15,353, an increase of 5,317, or a percentage increase of 53.

Richardson Street Looking South—1895

The population in 1900 was 21,108, an increase of 5,755, or a percentage increase of 37.5.

The population in 1910 was 26,319, an increase of 5,211, or a percentage increase of 24.7.

In June, 1913, the suburbs of Shandon, Waverley, South Waverley and a part of Eau Claire were annexed to Columbia by an election of the people of the city and of the suburbs which was ratified by the city council of Columbia, June 13, 1913.

The vote to annex Shandon was, in the city, 366 for and 7 against; in Shandon 49 for and 9 against.

For Waverley the city vote was 364 for and 7 against; in Waverley 28 for and 10 against.

For South Waverley the city vote was 362 for and 9 against; in South Waverley 17 for and 8 against.

For Eau Claire the city vote was 362 for and 5 against; in Eau Claire 39 for and 32 against.

As a result of these additions to Columbia the census of 1920 showed a population of 37,524, an increase of 11,205, which was nearly twice the average of the increases at the three preceding censuses. The percentage increase was 42.6.

Although the total vote cast in all four of the suburbs taken in was but 188, which, at the rate of one-fifth of the population as voters, would give a population of only 940, it is well known that at most only fifty per cent of the qualified voters exercised the suffrage at this election. Very few negroes voted, and, in the case of Waverley and South Waverley, negroes constituted a large percentage of the population.

The following are the descriptions of the tracts taken in, as recited on the minutes of the city council of Columbia for June 13, 1913:

Shandon,[2] commencing at the intersection of Harden Street of the City of Columbia with the southern line of Wheat Street on lands of the Columbia Land and Investment Company, as delineated on a map of said lands on record in the office of the Clerk of Court for Richland County in said State, in Plat Book A, page 113; thence eastwardly along the southern line of said Wheat Street in a straight line to the eastern boundary of the lands of said Company, thence in a straight line to the Garner's Ferry Road on the boundary line of the lands of said Company and of the Epworth Orphanage lot, and across said road; thence along the northern line of the Garner's Ferry Road to the western line of King Street where it intersects said road; thence along western boundary line of said King Street to the northeastern boundary line of the Columbia Land and Investment Company (formerly Kleinbeck), designated by deep black line on said plat; thence northwestwardly along said line to the next corner thereon, about 175 feet from the Garner's Ferry Road, as shown by said plat; thence in a straight line to where the northwestern boundary of the said Company's land intersects said Harden Street, and thence along the eastern side of Harden Street to the beginning corner. That area is about three-fourths of a square mile, and the center thereof is distant less than one mile from any and every point on the said proposed boundary lines.

Waverley, commencing at a point where the eastern line of Harden Street intersects the southern line of a street which is an extension of Gervais Street; thence along the southern line of the extension of Gervais until it intersects the eastern line of Heidt Street; thence in a northerly direction along the eastern line of Heidt until it intersects the southern line of the extension of Taylor Street; thence in an easterly direction along the southern line of Taylor until it in-

---

[2] Shandon had been incorporated under the terms of "An Act to Provide for the Corporation of Towns of Less than One Thousand Inhabitants," approved March 2, 1896, on the basis of a petition for municipal commission by U. R. Brooks *et al.,* filed October 6, 1903, upon which a commission was issued the same day.

tersects the eastern line of the Two Notch Road; thence in a northeasterly direction along the eastern line of said road until it intersects the northern line of the extension of a public road known as
the extension of the Barhamville Road and along the northern line
of said Barhamville Road until it intersects the eastern line of Harden Street; thence in a southerly direction along the said eastern line
on Harden to the point of beginning.

Main Street, Looking South

South Waverley, beginning at the eastern side of the intersection
of Gervais and Harden Streets, at the eastern boundary of Columbia, and running thence easterly along the northern side of the extension of Gervais to the middle of Heidt Street to the line of the
street railway; thence turning and running with and along said
street railway in a southerly direction to the point where the said
street railway first intersects the boundary line of the town of
Shandon; thence turning and running in a westerly direction with
the said boundary line of Shandon to the point where said boundary
line intersects the eastern boundary line of Columbia; thence turning and running in a northerly direction along the eastern boundary
line of Columbia to the point of commencement.

Part of Eau Claire, beginning at a stake on Broad River Avenue
75 feet, more or less, northwest of Second Avenue; thence running
westwardly parallel to the northern boundary line of the corporate
limits of Columbia to its intersection with a prolongation of the
western boundary line of the corporate limits of Columbia; thence
southwardly down said prolongation of said western boundary line

of Columbia to the northern boundary line of Columbia; thence easterly along the northern boundary line of the corporate limits of Columbia to a point 600 feet east of Main Street; thence a line perpendicular to the northern boundary line of Columbia, to its intersection with a prolongation of the first described line in an easterly direction; thence said prolongation of said first described line to the beginning point on Broad River Avenue, the shape of said territory being rectangular.

The census of 1930 gave Columbia a population of 51,581, an increase of 14,057, and a percentage increase of 37.5.

Between 1920 and 1930 much surburban population was added to Columbia by the annexation of additional territory. The following tracts were annexed May 26, 1925:

North Columbia, from the northern limits of the city a tract bounded east by North Main Street for 1,250 feet, thence westwardly through the northeast corner of Newman Park to the intersection of Broad River Road and Fourth Street, thence southwestwardly along Fourth Street 575 feet to its intersection with Lyles Avenue; thence southeasterly along Lyles Avenue for approximately 960 feet to its intersection with Madison Avenue; thence in a southwesterly direction in a straight line to the center of the Southern Railway track where the then northern limits of Columbia intersected it; thence easterly along the then northern limits to Main Street.

Newman's Field, from the point where the then northern limits line intersected the northern side of Columbia Avenue; thence easterly for approximately 240 feet to the property line of the Confederate Infirmary; thence southwardly along the property line of the Confederate Infirmary to the point where the then city limits line intersected the property line of the Confederate Infirmary; thence westerly along the then city limits approximately 470 feet to the corner of the then city limits line; thence northerly along the then city limits line to the starting point on Columbia Avenue.

The following tracts were annexed May 17, 1926:

All that territory beginning at the intersection of Wheat and Harden Streets and running easterly along Wheat Street to its intersection with King Street; thence south on King for 1,482 feet to the intersection of King Street and on unnamed street running east and west; thence westwardly on that street to its intersection with the southern line of Heyward Street; thence along Heyward to Harden; thence northwardly on Harden to Wheat, known as "the New Chicora College Property."

All that territory beginning at the intersection of Heyward and Gregg Streets and running southwardly on Gregg 1,915 feet to its intersection with Altee Street; thence easterly along Altee for 2,140 feet to a point on the south side thereof; thence northwardly along the boundary line of the property of the Liberty Realty Company, parallel with Etiwan Avenue, for 2,110 feet to a point on the south side of Heyward Street; thence along the south side of Heyward Street to the beginning point, known as Rose Hill.

Carolina Life Insurance Company Building

All that territory beginning at the southwest cornor of Heyward and South Bull Streets and running in a southeasterly direction along the west side of West Bull Street for 2,150 feet to a point on the south side of Altee Street; thence in a westerly direction along the south side of Altee Street for a distance of 359 feet to a point where the south side of Altee Street intersects the west side of Palmetto Lane; thence northwesterly along the west side of Palmetto Lane to its intersection with the south side of Heyward Street; thence easterly along Heyward to the beginning point, known as Atlantic Building Company lands.

All that territory beginning at a point in the center of Devine Street on a line with the western side of Sims Avenue, and running in an easterly direction for an approximate distance of 952 feet to the intersection of Devine Street and Wilson Avenue; thence in a southerly direction along Wilson Avenue 1,125 feet to its intersection with Wheat Street; thence westerly on Wheat for 200 feet to its intersection with Walker Street; thence southerly on Walker for approximately 400 feet to its intersection with First Street; thence westerly along First Street 548 feet to its intersection with Moore Street; thence along Moore Street in a northerly direction for approximately 400 feet to its intersection with Wheat Street; thence westerly along Wheat 183 feet to the western property line on Sims Avenue; thence northerly on Sims Avenue 1,125 feet to the starting point, known as Capital Heights.

All that territory beginning at the intersection of Heyward and South Gregg Streets and running southerly along the eastern boundary of Gregg Street approximately 1,862 feet to the south side of Altee Street; thence westerly along Altee for approximately 1,050 feet to its intersection with South Bull Street; thence northwesterly

Main Street, Looking North From Capitol

along South Bull to the south side of Heyward Street, thence easterly along Heyward to the starting point, known as Hollywood.

The following tracts were annexed January 25, 1927:

All that tract of land starting at the intersection of Harden and Heyward Streets and running southeasterly along Harden to its intersection with Altee Street; thence easterly on Altee to its intersection with Fifth Avenue; thence along Fifth Avenue to its intersection with Ott Road and thence to the intersection of Ott Road with the southeastern boundary of the lands formerly of Frank Sims; thence in a southeasterly direction to the Millford Road; thence along Millford Road in a northeasterly direction to the Garner's Ferry Road; thence along the Garner's Ferry Road in a southeasterly direction to the eastern boundary of the lands, of M. C. Heath; thence northerly along the said property line to the Devereaux Road; thence along the Devereaux Road for approximately 1,400 feet to a bend therein; then northeasterly between the lands of Emerson and Reeves and Williamson to Kilbourne Avenue; thence westerly along Kilbourne Avenue

Central Union Building Tallest of Columbia.

to Clairmont Avenue; thence along Clairmont to the Trenholm Road; thence northwesterly along Trenholm Road to the road leading "to the home and through the property of R. B. Jennings"; thence along said road to the Camden Road; thence westerly along the Camden Road to the city limits.

All that tract from the southwest corner of the intersection of Altee Street and Edisto Avenue south along the western side of Edisto Avenue to the intersection of Edisto Avenue and B Street; thence east along B Street to its intersection with Fifth Street; thence north on Fifth Street to its intersection with Altee Street; thence along Altee Street to the starting point, known as South Wales.[3]

As Columbia has grown there have been efforts to beautify its streets and public squares. The parking of the State House grounds has added much to the dignity and appeal of that building.[4]

Memorials and monuments have done their share to improve and beautify such places. The three monuments on the State House grounds: the equestrian statue of General Wade Hampton; that to Generals Sumter, Marion and Pickens, three militia generals of South Carolina who fought with conspicuous achievements in the Revolution, and to the soldiers of the State; and the one to the Women of the Confederacy, were executed by Frederick W. Ruckstull. The inscriptions on the last named statue, written by William

---

[3] *The Revised Ordinance of the City of Columbia,* 1933, pp. 263-266.

[4] The information concerning the monuments was supplied by Mrs. A. S. Salley.

E. Gonzales, are of rare literary quality, enriching the fine execution of the design with a fitting memorial inscription.

Right: General Hampton. Below: Monument to Men of the Confederacy

The memorial to Doctor J. Marion Sims, erected in 1929 with an appropriation by the State and funds collected through the efforts of the South Carolina Women's Auxiliary to the Medical Association, was the work of Edmond Quinn. It stands at the very edge of the grounds, on the northwest corner of Senate and Sumter streets.

The services of the Palmetto Regiment, which participated in the war with Mexico, are memorialized in a remarkably life-like representation of a palmetto tree executed in iron, bearing the names of the men of the regiment who were killed or died in service. It stands guard over the western wing of the State House. It was designed by Christopher Werner.

Monument to Women of the Confederacy

The monument to the Confederate dead which stands directly in front of the State House bears beautiful inscriptions written by William Henry Trescot. The face on it is the work of Nicoli, an Italian sculptor. The bronze statute of George Washington is a copy of the marble by Houdon in the capitol at Richmond and was bought by the State of South Carolina from W. J. Hubard, of Richmond, for ten thousand dollars.

The monument to Jonathan Maxcy on the University Campus is from a design by Robert Mills.

At the corner of Senate and Sumter Streets stands a shaft to the memory of N. G. Gonzales.

At the southeast corner of Sumter and Pendleton is the most elaborate monument in the State. It is the World War Memorial "dedicated to the men and women of South Carolina who offered their lives in the winning of the war." This monument has a utilitarian feature. The historical records of the State are housed on the basement floor and the Historical Commission of South Carolina is in charge. The upper floor is a beautiful memorial chapel to those who made the supreme sacrifice in the war. On the left of the entrance to the chapel door is a tribute to the men of South Carolina who participated in the war; to the right is one to the Spiritual Union of the dead; while a third graces the back of the "shrine" at the east end of the chapel. These beautiful inscriptions for the marble tablets that carry them were written by William E. Gonzales, Esq.

CHRONOLOGY

The preliminary work for this table was done by the following pupils of the Columbia High School under the direction of Miss Sadie Magill:

Hazel Chavis, Edith Smith, Cecil Dorn, Henry B. Carson, Alice Bryant, Lewis Pennell, Edward Alexander, Spier Daughtry, John B. Paysinger, Eleanor Lykes, Elizabeth Moseley, Martha Ebaugh, Doris Wev, Beth Herzog, Mamie Thomas, Eva Bryan Wilson, Florence Daniel, Blanche Penick, Catherine Webster, Leo M. Traynor, C. E. Graybill, and Howard Dutrow.

The work was completed and tabulated by Irving Stebbins.

1786

Mar. 22 Columbia created capital by legislative act
Sept. 26 First sale of Columbia lots in Charleston
Oct. "Married in Columbia, Mr. Jacob Seibels to Miss Sally Temple from New York"

1787

Columbia laid out, John Gabriel Guignard, surveyor
First religious services held by Rev. Isaac Smith at home Col. Thos. Taylor
Jan. 13 Col. Hampton's horse "Columbia" won purse of 35 guineas at Newmarket

1788

First story of State House completed
Apr. 17 Nearly fifty houses under construction

1789

Public records moved to Columbia

1790

State House ready for use
Constitutional convention held May 12–June 3
Stage line between Columbia and Charleston well established
Jan. 4 First meeting of Legislature in Columbia
Jan. First Columbia races
Jan. Subscription Ball at the State House

1791

Flood swept away Wade Hampton bridge over Congaree
Mar. 5 *Columbia Gazette* founded by Robert Haswell
Apr. 21 Wade Hampton II born in Columbia
May 22 George Washington's visit

1792

Population of Columbia, 2,479 whites, 1,451 negroes
Permission given by Legislature to conduct lottery for "free" school
Aug. 6 Site chosen for County Court House
Dec. 21 Legislature set aside one block for free school
Dec. 21 Legislature gave power to commissioners to sell lots at auction
Dec. 21 Provision made for Columbia Academy

1793

State Gazette and Columbian Advertiser begun by Faust
Mar. 29 "Married at Camden, John Taylor, Esq. of Columbia, to Miss Sarah Chestnut"
Apr. 5 Died in Columbia, Mrs. James Green Hunt, only daughter of Col. Thos. Taylor
May 27 Federal Court held in State House

1794

Mar. 30 Rev. David E. Dunlap called for Presbyterian Church
Oct. 31 Death of Mrs. Harriet Hampton, wife of Wade Hampton, Sr.

1795

Wade Hampton Sr., representative to Congress
Wm. C. Clifton, teacher from near Hopkins, erected school on northwest corner, Main and Taylor
June 4 Rev. David E. Dunlap ordained and installed as pastor of First Presbyterian Church
Dec. 19 Act of incorporation of "Academy of Columbia"

1796

Flood washed away 700 foot bridge built by Wade Hampton over Congaree
Daniel Morgan visited Wade Hampton

1797

Trustees of Columbia Male Academy announced that they had found a teacher
During session of Legislature mail between Columbia and Charleston was carried twice a week
Dec. 16 Board of nine commissioners of streets and markets created
Dec. 16 Public burial ground established
Dec. 16 Inspections and warehouse for tobacco provided

1798

James Sanders Guignard, 17 years old, first postmaster
Burial ground prepared

John Compty empowered to build bridge above Columbia near site
            of present Broad River Bridge
Jan.   Male Academy established by Abram Blanding
Dec. 21   Act passed providing for annual election of 7 commissioners of
            streets and markets, empowered to give licenses, suppress gam-
            bling, fine, make rules and regulations and appoint clerk of
            market

1799

Columbia Ferry authorized, half profits for Academy of Columbia
Col. Hampton erected a cotton gin at his mill just below Southern
            Rail Road crossing at Gill Creek
County Courts declared forever abolished by Legislature
Aug. 7   Swanson Lunsford, one of town commissioners, died during legisla-
            tive session and buried on State House grounds
Dec. 18   Act passed making Columbia Richland county seat

1800

James Sanders Guignard appointed treasurer for upper division of
            South Carolina
Legislative library established
Aug.   Contract made with Jesse Arthur to erect gaol, costing not more
            than $3,570 and to be completed by September 1, 1801

1801

James Sanders Guignard elected Surveyor General of S. C.
$50,000 voted by General Assembly for the establishment of S. C.
            College
South Carolina College established by legislative act
May 16   Boat arrived at Charleston from 90 miles above Granby
Dec. 19   Commissioners of Columbia given power to grant licenses to keepers
            of billiard tables and to appropriate money for public wells and
            a fire engine

1802

Rope walk in operation by Stephen Brown
Oil mill in operation by Benj. Waring
James B. Richardson took office as Governor
Methodist services held in the State House by Rev. J. Harper
Approximately 200 houses and about 10 stores in Columbia
Feb. 12   First meeting of Board of Trustees of S. C. College held in Charles-
            ton
Dec. 18   Legislature provided for condemning of lands for S. C. College and
            authorized the Comptroller to buy mathematical and philoso-
            phical apparatus and a library for the college

1803

Methodist church organized with six members

1804

Paul Hamilton governor
Regular weekly mail coach between Columbia and Charleston
Mar.-Apr. Three destructive fires in Columbia
May 4 Dr. Jonathan Maxcy elected president S. C. College
May 15 Banquet at Green's Tavern to celebrate Louisiana Purchase

1805

People of Columbia petitioned Legislature for self government
Edward Hooker's visit
Jan. 10 S. C. College opened to students with a faculty of two members
Dec. 19 Law creating commissioners of Columbia repealed and Columbia incorporated as a town. Government under an intendant and six wardens

1806

Charles Pinckney governor for 4th time
Euphradian and Clariosophic literary societies founded at S. C. College
Paper manufactory erected by Benj. Waring
A brick kiln established
Dr. Samuel Green postmaster
May 1 John Taylor, Esq., elected first intendant of Columbia
May 1 First session of town board: Ordinance I passed
Dec. 12 James Boatwright and Middleton Glaze engaged in the manufacture of cotton gins
Dec. 19 Law required purchasers of Columbia lots to register their titles

1807

First Baptist Church organized
House erected for president of S. C. College
Apr. 11 Abraham Nott elected intendant
June 9 Claiborne Clifton elected intendant
July 30 Strict tax enforcement laws passed

1808

State patrol law passed
Apr. 14 John Hooker elected intendant
July 11 Daniel Faust elected intendant
Dec. 17 Law gave the governor power to appoint a commissioner for Columbia to execute titles of land sold by former commissioners. He was also to investigate the former commissioners and to obtain from them all money accruing from the sale of Columbia lots

1809

First Baptist congregation organized
Apr. 7 Simon Taylor elected intendant
Dec. 19 Unlicensed billiard tables in Columbia prohibited

1810

Henry Middleton governor
First house for professors erected at S. C. College
Apr. 3 Robert Stark elected intendant

1811

Building at S. C. College cracked by an earthquake
First Baptist Church building erected
Apr. 8 Simon Taylor elected intendant
Dec. 21 Laws passed forcing inhabitants of Columbia to keep the streets in repair and providing an assize on bread

1812

Joseph Allston governor
Apr. 21 Daniel Faust elected intendant
Aug. 8 First Episcopal congregation formed in Columbia. Services held in the State House by Rev. Andrew Fowler
Dec. 9 Columbia branch of the Bank of the State of S. C. authorized and the bank opened in the brick basement of the State House

1813

Apr. 10 Daniel Faust elected intendant
Aug. 8 Richland Volunteer Rifle Corps formed

1814

First Presbyterian Church building dedicated
First steps for fire prevention taken
Mar. 7 Trinity Episcopal Church completed
Apr. 6 Daniel Faust elected intendant
Dec. 14 Trinity Episcopal Church dedicated and consecrated

1815

Jan. 8 Col. Wade Hampton sent to Washington with a report of the Battle of New Orleans
Apr. 6 William E. Hayne elected intendant
Dec. 19 *The Telescope,* started by Thomas W. Lorrain

1816

"Female Benevolent Society" established
Commissioner of Columbia required to convey all unsold land in outer Columbia to the trustees of the Columbia Academy
Fire department created
Morgan & Guiry's bookstore well established; first bookstore in S. C. outside of Charleston
Apr. 3 James Gregg elected intendant
Dec. 6 Colonel Andrew Pickens governor

1817

Magnetic telegraph introduced
Female Academy under Dr. Elias Marks established
First observatory completed at S. C. College
Apr. 10 Daniel Morgan elected intendant

1818

Apr. 7 James T. Goodwyn elected intendant
Dec. 16 Lot set aside for a building to be used by Agricultural Society, Medical Board, and Masonic Lodge 68; town clock with bells ordered
Dec. 18 Law passed enabling the intendants and wardens to borrow money for the town waterworks. No licenses for billiard tables to be issued in a fifteen mile radius of Columbia
Dec. 18 Act providing for town hall

1819

S. C. College faculty increased to five members
Waterworks contracted for, supplying Richardson, Senate, Bull and Taylor streets
Apr. 10 James T. Goodwyn elected intendant
Dec. 14 Law giving intendant and wardens of Columbia power: to impose a tax on real property not exceeding fifty cents on every hundred dollars; to fine up to fifty dollars; to prohibit blacksmith shops in the public part of town; to require licenses for the sale of spirits

1820

Peter Clissey manufactured coaches
Thos. Cooper president of S. C. College
Jan. 1 County seat abolished
Apr. 4 James T. Goodwyn elected intendant for third time
Dec. 12 First demonstration of steam engine water pump

1821

Steamboat "City of Columbia" made trip up Santee and Congaree Rivers to Columbia
First Catholics came to Columbia, Roman Catholic Church organized
State Asylum organized by Samuel Farrow and William Crafts
Apr. 3 James T. Goodwyn elected intendant for fourth time in succession
Dec. 20 Law passed authorizing the erection of suitable buildings for a lunatic asylum and a school for the deaf and dumb

1822

Charter granted for a bridge over the Congaree
Male Academy situated on Sumter Street between Blanding and Laurel

Female Academy situated on corner of Washington and Marion
    streets
Hebrew Benevolent Society formed
A horse powered street railway for transportation of cotton run
    by John McLean
Apr. 3 David J. McCord elected intendant

1823

Not less than 30,000 bales of cotton handled
Apr. 10 James T. Goodwyn elected intendant for fifth time
Dec. 20 Laws passed transferring the power over the patrol to the intendant
    and wardens, and constituting them commissioners of the poor

1824

Waterworks begun by Colonel Blanding
Society formed for the "Encouragement of Industry Among the
    Female Poor"
Jan. 1 Columbia Canal completed
Apr. 9 David J. McCord elected intendant
May 15 Roman Catholic congregation organized and church built
Dec. 17 Laws passed providing for the division of Columbia into wards
    and for a tax on all personal property in the town

1825

Marquis de Lafayette visited Columbia
Apr. 5 James T. Goodwyn elected intendant for the sixth time
Dec. 20 Act passed condemning land for the Columbia Canal

1826

Five religious denominations with churches: Methodist, Baptist,
    Episcopal, Presbyterian and Roman Catholic
Apprentices' library society projected
A female school established by Mrs. Edmunds
Apr. 4 Wm. F. DeSaussure elected intendant

1827

South Carolina Canal and Railroad Company chartered
Apprentices' Library Society organized
Apr. 3 Wm. F. DeSaussure elected intendant
Apr. 4 Bridge across Congaree opened
July and Aug. Protest meetings held against increased tariff
Dec. 15 Bronze monument to Dr. Maxcy dedicated on S. C. College campus
Dec. 18 Law passed authorizing the town council of Columbia to establish
    public scales

1828

Law passed giving the intendant and wardens of Columbia the
    power to grant licenses to auctioneers, levy taxes on sales at

auction, tax public conveyances, and to prevent the keeping of bawdy and gaming houses in a ten mile limit of S. C. College

Apr. 8   E. H. Maxcy elected intendant
May 28 Lunatic Asylum ready for patients
Oct. 8   Barhamville Academy erected by Dr. Elias Marks
Dec. 12 First patient received at the Lunatic Asylum

1829

Columbia Male Academy moved to lot donated to the city by John Taylor
Presbyterian Theological Seminary located in Columbia

Feb. 2   Saluda bridge opened
Mar. 4   Jackson's inauguration celebrated with fireworks, cannon, etc
Apr. 7   E. H. Maxcy elected intendant
Aug. 14 Broad River bridge opened for traffic

1830

Traffic regulations started
Population, 3,310
Landrum Pottery Company begun

Apr. 7   Wm. C. Preston elected intendant
Sept. 20 "States' Rights" meeting held

1831

Mrs. Ann Royal visited Columbia
Main building of Presbyterian Theological Seminary erected

Apr. 5   Wm. C. Clifton elected intendant
Dec. 5   States' Rights and Free Trade party met in Columbia
Dec. 17 Law passed by the Legislature to establish a bank in Columbia

1832

Methodist Church rebuilt in brick
Washington Irving visited Wm. C. Preston
The South Carolinian published

Apr. 3   E. H. Maxcy elected intendant
Sept. and Dec. Union Party held meetings in Columbia

1833

First preparatory school of medicine established in Columbia by Doctors Nott and Gibbes
First class graduated from the Columbia Theological Seminary

Apr. 2   M. H. DeLeon elected intendant
Nov. 16 Colonel Thomas Taylor died
Dec.   Columbia Railroad Company chartered

1834

Stage coaches run on schedule

Apr. 8   M. H. DeLeon re-elected intendant

1835

Wade Hampton died
Brick wall around S. C. College finished
S. C. College reorganized
Waterworks sold to Columbia by Col. Blanding for $24,000
Apr.   6   M. H. DeLeon elected intendant for third time

1836

"Independent" fire company established—first in Columbia
Jan.   Surveying of railroad from Columbia to Charleston begun by James
              Clark
Feb. 11   Columbia men in the Richland Volunteer Rifle Corps left for the
              Seminole War
Apr.   4   John Bryce elected intendant

1837

Elliot and Harper Colleges completed at S. C. College
P. T. Barnum began career by reorganizing Napoleon Turner's
              Circus
Summer: Members of Richland Volunteer Rifle Corps returned from Seminole
              War without entering action
Apr.   3   John Bryce elected intendant

1838

Mar. 20   Contracts for railroad from Columbia to Charleston let and work
              begun with ceremonies in Columbia
Apr.   4   John Bryce re-elected intendant

1839

Dr. Thomas Cooper died while compiling the statutes of S. C.
Apr.   1   Dr. R. W. Gibbes elected intendant

1840

Population of Columbia, 4,340
Library of S. C. College completed—first college library under a
              separate roof in the U. S.
Apr.   6   Dr. R. W. Gibbes re-elected intendant
Aug.   1   Columbia Branch Bank established
Dec.   8   Bible convention held in Columbia

1841

Feb. 17   Nine delegates of the Tippecanoe Club of Columbia sent to attend
              Harrison's inauguration
Apr.   5   Colonel Benj. T. Elmore elected intendant
Sept. 20   Colonel R. H. Goodwyn elected intendant

1842

Columbia's first extensive fire
Arsenal Academy established
Apr.   4   William M. Meyers elected intendant
May   8   Odd Fellows Society organized
June 28   First train reached Columbia—"Robert Y. Hayne"; elaborate cele-
          bration
July   1   First freight train reached Columbia

1843

Apr.   3   William M. Meyers elected intendant
Dec. 19   Law passed vesting the Columbia Canal in Frederic William Green
          for twenty years
Dec. 19   Governor's Guards chartered

1844

First commercial daguerreotype made in Columbia by Mr. Libolt
Visit of Professor Frederick Von Raumer of the University of Berlin
R. L. Bryan Company established
Palmetto Lodge School opened by Odd Fellows
Apr.   1   William M. Meyers elected intendant
May   Columbia Commercial Association (Chamber of Commerce) formed

1845

Girls' School begun by Mr. and Mrs. Hassell
Attempt to pave the sidewalks of Main Street made by the city
      council without referring the matter to the citizens; protest
      meeting held and paving prevented
Arsenal Military Academy housed in what is now the governor's
      mansion
Electric telegraph was demonstrated by Professor Ellet
Apr.   5   William B. Stanley elected intendant

1846

Greenville and Columbia Railroad Company chartered
Apr.   6   William B. Stanley elected intendant
Dec. 12   Joel Stevenson elected intendant

1847

C. O. Brown and Company established
Trinity Episcopal Church dedicated
Apr.   5   Edward Sill elected intendant
May   Daniel Webster's visit

1848

Methodist Church, now Main Street Methodist, built on the corner
      of Marion and Calhoun streets

Buildings at S. C. College named
Apr.   1   Edward Sill re-elected intendant
July 27   Return of the Palmetto Regiment celebrated
Dec. 19   Act passed increasing the powers of the city council by permitting
           it to borrow money, issue stock, and to lay tax for railroad
           subscription

1849

Columbia Daily Telegraph printed
Joe Jefferson's company played season in Columbia
Track laying of the Greenville and Columbia Railroad Company be-
gun from the Columbia end
Apr.   2   Edward Sill re-elected intendant

1850

Population, 6,060
Palmetto Armory built to convert old style firearms into newer types
Apr.   1   Henry Lyons elected intendant
Aug.   5   Law passed allowing the Charlotte and South Carolina railroad
           company to lay down a railroad through the streets of Co-
           lumbia and build a station

1851

Columbia and Newberry linked by the Columbia and Greenville
   Railroad
Saint Mary's College chartered and opened
Apr.   7   Colonel A. H. Gladden elected intendant
Dec. 15   Corner stone of the State House laid

1852

A manufactory for rifles in Columbia
Exchange Bank of Columbia chartered
Charlotte and South Carolina Railroad completed connecting Co-
   lumbia and Charlotte
First illuminating gas plant established in Columbia
Apr.   7   Colonel A. H. Gladden elected intendant
Apr. 26   Convention held to elect delegates to the Southern Convention
July   Columbia and Greenville Railroad completed

1853

Columbia and Hamburg Railroad chartered to connect Columbia and
   Augusta
Apr.   William Maybin elected intendant

1854

Clash between the students of South Carolina College and the police
Mar. 13   First meeting of the Medical Society of Columbia
Apr.   William Maybin re-elected intendant

Dec.   7   "A destructive conflagration took place and every store and dwelling
           on one whole square was destroyed with two exceptions." *The
           South Carolinian* office and machinery completely destroyed with
           a loss of $40,000
Dec. 21   Columbia Female College founded (now Columbia College)
Dec. 21   Columbia chartered as a city

1855

           Term Mayor used for first time
Apr.   Edward J. Arthur, mayor of Columbia
Dec. 19   An Act passed to aid the city of Columbia to construct new water-
           works by the issuance of bonds to the amount of $100,000

1856

Nov. 11   First State Fair in Columbia
           Elmwood Cemetery Company formed
           Nine policemen in Columbia
Dec. 20   An Act to provide water for the public buildings of Columbia

1857

           First library "The Athenaeum" opened, corner Main and Washing-
           ton streets
Apr.   James B. Tradewell, mayor

1858

           Columbia and Hamburg Railroad rechartered, but unable to raise
           funds for construction
           First Baptist Church built
           First work house established
           The Ursuline Convent founded at Columbia by Rt. Reverend John
           Lynch
Apr.   James B. Tradewell, mayor
May   3   General John A. Quitman visited Columbia

1859

           Columbia College built and put in operation
           Mayor's tenure of office extended to two years
           Law passed requiring death certificates
           Ambrotypes and photographs made by Mr. Zealy
Apr.   Allen J. Green, mayor

1860

           Military company formed by South Carolina College students
           Population, 8,052
Dec. 17   Meeting of the Secession Committee held in the First Baptist Church
Dec.   Smallpox epidemic in Columbia

1861

Dr. John Boatwright, mayor
First Wayside hospital in the world established in the Charlotte
    Depot by Columbia women to aid passing wounded
The Ursuline Institute incorporated by the Legislature

Jan.   7 Columbia Grays military company formed
June   Concert held to raise funds for Confederate relief work

1862

The "Ladies' Hospital" established in Columbia, caring for over
    1,000 wounded the first year

June 25 South Carolina College taken over by the Confederate government
    for use as a general hospital
Oct.   8 Meeting held establishing a central association for the relief of South
    Carolina soldiers at the fronts

1863

Dr. Thomas J. Goodwyn, mayor
The Columbia and Augusta Railroad chartered

Apr.   A "Corn Association" established to provide the poor with food at
    reasonable prices
July   South Carolina College closed

1864

Jefferson Davis' visit
Columbia College closed and buildings rented for use as a hotel
Great distress in Columbia due to the high prices of food and fuel

May   Military review given by the Hampton Legion

1865

Jan.   "Great Bazaar" held in the State House, raising $350,000
Feb. 16 Columbia shelled by Sherman
Feb. 17 Columbia surrendered to Sherman by Mayor Goodwyn
Feb. 17 Columbia devastated by fire
Feb. 21 City council met to secure foodstuff
Mar. 21 First issue of the *Phoenix*
Apr. 18 James G. Gibbes elected assistant mayor
May 26 James G. Gibbes elected mayor
Dec.   South Carolina College granted a new charter as the University
    of South Carolina

1866

Jan 10 University of South Carolina received students
Apr.   Theodore Starke, mayor
Dec. 19 An act providing that notes payable on taxes or dues to the city be
    put in circulation by the city council

1867

Last public hanging
University of South Carolina closed

Work of construction begun on Columbia and Augusta railroad

Oct.   6   Henry Timrod died at his home

1868

South Carolina College reopened
Constitutional convention
Columbia and Augusta railroad completed
First velocipedes brought to Columbia

May 11   Carolina National Bank chartered
July   Colonel Gunther appointed mayor by the military
Aug.   C. H. Baldwin appointed mayor by the military
Nov.   John McKenzie appointed mayor for four years by the military

1869

A map of Columbia made by Alex Y. Lee
A cotton oil mill established by General E. P. Alexander which had
    an output of 3,000 gallons per week

1870

Broad River Bridge rebuilt
Population, 9,298
Y. M. C. A. established

Feb. 26   City limits of Columbia extended
Mar. 30   General R. E. Lee passed through Columbia
Apr.   John Alexander elected mayor
Apr.   Two year term for mayor re-established—McKenzie legislated out of
          office
Nov. 13   First dance of the South Carolina Club
Dec. 30   Licenses required for all business enterprises

1871

Benedict Institute founded
Central National Bank incorporated
Eight newspapers published in Columbia
John Alexander, mayor

May   9   First city ordinances passed by city council: concerning nuisances,
          regulating the alms house, for the better observation of the
          Sabbath day, and establishing a board of health
June 6   Ordinance passed to punish offenders by confinement in the work
          house at hard labor
June 27   The offices of City Clerk, City Treasurer, and City Assessor con-
          solidated into one office

1872

Four banks in Columbia, not including one private bank
Knights of Pythias chapter founded
Third court house established

Aug.   The Savings Bank of Columbia founded

1873

General bank panic
Citizens' Savings Bank bankrupt
Payments exceeding $100 suspended by the National banks in Columbia
Columbia College re-opened
1873-77 negroes had free access to the University of South Carolina
Oct.   Three professors of the University of South Carolina resigned because of the enrollment in the law school of the negro secretary of state

1874

City Hall erected
Court House erected at a cost of $30,000
Jan. 15 Knights of Pythias chartered

1875

First Presbyterian Church spire blown off by a cyclone
Publication of the *Columbia Register* begun
Sixty-second anniversary celebration of the Richland Rifle Corps
Governor's mansion repaired
"Young America" colored fire company organized
Main Street improved
New United States Court House and Post Office opened
First annual meeting of the Columbia Jockey Club
Washington Street M. E. Church dedicated

1876

Session of the Wallace House
Wade Hampton inaugurated governor
John Agnew, mayor
Art Gallery opened under the Opera House
South Carolina Historical Society began publication of historic papers
Columbia Artillery Club organized
Federal troops placed around the State House
Legislature met at the Choral Union hall
Columbia Street Railway chartered

1877

Columbia Female College reopened
June   University of South Carolina closed and the buildings rented

1878

Captain W. B. Stanley, mayor
Legislature appropriated money for improving the Columbia Canal
Ursuline Institute chartered as a college
Feb. 1 Paid Fire Department in operation

1879

Columbia and Lexington Water Power Company awarded exclusive
rights to the Broad and Congaree Rivers and the Columbia
canal, free use of 250 convicts for three years, and exemption
from taxation for several years

1880

College of Agricultural and Mechanical arts established at the University of South Carolina

Population, 10,036

Jan. 1 General Grant passed through Columbia
Apr.   Captain R. O'Neale elected mayor
July   Southern Bell Telephone Company established in Columbia
Dec. 24 New school district created and called "School District of the City
of Columbia"; school commission of Richland County limited to
territory outside of Columbia

1881

Allen University founded

Carolina National Bank reorganized

July 28 General Eaton, U. S. Commissioner of Education in Columbia

1882

State Military Academy at Charleston added as third branch of the
University of South Carolina

University of South Carolina changed to South Carolina College

First street railway for passengers built and operated by horses

City waterworks purchased from Pearce

Apr.   John T. Rhett elected mayor

1883

Columbia Male Academy property leased to the public schools

Commercial Bank established

June 23 D. B. Johnson elected superintendent of Columbia city schools
Sept. 28 Public schools open for first time
Dec. 23 Second Presbyterian Church begun as a mission Sunday school

1884

Van Metre's Furniture Company established

Cotton Compress Company founded

The "Columbia Club" formed

First graduation of Allen University students

Edgewood Methodist Church founded

Law department of the University of South Carolina founded

Apr.   John T. Rhett, mayor
Dec.   First local tax (one mill) for public schools authorized by Legislature

1885

Columbia, Newberry and Laurens Railroad chartered
Special levy for schools increased to two mills
Feb. 28 Second Presbyterian Church dedicated
July   Y. M. C. A. organized

1886

Apr.   John T. Rhett, mayor
May   First meeting of the Farmers' Association held in Columbia
Oct.   1 Loan and Exchange Bank organized
Nov. 15   Winthrop Training School for Teachers organized in Columbia
Dec. 12   St. Paul's Lutheran Church organized

1887

Southern Cotton Seed Oil Company established
Columbia College enlarged
Columbia Compress Company organized

1888

South Carolina College changed to University of South Carolina
Electric lights turned on for first time

1889

The Assembly Ball organized
Columbia Phosphate Company organized by Dr. T. C. Robertson

1890

B. R. Tillman Governor
Second Baptist Church organized
Columbia Zouaves reorganized
Agricultural and mechanical branches removed from the University
The University of South Carolina reorganized as South Carolina
    College
The State founded by N. G. and Ambrose Gonzales
College for Women founded
Population, 15,353
Apr.   Colonel F. W. McMaster, mayor
Oct.   1 South Carolina Institute for young ladies opened
Oct. 27   Columbia, Newberry, and Laurens Railroad completed

1891

Columbia Mills and Olympia Mills constructed
Balls forbidden in the State House
Feb. 18   First issue of *The State*
May 13   Centennial celebration of founding of Columbia
Oct.   Columbia to Savannah railroad completed
Dec. 11   Columbia Canal completed

1892

Jan. 11 Columbia Canal formally opened
Apr.   Dr. W. C. Fisher elected mayor
May   The Bank of Columbia organized
May 24-Sept. 17 Columbia Hospital Association formed, land leased for 99
                years, hospital chartered

1893

         Electricity generated from the Columbia Canal
Jan. 6 Thomas Nelson Page in Columbia
May   3 Cornerstone of Columbia Hospital laid
May   6 First electrical street railway in the state inaugurated at Columbia;
                Alfred Wallace, driver
Nov. 1 Columbia Hospital formally opened

1894

         Columbia Rifles formed
         913 male, 1,161 female students enrolled in the city schools
         South Carolina College admitted women students
Mar. 8 Street railway electrified
Apr.   W. McB. Sloan elected mayor

1895

         Mrs. "Stonewall" Jackson in Columbia
         955 male, 1,192 female students enrolled in Columbia schools
         Columbia College modernized
         E. S. Dreher became Coumbia's second superintendent of schools
Feb.   Susan B. Anthony visited Columbia
May 22 City school board organized high school—co-educational—corner
                Marion and Washington streets

1896

         Columbia Library Association opened
                library in city hall. Mrs. Eugene Cramer, librarian
         Tree of Life Jewish Congregation organized
         Granby Methodist Mission organized
Jan. 15 Columbia Hospital Bazaar
Mar.   Electric belt line proposed for Columbia
Apr.   W. McB. Sloan, mayor
Apr. 11 Old opera house converted for use as police headquarters
June   Car line between Columbia and Hyatt's Park completed

1897

         Richland Volunteer Rifle Corps disbanded and reorganized
Feb. 1 Associate Reformed Presbyterian Church organized
Apr. 11 William Jennings Bryan in Columbia
Apr. 26 *The Columbia Record* founded by George R. Koester
June 10 First high school commencement exercises: Edward S. Cardwell,
                J. Waties Thomas and James A. Cathcart on the program

1898

Colonel T. J. Lipscomb elected mayor
1,038 male, 1,300 female students enrolled in city schools
May 10   Door of Hope founded by Dr. J. M. Pike
Sept. 7 Booker T. Washington in Columbia
Sept. 21 W. J. Bryan passed through Columbia
Oct. 25 Marion Street Methodist Church completely destroyed by fire
Dec. 19 President McKinley passed through Columbia

1899

Y. M. C. A. building begun
Marion Street Methodist Church rebuilt on Main Street
Direct railroad connecting Columbia and Savannah established
1,115 male, 1,414 female students enrolled in the city schools

1900

Columbia to Cheraw railroad completed
Contract awarded for completion of State House
Population, 21,108
Knowlton Infirmary begun by Dr. A. B. Knowlton
1,181 male, 1,448 female students enrolled in the city schools
Feb. 15 Wm. Jennings Bryan made several speeches in Columbia
Apr.   F. S. Earle elected mayor
June   Union Station begun

1901

Steward's Hall for South Carolina College
Kindergarten opened by Miss Louly Shand

1902

Epworth Orphanage Methodist Church erected
Columbia Chamber of Commerce chartered
Jan.   Steward's Hall opened at South Carolina College
Jan. 14 Union Station completed
Apr.   F. S. Earle elected mayor
Apr. 11 President Theodore Roosevelt passed through Columbia

1903

Glass factory built to supply state dispensary with bottles
Whaley Street Methodist Church erected
Seaboard Air Line Railway built
State House completed
June 23 Waterworks Commission created

1904

Arsenal Hill Presbyterian Church built
First large addition made to Columbia Hospital

New site chosen for Columbia College and new buildings erected
Medical Society of Columbia made part of the American Medical
   Association
Apr. T. H. Gibbes elected mayor
June Nine graduates from Columbia High School

1905

Centennial of South Carolina College celebrated
Jan. 6 New Columbia Hospital opened
June   Twelve graduates from Columbia High School
Sept. 24 Tree of Life Synagogue dedicated
Oct. 18 Captain R. P. Hobson visited Columbia

1906

Statue of Wade Hampton erected on State House grounds
Congaree Hotel burned
Taylor School completed
Mar. Building of St. Peter's Church begun
Apr. T. H. Gibbes elected mayor

1907

Columbia Clearing House issued certificates to be used as money
   during panic
Nov. 27 Corporate limits of city of Columbia extended

1908

First surfacing of city streets
Wallace Thomson Memorial Infirmary completed at University of
   South Carolina
Apr. W. S. Reamer elected mayor

1909

Shandon Methodist Church organized
Shandon Baptist Church organized
Davis College completed
University preparatory school for boys in operation
Mar. 19 Dr. Charles W. Eliot of Harvard in Columbia
Sept. 9 Large buildings of Columbia College destroyed by fire
Nov. 6 President Taft in Columbia

1910

Elmwood Park Baptist Church organized
Maxcy Gregg Park development begun
Means Davis College dedicated
Population, 26,319
Apr. W. H. Gibbes elected mayor
Sept. 29 New Columbia College buildings completed

1911

Southern Lutheran Theological Seminary moved to Columbia
LeConte College dedicated
McMaster School built
Apr.   9   Tabernacle Baptist Church organized
June   2   Woodrow Wilson in Columbia
Oct. 24   Alfred Tennyson Dickens in Columbia

1912

Y. W. C. A. established
Columbia had 83 miles of streets
Lutheran Church of the Ascension organized
Davis High School established
Congaree toll bridge bought by Richland County and made a free
    bridge
Work begun on the Palmetto Building
Wales Gardens section begun by the City Development Company

1913

College Place Methodist Church organized
Old city market razed
Logan School built
Addition of Shandon and Waverley sections
Jan.   Columbia Male Academy reunion
Jan.   3   Palmetto Building, under construction, twisted several inches by
    high winds
Jan. 16   Charles Francis Adams, president of the Massachusetts Historical
    Society, in Columbia
Jan. 31   Walter Hines Page in Columbia
Mar.   1   W. J. Bryan in Columbia

1914

Waverley Sanitarium founded by Dr. James Woods Babcock
Over three miles of pavement laid in Wales Gardens
Clearing house certificates issued for the second time due to lack
    of cash
Knowlton Infirmary purchased by the South Carolina State Baptist
    Convention
Mar. 11   Equal Suffrage League formed
Apr.   T. L. Griffith elected mayor
Apr. 24   Otis Skinner in Columbia
Apr. 25   Auto races held in Columbia
Sept.   Knowlton Infirmary opened as the Baptist Hospital

1915

R. I. Manning elected governor
$250,000 voted for a new high school and to enlarge and repair
    grammar schools
Elmwood Park Baptist and Second Baptist Churches consolidated
    into the Park Street Baptist Church

Woman's Building exempted from city taxation and campaign started
to raise funds

Maude Adams in Columbia

Chamber of Commerce budget set at $9,000

Miss Euphemia McClintock retired from presidency of College for
Women

Radio receiving station installed at the physics department of University

George M. Cohan in Columbia

Masonic Temple on Main Street burned

1916

Jan. 27 President Bryan of Colgate University in Columbia

Feb. 3 Flood of Congaree caused freight boats, the "Ruth II" and "City
of Columbia" to break moorings and float away. Both were
recovered

Eau Claire Presbyterian Chuch organized

Ridgewood club house begun

Columbia High School added the eleventh grade. New building built
on old site

Special levy for schools increased to 5 mills

Feb. 6 South Carolina Convention of Second National Missionary Conference held. Many famous speakers and registration of 1,956

Mar. 15 First annual auto show

1917

Camp Jackson established

Shandon Presbyterian Church organized

June 6 Major General Leonard Wood in Columbia

Aug. 29 81st Division arrived for training at Camp Jackson

Dec. 2 Newton D. Baker in Columbia

1918

70,000 men at Camp Jackson

W. H. Hand became third superintendent of city public schools

Apr. R. J. Blalock elected mayor

1919

Richland Shale products company founded

Paving of residential sections of Columbia begun

Town Theater and Stage Society inaugurated

Oct. 31 Rose Hill Presbyterian Church organized

1920

Population 37,524

Jan. 13 Colonia Hotel formally opened

Jan. 28 Strike of motormen

Apr. 13 Bank of Columbia and the Commercial Bank of Columbia consolidated

June 23 Dr. Frederic Cook, "discoverer" North Pole 1909, visited Columbia

Sept. 27 Carolina Band organized
Dec. 16 Work begun on remodeling a house into Town Theater

1921

Lutheran Church of the Incarnation organized
Control of Columbia Hospital vested in Legislative Delegation of
      Richland County
May   1 Southeastern Express Company came to Columbia
June 26 Eau Claire Baptist Church organized
July   3 Rose Hill Presbyterian Church completed
Sept. 30 Columbia Post Office built
Nov. 16 Council assumed charge of the opera house

1922

New Masonic Temple built
Dial telephone system installed in Columbia
Bond issue of $75,000 for addition to Columbia High School
Jan.   2 Bon Air School reopened
Feb. 12 First Dollar-Day held
Feb. 15 Street railway carmen strike
Feb. 15 John Phillip Sousa in Columbia
Apr.   2 W. H. Coleman elected mayor
July   2 Arc lights replaced by mazda in street lamps

1923

Columbia Bible College opened
Bond issue of $300,000 for general school improvement
Mar. 4–April 8 Billy Sunday in Columbia
Oct.   6 Cornerstone of Salvation Army building laid
Oct. 16 National convention of the American Cotton Association met in
      Columbia
Nov. 3 Geraldine Farrar sang in Columbia
Nov. 27–28 Madame Ernestine Schumann-Heink in Columbia
Dec. 30 Shandon Lutheran Church dedicated

1924

Timrod Library became Columbia Public Library, supported by City
      Council and Chamber of Commerce
Jan.   1 Enlargement of the Presbyterian Church begun
Mar. 17 Work begun on Science Hall at Benedict College
May   1 Tornado kills twenty people in Richland County
May 15 St. Peter's Church consecrated
July 22 Santee River bridge officially opened
July 18 "Uncle Jaggers" died
Dec. 18 New Town Theatre opened

1925

New Congaree bridge planned
Rose Hill, Olympia, and Heathwood schools built
Loyal Order of Moose open a new radio station
Forest Hills development begun
Broad River bridge destroyed by fire
Cornerstone of Trinity Parish House laid
Historical pageant—The Making of America
Senator Thomas J. Walsh spoke in Columbia
Hamilton Holt in Columbia

Jan.	10	Paul Whiteman in Columbia
Jan.	15	Dusolina Gianini in Columbia
Feb.		Major General Hines in Columbia
Feb.	10	Walter Damrosch in Columbia
Dec.	28	Woodrow Wilson home marked by a granite boulder
Dec.	30	Rebuilding of the Broad River Bridge begun

1926

First Presbyterian Sunday School cornerstone laid
Bond issue of $300,000 for school building program
Lutheran Church of the Incarnation organized
College Place Methodist Church erected
American Bank and Trust Company closed

Feb.	1	Work begun on the new Congaree bridge
Apr.	2	Will Rogers in Columbia
Apr.		L. B. Owens elected mayor
Dec.	31	Man killed while at work on Congaree bridge

1927

Buxton Stables established winter training quarters in Columbia
Second fatality at Congaree bridge
Bridge over Congaree river completed
$1,500,000 shops begun by Southern Railway
Observatory built at University of South Carolina
Dreyfuss Field dedicated
Work begun on Lake Murray dam

Feb.	14	Will Rogers in Columbia
Dec.		Claussen's Bakery begun
Dec.	9	Wardlaw Junior High School dedicated
Dec.	10	Royster's sulphuric acid factory burned

1928

Columbia struck by a hurricane
Washington Street Methodist Sunday School built
Sergeant Alvin C. York in Columbia
People's Bank of Columbia opened
Development of "Five Points" begun
Claussen's Bakery completed
Columbia divided into ten wards

Jan. 1 All motor busses withdrawn from Columbia due to a mortgage held
on them

Jan. 6 Columbia motorists asked to help solve the transportation problem
by giving free rides. Regular stations established

Aug.   A. C. Flora elected superintendent of public schools

1929

Part of temporary Broad River bridge washed away

Campaign started to buy Woodrow Wilson home

Columbia Public Library moved to Woodrow home

Jan.   Radio Station W.R.B.W. began weekly broadcasts

Feb. 8 First shovel of earth for new airport dug by Mayor Owens

Feb. 18 Concert by Marion Talley

Mar. 8 Harvey Firestone in Columbia

1930

Statue "American Doughboy" erected in Olympia

Columbia Township Auditorium built

Hand Junior High School built

New Ebenezer Lutheran Church begun

Municipal Airport built

Radio station W.I.S. began operation

Al Smith in Columbia

"Los Angeles" dirigible passed over Columbia

Chicora College transplanted to Charlotte

Population 50,581

1931

Standard Oil Company office moved to Columbia

Street cars resumed operation

Heathwood School bought by Shandon Methodist Church for use
as church

Bon Air school discontinued

Educational Building completed at the University of South Carolina

Veterans' Hospital located near Columbia

Columbia Hotel built

1932

Veterans' Hospital completed

Public School Administration Building built

Professional baseball team organized

Peoples' Bank chain closed with two branches in Columbia

City busses started in Columbia

Opera house remodeled into a moving picture theatre

University High School built

Mar. 3 Governor Albert Ritchie in Columbia

1933

Transient camps established

Y.W.C.A. camp established

Y.M.C.A. camp established
Mar. 27 South Carolina State Bank reopened
June 19 Central Union Bank ordered to liquidate
Nov. 1 New Columbia Hospital opened

1934

Municipal Stadium built
One of world's largest water tanks constructed at Melrose Heights
"Cavalcade" trained in Columbia
Main Street repaired
State House exterior cleaned by sand blasting
New Federal Land Bank built

1935

Liquor stores re-opened
Police radio installed—W4XAH
"House of Peace" synagogue built
Citizens and Southern Bank chartered
State Highway Department placed under military rule
Columbia visited by Senator Huey Long
Seed Loan Office obtained for Columbia
New curb market built
"Women of the Confederacy" statue moved
Old county court house demolished
World War Memorial completed
12,628 pupils enrolled in public schools
Work started on fourth Court House
Jan. 15 Olin D. Johnston inaugurated governor
Mar. 24 "Burlington Zephyr" streamline train in Columbia
Apr.   1 Paul Whiteman in Columbia

1936

University enrollment, 1,348
Public school enrollment, 13,266
Bank clearance for 1935, $76,797,514.28
Postal receipts for 1935, $493,077.74
Main Street property valued at $2,250.00 front foot, compared to
    $100.00 in 1886

Editor's note: This table is necessarily limited, omitting items of interest which would have been been included had space permitted.

Sources of information: Newspapers, memoirs, statutes, minutes of institutions, general books about Columbia, and chapters in this volume.

BIBLIOGRAPHY

Allen, Walter, *Governor Chamberlain's Administration in South Carolina. A Chapter of Reconstruction in the Southern States,* New York, 1888.

Andrews, Matthew Page, ed., *The Women of the South in War Times,* Baltimore, 1920.

Andrews, Sidney, *The South Since the War; As shown by fourteen weeks of travel and observation in Georgia and the Carolinas,* Boston, 1866.

Angell, James Burrell, *The Reminiscence of,* New York, 1912.

Ball, William Watts, *A Boy's Recollection of the Red Shirt Campaign,* Columbia, 1911.

——————, *The State That Forgot, South Carolina's Surrender to Democracy,* Indianapolis, 1932.

Barker, Theodore G., *Treaty of Washington. Before the Mixed Commission on British and American Claims. George Wood, Jr., and Lawrence Heyworth vs. the United States. No. 103. Brief for the Claimants,* Charleston, 1873.

Bateman, John M., *Columbia Scrapbook,* Columbia, 1915.

——————, *A Sketch of the History of the Governor's Guards of Columbia, S. C., 1843–1898,* Columbia, 1910.

——————, Alston, J. K. and Frost, J. D., *Military Report of Sub-Committee on Citizens' Fair,* Columbia, 1897.

Blease, Cole L., *Destruction of Property in Columbia, S. C., by Sherman's Army. Speech . . . delivered in the Senate, May 15, 1930.* Senate Doc. No. 149, 71st Congress, 2nd Session, Washington, 1930.

Boucher, Chauncey Samuel, *The Nullification Controversy in South Carolina,* Chicago, 1916.

Bowers, Claude G., *The Tragic Era,* New York, 1929.

Brigham, C. S., "Bibliography of American Newspapers, 1690–1820." *Proceedings of the American Antiquarian Society, 1824.* n. p. n. d.

Brooks, U. R., *Butler and His Cavalry in the War of Secession, 1861–1865,* Columbia, 1909.

——————, *South Carolina Bench and Bar.* Vol. I, Columbia, 1908.

Bryce, Mrs. Campbell, *The Personal Experiences of, During the Burning of Columbia, South Carolina, by General W. T. Sherman's Army, February 17, 1865,* Philadelphia, 1899.

——————, *Reminiscences of the Hospitals of Columbia, S. C., During the Four Years of the Civil War,* Philadelphia, 1897.

Caldwell, J. F. J., *The History of a Brigade of South Carolinians Known First as "Gregg's" and Subsequently as "McGowan's Brigade,"* Philadelphia, 1866.

Capers, Brigadier-General Ellison, "South Carolina," Vol. V of *Confederate Military History,* ed. by Gen. Clement A. Evans, Atlanta, 1899.

Carroll, James Parsons, *Report of the Committee Appointed to Collect Testimony in Relation to the Destruction of Columbia, S. C., on the 17th of February, 1865,* Columbia, 1893.

The Centennial Celebration of the Granting of the Charter to South Carolina College Held in Charleston, S. C., Dec. 19–20, 1901, at the South Carolina Interstate and West Indian Exposition, Charleston, 1902.

[399]

Central Association for the Relief of the Soldiers of South Carolina, *The Plan, and Purpose, and Address, adopted October 20, 1862,* Charleston, 1862.

Chesnut, Mary Boykin, *A Diary From Dixie, as written by Mary Boykin Chesnut, wife of James Chesnut, Jr., U. S. Senator from South Carolina, 1859–1861, and afterward an Aide to Jefferson Davis and a Brigadier-General in the Confederate Army,* edited by Isabella D. Martin and Myrta Lockett Avery, New York, 1905.

Childs, Arney R., *Robert Wilson Gibbes, 1809–1866,* University of South Carolina Bulletin, No. 210, October, 1930.

Claiborne, J. F. H., *Life and Correspondence of John A. Quitman.* 2 vols., New York, 1860.

Clark, W. A., *The History of the Banking Institutions Organized in South Carolina Prior to 1860,* Columbia, 1922.

Columbia, S. C., Board of Trade, *Columbia, S. C., the Future Manufacturing and Agricultural Center of the South,* Columbia, 1871.

———————, Chamber of Commerce, *Chronicles and Comments, 1786–1913,* Columbia, 1913.

———————, *City of Columbia Annual, 1910–1914.*

———————, *City Directories, 1875–1934.*

———————, *Ordinances of Town of Columbia,* Columbia, 1823.

———————, *Revised Ordinances of the City of Columbia, S. C.,* Columbia, 1895.

———————, School Commissioners. Minute Books, MS.

———————, *Triennial Report of Public Schools of Columbia . . . 1922–1923, 1923–1924, 1924–1925,* Columbia, 1926.

"Columbia's Volunteer Fire Department, History of," *Annual State Fireman's Association,* Charleston, 1926.

Davis, R. Means, "A Sketch of Education in South Carolina," *South Carolina: Resources and Population, Institutions and Industries,* Charleston, S. C., 1883. pp. 445–549.

De Leon, Edwin, *Thirty Years of My Life on Three Continents,* London, 1890.

Dickert D. Augustus, *History of Kershaw's brigade, with Complete Roll of Companies, biographical sketches, incidents, anecdotes, etc.; with an introduction by Associate Justice Y. J. Pope,* Newberry, 1899.

Dictionary of American Biography, New York, 1928–1935.

Drayton, John, *A View of South Carolina . . . ,* Charleston, 1802.

Edwards, W. H., *A Condensed History of the Seventeenth Regiment, S. C. V., C. S. A., From its Organization to the Close of the War,* Columbia, 1908.

Elzas, Barnett A., *The Jews of South Carolina From the Earliest Times to the Present Day,* Philadelphia, 1905.

English, Elizabeth D. and Clark, B. M., *Richland County, Economic and Social,* Bulletin of University of S. C., Columbia, 1924.

Gamewell, J. A. and Wallace D. D., *Richland Almanac,* Spartanburg, 1903.

Garrett, C. G., Reminiscences, MS.

Gibbes, James G., *Who Burnt Columbia?* Newberry, 1902.

Gilmer, Gertrude C., *Checklist of Southern Periodicals to 1861,* Boston, 1934.

Gonzales, Narcisco G., *In Darkest Cuba,* Columbia, 1922.

Gonzales, Robert E., *Poems and Paragraphs,* Columbia, 1918.

Governor's Guards, Minutes, 1874–1899, MS. University of South Carolina Library.

Green, Edwin L., *A History of Richland County,* Vol. I, Columbia, 1932.

——————, *A History of the University of South Carolina*, Columbia, 1916.

Gregg, Alexander, *History of the Old Cheraws*, Columbia, 1905.

Hall, Margaret (Hunter), *The Aristocratic Journey*, New York, 1931.

Hampton, Wade, *Burning of Columbia; Letter of General Wade Hampton, June 24, 1873*, with appendix, Charleston, 1888.

Henderson, Archibald, *Washington's Southern Tour, 1791*, Boston and New York, 1923.

Hennig, Helen Kohn, Edwin De Leon, M.A. Thesis, University of South Carolina. MS., 1928.

Hill, James D., "The Burning of Columbia Reconsidered," *The South Atlantic Quarterly*, Vol. XXV, July, 1926.

History of the 55th Field Artillery Brigade, Nashville, n. d.

Hitchcock, Henry, *Marching with Sherman; Passages from the Letters and Campaign Diaries of Henry Hitchcock, November, 1864–May, 1865*. Edited with an introduction by M. A. DeW. Howe, New Haven, 1927.

Hodge, Frederick Webb, *Handbook of American Indians*, United States Bureau of American Ethnology, Bulletin 30, Washington, 1907–1910.

Hooker, Edward, "Diary of Edward Hooker," *Annual Report of American Historical Association, 1896*, Washington, 1896.

Houston, David Franklin, *A Critical Study of Nullification in South Carolina*, New York, 1896.

Izlar, William V., *Sketch of the War Record of the Edisto Rifles, 1861–1865*, Columbia, 1914.

Jervey, Theodore D., *Robert Y. Hayne and His Times*, New York, 1909.

Johnson, Joseph, *Traditions and Reminiscences of the American Revolution in the South*, Charleston, 1851.

Jones, Cadwallader, *A Genealogical History*, Columbia, 1900.

Joynes, E. S., "Origin and Early History of Winthrop College," *Winthrop Normal and Industrial College Bulletin*, Rock Hill, September, 1912.

King, William L., *The Newspaper Press of Charleston, S. C.*, Charleston, 1882.

Knight, Edgar W., "The Academy Movement in the South," *North Carolina High School Journal*. Vols. I and II. n. p. n. d.

LaBorde, Maximilian, *History of the South Carolina College*, Columbia, 1859.

——————, *History of the South Carolina College*, 2d ed., Charleston, 1874.

Ladies' Memorial Association of Charleston, S. C., *Memorials to the Memory of Mrs. Mary Amarintha Snowden* . . . Charleston, 1898.

Lathan, Robert, *Proceedings of the 37th Annual Meeting of the South Carolina Press Association, 1911*. n. p. n. d.

Lathers, Richard, *Reminiscences; Sixty Years of a Busy Life in South Carolina, Massachusetts and New York*, edited by Alvin F. Sanborn, New York, 1907.

Lavasseur, A., *Lafayette in America*, New York, 1929.

Lebby, Robert, "The First Shot on Fort Sumter," *South Carolina Historical and Genealogical Magazine, July, 1911*.

Leconte, Joseph, *Autobiography*, edited by William Dellam Armes, New York, 1903.

Leiding, Harriette Kershaw, *Historic Houses of South Carolina*, Philadelphia and London, 1921.

Leland, John A., *A Voice from South Carolina. Twelve Chapters Before Hampton. Two Chapters After Hampton*, Charleston, 1879.

Lesesne, J. M., "The South Carolina State House," *South Carolina Education,* Vol. XVI, 288–291.

Logan, John H., *A History of the Upper Country of South Carolina,* Vol. 1, Charleston, 1859.

Lowery, I. E., *Life on the Old Plantation,* Columbia, 1911.

McClure, A. K., *The South, its Industrial, Financial and Political Condition,* Philadelphia, 1886.

Mackey, Albert G., *History of Free Masonry in South Carolina,* Columbia, 1856.

McKissick, J. Rion, "Some Observaitons of Travelers in South Carolina, 1800–1860," *Proceedings of the South Carolina Historical Association, 1932,* Columbia, 1932.

McMaster, F. H. and Bateman, J. M., *History of the First Presbyterian Church and Its Churchyard,* Columbia, n. d.

Malone, Dumas, *The Public Life of Thomas Cooper, 1783–1839,* New Haven, 1926.

Mason, Edward G., "A Visit to South Carolina in 1860," *Atlantic Monthly,* February, 1884.

Merritt, Elizabeth, *James Henry Hammond,* Baltimore, 1923.

Michaux, F. A., *Travels to the West of the Alleghany Mountains . . . ,* London, 1805.

Mills, Robert, *Statistics of South Carolina Including a View of Natural, Civil, and Military History,* Charleston, 1826.

Moore, Maude, History of College for Women, M.A. Thesis, University of South Carolina. MS., 1932.

Moore, Dr. Maurice A., *Reminiscences of York,* Yorkville, S. C., n. d.

Mott, Frank Luther, *A History of American Magazines, 1741–1850,* New York, 1930.

Nichols, George W., "The Burning of Columbia," *Harpers Magazine,* August, 1866.

——————, *The Story of the Great March, From the Diary of a Staff Officer,* New York, 1865.

Nicholson, William A., *The Burning of Columbia,* Columbia, 1895.

O'Connell, J. J., *Catholicity in the Carolinas and Georgia,* New York, 1879.

O'Neall, John Belton, *Bench and Bar of South Carolina,* 2 vols., Charleston, 1859.

Palmer, Benjamin M., *Address Delivered at the Funeral of General Maxcy Gregg, in the Presbyterian Church, Columbia, Dec. 20, 1862,* Columbia, S. C., 1863.

——————, *The Life and Letters of James Henley Thornwell,* Richmond, 1875.

Parkinson, B. L., *History of the Administration of the Public Schools of South Carolina,* Bulletin of the University of S. C., Columbia, 1912.

Peay, Mary Elizabeth, "W. H. Hand and His Influence Upon Public Education in South Carolina." M.A. Thesis, University of South Carolina, MS., 1932.

Perry, B. F., *Reminiscences of Public Men,* 2d series, Greenville, 1889.

Perry, Thomas S., ed., *The Life and Letters of Francis Lieber,* Boston, 1882.

Pike, James S., *The Prostrate State: South Carolina Under Negro Government,* New York, 1874.

Pleasants, William H., *The Destruction of Columbia, S. C., A Translation from the German . . . of the 19th, 20th, 21st and 22nd Chapters of*

"Lights and Shadows in American Life During the War of Secession," by August Conrad, published at Hanover, 1879, Roanoke, 1902.

Porter, A. Toomer, *Led On! Step by Step. Scenes from Clerical, Military, Educational and Plantation Life in the South, 1828–1898. An Autobiography,* New York, 1899.

Pratt, Waldo S., *New Encyclopedia of Music and Musicians,* New York, 1924.

Preston, John S. *(et al.), Addresses Delivered Before the Virginia State Convention by Hon. Fulton Anderson, Commissioner from Mississippi; Hon. Henry L. Benning, Commissioner from Georgia, and Hon. John S. Preston, Commissioner from South Carolina, February, 1861,* Richmond, 1861.

Preston, William C., *Reminiscences of,* edited by Minnie Clare Yarborough, Chapel Hill, 1933.

Reynolds, John S., *Reconstruction in South Carolina, 1865–1877,* Columbia, 1905.

Rhodes, James F., *Historical Essays,* New York, 1909.

——————, *History of the Civil War, 1861–1865,* New York, 1917.

——————, *History of the United States from the Compromise of 1850 to the End of the Roosevelt Administration,* New Edition, 9 vols., New York, 1913–1928.

Robbins, D. P., comp., *Historical and Descriptive Sketch of the Leading Manufacturing and Mercantile Enterprises, Public Buildings, Officials, Professional Men, Schools, Churches, etc., Railroads, Canals, Rivers, Advantages and Surroundings of Coulmbia, S. C.,* Columbia, 1888.

Robertson, Mrs. A. I., "Columbia, a Short History," *The New South,* Nashville, Tenn., 1899.

Robinson, William C., *Columbia Theological Seminary,* Decatur, Georgia, 1931.

Royall, Mrs. Anne, *Southern Tour or Second Series of The Black Book,* 3 vols., Washington, 1830–1831.

Sabre, G. E., *Nineteen Months a Prisoner of War . . . List of Officers Confined at Columbia During the Winter of 1864 and 1865,* New York, 1865.

Salley, A. S., *President Washington's Tour Through South Carolina in 1791,* Bulletin 12, Historical Commission of South Carolina, Columbia, 1932.

——————, *South Carolina Troops in Confederate Service,* 3 vols., Columbia, 1913–1930.

Scott, Edwin J., *Random Recollections of a Long Life, 1806–1876,* Columbia, 1884.

Selby, Julian A., *Memorabilia and Anecdotal Reminiscences of Columbia, S. C.,* Columbia, 1905.

Shand, P. J., Letters and Statement Regarding the Burning of Columbia, MS., University of South Carolina Library.

Sherman, William T., *Memoirs . . .* 2 vols., New York, 1892.

Simkins, Francis B., *The Tillman Movement in South Carolina,* Durham, 1926.

Simmons, J. Andrew, Professional and Cultural Background of Teachers in South Carolina High Schools for Negroes. M.A. Thesis. MS., Columbia University, 1935.

Simms, William Gilmore, *The Geography of South Carolina,* Charleston, 1843.

——————, *Sack and Destruction of the City of Columbia, S. C., to which is added a List of the Property Destroyed,* Columbia, 1865.

Snowden, Yates, *Marching with Sherman. A Review of the Letters and Campaign Diaries of Henry Hitchcock, Major and Assistant Adjutant General of Volunteers as edited by M. A. DeWolfe Howe and published by the Yale Press,* Columbia, 1929.

——————, *South Carolina School Books, 1795–1855,* Columbia, 1910.

——————, *War Time Publications,* Charleston, 1922.

Sonneck, Oscar G., *Early Concert Life in America,* Leipzig, 1907.

——————, *Early Opera in America, Boston,* 1915.

South Carolina Female Collegiate Institute, Records of (MS. owned by Professor Henry C. Davis), Columbia.

South Carolina Convention, 1832–1833, *Journal of the Convention of the People of South Carolina, Assembled at Columbia on the 19th November, 1832, and again on the 11th March, 1833,* Columbia, 1833. (Reprint, Columbia, 1860.)

South Carolina Convention, 1852, *Journal of the State Convention of South Carolina Held in 1852, together with the Resolutions and Ordinance,* Columbia, 1860.

South Carolina Convention, 1860–1862, *Journal of the Convention of the People of South Carolina, held in 1860, 1861 and 1862, together with the Ordinances, Reports, Resolutions, etc.,* Columbia, 1862.

South Carolina Constitutional Convention, 1865, *Journal of the Convention of the People of South Carolina, held in Columbia, S. C., September, 1865, together with the Ordinances, Reports, Resolutions, etc.,* Columbia, 1865.

South Carolina Department of Agriculture, Commerce and Industries, *Twenty-seventh Annual Report,* Columbia, 1934.

South Carolina General Assembly, House of Representatives, *Journal,* Columbia.*

——————, *Reports and Resolutions,* Columbia.*

South Carolina General Assembly, Senate, *Journal,* Columbia.

——————, *Statutes at Large,* Columbia.*

South Carolina Historical and Genealogical Magazine, Charleston, 1900–date.

South Carolina Hospital Aid Association in Virginia, *Report, 1861–1862, Embracing Report to the Legislature, Sketch of Hospitals, Accounts, Lists of Contributions, and Catalogue of Deceased South Carolina Soldiers,* Richmond, 1862.

South Carolina Press Association, *Minutes, 1877–1888,* Newberry, S. C., 1903.

South Carolina, University of, *Faculty Research and Productive Scholarship,* Bulletin, Columbia, 1931.

——————, *The Clariosophic and Euphradian Societies, 1806–1931. 125th Anniversary Celebration, November 6–7, 1931,* Columbia, 1931.

----

* The records familiarly known as the "Acts" and the "Reports and Resolutions" were printed together until 1839 with the following title page: *Acts and Resolutions of the General Assembly of the State of South Carolina.* Beginning with this year the "Acts" were printed separately to conform to an ever growing series known as *The Statutes at Large of South Carolina.* The title page of the "Acts" now became, *Acts of the General Assembly of the State of South Carolina,* and the title page of the "Resolutions" became *Reports and Resolutions of the General Assembly of the State of South Carolina.*

In 1866 the joint resolutions began to be printed with the "Acts" and the title page became *Acts and Joint Resolutions of the General Assembly of the State of South Carolina.* In 1917 the title page of the *Reports and Resolutions* became *Reports of the State Officers, Boards and Committees to the General Assembly of the State of South Carolina.*

There were no journals of the legislature printed before 1831. In that year the journals were first printed together with the title page, *Journal of the Proceedings of the Senate and House of Representatives of the General Assembly of South Carolina.* These were not the records of the regular clerks but only notes of reporters. (See *Reports and Resolutions,* 1841, pp. 120-123.) Beginning with 1842 the journals of the Senate and the House were printed separately from the manuscript copies in the hands of the clerks. The title pages are: *Journal of the House of Representatives of the State of South Carolina,* and *Journal of the Senate of the State of South Carolina.*

The laws of the province and state of South Carolina, up to and including 1838, were collected and edited (1836-1841) in ten volumes by Thomas Cooper and David J. McCord (Vol. X is the index). Each year since 1838 the acts have been printed to continue this series, which is known as the *Statutes at Large of South Carolina.*

(This note was prepared by J. M. Lesesne.)

————————, *Report of the Faculty of, on Free School System,* Columbia, 1826.

Stevens, Neil E., *The Mycological Work of Henry W. Ravenel,* (Reprint from *Isis,* Bruges, Belgium, July, 1932.)

Stoddard, J. A., *Backgrounds of Secondary Education in South Carolina,* Bulletin of the University of South Carolina, No. 150, Columbia, 1924.

Taylor, Alrutheus A., *The Negro in South Carolina Military Academy,* Charleston, 1893.

Thomas, John Peyre, *The History of the South Carolina Military Academy,* Charleston, 1893.

————————, *Report of the Historian of the Confederate Records to the General Assembly of South Carolina,* Columbia, 1899.

————————, ed., *Rivers' Account of the Raising of Troops in South Carolina for State and Confederate Service,* Columbia, 1899.

Thomason, John Furman, *Foundations of the Public Schools of South Carolina,* Columbia, 1925.

Thompson, Henry T., *The Establishment of the Public School System of South Carolina,* Columbia, 1927.

————————, *Henry Timrod, Laureate of the Confederacy,* Columbia, 1928.

————————, *Ousting the Carpetbagger from South Carolina,* Columbia, 1926.

Thornwell, J. H., *The State of the Country,* Columbia, 1861.

Townsend, John, *et al., Memorial of Honorable John Townsend, Rev. Benjamin M. Palmer, Hon. W. F. DeSaussure, and Prof. M. LaBorde, on Behalf of the "Central Association for the Relief of Soldiers of South Carolina," Praying for an Appropriation of Money for that Object,* n. p., 1862.

Trent, William P., *William Gilmore Simms,* Boston, 1892.

Trezevant, D. H., *The Burning of Columbia, S. C. A Review of Northern Assertions and Southern Facts,* Columbia, 1866.

United Daughters of the Confederacy, S. C. Division, *South Carolina Women in the Confederacy,* 2 vols., Columbia, 1903, 1907.

————————, *Memorial Pamphlet. Confederate Soldiers Who Died in the Service of their Country and are Buried in Columbia, S. C., 1861–1865,* Columbia, 1924.

United States Bureau of the Census, Census of the United States.

————————, War Department, *The War of the Rebellion: A Compilation of the Official Records of the Union and Confederate Armies,* 130 vols., Washington, 1880–1901.

Wallace, David Duncan, *The History of South Carolina,* 4 vols., New York, 1934.

Wauchope, George Armstrong, *The Writers of South Carolina,* Columbia, 1910.

————————, *Literary South Carolina.* University of S. C. Bulletin, 1923.

Wells, Edward L., *Hampton and His Cavalry in '64,* Columbia, 1899.

————————, *Hampton and Reconstruction,* Columbia, 1907.

Whilden, Mary S., *Recollections of the War, 1861–1865,* Columbia, 1911.

Who Burnt Columbia? Official Depositions of William Tecumseh Sherman . . . and General O. O. Howard, U. S. A., for the Defense; and Extracts from Some of the Depositions for the Claimants, filed in Certain Claims vs. United States, pending before "The Mixed Commission on British and American Claims" in Washington, D. C., Charleston, 1873.

Williams, Alfred B., *Hampton and His Red Shirts,* Charleston, 1935.

Williams, J. F., *Old and New Columbia,* Columbia, 1929.

Willis, Eola, *Charleston Stage of the XVIII Century,* Columbia, 1924.

Woodrow, James, *Dr. James Woodrow as Seen by His Friends. Character Sketches of His Former Pupils, Colleagues, and Associates,* Columbia, 1909.

INDEX

By Bess Glenn

Horine, J. W., 99, 222.
Horse racing, 244, 297.
Hort, E. B., 150.
Hospital Aid Association, 32.
Hospital at University of South Carolina, 89.
Hospitals, 33-34, 89, 153-160, 314.
IIouse of Peace (Synagogue), 149-150.
Houseal, W. P. (note), 222.
Howard, O. O., 39, 42.
Howard School, 117, 123, 128, 131, 311.
Howe, Mrs. Annie J., 278.
Howe, George (1802-1883), 94, 197, 140; *History of the Presbyterian Church in South Carolina*, 197.
Howe, George (1893), 158, 278.
Hoyt, J. A., 221, 236, 237, 241.
Huet, Dr., 154.
Huger, F. K., 263.
Huger, Isaac, 9.
Hughes family, 174.
Hughey, W. B., 84.
Hunt, B. F., 61.
Hunt, J. G., 58, 69.
Hunt, Sue E., 114.
Hunting, 298.
Huntt, S. G., 110.
Hyatt, F. H., 97.
Hyatt Park Casino, 214.
Hyatt Park School, 133.
Hyde, Helen, 189.

Ice manufacture, 326.
Ideal Theater, 213, 279.
Imperial Theater, 213.
Independent Fire Company, 77.
Indians, Trade with, 315-316.
Inglesby, Mrs. Legare, 188.
Inman, Henry, 183, 185.
Innes' Band, 178.
Insane Asylum. *See* State Hospital.
Iron Works, 323-324.
Irving, J. B., Jr., 185.
Irving, Washington, in Columbia, 269.
Irwin, May, 217.
Israels, Joseph, 189.
Izard, Mattye, 181.

Jackson, Andrew, 22.
Jackson, C. A. G., 241.
Jackson, J. W., 140.
Jackson, Robert, 314.
Jackson, Mrs. T. J., in Columbia, 272.
Jacquier, L., 149.
Jaggers, Charles, 309.
Jaggers' Home, (illus.) 304, 309.

Jail, 67-68, 73, 83-84.
James, James, 307.
James, Louis, 217.
James, Marquis, 281.
Janney, Ellen, 112.
Jaquins, W. A., 181.
Jefferson, Joseph, 216, 217.
Jefferson, Thomas, 187.
Jenkins, Micah, 273.
Jenkins, N. A., 314.
Jenkins, Robert, 146.
Jewish Cemeteries, 85, 150.
Jewish Synagogues, 135.
Jews, 149-150.
Johnson, Mrs. Boyd, 182.
Johnson, C. A., "Negroes," 303-314.
Johnson, C. C., 313.
Johnson, C. E., 127.
Johnson, D. B., 116, 122-127, 277.
Johnson, David, 268.
Johnson, Frank, 314.
Johnson, H. P. (note), 127.
Johnson, M. G., 309.
Johnson, W. C., 308.
Johnson, William, 161.
Johnson-Bradley Funeral Home, 308.
Johnston, A. S., 208, 224, 236, 240.
Johnston, E. W., 207-208, 224.
Johnston, W. B., 240, 241.
Johnston & Cavis, 224. *See also* Printers, Publishing houses.
Johnston, Du Bose &., 224.
Jones, C. C., 94.
Jones, Cadwallader, 265.
Jones, Mrs. Curran, 182.
Jones, I. B., 274.
Jones, J. L., 96.
Jones, James, 62.
Jones, S. B., 96.
Jones, Samuel, 103.
Jones, W. H., 222.
Jones, W. R., 241.
Jones, Wilie, 272, 273, 292, 293.
Joynes, E. S., 90, 119, 121, 125, 195.
Judd, H. O., 146.
Judge, John, & Company, 36.
Judiciary, 161-170.
Junior League, 255.

Kaminer, Mrs. H. G., 182.
Karesh, Coleman, 219.
Karesh, David, 149.
Kasparides (Painter), 189.
Kean, C. J., 215.
Kean, Clara, 175.
Kean, Ellen T., 215.
Kean, Black &., 224.
Keenan, R. C., 86.
Keene, Laura, 216.

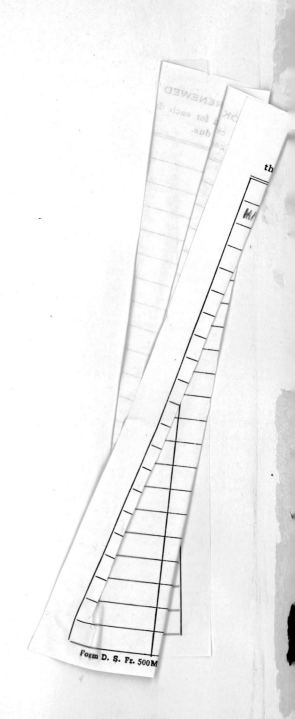

Form D. S. Fr. 500M